FICTION AND PURPOSE IN *UTOPIA*, *RASSELAS*, *THE MILL ON THE FLOSS* AND *WOMEN IN LOVE*

By the same author

GEORGE CRABBE'S POETRY

FICTION AND PURPOSE IN
UTOPIA, *RASSELAS*,
THE MILL ON THE FLOSS
AND *WOMEN IN LOVE*

Peter New

MACMILLAN

First published 1985 by
THE MACMILLAN PRESS LTD
London and Basingstoke
Companies and representatives
throughout the world

Typeset by
Wessex Typesetters Ltd
Frome, Somerset

Printed in Hong Kong

British Library Cataloguing in Publication Data
New, Peter
Fiction and purpose in Utopia, Rasselas,
The Mill on the Floss and Women in Love.
1. English fiction—History and criticism
I. Title
823'.009   PR821
ISBN 0-333-38450-4

'One slim volume'
for my family

The poor woman was not content simply to write amusing stories. She is convicted upon conclusive evidence of having indulged in ideas; she ventured to speculate upon human life and its meaning, and still worse, she endeavoured to embody her convictions in imaginative shapes, and probably wished to infect her reader with them. This was, according to some people, highly unbecoming in a woman and very inartistic in a novelist. I confess that, for my part, I am rather glad to find ideas anywhere. They are not very common; and there are a vast number of excellent fictions which these sensitive critics may study without the least danger of a shock to their artistic sensibilities by anything of the kind.

Leslie Stephen, obituary article on George Eliot, *Cornhill Magazine*, vol. 153 (February 1881).

Contents

Texts and Acknowledgements

For *Utopia* I have used the major Yale edition by Edward Surtz and J. H. Hexter (1965, revised 1974) and the translation printed with it. For *Rasselas* I have used J. P. Hardy's Oxford edition (1968), and for *The Mill on the Floss* the Clarendon edition by Gordon S. Haight (1980). Quotations from *Women in Love* are taken from the Penguin edition.

Two chapters have previously been published, with minor differences, in periodicals: Chapter 9 in *English* (Oxford, 1978) and Chapter 2 in *Organon* (Warsaw, 1983). I am grateful to the editor of *English*, Martin Dodsworth, and to the Polish Academy of Sciences for permission to reproduce the material. My debts to previous critics of the four fictions discussed here are extensive, and only the most specific can be acknowledged without ostentatious pedantry: references will be found in the notes. I should also like to thank the inter-library loan department of Exeter University Library for their prompt and efficient help.

My greater debts are, in order of increasing magnitude, to Myrddin Jones for intelligent tact, to my students for obstinate honesty, to my family for more than diversion, and to those I most wished to please, who from my beginning showed me the end.

1 Introduction

The basic assumptions underlying this book are, that man is an animal needing by nature to have a purpose or purposes in view, and that what he takes as his ultimate purpose has an intimate relationship with what he does and becomes, that is, with his nature as a whole. The first assumption is subject to empirical challenge, though the room for doubt seems small: people who can envisage no short-term or long-term purpose are more often found inside psychiatric hospitals than outside. But the second assumption is contentious, and one of my aims here is to throw some light on it by examining at length four relevant works of fiction. The fictions selected all explore profoundly questions concerning human purposes and what happens to men who give various answers to those questions. But different forms of fiction have interestingly different ways of relating human purposes to various obstructions, external and internal – the recalcitrance of the brute world to human will, and the confusion of purpose with fantasy. So what is also involved is a discussion of how fictional form can embody, shape, refine conceptions of human purpose, which I hope will provide some insight into certain general aspects of fictional technique.

Each of the writers I shall concentrate on has shown awareness of a paradox which recurs in normal human attempts to think about purpose. On the one hand, reflection about purpose naturally tends to widen in range: a person who is sufficiently reflective to ask questions about a limited purpose (why do I want more money?) frequently moves or drifts towards much larger questions (what is the purpose of my life?). On the other hand, there is a natural inclination not to ask questions about purpose at all, or to repress any impulse to ask them: a limited end becomes so absorbing that any question of its value within a wider perspective is repressed either before it can obtrude or immediately it has obtruded. I am not contrasting two kinds of individual: both things normally happen within the same mind. A

1

miser might seem to be a very clear example of the second habit. But when Silas Marner loses his hoard and finds Eppie, his sense of purpose does not stop at keeping her safe; it extends outwards into a new sense of his role within the Raveloe community and ultimately in fact into a renewed and matured faith in a divine purpose giving shape to what had seemed the meaningless injustice of events. George Eliot, of course, did not share Marner's faith, but she found substitutes, the adequacy of which I shall discuss later. In our century scepticism has increased. It may now be said that the movement from reflection on a limited purpose to reflection about a larger one is merely a habit based on an obsolete metaphysic. Previous centuries may have encouraged beliefs like Marner's, but there is no reason for assuming that an answer to a small question why? makes it sensible to ask a larger question why? about that answer. Very many people of our time believe that the largest question why? concerning us (why does man exist?) is not a sensible question. There is, it may be said, no purpose in our existence: we are one result of events occurring over vast stretches of space and time, and the concept of 'purpose' has only existed in the tiny fraction of those stretches in which we have been using such abstract language. If the concept is only our invention, it is clearly senseless to apply it to events which preceded its invention. This and many other lines of thought, too numerous to list here, have led to the fact that we, more than any age of recorded history, are faced with the possibility that life has, in the longest perspective, no purpose at all.

Two of the writers I am going to discuss saw life as having ultimately a Christian purpose; the other two did not believe in Christianity and found alternative purposes which they, and others, have thought adequate. Another book would be required to examine fully some recent responses to questions of purpose, but to put into perspective those which I want to discuss here, two modern extremes can be briefly mentioned. Samuel Beckett is a writer who believes that life is without purpose, yet who feels a compulsive urge to set up fictional situations which repeatedly ask the same question expecting the answer no. He is, in his writing, permanently in the first stage of the paradox I mentioned above. The minds of his characters perpetually drift from trivia towards huge questions about the nature of existence, and when the questions are always unanswered, back to trivia, and so on in deliberate circularity until an arbitrary length of time has passed.

The proposition that life is without purpose is not, at this date, in itself very interesting: it has been made rather often in our time. What is interesting is that Beckett should feel this need to go on asking whether it is, and repeating the same answer to himself. I have used the word 'need' which suggests it is a psychological matter; his word is 'obligation', which is strange, because one is normally only *obliged* by something outside oneself. 'The expression that there is nothing to express, nothing with which to express, nothing from which to express, no power to express, no desire to express, together with the obligation to express.'[1] Perhaps it may seem excessive to say that the sense of obligation has been transferred, since that may imply a degree of self-consciousness Beckett does not have; but his words certainly seem to convey a feeling of resentment. Beckett clearly feels that life *ought* to have purpose. It ought but it does not; so the tone in his works is one of consistently implied accusation. 'We have kept our appointment', says Vladimir. Such lines only have force because Godot has *not* kept the appointment, or because there *was* no appointment. Life has not met its obligations. But Beckett will: night after night he will stand at the same tree and ask the same questions, to which he knows the answer, until he dies at life's final, inevitable moment of failure. In such strength of purpose, absurd as it is, there is something to admire. But he can only speak very directly to those who share his resentment, for he deliberately empties his world of everything admirable except the defiantly punctilious writer. Most people who share his absurdist philosophy feel, like Camus, for example, that there remain other things which can be admired; so a common response is to transpose the qualities of the writer to his characters. Vladimir and Estragon actually try not to keep their appointment, but that does not stop critics from trying to admire their perseverance.

But such a response is too sophisticated to be credibly attributed to all the enormous numbers of people who enjoy the works of this strange man. It is probable that more of them actually lie at the opposite extreme from Beckett. Most people in an affluent society are more likely to suppress questions concerning purpose than to torment themselves with them. Yet thanks to writers like Beckett, they are not so permanently fixed in the second stage of the paradox I mentioned as he is in the first. Beckett can work for them as a kind of Consumer Man's Sunday. On most days, life in Western society is not at all made up of dustbins and mud. That is not at all How It Is. But on Beckett days one can show how clearly one sees behind the car, colour television and mock-Tudor pub to the reality of dustbins and mud. And since life is clearly to blame (it ought to have purpose and does not), then clearly one cannot change anything when one leaves the theatre and returns to the pub. How long such people will be able to continue on a diet of short-term purpose and occasional therapeutic dose of 'reality' I am not competent to prophesy. But money is the best opiate, and when famous writers, acclaimed by the critics, show that if you ask further questions the answer is mud, it is comforting to return to it.

Beckett, then, shows one possible response to the assumption that life is without ultimate purpose, and Consumer Man shows an opposite extreme which is obviously more common. Both are content with shorter-term purposes; but it seems unnecessary to argue that one can hardly use the word 'content' of either without irony.

As the assumption of ultimate purposelessness has grown, so has the idea that fiction will to some extent provide a substitute form of content. Nietzsche put it most succinctly: 'we have art in order not to die of the truth'. Frank Kermode's book, *The Sense of an Ending*, is one of the most interesting recent sophistications of this idea. He starts with an assumption apparently close to mine: 'there is still a need to speak humanly of a life's importance in relation to [time] – a need in the moment of existence to belong, to be related to a beginning and to an end'.[2] But it is the word 'end' which interests him, not the related word *purpose*. *Purpose*, in the sense which interests me, he sees as a rather small variant of the recurrent human need for the myth or fiction of an apocalypse. The need, as he understands it, is so exclusively psychological that fiction, provided it is sufficiently subtle, can meet it with total adequacy: 'the need we continue to feel is a need of concord, and we supply it by increasingly varied concord-fictions'.[3] Following (at some distance) I. A. Richards, he sees the effect of fiction as restoring the psychological equilibrium which is upset by glimpses of 'reality' as chaos. Sophisticated fiction must acknowledge the glimpses, but beyond that it is not dependent on truth: its importance lies in the degree to which it meets the psychological need for feelings of 'concord'. But Kermode goes further than Richards: literary fictions, he says, meet this need 'for some of us, perhaps better than history, perhaps better than theology, largely because they are consciously false'.[4] One could only say 'because' there if one has made the prior assumption (and the next sentence shows that Kermode has made it) that what actually surrounds us is chaos. If the truth is chaos, it is better to derive our needed concord-feelings from what we know to be false. But if, as he thinks, we can only see at all by means of fictions (in a general, not an exclusively literary sense of the word fiction), it is difficult to understand why the chaos is less fictional than the order. Kermode sees (p. 37) that Nietzsche is in some danger of resembling the Cretan Liar, yet he himself, aware that he is making patterns (p. 31), wants to call pattern-making 'consciously false'.

That will seem very strange until we understand that Kermode, like so many of our contemporaries, has a *need* to believe that even the most demanding works of literature require of us only what he calls 'experimental assent'.[5] If one is not careful, they might disturb one's hold on the slippery 'truth' of ultimate chaos. His need to provide them with a form of insulation, which he later elaborates with great ingenuity in terms ranging from medieval Scholastic philosophy to quantum physics, is demonstrated in a touchingly vulnerable way by the clumsy manoeuvre of threatening us with Buchenwald. Arian anti-Semitism and *King Lear* are both fictions, and Kermode wants to distinguish them by calling the first myth and the second fiction. 'Fictions can degenerate into myths whenever they are not consciously held to be fictive. In this sense anti-Semitism is a degenerate fiction, a myth; and *Lear* is a fiction.'[6] The distinction later commands some sympathy when Kermode writes, with an honesty and cogency which are still rare about the artistic radicalism of the modernist movement of the earlier twentieth century and the fascism which is the degenerate expression of such radicalism transposed into the world of active politics. But it will clearly not do to use this as a general argument: 'You neither rearrange the world to suit [fictions], nor test them by experiment, for instance in gas-chambers.'[7] Not all experiments are conducted in gas-chambers. This is an argument for cautious reading and uncowardly criticism; not for insulating fiction from life. More was highly sceptical about the possibilities of rearranging the world and he would have found some of the utopian experiments conducted in the nineteenth century very comic. But to prevent an intelligent understanding of *Utopia* from interacting with actual political conduct would make one guilty of the irresponsibility which is so penetratingly analysed in the character of Hythloday.

In Kermode's book, then, the aesthetic experience of the 'sense of an ending' has become an alternative to any sense of personal purpose (end-in-view) or any ultimate End in human life. He prefers the 'consciously false' because that way he can have the experience but keep his hands clean. He is much more intelligent than the aesthetes referred to by Leslie Stephen in the passage quoted as the epigraph to this book; but he has more in common with them than with the four writers I shall be primarily concerned with. They all, in Stephen's words, 'ventured to speculate upon human life and its meaning', to use the aesthetic forms they chose, not to convey the 'sense of an ending', but to explore the possibilities of certain human ends. They have to be convicted guilty of writing in their fictions, not about the 'consciously false', but either directly or indirectly about what they considered to be most importantly true about the purpose of human life. And I plead guilty to the charge, which will be levelled at me, of being infected with their convictions, since I have foolishly disregarded the antiseptic precautions of 'experimental assent'.

There are, however, limits to my foolishness. I do not wish to claim that Stephen's words can sensibly be applied to all fictions which are worth reading. The furthest I should wish to go would be to accept in part the irony in his use of the words 'excellent' and 'sensitive'. One must set limits to the irony since there are obviously very many fictions with do not address themselves to anything resembling a speculation upon human life and its meaning; though I do not think it is a coincidence that a large proportion of those which by common consent are felt to be most truly 'excellent' do. There are also some literary critics to whom one feels grateful precisely because they have not concerned themselves with such speculations, concentrating instead on matters of form or on patiently demonstrating, to those of us who are slow to learn, that content and form cannot be so separated as I may seem to be implying; though I am more interested in criticism which has as its ultimate question in view something more like 'What is the human importance of this work?' than 'Is this work a Menippean satire or a bourgeois romance?' I am fully aware that there are other kinds of fiction and other kinds of criticism which are worthwhile; but I have, in that awareness, quite deliberately chosen mine.

This is not a suitable place to attempt a full defence of that choice, but a partial one is relevant and perhaps owed. Creative writing is (as Kermode and many others have shown) a special and peculiarly intense case of human purposive activity. The making of something requires a sense of purpose, and only in certain avant garde experiments, which seem to me sterile sports, is there any attempt to remove human intentionality from art. If one believes purpose to be untrue to non-human reality, there is a certain logic in trying to eliminate it from art. I think that success would entail untruth to human reality; but even if that were not conceded, the attempt is essentially doomed to failure. One has to intend to remove intentionality. The only hope would lie in total accident, such as *unintentionally* knocking over a bottle of ink, or standing silent on stage and perhaps yawning, perhaps not. I should not find that very interesting. Interest seems to me to increase not as purpose is eliminated but as it is compounded. Much recent fiction has moved in this direction, reflecting on its own process – fiction reflecting on the purpose of fiction. But fascinating as some of the results have been, there remains an element of sterility in such activity. The range of reflection can move, and in the works I shall examine has moved, beyond that, to much wider questions. It is at this point that I become most grateful to those who remind me that form and content are inseparable: the form in the hands of a great writer can be the irreducible means of posing the questions. Form and the analysis of form can of course both be ends in themselves; as such I find neither very interesting, though others do. But they can also be means towards something else; and form as a means of discovery (to adapt phrases used by critics as diverse as Yvor Winters and Mark Schorer) seems to me both absorbing and willy-nilly an essential object of critical attention. Yet the final question remains, for me, discovery of what? – even though the answer, in dealing with great literature, will often have to consist only of painfully retracing the process of discovery. Or to put it differently, even though I may not be able to express the answer in terms, as it were, of a destination, I shall want to know whether the voyage was worth making. Clearly, that depends very largely on its purpose.

The question of whether the purpose which matters is that of the author or of the work, is one which exercises many, but is tangential to my interests. I wish only to make four general points. Firstly, these two purposes coincide in pre-Symbolist writing more frequently than the fuss over the 'Intentional Fallacy' of a few decades ago suggested: if they were found to differ, most pre-Symbolist writers would have thought an adverse criticism had been registered. Secondly, information, other than from the work, about the author's purposes is often the quickest way to identify assumptions which he may have regarded as self-evidently shared with his contemporary readers, but which are not so shared in our time. Thirdly, external information is more commonly useful in a negative than a positive way: that is to say, it is extremely seldom an adequate means of establishing what the work is intended to mean, but is sometimes helpful in exposing what it is unlikely to mean. Fourthly, aesthetic form, like all works of man, is subject to imperfection, so one can sometimes see what a writer meant to say, though his writing inadequately expresses it. With these qualifications made, I accept the general argument that the concern of the literary critic, as opposed to the biographer, is primarily with the purpose of the work rather than the purpose of the author. To repeat: it is often impossible to find out the purpose of the author except through retracing the process of discovery in the work, recreating the form as one reads.

But there is a problem here which requires further investigation. One of the basic difficulties facing the literary critic is that a major distinguishing feature of the object of his enquiry is its instability. The distinctively aesthetic quality of a literary text is that part of the creative act is left to the reader. That notorious statement by Archibald MacLeish, 'A poem should not mean But be', which has so often been used to justify the aesthetic insulation of literature, is misguiding in many ways, but not least in that the last word should be 'becomes'. Leavis's patient insistence on this point remains ignored even now, when his general importance is more widely conceded. The distinctively aesthetic quality of a literary text is not that it *is* like a vase instead of *means* like a military message but almost the contrary: it is by nature unstable. Clearly in a wider sense all documents are unstable: a laundry-bill which is only a laundry-bill to one generation may seem to a historian belonging to another to demonstrate the exploitation of

the working-classes or the fastidiousness which Conrad's Mar-
lowe would have regarded as an 'achievement of character'. But
in such a wide sense all objects whatever are unstable, that is,
subject to various kinds of interpretation. To narrow the field: the
success of writing which has little or no aesthetic purpose can be
measured by the degree to which the writer has ensured that the
envisaged addressee knows how to decode his message in the
intended manner. In complex non-aesthetic messages, in which a
number of parts have to be articulated, it is incumbent on the
writer to include articulating signs which unambiguously indicate
his intention. If he omits such signs, one can say without
hesitation that he has written badly. But in writing which has
aesthetic purpose relatively high in its order of priorities, it is
normal for an important proportion of such signs to be absent or
deliberately concealed or inconspicuous. So reading becomes
creative in the very direct sense that the reader has to an
important degree to work out for himself the relative significance
of parts and the relation between parts.

Why this should be so, is another very large question which
cannot be discussed adequately here. But although the degree
varies greatly from author to author (More and George Eliot are
nearly at opposite extremes: *Utopia* notoriously enigmatic; George
Eliot notoriously explicit through the voice of her omniscient
narrator), and although the degree is not a reliable basis for
comparative value-judgement, the fact seems incontrovertible.
Imagist poetry is not superior to a Johnson essay or a Jonson
poem because its syntactic omissions are very extensive, but
aesthetic appreciation of the latter is largely a matter of fully
registering a syntax which in its finer details is initially inconspicuous (*ars est celare artem*). A general reason which may be put
forward without entailing the obligation of a longer explanation
than can be given here is that the purposive activity of creative
reading is obviously pleasurable. All purposive activities are to
some degree pleasurable, since purposive activity is natural to
man; but a collaborative purpose, reader meeting writer, is
especially pleasurable. A particular reason, which I shall discuss
below since it is clearly present in *Utopia*, is that by making the
reader work, the writer can sometimes affect the reader in an
interesting way: if the writer wants to communicate not so much a
thought as a way of thinking, then a good way of proceeding is to

make the reader do it. In George Eliot, something analogous
happens, but the reader is made to adopt more a way of feeling
than a way of thinking.

The consequences for the critic of the omission or hiding of
articulating signs are enormous, and I shall mention only two.
Firstly, it gives him something to do. Secondly, it gives him a
freedom fatally easy to abuse. Over-ingenious critics tend naturally to cluster round the poets who give the fewest articulating
signs or the most ambiguous ones; but it is not hard to impose a
totally false order on even a Jonson poem. Here again the concept
of purpose seems to me indispensible. If the purpose of the critic is
not to clarify what he honestly believes to be a purpose of the work
he is criticising, then either he is engaged in another trade or he is
abusing his freedom. I say '*a* purpose' because great works of
literature commonly have more purposes than one, and the critic
has no obligation to be interested in all of them. The only
obligation is honesty.

To that I can see only three objections. Firstly, the work must
have purpose. I have already suggested that that is inevitable. On
a half-way attempt, a deliberate attempt at the random, my
honest observations would be brief. Secondly, it only makes sense
to say that honesty is an obligation if one pre-supposes that one
can use words such as *correct* and *mistaken* about particular
opinions of the purposes of the work; and that in turn pre-
supposes that those purposes are, despite the omission of signs,
verifiable. No interpretation will ever be definitive, since individual response is part of the meaning; but one interpretation can
be said to be more accurate or more adequate than another, on
appeal to the text. If so, honesty is clearly crucial. But it is quite
possible to argue from an opposite assumption, that given the
omission of signs, the choice of interpretation is virtually infinite
and wholly subjective, so one cannot be more correct than
another. In that case, ingenuity and novelty are more important
than honesty. To someone who thinks in this opposite direction, I
regret that what I have to say will be very dull; but he can find
abundant consolation elsewhere – most of all in those modern
writers who regard the omission of signs as an end in itself
because, they have gathered, that way lies infinite profundity.

The third objection is more mundane, but I shall record it since
it strikes nearer home. How can a critic be honest to four very

different fictions and simultaneously pursue a consistent purpose of his own? Others have done it; of myself I can only say that I have intended it.

2 *Utopia*: Form as Model

To write with any confidence about the purposes of a book as notoriously enigmatic as *Utopia* may seem a very foolhardy enterprise even at this date. Some of the more tendentious interpretations which were put forward in the past have been so convincingly challenged that they can no longer be regarded as seriously tenable: it would require wilful blindness to believe now that More's book was either a blueprint for a proto-Marxist state or an early plan for British imperialism. Yet disagreement remains such that of the two editors of the standard modern scholarly edition, one regards the passages on Utopian religion and philosophy as a relatively insignificant *tour de force* ('humanistic intellectual fancy-work')[1] and the other thinks them so important that he has written two books about them. And I shall have the temerity to argue that the first is mistaken and the second very gravely misinterprets what he rightly sees as important. As I suggested above, literary texts are by nature permanently open to varied interpretation; but of *Utopia* there is not a normal variety but a quite abnormal multiplicity of mutually contradictory interpretations. The reason, I think, lies not in an incompetence in either More or his critics, but in the particular nature of the book's form. Although it is concerned much more directly with ideas than with narrative, character or feelings, it does not present the ideas as an articulated body of thought to which responses might vary within a limited range. The reader is in fact quite deliberately made radically unsure how to respond. The man who describes the island of Utopia has two names, one of which means *Messenger of God* and the other *Distributor of Nonsense*. Even those critics who can resist the temptation to convert the complexity of *Utopia* into the simplicity of a programme often find it difficult not to make in effect an exclusive choice between the two names. But like Erasmus's Moria (Folly) in the book he dedicated to his friend More, *The Praise of Folly*, Raphael Hythloday speaks both sense and nonsense; and in both books it is very largely left to the reader

12

to sort out the sense from the nonsense. The reader is not told what to think; but is made to think.

The chief disadvantage of such a form is sadly obvious from the history of critical accounts and indeed from the history of the word *utopia* itself: the point on which more critics are agreed than on any other is that More's imaginary island does not correspond to the current dictionary definition, 'an ideally perfect state'. The chief advantage is that the very act of reading becomes an educative intellectual effort. The reader is made to work through certain intellectual problems concerning political and moral life, just as in different sorts of fiction he is made to live through certain emotional problems concerning personal relationships. Throughout his life More was profoundly interested in education, and he was well-acquainted with the ancient principle that one learns better what one is made to think through than what one is merely told. It is also not merely more effective but far more pleasurable. In fact the intellectual involvement required to sort out sense from nonsense takes the place of the imaginative involvement demanded by most forms of drama and novel. The writer of fiction of this kind is as dependent on suspiciousness in the reader as the novelist is on imagination. Creative reading is in general more pleasurable than passive reading, and the particular kind of creative response required by a work such as *Utopia* can be seen as one of the primary sources of its aesthetic power. So the difficulty of form which has made criticism look more than ordinarily foolish has in itself two important purposes: to stretch the reader's moral intelligence and to give a distinctive aesthetic pleasure.

In this chapter I shall be concerned primarily with an analysis of Book I, since its function within the economy of the whole seems to me to be to create in the reader the frame of mind in which More wanted Book II to be read, that is, a radically questioning state of mind in which certain moral issues are seen to be profoundly difficult, but not ultimately insoluble. But before proceeding, I want to clarify the kind of literary reading which seems to me appropriate to a rather short tradition, confined, I think, in its pure form, to Erasmus, More and Swift, by dwelling briefly on the ancient paradox of the Cretan liar (A Cretan said, 'All Cretans are liars.') Discussion can be facilitated by setting it out thus:

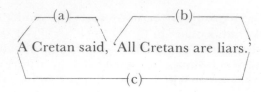

On the face of it, this is a rather trivial puzzle: if the statement (b) is true, the Cretan (a) must be lying, therefore the statement (b) is untrue. But if we do not regard it as an isolated puzzle and try instead to envisage it in a literary context, we shall see some things central to the mode of works like *Utopia*. If, from knowledge of his context, we think the Cretan (a) is trying to speak the truth, we shall have to say that, since he has not noticed his statement (b) includes himself, he must be regarded as foolish; yet, at the same time, he may well be largely correct (have the wisdom of the Fool). Alternatively, if we think the Cretan is lying, statement (b) may confirm our suspicions, but can tell us nothing reliable about other Cretans (application of the text to the world may be perilous). But so far 'liar' has been taken to mean someone who always lies, whereas everyone knows that no such person has ever lived. If we take 'liar' to mean only someone who lies sometimes, then clearly the Cretan (a) is almost certainly right and the form of the statement (c) would indicate, in a literary context, that the Cretan has the self-knowledge of a wise man. In order to appreciate fully the total statement (c), we have, then, firstly to decide, on the basis of what else we know of the Cretan, how reliable the speaker (a) is, and secondly to bring to bear some of our independent knowledge of human nature, though in the awareness that such a procedure is perilous. If Folly says, 'All things are foolish', we shall have to be careful in deciding how far to believe her.

We can, however, go a little further. Statements of the form of (c) are only interesting when truth has the status it would self-evidently have had for More: that is, when it is agreed to be both verifiable and objective. If it is held that truth cannot be clearly distinguished from falsehood, the statement (b) becomes empty and (c) therefore totally uninteresting. If truth is held to be subjective, the statement (c) can only tell us that the Cretan (a) has a low opinion of his compatriots. Unless the Cretan is a character in a quite different sort of fiction, such as a modern novel, this also is uninteresting. The form is thus one which is enjoyed by those who perceive complexity but who envisage truth as verifiable and objective. It is not difficult to understand why in its pure shape it did not remain attractive to Romantic and post-Romantic writers.

The following analysis will, then, be based on the dual assumption that More wished to emphasize the immense difficulty of the questions raised by Raphael Hythloday's discourse, but that he did not regard them as ultimately unanswerable. This will place me in the unenviable position (unenviable because so frequently claimed by previous, mutually contradictory crticis) of implying that I have understood the intentions of the book better than anyone else who has written about them. My own procedures will provide fitting amunition to punish such arrogance where needed.

The relation between the two Books of *Utopia* is far from obvious. J. H. Hexter has demonstrated beyond all reasonable doubt that the work falls into two parts, roughly but not exactly corresponding to the division into two books. One part is written in a discursive manner and consists of the description of the Utopian commonwealth; the other is in the form of a dialogue which is concerned with the question of counselling princes in sixteenth-century Europe. Hexter proves that the description was written first, in the Netherlands in 1515, and the dialogue some months later, when More had returned to London. But it remains uncertain whether More merely added the discussion of a problem which had become more directly important to him, or whether he had an aesthetic purpose in placing it where he did. I think the second of these views is correct, but I do not think that proof is available: all I hope to do is to persuade by accumulation of probability. Firstly, there is on the face of it little connection between the two parts. If More's preoccupations changed completely because his personal circumstances presented him with a new and difficult dilemma, one would expect him to have written a separate work in dialogue form, rather than to have cobbled a discussion about the political responsibility of a philosopher to a traveller's tale about a land with alien institutions. But secondly, there are in fact several connections between the parts which I shall discuss below. If he merely added, then he spoilt the coherence of what he had written in the Netherlands, which was foolish; but if the two parts interact, then he had good reason for joining them. Thirdly, Hexter can separate the parts so conclusively only because the seams are visible four centuries after they were made. This shows Hexter's intelligence; but it also shows that integration was not wholly successful. It would have been much easier, much more natural and much more likely to be undetectable, if More had simply written a Book II of dialogue between the characters referred to in a Book I of description, the dialogue taking up some aspects of the description and then moving into a more particular political issue. If a man, who as a Northern European Humanist regarded good writing as educationally and morally crucial, adopted a more difficult means of achieving an untidier result, it seems sensible to assume he had good reason. I shall, then, assume that, in addition to its intrinsic interest, Book I has relevance to Book II. What I hope to prove is that, granted this assumption, the specific intention is that Book I should provide the reader with important clues as to how to respond to the more enigmatic Book II.

The most important of these clues is an emphasis on the dual nature of Raphael Hythloday, the man who can at times be taken to be speaking in praise of wisdom, in contrast to Moria speaking in praise of folly, yet who also distributes nonsense. But there are also other pointers to an ambivalent response.

In Book I Hythloday describes at some length the penal system of another country he has visited. As a system it is in some respects superior to what was current in Europe, though a certain scepticism must be reserved for something developed by a people whose name, Polylerites, may be translated *People of much nonsense*. But in addition to providing a perspective on Europe, as Hythloday intends, the passage also provides a perspective on Utopia as he describes it later. The life of convicted criminals in the land of the Polylerites resembles extremely closely the life of honest citizens in Utopia. They are fed by the community; they are all dressed alike; they live in effect without money; they are confined to particular districts; the punishment for plotting to escape is just as severe as for actually escaping; informing is encouraged by high rewards; in general they are so regimented 'that they necessarily become good' (*ut bonos esse necesse sit*). The most substantial difference is that, unlike the Utopians, the Polylerite criminals have some prospect of ultimately earning liberty by good behaviour; though even this bears an ironic resemblance to the Utopians' use of the prospect of a happy after-life as an ultimate argument for behaving well. In short, the implication is that the Utopian social organisation is more suitable for criminals than for free men. It is as a system for dealing with criminals and vagrants that such an organisation has the provisional approval of Cardinal Morton.

Almost immediately, however, this perspective on life in Utopia is displaced by an opposite. In response to the proposal that English criminals and vagrants might be treated in this way, the hanger-on at the Cardinal's table suggests that a third category of public nuisances, beggars, could be removed by forcing them to become monks and nuns. There is clearly in Utopia an element of the monastic way of life which is well known to have been admired by More. What may seem fitter for thieves than for honest citizens may in another perspective be a desirable means of achieving spiritual discipline.

But there are other pointers more specific than such vague indications of both approval and disapproval. One of the very few fictional proper names used in the book which is not pejorative is that of the Macarians, which means *blessed*. Their king has to swear an oath at the beginning of his reign that he will never keep more than £1000 in his treasury at one time. The purposes of this are partly that he should have enough to quell any rebellion or invasion which might occur and to keep his country's economic system active, but primarily that he should not have enough to 'encroach on the possessions of others'. By this less drastic means they would achieve the public justice, which is the best purpose of the Utopians' total abolition of money, without substituting an almost penal austerity and regimentation for personal profit as a motive to work. But the specific reference is in the Macarians' primary purpose: the Utopians, as I shall emphasise later, do 'encroach on the possessions of others' in ways which are of very dubious morality. In the form of an unadvertised cross-reference the reader is given the means of questioning the desirability of a Utopian institution and the consequent behaviour.

The clearest general indication of the complex response demanded by the book is in the passages concerning Cardinal Morton. He is described for us by Hythloday as a man whose wisdom, integrity, public service and congenial company command the admiration and liking not only of More but also of Hythloday himself. Unlike the lawyer, Morton responds with open though critical mind to Hythloday's description of the Polylerite penal system: it might be worth experimenting along such lines, though only experience would show if it would work, so the present system would have to remain in reserve in case the new one broke down. His wise caution is clearly contrasted with Hythloday's failure to see any reason why the new one should not be immediately adopted, as well as with the lawyer's irrational conservatism. As for the proposal of the hanger-on that beggars should be forced to become monks, Morton's guests all take it 'in earnest'; only Morton himself has the sense to take it 'in jest'. His subsequent remarks to the friar make it clear that it is unprofitable to answer a fool with further folly. The proper response is to select from the words of the fool what wisdom one may, to laugh at the folly which remains, and then courteously to transfer one's attention to one's responsibilities: the episode is concluded with Morton 'tactfully' changing the subject and soon leaving to attend to his public duties. Neither the bigot, to whom anything new is folly, nor the fool, who takes folly 'in earnest', will be silenced; the wise man listens critically and in due course returns to his own tasks.

But the Morton episode provides an essentially simplified paradigm. It indicates the kind of response which is appropriate, but not the difficulty of making it when the issues are as demanding as they are in Hythloday's description of the island. The difficulty is registered by the form of the dialogue between Hythloday and the character to whom More gives his own name. One of the main unifying strands running through Book I is a debate between 'More' and Hythloday concerning the role of a wise man in a political system dominated by fools, and although it has great intrinsic interest as an issue which faced More personally and has faced many others, its rhetorical function within the book as a whole is to emphasise that on difficult questions there is much which is cogent to be said on both sides. This intention is so successfully carried out that critics remain in almost exactly balanced disagreement about which character finally wins the argument, and some think the issue is deliberately left unresolved. As I suggested in considering the paradox of the Cretan liar, it seems to me, however, that More believed the matter to be finally resolvable despite its difficulty, and I shall therefore concentrate on trying to prove that the character 'More' wins. The importance of this to my main line of argument is that one effect of 'More''s victory here is to throw doubt on the validity of Hythloday's convictions about Utopia. In the following chapters I shall, similarly, concentrate on trying to show what there is in Book II which undermines Hythloday's views. Ultimately Utopia is to be taken as a false ideal; but the route to that conclusion is not meant to be obvious. Many of the details are in fact never conclusive but remain provocative. (A society where all wear a kind of uniform is not attractive; but is the reason for that human vanity or a harmless desire for trivial expression of individual freedom?) Other details, as I shall try to show, are, after strenuous questioning by the reader, conclusive. But the effort is an essential part of the aesthetic and moral demand of the book.

Much of what Hythloday says in Book I clearly commands assent. In his very perceptive analysis of Book I, David Bevington[2] divides the main body of the argument into three stages, concerning respectively domestic policy, foreign policy and fiscal policy. In the second and third stages, 'More' capitulates so completely that he can put forward no answer at all. Hythloday's assertions that it would be hopeless for a wise man to attempt to moderate the desires of kings to conquer foreign land and to increase taxes are unchallenged in the book. On matters incidental to the main argument also, it is impossible to doubt that More the man and the writer wholly agreed with him. When Hythloday speaks of a king as being chosen for the people's sake rather than for his own and as a shepherd who should care more for his flock than for himself, the Yale editors can produce very direct parallels from words written and spoken by More in his own voice. When he particularly emphasises the vices of Pride, Greed and Sloth as the roots of social and political evil, it is unthinkable that More would have wished him to be regarded as mistaken. In Chapter 4, I shall discuss some other areas in which the reader is clearly expected to agree at least partly with Hythloday.

More's chief means of counterbalancing the weight of this body of sound thought, and thus holding open the more contentious issues, is the characterisation of the two figures. This is not a novel and I do not wish to imply by the word 'characterisation' that we are made emotionally interested in them as individuals. But moral characteristics are attributed to them which should, I think, influence our response to the opinions they express more than is allowed for in previous critical accounts.

Apart from what he says on the contentious matters, little direct evidence is given concerning the moral character of 'More', but what does emerge is very important. At the beginning of Book I, he comes across as a modest man, anxious primarily to emphasise the good qualities of others, and as fond of the company of friends. He is engaged in public service, on a diplomatic mission of some importance, but he is eager to return to his family, despite the strong pleasure he takes in the conversation of such men as Peter Giles. Although there is no question of name-dropping, his friends are well-known men of great moral and intellectual stature. In particular, Tunstal, already renowned for integrity and learning, has just been promoted to high office by Henry VIII, and Peter Giles holds a high position in the public life of Antwerp. Emphasis is also put on Giles's modesty and hospitality and his desire to give pleasure to 'More'. 'More' is thus set in a historical context, among actual people, in a situation of honour, hospitality and good company. His fictional status is not that of, for example, Moria; he is as the title-page expresses it, 'the renowned figure, Thomas More, Citizen and Sheriff of the famous city of Great Britain, London'. This being so, I shall cease my concession to 'sensitive critics' and put inverted commas round More's name from now on only when I think there is point in distinguishing the persona from the writer. For the most part I think there is no point: the More apparent to me is only once put in the position of stooge. It is Hythloday who has the fictional status of Moria, though he is by no means altogether a fool. The hints at a resemblance between More and the clearly idealised Cardinal Morton are emphasised at the end of Book II, when, though expressly disagreeing with Hythloday, he thinks it best not to argue and with quiet tact and protective courtesy, 'taking him by the hand', leads him in to supper.

In the prefatory letter from More to Giles,[3] these impressions are confirmed: in excusing his delay in publishing, More explains that his public duties are very extensive and that he believes spending time with his family to be a responsibility as well as a pleasure. But two other points of importance are added. More says he thinks Hythloday said the bridge at Amaurotum was 500 paces long. His servant thinks 200 must be deducted as the river there is only 300 paces wide, and More says he will be guided finally by Giles's memory as he would prefer repeating an inaccuracy of Hythloday's to making deliberate alterations. Obviously this is not altogether serious: it is the sort of question which would have interested that fictional bishop who complained that he could not find on his map the countries visited by Gulliver. But at the same time, it does have the effect of establishing, with appropriate absence of solemnity, that Thomas More, Citizen of London, takes no responsibility for what he reports Hythloday as having said. The second point is even more important. More asks Giles to try to find Hythloday again so that he can check details, but also so that More can be sure he is not planning to publish a description of Utopia himself: More does not wish to steal the glory by forestalling him. He then goes on, in a passage aimed ostensibly at readers who will be unable or unwilling to understand the book, to imply a contrast between himself and Hythloday: 'those persons who pleasantly and blithely indulge their inclinations seem to be very much better off than those who torment themselves with anxiety in order to publish something that may bring profit or pleasure to others, who nevertheless receive it with disdain or ingratitude'. Writing up Hythloday's account has been largely a responsibility undertaken at personal cost; what pleasure it has included, More is prepared to resign to Hythloday if he chooses to claim it. But Hythloday evidently does not think the pleasures of writing outweigh the pains.

This is central to the moral character of Hythloday. When Peter Giles asks him, in Book I, why he does not put to use the wisdom he has acquired from his travels, by engaging in public service, the centre of Hythloday's reply is 'I now live as I please' (*nunc sic vivo ut volo*). He has seen very clearly that the way to remain free to do as he pleases is to decline all responsibility and stay independent. There may be some irony in his contempt for court parasites: he is currently the guest of Giles and More; he gained provisions and a guide for his travels to Utopia through a 'ruler's generosity'; in fact he has spent his life, and intends to continue, as a permanent itinerant guest. But the important contrast is with More, sheriff, diplomat, and, in what time remains, writer of books he intends to benefit and please others. Hythloday's fundamental aim is to please himself. The difference extends to his attitude towards his family: in place of More's concern, Hythloday is 'not greatly troubled about' his relatives and friends. With a very strong irony, in view of his admiration for the Utopians' contempt for possessions, he considers he performed all his duty towards his family long ago by distributing his possessions among them in his youth. Hythloday's personal

isolation might be compared with the geographical isolation of
Utopia, made as it was into an island by human effort under the
direction of Utopus.[4] But Hythloday comes off worse even from
that comparison: as the 'Quatrain in the Utopian Vernacular'
added by Peter Giles makes clear, Utopia is willing to share its
benefits with others. Hythloday does not write a description of
what he learnt there; indeed he is only drawn into giving an oral
description of it in the course of defending his own choice of life.

The important contrast is, as I have stressed, with More, but
the main debate is opened by Peter Giles in order to clarify the
basis of Hythloday's thinking while keeping More's consistent.
Peter Giles first puts the question less in terms of public service
than of personal and family advancement. Hythloday's response,
radically utilitarian, is that the greater pleasure lies in isolation. It
is only then, when More introduces the alien concept of a *duty* to
the commonwealth, that Hythloday starts arguing that no-one
would listen to him. His ultimate end is his own pleasure.
Consequently he never really understands what More says.

More's presentation of himself has been careful. He does not
reject pleasure: he finds it in the company of his friends and
family, and is grateful when Peter Giles finds it for him in the
acquaintance of Hythloday. The primary difference is that it is
not his ultimate end. Cardinal Morton, too, enjoys the company
at his table, though in due course he leaves it, to attend to his
responsibilities.

One can see how deeply Hythloday's thinking is infected with
the principle of self-interest by glancing at the end of Book II,
where he is introducing his diatribe against Pride: 'Nor does it
occur to me to doubt that a man's regard for his own interests or the
authority of Christ our Saviour . . . would long ago have brought
the whole world to adopt the laws of the Utopian commonwealth,
had not one single monster . . . striven against it – I mean, Pride.'
The order of thought in the first part of the sentence is radically
characteristic of Hythloday. But the end of it is also ironic, for this
diatribe against Pride is being delivered by a man who thinks all
kings too corrupt ever to be influenced in the slightest by his
borrowed wisdom. In his prefatory letter to Lupset, Budé
elegantly contrasts More's modesty with Hythloday's pride by
switching briefly from Latin into Greek for the purpose. But the
point is made more delicately and with a fine dramatic sense when

More takes the hectoring Hythloday by the hand and leads him in to supper, with the tactful flattery he clearly needs.

So in three important respects Hythloday resembles Moria: we know he is wholly fictional (unlike More); his ultimate good is pleasure; and he is proud. Moria names three of her attendants Pleasure, Self-love and Flattery. As I have stressed, this does not prevent Hythloday from being often right: even Moria is often right and Raphael Hythloday's name itself suggests he is likely to be more often right than Moria. But when his views conflict with those of Thomas More, sheriff, diplomat, husband, father, and friend of famous Humanist scholars, the pressure to question them is extremely strong. As in *The Praise of Folly*, the reader is left to do much of the work of selecting wisdom from folly; but here the pull in both directions is stronger. As Hythloday speaks more sense than Moria, so More is introduced to indicate more firmly the basic form of the nonsense. How finely More calculated the balance is shown by the continuing disagreement among critics about where the sense ends and the nonsense begins. It now remains to attempt proof that the balance is tipped slightly, but nonetheless crucially, against Hythloday.

The basic premises of the two men are unmistakably clarified at the beginning of the major confrontation: self-interest against obligation. To Hythloday's *sic vivo ut volo*, More's immediate response is that it would be more worthy of a wise man to serve 'the public interest, even if it involves some personal disadvantages'. But Hythloday immediately deflects the argument into questions of possibility rather than desirability. The line of his argument is: even if I preferred to serve, no one would take any notice ('in disturbing my own peace and quiet, I should not promote the public interest'). The line of More's is: even though the possibilities of success are limited, the obligation remains. There is thus a damaging but not immediately apparent circularity in Hythloday's case: the counsel he proposes to offer is impossible, and he argues that since it is impossible that his counsel will be welcomed, it is not worth offering it. More replies that it would therefore seem sensible to offer counsel which is possible.

Initially, Hythloday puts forward two reasons why he will not be listened to: kings prefer conquering more kingdoms to administering well what they already have, and royal councillors are both bigotted and obsequious towards the chief royal favourites. In calling others bigotted he is not on strong ground. When he says, 'it is but human nature that each man favor his own discoveries most', the reference to himself is obvious. And even he slips in a qualification, which he later forgets, to the point about kings: he says here '*almost* all monarchs' (my italics). But on the whole More accepts this point. As I have mentioned already, he agrees, in the second and third stages of the argument clarified by Bevington, that it is futile to oppose the territorial ambitions of kings or to reduce their income by moderating taxation. Or to be more precise, he agrees that it would be futile to oppose them head-on in the way Hythloday suggests. It is in the first area that he will not give ground ('I cannot change my mind'), the area of domestic policy concerning enclosure and the death-penalty for theft. This is clearly to one of More's persuasion the most important area, for what is at issue is justice. Through war and through heavy taxation, kings can cause suffering, but an unjust legal system can do worse than that: it can cause men not only to suffer but to do evil. Suffering is ultimate evil to one whose ultimate good is pleasure; to More suffering was an evil, but not ultimate evil.

One of the means by which More's victory, in this part of the dialogue, is indicated for the careful reader has been clarified very well by Bevington. Hythloday is here not only speaking to More in 1515; he is reporting a discussion at the table of Cardinal Morton which took place in 1497. In 1497, enclosure was a social evil about which nothing was being done by the king or his councillors. But by 1515–16, the government, under the direction of Wolsey, was acting on a large scale to remedy the evils of enclosure and to prevent further enclosure. Hythloday had every right to speak with such passion in 1497, but as an argument in 1515 that kings take no account of good counsel, the passage backfires on him. Much of course remained undone, but enough had been done to destroy his argument that good counsel is always rejected.

The other means is aimed very precisely at Hythloday's point about royal councillors. The most obvious is sometimes the most subtle. Morton is praised highly as a wise and virtuous man by Hythloday, who is arguing that wise men stay out of politics. But Morton, as he tells us, was in 1497 Lord Chancellor of England. In fact Hythloday even adds, 'The king placed the greatest confidence in his advice, and the commonwealth seemed much to depend upon him.' A man who can both say this and argue that it is pointless for a wise man to attempt to influence a king cannot altogether be relied on for accuracy of judgement or clarity of thought. A man who says this in the middle of such an argument might even be said to seem rather foolish. Morton is in fact so far from being bigotted that he is willing to entertain the possibility of experimenting with penalties against theft along the lines mentioned by Hythloday. The detail is of course fictional, like Hythloday. But Morton, though he has a function within the fiction, is not fictional: he stands as a factual, historical contradiction of Hythloday's argument that a truly wise and honest man will not succeed in public office. As to Hythloday's point about the obsequiousness of councillors towards court favourites, the episode registers that here he has hold of a half-truth. When the lawyer expresses disapproval of Hythloday's views, everyone present follows suit. But when Morton expresses approval immediately afterwards, they all vie in praising what they had just rejected with contempt. Hythloday's point is correct in so far as they praise particularly the detail added by the Cardinal; but another tacit implication is that when a wise man has attained the position held by Morton, the fools, flatterers and former bigots will follow his lead. Again the fundamental point is that a wise man *can* have effective political influence. Characteristically, it is made silently: the reader has to reflect in order to perceive it. Neither More nor Morton says very much, which might seem on a hasty reading to make the dialogue one-sided; but Hythloday's loquaciousness puts him in the unenviable company of the lawyer, the hanger-on and the friar. 'A fool uttereth all his mind.'[5]

At the end of this first stage of the argument, the differences between the two men are again stressed. More uses the concept of *duty*: giving counsel which will benefit the commonwealth, he tells Hythloday, 'is the most important part of your duty as it is the duty of every good man'. Hythloday's reply is very much in character: he thinks first of advising through books rather than in person, and he would give his advice if kings were 'ready' to take it – in other words if it were an easy undertaking. Yet he then goes on to reveal the total impossibility of the advice he has in mind: 'If I proposed beneficial measures to some king and tried to uproot from his soul the seeds of evil and corruption'. The difference between proposing beneficial measures and uprooting the seeds of evil in a man is a difference between the possible and the impossible, and Hythloday, characteristically, does not perceive it. Hythloday is in effect arguing as follows: 'Benefitting the commonwealth requires a change in human nature; but human nature cannot be changed by offering counsel to kings; therefore there is no point in trying to benefit the commonwealth.' This is not an entirely foolish line of argument; but there is an element of childishness in it ('If I can't make up the rules, I shan't play'). Even though Hythloday clearly does win the next two stages of the argument, since More agrees that in foreign and fiscal policy a councillor will have little influence, this tendency to simplify and exaggerate persists and at least slightly weakens his case. The French king whom he uses as an example has, in his own words, 'already for a long time' (*iam olim*) thought of usurping foreign territory. Similarly on fiscal matters, he says that his ideas will have no effect on 'men strongly inclined to the opposite way of thinking' (*in contrariam partem vehementer inclinatos*). That this is certainly true of many kings does not imply that it is necessarily so of all.

The major statement of More's position is directed at the unreality and wilful hopelessness of Hythloday's. He generalises, from his agreement that Hythloday's proposed fiscal counsel will not be welcome, to the point that advice should not be given when one is 'positive [it] will never be listened to', and he twice repeats that it is useless to force new ideas on people who are of 'opposite conviction'. This already implicitly diagnoses Hythloday's case as that of a man who excuses himself from the possible by declaring that the impossible is impossible. But More emphasises the point by making a distinction between bookish philosophy and practical philosophy: the bookish philosophy Hythloday has had in mind is only appropriate in the company of like-minded friends; in the world of practical politics one must do what one can with the situation as it is.[6] The primary implication of his famous image of political life as a play is that one must adapt to the play which is actually being performed, an adaptation which will require tact. The comic element implicit in Hythloday's stance is brought out very vividly by the image of him delivering a tragic speech in the middle of a low comedy. But More does not laugh at him. The tone is the same as when he takes him by the hand at the end of Book II: 'would it not have been preferable to take a part without words?' He is practising the tact he is preaching. Yet despite the tact, he is very firm and very precise in his rejection of the basic assumption Hythloday has made: there *is* a difference between improving a particular situation and changing the nature of reality. 'You must not abandon the ship in a storm because you cannot control the winds.' The final emphasis is again on the importance of duty ('You must not . . . desert the commonwealth'). He concedes the half-truth which Hythloday has clarified – 'it is impossible that all should be well unless all men were good, a situation which I do not expect for a great many years to come'. He does not, however, argue from impossibility to excuse but to realistic imperative: 'You must not abandon . . . because you cannot control.' And the nature of the imperative, as the language makes clear, is that of an emotive moral responsibility ('desert the commonwealth', 'abandon the ship'). Despite the tact, More speaks with emotional vehemence: 'you must seek and strive to the best of your power to handle matters tactfully' – as he is doing in this very speech.

The floor is then taken, again at length, by Hythloday. His manner is as mixed as his understanding. The senseless squabble between the friar and the hanger-on, which he reported earlier, has partly the function of emphasising by contrast the civilised nature of the present dialogue. But Hythloday's opening remark is the sort of adolescent debating-point in which the element of truth is so obscured that it is nearer falsehood: 'By this approach . . . I should accomplish nothing else than to share the madness of others as I tried to cure their lunacy.' On his own showing, Morton shared no trace of madness, and Hythloday had total freedom of speech in his company. The word which stood out before now recurs (*volo*): 'If I would stick to the truth.' What matters to him is what he wants to do. 'To speak falsehoods, for all I know, may be the part of a philosopher, but it is certainly not for me.' Apart from the arrogance of it, this is on a level with the friar: what More said was, 'take a part without words'. As it happened, More showed very vividly at the end of his own life that the difference between lying and remaining silent is not slight. Hythloday's sense of tact, however, *is* slight: 'what did my speech contain that would not be appropriate . . . to have propounded everywhere?' His sense of obligation is even shakier. The words I omitted from my last quotation are 'or obligatory'. To score a debating-point, he is now saying it is obligatory to propound everywhere what he has at length been arguing it is pointless to say anywhere. And in such a context it becomes easy to pretend that what More said implied that 'all the things which by the perverse morals of men have come to seem odd are to be dropped'. From that it is a very small step, via the friar's method of taking a biblical phrase out of context, to arguing that More is actually anti-Christian. In the Gospels, Christ commanded His disciples to preach His Truths from the housetops, yet More has suggested, according to Hythloday, that the truth should be accommodated to the perverse morals of men, and not spoken openly at all times.

Instead of meeting More's argument, Hythloday, like the friar, concentrates his attention on making a rhetorical impact. Through a combination of question-begging and simplification, he gives a surface impression of an unanswerable case. He would not have any effect in council meetings, he says, 'For I should hold either a different opinion, which would amount to having none at all, or else the same, and then I should . . . help their madness.' This seems to leave little room for answer, but it is wholly specious. For a start, when he expressed a different opinion, it was listened to intelligently by Morton. Secondly, if he held the same opinion as others he would (if he was right) not help any madness: it would not be mad. But the tacit assumption here in fact is that everyone else is always wrong: if he thought as they did, he would also be wrong. The pride is grotesque. He seems determined to be in the strict sense of the word an idiot, that is, one who thinks in a manner peculiar to himself. Finally, the alternatives are not of course exclusive: as always, Hythloday thinks in black and white terms – either he will think the same or he will think so differently that no one will listen. More's quietly insistent point about tact is simply not confronted.

As Hythloday reaches the nadir of his specious rhetoric, there are two very pointed references to what happens in the description of Utopia. Hythloday both complains that men have accommodated Christ's teaching to their own perverse morals and says he cannot see what has been gained in this way, 'except that men may be bad in greater comfort'. In describing the Utopian way of life one of his main efforts is precisely to accommodate Christ's teaching to it; the nature of Utopian 'bad'ness and the significance of 'comfort' to it will be discussed in the following chapters.

Thus far he has grossly mis-represented what More has said, and has damaged his own case by self-contradiction and disreputable modes of argument. But just where one might be relaxing into the assumption that he is merely distributing nonsense, there is placed a passage in which he not only confronts directly More's point about tact, but brings out extremely powerfully both the difficulties and the dangers of acting in the way More has proposed. It would be very difficult in a court situation where, flattery being the convention, even faint praise is likely to be regarded with suspicion: one is likely to be forced into open approval of what one knows to be evil. Worse still, there is danger of being corrupted, or, more subtly, of one's integrity being used as a 'screen for the wickedness and folly of others'. Although he wins the argument, More was not only aware that what he proposed was difficult and dangerous, but wished to make the reader appreciate directly how hard a question is at issue. The attractions of Hythloday's point of view are largely specious; but they are by no means wholly so.

Accordingly, the climax of his speech is the reference to Plato's image of philosophers keeping themselves dry indoors, while the people rush about outside in the rain, getting wet: 'They know that, if they go out, they can do no good but will only get wet with the rest. Therefore, being content if they themselves at least are safe, they keep at home, since they cannot remedy the folly of others.' In imaginative force, this seems to balance More's image of life as a drama, and it carries in addition the authority of Plato. But more is happening than Hythloday is aware of. In context, Plato's image is the climax of an argument that the philosopher can do nothing in such societies as at present exist. What follows is an argument that in a changed society his wisdom could prevail. The nature of the change envisaged by Plato is nearer to Hythloday's dreams of changing the human character than to More's realism, but Plato is arguing fundamentally that the philosopher has a responsibility to bring it about. So the image is working thus far in a complex way, partly supporting Hythloday's argument and partly undermining it. But to anyone acquainted with Plato's *Republic*, the image Hythloday refers to will immediately bring to mind also the one which follows quite shortly afterwards: the image of the present life as inside a dark cave and of truth as the light outside, where the primary implication is quite the reverse of Hythloday's argument. The philosopher there has an unquestionable moral obligation to go back into the cave and share with the common people the wisdom he has gained in the daylight. Hythloday cannot really enlist Plato in support of the main line of his argument.

But the image of the rain in fact moves even further beyond his control. He has just referred to St Matthew's Gospel in his tag about preaching from the roof-tops. A little earlier in the same Gospel, there is a famous image which defines with great clarity a profound difference between Christian belief and the thinking of Hythloday and the Utopians he admires. '[God] maketh his sun to rise on the evil and on the good, and sendeth rain on the just and the unjust. For if ye love them which love you, what reward have ye? do not even the publicans the same?'[7] What Hythloday wants, fundamentally, is justice in the very naive sense of each man getting due reward in terms of prosperity. The words *justice* and *prosperity* are almost interchangeable in his vocabulary: in a society based on cash values, he says, 'it is scarcely possible . . . to have justice or prosperity'; whereas in Utopia 'virtue has its reward'. In Christian thinking, on the contrary, as More expounds at length in his *Dialogue of Comfort*, there is no guarantee at all that good behaviour will lead to prosperity. Good is to be done because it is good, not because it will be rewarded; to do good on the assumption that good will be returned is in fact the cash morality of the publican. We found before of Hythloday that his mode of thought was to weigh up which course would be of most advantage, which would repay him best. Despite his contempt for money, his moral thought is essentially based on an account-book principle. It is More, with his concept of duty, so radically alien to Hythloday, who really escapes money-values. Yet at the same time it is More who is living in the world of reality. Hythloday is certainly unaware of the play he is acting in if he conceives it possible that the rain will ever not fall equally on the just and the unjust.

How far he has lost sight of reality is emphasised at the end of his long speech. After mentioning a number of expedients which might lead to a possible improvement in social justice (expedients which are listed in a throwaway manner, but which indicate the sort of thing More would have thought it sensible to attempt) he says, 'By this type of legislation, I maintain, as sick bodies which are past cure can be kept up by repeated medical treatments, so these evils, too, can be alleviated and made less acute. There is no hope, however, of a cure and a return to a healthy condition as long as each individual is master of his own property.' 'Sick bodies which are past cure' – this, as More stresses at length in *The Four Last Things*, is what we inescapably are. 'A return to a healthy condition' – what, in a Christian frame of thought such as Hythloday professes to be thinking in, could this be a return to? He cannot really mean a reversal of the Fall, but the image prevents him from meaning anything else. He has lost all sense of the direction of his argument as well as all sense of reality. He is talking about No Time as well as No Place, never as well as nowhere. He does not want to act in any play which has ever been performed; he wants to write his own. *Sic vivo ut volo*.

But again, in case we are inclined to think that what he has to say is too easily to be regarded as nonsense, our sense of security is shaken. More raises two objections to Hythloday's preliminary hints about the organisation of Utopian society, that it does not provide motivation for work and that there could be no respect for magistrates if all men were 'on the same level'. The first objection is intelligent: the Utopians have largely to substitute regimentation for incentive. But the second is stupid: respect for magistrates should be based on their degree of integrity, not on a social rank dependent on personal wealth. This is the only time 'More' speaks foolishly,[8] so the effect is a sharp warning that the reader is likely to trip unless he walks with the greatest care. We must follow the hint dropped by Peter Giles in a letter to Busleyden: 'in all the five years which Raphael spent on the island, he did not see as much as one may perceive in More's description'. Perceiving more than Raphael saw is not a matter of breaking a simple code, but of sustained intellectual effort. In Raphael's dream-play he would like the rules to be very simple; More knew that the real play is not simple at all.

3 *Utopia*: the Pleasure Ethic

The ultimate end of the Utopians is pleasure. It is characteristic of our time that this should generally be thought either to be not very important, or (after some minor qualifications have been made) to be easily and directly assimilable into Christian belief. 'It is not extravagant to say that the whole Utopian state is waiting breathlessly, as it were, for fulfillment in the reception of Christ's faith and morals. Christ would not come to destroy the Utopian law and the Utopian prophets but to fulfill (Matt. 5.17). Little would have to be discarded: nearly all could be retained.'[1] Fr Surtz does register some reservations about euthanasia and divorce by mutual consent (which are entirely logical extensions of the pleasure ethic), but if the secularisation of Christian thought continues at its present pace, it is unlikely that these too will not soon be discovered to be entirely compatible with Christianity. In his discussion of hanging in Book I, Hythloday complains about the way some men 'determine in everything how far it suits them that God's commandments should be obeyed'. In so far as they bring God in at all, that is essentially the way the Utopians think. The failure to see anything amiss about it cannot be attributed merely to an incompetence in literary criticism: it is essentially the direction of most modern moral theology. Historically we are not well-placed to see *Utopia* very clearly: the East has notorious grounds for mis-reading it, but the West has a beam in its own eye. Welfare has become so unquestioningly our ultimate end, that we can think we are being appropriately critical if we point out that the Utopian understanding of the word is morally superior to our materialism. They recognise that the pleasures of the mind are superior to those of the body, that natural pleasures are superior to the depraved ones of European civilisation. Their end is true pleasure; ours is false pleasure; therefore they are (with a few slightly embarrassing exceptions) right. We have had the benefit of Revelation, so have the advantage in a few ecclesiastical details; but it is they, even without Revelation, who really live as

Christians should. Their ignorance of the Cross, and the absence from their thought of any concept corresponding to its implications, creates so little difference between them and modern theologians that it can be passed over without mention.

More certainly intended his book to be witty, and he was fond of pretending to be in earnest when he was joking; but I am not sure he would have been pleased to see the joke go this far. Of course there are some desirable things in Utopia, just as Hythloday makes some valuable proposals in Book I. Of course pleasure is a good: we saw Morton and More enjoying it in Book I. But, as I stressed, More was at some pains to indicate, in the moral character of Hythloday, the centre of what is wrong in the nation he admires. In order to live as he likes, Hythloday is prepared to 'desert the commonwealth'. The Utopians cannot desert – strict regimentation prevents them – and they have been conditioned to be discerning in their choice of pleasures; but they will do what gives the greatest real pleasure. If that involves treachery, judicial murder and mass deportation, so be it: love of God and of their neighbour is not their ultimate end. The difference between loving one's neighbour because it gives pleasure, and deriving pleasure from loving one's neighbour, is one which leads to very crucial differences of behaviour, when one's own interests conflict with one's neighbours'. Even the *communism* which has seemed to so many readers their ultimate end is, as Fr Surtz himself has pointed out, essentially a sharing of the 'matter of pleasure' (*materia voluptatis*). Their whole social structure is a precaution against the personal selfishness of a Hythloday. Utopus knew that selfishness is self-defeating. Yet man is by nature selfish. So the most efficient means of achieving a genuine sharing of the *materia voluptatis* is to abolish all possibility of possession. The Utopians are not crude in their pursuit of pleasure. But the intelligent pursuit of a mistaken end is still a pursuit of a mistaken end.

In this chapter, I shall attempt to prove that pleasure *is* their ultimate end, by analysing a few passages of crucial importance, and to confirm by external evidence that More would have regarded it as a mistaken ultimate end. Internal evidence will accumulate in Chapter 4, when I examine the consequences of pursuing this end on other aspects of Utopian thought.

Proof is less straightforward than I have suggested in these opening remarks. What most impresses Hythloday about Utopia is, of course, its *communism*, and one might expect to discover the ultimate end of the Utopians by asking a question about the intention of the *communism*. Why have no private property and no money? To this, the immediate answer is, 'To achieve a just distribution of the *materia voluptatis*' ('Though no man has anything, yet all are rich.'). But it will not do to stop there: this is not their ultimate end, for to the further question, 'Why do you want a just distribution of the *materia voluptatis*?' they would answer, 'To exclude the evils of pride, greed and sloth', or (making specific reference to what Hythloday has on his mind) 'To remove the causes of theft and the crimes caused by enclosure.' In the words Hythloday used of the Polylerites, they intend to make the people 'necessarily become good'. Leaving aside for a moment the implications of the word 'necessarily', one would expect, if Utopian thought were really in effect Christian, to have reached a conclusion here: it is desirable to become good because that is the will of God. Yet in fact, for the Utopians, the purpose of becoming good is not *amor Dei*: instead it is, in their view, sensible to remove pride, greed and sloth because that is the way to achieve the greatest happiness of the greatest number. Hythloday does not, of course, use this eighteenth-century formula, but in his final peroration in Book II he makes it clear that ease, comfort, pleasure are the ends which make it sensible to 'become good'. The extirpation of crime leads to an easier life: 'Who does not know that fear, anxiety, worries, toils, and sleepless nights will also perish at the same time as money?' Even the rich would be better off: they would be relieved of 'numerous troubles'. The Utopian commonwealth is founded in the 'happiest way' (*modo felissime*), or as Robinson has justification for translating it 'wealthily'. When Hythloday contrasts conditions in Utopia with the effects of greed in Europe it is the difference in degree of happiness which is put forward as significant: 'how far are they from the happiness of the Utopian commonwealth!' Evil is to be removed because it makes people unhappy. Welfare – the commonwealth – is the ultimate good.

Before looking in detail at the passages about Utopian philosophy which expound the thinking behind this conclusion, it is important to pursue the implications of the word 'necessarily' in that phrase 'necessarily become good'. Into the sentence I have partly quoted before – 'Nor does it occur to me to doubt that a man's regard for his own interests or the authority of Christ our Savior . . . would long ago have brought the whole world to adopt

the laws of the Utopian commonwealth, had not one single monster, the chief and progenitor of all plagues, striven against it – I
mean Pride' – Hythloday inserts, as what is evidently to him a
mere gesture of orthodoxy, a parenthesis which is actually crip-
pling to the whole Utopian enterprise: 'who in His wisdom could
not fail to know what was best and who in His goodness would not
fail to counsel what He knew to be best'. Christ would have coun-
selled Utopian laws had it not been for Pride; but the purpose
of Utopian laws, we are being told, is to extirpate Pride. The
implication of that parenthesis, if one takes it as a serious
statement of belief, is either that Christ is powerless against Pride,
which cannot be intended by either Hythloday or More, or that in
His wisdom He knew that it was not best to extirpate it by means
of legislation. Christ did not come as a legislator; on the contrary,
He stated, in summary of a clear pattern of behaviour, 'My
kingdom is not of this world.'[2] The idea that the worst of the Seven
Deadly Sins, and by implication most other sins, could be
eradicated by a system of law is in fact very precisely opposite to
Christian thinking as set out most fully in St Paul's *Epistle to the
Romans*. The Utopian social structure is designed to make men
'necessarily become good'; Christian belief is that by means of
laws men necessarily cannot become good. What Christ came to
do through His self-sacrifice, the Utopians, in an enterprise
against pride, achieve more efficiently by changing the conditions
of human life.

The Utopians, of course, profess humility – for example, they
pray that, if there is anything better than their system, God will
lead them to it. But even apart from Hythloday's pride, there are
clear alarm signals. The excavation of fifteen miles of land to make
Utopia into an island exceeds the feat of Xerxes, who also used his
soldiers for the digging, at Athos. Herodotus thought Xerxes was
motivated only by pride, and in subsequent literature he became
an example of foolish pride. Utopus was more intelligent: the
excavation made invasion much more difficult. But it also filled
the neighbouring peoples with 'wonder and terror'. A related
point is made in Book I when Hythloday tells of how he taught
another nation the use of the compass. He is concerned now at the
risks they take: 'trusting to the magnet, they do not fear wintry
weather, being dangerously confident'. What can help one to get
one's bearings will not alter the conditions under which one has to
sail. Good laws, like navigational instruments, are very useful, but

they will not make men into gods, or rough seas calm. In the discussion of the Utopian distinction between true and false pleasure, Hythloday says, 'it is impossible for any man's judgement, depraved either by disease or by habit, to change the nature of pleasure any more than that of anything else'. Quite: by the same argument, the Utopian judgement of what their citizens should be like cannot change the nature of man. Budé, in his letter to Lupset, draws attention more explicitly to the transformation in human nature which would have to take place if the Utopian system were really to exist: 'What sort of holiness did the Utopians possess to merit the heavenly grace of not having avarice and cupidity break or creep into that island alone for so many centuries?'

A question as bald as that exposes, more clearly than Hythloday ever cares to, an area of Utopian thought which they prefer, for their own reasons, to blur. Does 'necessarily become good' mean that a Utopian has become by nature good (is no longer, through Original Sin, inclined to fall), or only that he is prevented from doing evil by means of well-calculated legislation? But the possibility of confusion is greater still, for the Utopians argue, at some times and not others, that not just they, but man in general, is by nature good. It is crucial to notice their confusions and avoid them, in order to understand More. The elusiveness of Utopian ideas depends very largely on the interaction of two variables, the possible–impossible and the desirable–undesirable. More indicates these variables right at the end of Book II: 'there are many features in the Utopian commonwealth which it is easier for me to wish for in our countries than to have any hope of seeing realised'. A large proportion of what is impossible, is so, because it is based on assumptions about the nature of man which are unrealistic, so it is important to be clear about which account of human nature is in mind at each stage of their thinking.

The phrase *human nature* is in fact very widely used in two crucially different ways. Sometimes it refers to what man actually is and does: what he can be seen to be like in recorded history. At other times it refers to what man ought to be or would like to be. The gap between these two images of human nature is potentially very large, and Christianity has a clear, though complex, means of bridging it. But it is not immediately clear how the Utopians, whose thought was formed before they learnt of Christianity, could create an alternative bridge. The objection raised by More at the end of Book I is a special case of this general problem: what makes Utopians work when the incentive of personal gain is absent? Wise men, in the context of Christian or of Platonic thought, ought to know that it is their responsibility to work for the good of the community for no personal reward (though by one of More's characteristically silent strokes of wit, Hythloday, who admires Utopia, has been arguing against this); but what, asks More, will motivate ordinary men? Why should men work if no personal gain will come of it? Why should men as they are, with all the selfishness which is natural in one sense, behave as they should for the benefit of all, which is natural in the other sense?

The Utopians actually have three means of attempting to bridge this crucial gap, of trying to make what man *is* correspond with their notion of what he *ought to be*. The first is education. 'They take', says Hythloday, 'the greatest pains from the very first to instill into children's minds, while still tender and pliable, good opinions which are also useful for the preservation of their commonwealth.' Elsewhere he has already said, 'They have very few laws because very few are needed for persons so educated.' This is an attempt, in effect, to make Utopians become by nature good, to re-mould what they are. Strictly controlled education, especially of the very young has, of course, often proved a very powerful means of influencing adult behaviour. But the Utopians evidently do not find it sufficient, for they have to follow it up with a second bridge, that is, despite what Hythloday says, an extremely rigid legal system. To make sure that no one becomes possessive about his house, everyone has to move every ten years. If a family becomes too big to suit the social structure, some adult members are arbitrarily transferred to another family which is smaller. In order to ensure that there are no private possessions, they are denied privacy: no door can be locked, and anyone can walk into any house. If the Utopians keep to such rules they are quite safe; but if they break them the penalties are extreme. A citizen who is twice caught outside his assigned city boundaries without a permit is sentenced to slavery. Discussion of matters of public importance outside the senate or the popular assembly is subject to the death penalty. Opinion has varied notoriously about whether the disadvantages of such rigidity outweigh the advantage of removing the evils which result from unequal distribution of private property. But there are two more important points to note. This attempt differs from the first, in that the

intention is not to make the Utopians by nature good: it is based
on the assumption that they will retain private inclinations which
will conflict with the interests of the commonwealth they should
serve. The purpose of the legislation is to counterbalance by
external sanction the pull of natural inclination. Man is legally
restrained in order to make him behave as he should. This second
means of bridging is therefore less optimistic than the first. But the
other important point is that the Utopians find it also inadequate.
Ultimately they find it necessary to require, from citizens who
hold full rights, a belief in immortality and reward or punishment
after death. A Utopian who does not have these beliefs is not
punished, but he is regarded as having fallen 'below the dignity of
human nature', and is allowed to hold no office. 'Who can doubt',
asks Hythloday, advocating Utopian beliefs, 'that he will strive
either to evade by craft the public laws of his country or to break
them by violence, in order to serve his own private desires when he
has nothing to fear but laws and no hope beyond the body?' Rigid
legislation will be thwarted by craft or violence: the pessimism
deepens. This is in fact a very ironic conclusion for the Utopians to
have reached. A good Utopian will not be rewarded with personal
gain in the form of money; but he is required to believe he will be
personally rewarded in heaven. In other words, they have failed,
ultimately, to find a reason why an individual should care more
about the community than about himself. On this account of
human nature, man will finally be brought to behave well only if it
pays him to do so.

There is a certain realism about this, even though it might seem
excessively cynical. But the central point is that it really will not
do to think this and at the same time base one's whole moral
philosophy on the premise that man is by nature good. The
pleasure ethic is, as I shall soon show, based on a premise which is
incompatible not only with Christian belief but with the Utopians' own political experience.

Utopia is, of course, being described to us by a man who does
not just emerge as morally inferior to More, but who is advocating
Utopian ways of thought in support of his own position. When he
says, 'We have taken upon ourselves only to describe their
principles, and not also to defend them', he is more than a little
disingenuous. As Hythloday's moral intelligence is limited, More
cannot use him directly to indicate that there is a crucial confusion
centring around the word *nature*; instead, in the manner of

Erasmus and Swift, he uses him indirectly, in some places as an obviously biased spokesman, and in others as the naive reporter of contradictions. So partly in Hythloday's opinion and partly in their own, the Utopians are represented in some places as by nature superior to Europeans and in others as normal human beings. There is a quite deliberate confusion about their nature in order to indicate that it is in this area that something very fishy is taking place in their thinking. In Hythloday's opinion, usually, they are by nature superior to Europeans. Although there is a sting in the tail (*ocio gaudens*), he is unaware of it and intends as straightforward praise: 'The people in general are easy-going, good-tempered, ingenious and leisure-loving.' What he reports objectively is more confusing. In the passage dealing with Utopian attitudes to gold, they appear in some respects normally human: gold is not kept locked up since 'it might be suspected that the governor and the senate – for such is the foolish imagination of the common folk – were deceiving the people by the scheme and they themselves were deriving some benefit therefrom'. If the common folk remain humanly suspicious, perhaps the governor and senate remain human enough for the word 'foolish' to be ironic. Yet on the next page the Utopian attitude towards precious stones is wiser than that of any human society in history. The decision not to lock up the gold they have accumulated in fact shows very wittily how slippery the word *nature* is. Hythloday has just reported the Utopian view that nature, 'like a most kind and indulgent mother', has exposed good things such as air and water, and concealed useless things such as gold. In the next sentence he begins to explain that the Utopians expose their gold, with the intention of inculcating a *natural* attitude towards it, as a rather useless and uninteresting metal. To achieve a *natural* attitude, they have to undo what nature has done.

This procedure is based on the assumption that the good attitude has to be inculcated through legislation, that it is not innate. Utopian views about treaties are based on the contradictory assumption, that innately good human nature is corrupted by legalistic contracts. There is a natural bond between nations deriving from universal human brotherhood; treaties only encourage men to find defects in the wording which will enable them to break faith. As satire on European abuse of treaties this is telling; but as far as the Utopians are concerned, the argument is of the form: laws are abused, therefore let us have no laws. It is not a very intelligent argument, and it completely contradicts the Utopians' second means of bridging the gap between what man is and what they would like him to be. A little later, the logic becomes even shakier. 'The result [of making treaties] is men's persuasion that they are born one another's adversaries and enemies and that they are right in aiming at one another's destruction except insofar as treaties prevent it.' The form of this argument is: if we have no laws, we will have no evil. It was, of course, put forward by the anarchist utopians of the nineteenth century, but the More of 1515 would have found it comic, and the More of twenty years later, who knew his only hope of protection from tyranny lay in law, would have regarded it as too grave a howler for even intelligent laughter.

In describing the Utopian philosophy of pleasure, Hythloday proceeds rather unsystematically, making first some preliminary points which I shall return to later. He reaches the premise of the major argument when he says, 'The Utopians define virtue as living according to nature.' The sense of *nature* in question becomes clear as he goes on to make the pun which is so helpful in creating confusion: 'humanity is the virtue most peculiar to man'. The possibilities of begging questions are legion when one can move silently from using *human* as a descriptive word to using it as a normative word. It is humane to relieve the misfortunes of others: the word *human* is often used in the sense of *humane*; and so it becomes apparently incontrovertible to say that it is human nature to relieve the misfortunes of others and restore them to pleasure. What follows needs such close analysis that I shall have to quote at length. 'If so,' continues Hythloday, 'why should not nature urge everyone to do the same for himself also? For either a joyous life, that is, a pleasurable life, is evil, in which case not only ought you to help no one to it but, as far as you can, should take it away from everyone as being harmful and deadly, or else, if you not only are permitted but are obliged to win it for others as being good, why should you not do so first of all for yourself, to whom you should show no less favor than to others? When nature bids you to be good to others, she does not command you conversely to be cruel and merciless to yourself. So nature herself, they maintain, prescribes to us a joyous life or, in other words, pleasure, as the end of all our operations. Living according to her prescription they define as virtue.'

The whole argument here is based on the premise that by

nature man is benevolent towards his fellows, a premise which, as I showed, is contradicted by the Utopians' own political experience. The next step is to say that *therefore* it is natural (and so, by current definition, good) to be benevolent towards oneself in the form of giving oneself pleasure. This depends on the fallacious assumption that something is *either* good *or* bad, irrespective of what it is directed towards. But the logic becomes even crazier with the introduction of the phrase 'first of all for yourself'. The end of the sentence, which one expects from the syntax to provide some justification for it, in fact cannot, and subsides lamely into paraphrase of the preceding point ('to whom you should show no less favor than to others'). As confidence returns with the waving of another specious alternative (either you are good to yourself in the form of seeking your own pleasure; or you are cruel to yourself), we reach the point where what was put forward as natural can be presented as obligatory: 'nature . . . *prescribes* to us . . . pleasure, as the end of all our operations' (my italics). It then becomes easy to loop back to the initial premise (virtue = living according to nature), so that the full equation seems established beyond doubt. Living according to nature = seeking pleasure ('first of all for oneself') = virtue. To regard pleasure as the ultimate end of human operations has become a matter of natural obligation. Pleasure *is to be* sought (the Latin gerund).

This was what was to be proved, but it puts the Utopians in an obvious difficulty: how is the individual's search for pleasure, primarily for himself, to be reconciled with the desire for a genuine commonwealth? The argument that it is natural to help other people has already been expended in the course of the proof that pleasure is the ultimate end of human endeavour. But it now has to be dragged rapidly back to counter-balance a line of thought which could so obviously be pursued undesirably far. The awkwardness of the manoeuvre is concealed by finding a synonym for pleasant – 'Nature calls all men to help one another to a merrier (*hilarior*) life' – and slipping into parenthesis the manifestly false explanation, 'she equally favors all whom she endows with the same form'. Even if it were true that nature favoured all men equally, it would not necessarily follow that men should therefore help each other. But the Utopians are in rather desperate need to find an argument which will have the same effect as Christ's second commandment. So it is simply asserted, '*Consequently* nature *surely* bids you take constant care not so to

further your own advantages as to cause disadvantages to your
fellows' (my italics).

Thus far in the Utopian moral philosophy, the assumption has
been that human nature itself leads to altruism: as in the
argument about treaties, law would seem unnecessary. But
without any admission that a different concept of human nature is
being assumed, Hythloday continues immediately after my last
quotation: '*Therefore* they hold that not only ought contracts
between private persons to be observed but also public laws for
the distribution of . . . the matter of pleasure' (my italics). As
in Swift's satirical writing, the accumulation of words such as
'surely' and 'therefore' is used as a signal that the logic is in need of
braces. In fact the need for contracts and laws depends on the
failure of the argument that altruism is 'surely' natural. This
momentary realism propels the Utopians into one of their genuine
approaches to Christian thinking. 'As long as such laws are not
broken, it is prudence to look after your own interests, and to look
after those of the public in addition is a mark of devotion.' That
contrast between prudence and devotion (*prudentia* and *pietas*)
does follow from the tacit difficulties the Utopians are having with
the word *nature*, and it is broadly Christian. But the point is that
the word *pietas* does not belong in any context established by
Utopian thought. Even if their argument for altruism worked, its
emphasis would be negative ('not so to further your own
advantages as to cause disadvantages to your fellows'). But the
contrast of *prudentia* and *pietas* implies that helping others is
morally better than helping oneself; and for this there is no
support at all in any of their arguments. A similar contrast occurs
elsewhere, most importantly in the passage about the two
Utopian religious orders which I shall discuss later. The Utopians
do have a sense that there is something more holy (*sanctior* is the
commoner word) which lies outside the boundaries of their own
philosophy. But it does lie outside: it cannot be incorporated.

In the present context the implications are not pursued.
Instead we are given the much more logical extension of their
pleasure ethic, which does not require the introduction of alien
concepts, but merely the weighing of one pleasure against
another. Utopian ethics are, with all their muddles, essentially
utilitarian: they decide what to do by working out what Bentham
called, in a suitably ugly phrase, the 'felicific calculus'. *Pietas* need
not really come into it. 'Remembrance of the love and good will of

those whom you have benefited gives the mind a greater amount of pleasure than the bodily pleasure which you have forgone would have afforded. Finally – and religion easily brings this home to a mind which readily assents – God repays, in place of a brief and tiny pleasure, immense and never-ending gladness. And so they maintain, having carefully considered and weighed the matter, that all our actions, and even the very virtues exercised in them, look at last to pleasure as their end and happiness.' This is not the very crudest form of utilitarianism, despite the phrase 'greater amount of pleasure' (*plus voluptatis*) and the contrast of 'tiny' (*exiguus*) and 'immense' (*ingens*). There is a qualitative calculation involved, not merely a quantative one: the pleasures of the mind are greater than those of the body (it is a qualitatively superior pleasure to be liked by others instead of snatching the physical goods) and 'gladness' is a rather inadequate translation of *gaudium* (the beatific vision is qualitatively superior to anything which could be covered by the word *voluptas*). It is Mill's utilitarianism rather than Bentham's; but it is still a matter of weighing up what brings the greatest pleasure. The Utopians, it is repeated again, 'look at last to pleasure as their end'.

One of the implications of thinking in terms of qualitatively superior forms of pleasure becomes clearer somewhat later, after the discussion of Utopian use of punishment. 'Not only do they discourage crime by punishment but they offer honors to invite men to virtue.' In particular, adds Hythloday, they set up, in the market-place, statues to men who have done conspicuous service to the country. This is clearly, from their point of view, a visible token of the 'good will of those whom [such men] have benefited' and a perfectly logical extension of an ethic based on the weighing of pleasure. The market-place is in fact where such statues would most appropriately be put. But a man who acted virtuously on the assumption that he was thereby in the running for such recognition is unlikely to be free of what the Utopians agree with Christians in regarding as the worst of sins. Even without a statue, the remembrance of the benefits one has brought to others would involve a degree of complacency which could hardly be kept short of pride. The Utopians profess humility, but this 'serpent from hell', as Hythloday calls it near the end of Book II, has insinuated itself into the centre of their moral thought: if they don't congratulate themselves on their own goodness, the pleasure-balance will not work properly.

At the end of his outline of Utopian moral theory, Hythloday repeats that they keep open the possibility that there may be something 'more holy' than their own thought. But the preceding paragraph emphasises very clearly that in Utopian ethics self-sacrifice, for any other motive than to achieve by it greater personal benefit in the long term, must be regarded as mad: 'unless a man neglects these advantages to himself in providing more zealously for the pleasure of other persons or of the public, in return for which sacrifice he expects a greater pleasure from God . . . this attitude they think is extreme madness'. This is a rather comically profit-orientated way of thought for a nation which has abolished the profit-motive provided by money. Even Hythloday seems to sense that all is not well, for this is the point at which he claims to be describing rather than defending their principles, and he quickly changes the subject to information about their height and the climate.

Before I discuss what happens when Utopian ethics are confronted with Christian ethics, there are a few further points arising directly from Hythloday's exposition which need to be stressed. Firstly, although they have an obscure sense of something 'more holy', the Utopian attitude towards their clearer religious principles is that they are essentially subservient to the main pleasure ethic. It is not an unfair vulgarisation of their religious thought to paraphrase it: God is useful because He makes the felicific calculus come out ultimately on the side of what is good for the commonwealth. When Hythloday first states that they regard pleasure as the ultimate human good, he immediately adds that they defend this opinion with religious arguments. In fact they have to, since according to the lower of the views of human nature they hold, their whole ethic of felicific calculus would otherwise collapse. If pleasure is the ultimate good, then to the individual it might seem foolish not to pursue it regardless of the common-wealth. So to maintain their equation pleasure = virtue, it becomes crucial that evil should not, in the long run, lead to individual pleasure. If one eliminated the concept of a God who finally punishes evil and rewards good in an after-life, they believe, it would be 'stupid' not to 'seek pleasure by fair means or foul' (*per fas ac nefas*). That this is not a very adequate conception of God is emphasised, for those who might not have noticed, only a few lines later. 'Now reason', says Hythloday, expounding Utopian views, 'first of all inflames men to a love and veneration of the divine majesty, to whom we owe both our existence and our capacity for happiness.' What reason does 'secondly' (urges men to seek pleasure) is what then occupies his attention, but this throwaway 'first of all' point has in fact stood Utopian thought on its head. If our whole 'capacity for happiness' is indeed owed to God, it is at the very least ungracious to reduce Him to a means of weighting the happiness in the direction we think most appropriate. The preceding sentence states that obedience to reason is following nature. ('That individual, they say, is following the guidance of nature who, in desiring one thing and avoiding another, obeys the dictates of reason.') So taken together the two sentences set up, as an alternative to the main Utopian equation (nature = seeking pleasure = virtue), something radically different: nature = reason = love of God. The Utopians cannot be blamed at this stage for not having thought through their conception of God: their glimpses of 'something more holy' are fitful before Revelation reaches them. But a reader acquainted with Christianity is not unreasonably expected to notice what is happening.

The second point to stress is that the Utopians persistently exploit the ambiguity of *nature* for the same purpose as they use God – to get themselves out of tight corners. It is crucial to their whole doctrine that the greatest real pleasure should lie in what they wish to be regarded as good. But they can only say that something ought to be done if it is natural; by their account of God (that is, underwriter to their own calculus), He cannot be an independent source of what ought to be done where what men commonly do is undesirable. So they have, rather desperately, to argue that although we must follow nature, some things which most men do are not natural. It is human to be humane, but actually most humans are not. At one point Hythloday uses an adroit turn of phrase to conceal the problem: men think by a 'futile consensus' (*vanissima conspiratione*) that perverse pleasures are sweet. At another, having conceded that the 'mob' prefers perverse pleasure to 'natural' pleasure, the escape is through use of analogy: it is a 'vitiated taste' such as pregnant women develop for unsavoury things. And from thus equating a permanent reality with a temporary aberration, he generalises to: 'it is impossible for any man's judgement . . . to change the nature of pleasure'. But it is a precarious manoeuvre: the man of 'vitiated taste' could reply in the same words to the Utopians.

A third point concerns the importance of health to the Utopians. 'Many hold it to be the greatest of pleasures.' As a reproach to the ingratitude of Christians, the passage on health as a positive pleasure is powerful. Certainly it works better aesthetically than the attacks on gambling and hunting, which are rather awkwardly introduced, since such things cannot exist in Utopian society. But it is emphasised more than is necessary for it to work as a reproach. 'Almost all the Utopians regard it as great and as practically the foundation and basis of all pleasures.' 'Those who have permanent health cannot be without pleasure.' It seems that Hythloday's words in Book I about a 'return to a healthy condition' are not so figurative as they appeared. But to talk in 1516, even granted good hospitals and sensible diet, of 'permanent health' would have been more obviously absurd than it might seem now. When he used the phrase 'sick bodies . . . past cure', Hythloday had not read More's *Four Last Things*; but his hearers would have read many works of a similar kind, in which it is made vividly plain that that is what men inescapably are. 'Many' Utopians have chosen a pathetically temporary end; and 'almost all' are in danger of losing their sense of proportion once again.

I hope that I have already made it plain that the philosophy of the Utopians cannot really be regarded as Epicurean Christianity. Epicureanism cannot be made effectually Christian by throwing in God and immortality as ultimate safety-nets to maintain the equation pleasure = virtue. What one regards as one's ultimate end makes a difference which nothing else can alter. When Peter Giles, as an afterthought to his doubts whether commonwealths in the new world could be superior to those in the old, adds, 'not to mention also the chance discoveries made among us, which no human mind could have devised', the throwaway tone is heavily ironic. The 'chance discovery' of Christ ought to have re-orientated totally the whole Utopian philosophy. Raphael is a *Messenger of God* to them; they pay no more attention than Europeans have. But before looking finally at the Utopian response to Christianity, it is necessary to confirm the drift of my analysis so far with some external evidence; for it is on external evidence that the commentators who think that the Utopians are Christian except in minor details mostly rely.

Against Utopian views about health one might set a quotation from *The Four Last Things* which almost repeats Hythloday's words: 'Consider that our bodies have so sore a sickness and such a continual consumption in themselves that the strongest were not able to endure and continue ten days together, were it not that once or twice a day we be fain to take medicines inward to clout them up withal and keep them as long as we can. For what is our meat and drink but medicines against hunger and thirst, that give us warning of that we daily lose by our inward consumption? And of that consumption shall we die in conclusion, for all the medicines that we use, though never other sickness came at us.'[3] Against the Utopian view that the point of acting well is that it leads to pleasure, one might set a quotation from the same work, indicating that for More virtue is the end and pleasure a by-product: 'the abandoning and refusing of carnal pleasure and the ensuing of labour, travail, penance and bodily pain, shall bring therewith to a Christian man, not only in the world that is coming but also in this present life, very sweetness, comfort, pleasure and gladness'.[4] As we saw, the Utopians profess humility while actually feeling a self-satisfaction, not only in their social system, but in, for example, their military tactics. In *The Four Last Things* this form of pride is diagnosed as the most pernicious: 'For how can he mend his fault that taketh it for none, that weeneth all is well that he doth himself, and nothing that any man doth else, that covereth his purpose with the pretext of some holy purpose . . .'.[5] It is always assumed that for the Utopians to have few written laws is wholly good. More would certainly have desired some simplification and clarification, but he would not have approved of this: 'For all other crimes there is no law prescribing any fixed penalty, but the punishment is assigned by the senate according to the atrocity, or venality, of the individual crime.' This is act-utilitarianism, as opposed to rule-utilitarianism: the calculus is done not by known rules but according to the assessment of every individual case. In the *Responsio ad Lutherum*, More is very explicit: 'if you take away the laws and leave everything free to the magistrates, either they will command nothing and they will forbid nothing, and then magistrates will be useless; or they will rule by the leading of their own nature and imperiously prosecute anything they please, and then the people will in no way be freer, but, by reason of a condition of servitude, worse, when they will have to obey, not fixed and definite laws, but indefinite whims changing from day to day. And this is bound to happen even under the best magistrates, whom, although they may enjoin the best laws, neverthless the people will oppose and murmur against as suspect, as though they govern everything, not according to what is just and fair, but according to caprice'.[6]

But the quotations I have so far adduced come from works later than *Utopia*, and it is often argued that the Erasmus-influenced, pre-Luther More must not be confused with the man whose views hardened in response to later events. In 1510, six years *before Utopia*, More published a *Life of Pico della Mirandola*, together with some very free translations of a few of Pico's writings. The Utopians have no conception of Original Sin: they assume, for example, that if a man dies 'cheerfully and full of good hope' he is certainly bound for heaven. From More's translation of Pico's First Rule:

> we must have war continual
> Against the world, the flesh, the devil, that aye
> Enforce themself to make us bond and thrall.[7]

The Utopians expect to get to heaven via pleasure; Pico's Third Rule:

> Consider well that folly it is and vain
> To look for heaven with pleasure and delight.
> Since Christ our Lord and sovereign captain
> Ascended never but by manly fight
> And bitter passion; then were it no right
> That any servant, ye will yourself record,
> Should stand in better condition than his lord.[8]

The Utopions base their arguments for acting well on profit; in Pico's Fourth Rule it is irrelevant

> How that thereby redound unto us might
> Any profit, but only for delight
> To be conformed and like in some behaviour
> To Jesu Christ our blessed Lord and Saviour.[9]

The Utopians regard fasting and mortification of the flesh as 'extreme madness'; the man who wore a hair shirt while he wrote *Utopia* had already written in admiration of Pico, 'he many days (and namely those days which represent to us the passion and death that Christ suffered for our sake) beat and scourged his own flesh in the remembrance of that great benefit and for the cleansing of his old offences'. A Utopian seeks pleasure 'first of all for [himself]', and Hythloday is of like mind. More's translation of the Twelfth Property of a Lover is:

> A very lover will his love obey:
> His joy it is and all his appetite
> To pain himself in all that ever he may,
> That person in whom he set hath his delight
> Diligently to serve both day and night
> For very love, without any regard
> To any profit, guerdon or reward.[10]

In Utopia there is no conception that to serve is in itself a good. This is understandable since it is a strictly Christian idea, deriving from the example of Christ's own life and death. But it puts an impassable gulf between Utopian behaviour, based on reward in terms of pleasure, and Christian behaviour, based on the belief that, as service is in itself a good, it is not to be offered with an eye to further reward. Hythloday in Book I thinks like a Utopian. The way More thinks is indicated in the Twelfth Property:

> Wageless to serve, three things may us move:
> First, if the service self be desirable:
> Second, if they whom that we serve and love
> Be very good and amiable:
> Thirdly, of reason be we serviceable
> Without the gaping after any more
> To such as have done much for us before.
>
> Serve God for love, then, not for hope of meed.[11]

In some respects the Utopians act as a reproach to European man in the manner indicated by R. W. Chambers: 'With nothing save reason to guide them, the Utopians do this; and yet we Christian Englishmen, we Christian Europeans . . .!'[12] But the centre of their philosophy represents the way we do think, rather than the way More believed we ought to think. In Utopia, as commonly in Europe, God is invoked to serve the interests of man;

in true Christian thinking, man is to serve God and his fellows. The difference is uncomfortable, easily blurred, but absolute.

The nearest the Utopians come to Christian thought is in the two religious groups they call Buthrescae. The thinking of these two groups has a recognisably Utopian basis: 'It is only by keeping busy and by all good offices that they are determined to merit the happiness coming after death.' But they have both carried it to a point where the emphasis undergoes a crucial change. Service has become in itself a desirable end: 'they behave as servants and as more than slaves. If anywhere there is a task so rough, hard, and filthy that most are deterred from it by the toil, disgust, and despair involved, they gladly and cheerfully claim it all for themselves'. The more austere group 'entirely reject the pleasures of this life as harmful'. And the other also has a concept of 'duty' which is otherwise absent from Utopian moral vocabulary ('their duty to nature requires them to perform the marital act and their duty to the country to beget children'). Of course the Utopians regard the second group as 'saner' (*pruentiores*) and the first as 'holier' (*sanctiores*). But it is important that they respect both, and in particular that they do use the word 'holier' of what, according to the main line of their thinking, is only more mad. The Utopians do not let these ways of thought trouble the main stream of their philosophy, but they have a clear sense that they represent something, beyond the limits of their own understanding, which demands reverence.

The same cannot be said of their response to the Christian teaching brought to them by Raphael Hythloday. At the end of Book I, Hythloday says they are very ready to absorb anything new which is superior to what they have already. But this is significantly not their response to Christian instruction. All critics who try to argue that the Utopians are Christian in deed if not in name, seem to me to be faced with an insuperable difficulty here. 'After they had heard from us the name of Christ, His teaching, His character, His miracles, and the no less wonderful constancy of the many martyrs whose blood freely shed had drawn so many nations far and wide into their fellowship, you would not believe how readily disposed they, too, were to join it, whether through the rather mysterious inspiration of God or because they thought it nearest to that belief which has the widest prevalence among them. But I think that this factor, too, was of no small weight, that they had heard that His disciples' common way of life had been pleasing to Christ and that it is still in use among the truest societies of Christians.' It will not do to pounce on 'readily disposed' and ignore the rest of this account. It is, of course, characteristic of Hythloday to omit the Crucifixion from his account of Christ, but to do him credit, he does mention the martyrs. What draws the Utopians to Christianity is not the element of self-sacrifice, which is outside their previous orbit of thought, but what corresponds most to things they already think and do. This is precisely the form of pride diagnosed in the quotation I made above from *The Four Last Things*: 'For how can he mend his fault . . . that weeneth all is well that he doth himself . . . ?'[13]

It is, of course, possible to ignore the throwaway phrase 'whether through the rather mysterious inspiration of God', and argue that the passage I have quoted proves that the Utopians are in fact near in belief and conduct to Christianity. But the description of the Utopian response to Christianity is then concluded with two further passages which indicate that both in matters of belief and in matters of conduct, they remain mistaken. If they were basically right before, one would expect here a unanimous recognition that what Raphael reveals is indeed the Gospel. What we are given instead in the first passage is a heretical debate which seems likely to lead to schism: they debate whether they can ignore the Apostolic Succession and elect a priest who has not been ordained by a bishop. In the second passage, the man who is, as far as we know, the only Utopian to grasp the implications of what he has been taught ('He proclaimed them [the kinds of worship previously practised in Utopia] to be prophane in themselves and their followers to be impious and sacrilegious and worthy of everlasting fire'), behaves in a manner more likely to cause a riot than win converts, and is exiled according to Utopian law. Christianity does provide a new topic for debate, but Utopian order prevails as usual over a minor disturbance.

4 *Utopia*: Proximate Ends and Means

What one takes as one's ultimate end does not merely affect matters of belief: it also affects one's choice of more immediate ends and of the means by which such ends are to be pursued. In fact it affects the whole direction of one's life. My concern in this chapter will be with what I shall call proximate ends and means: that is, both with the undesirable consequences, on other aspects of their behaviour, of the fact that the ultimate end of the Utopians is pleasure, and also with other ends, logically but not necessarily, dependent on Utopian premises, which More can be taken to have regarded as to some extent undesirable.

The Utopian practice which it is most notoriously difficult to reconcile with a Christian conception of the end of life is euthanasia. Euthanasia is a wholly logical deduction from the basic principle of their thought. If a life becomes so painful that there is no possibility that any pleasure could outweigh the pain, then the felicific calculus indicates very obviously that the solution is to terminate the life. The advantage in staying alive is that one has the capacity for pleasure; if the possibility of pleasure is removed and the remaining capacity is for pain, the point of continuing to live has disappeared. A man in extreme and incurable pain, who takes his own life or lets others take it for him, 'act[s] wisely since by death he will put an end not to enjoyment but to torture'.

But considerable emphasis is put on the requirement that permission for euthanasia must be obtained from the priests and senate. The priests here, of course, are the representatives of a God whose function is to hold the balance of pleasure, so the phrase 'pious and holy action', used, as elsewhere, in conjunction with 'wisely' (*prudenter*) is on this occasion ironic. God is being used to underwrite what is prudent. Since God is conceived of as merely a supernatural utilitarian safety-net, there can be no religious value in apparently useless suffering. The discussion of tribulation in More's *Dialogue of Comfort*, and all such works of Christian apologetics concerning suffering, are simply mad in a Utopian perspective. But the senate is involved as well as the priests, because the greatest good of the greatest number is crucial: a man who qualifies for euthanasia must be 'a trouble to others' as well as 'a burden to himself'. Anyone who thinks he can decide for himself, independently of the interests of society, that he can take his own life, is treated with extreme ignominy and denied proper burial. At the time Hythloday makes his report, 'they do not make away with anyone against his will'. They hold a balance between the interests of the individual and the interests of society, and a negative on either side decides the case as a whole in the negative. But it is a very precarious balance, requiring magistrates of much greater probity than More thought possible when he replied to Luther. In other matters where the rights of the individual conflict with the rights of the greatest number, the Utopians do not give equal weight to the former; and in most respects they are very ruthlessly consistent.

Utopian attitudes towards sexual relationships are at first sight curiously out of step with European attitudes of More's time. Fornication incurs extremely severe punishment: offenders are usually forbidden to marry at all, so that a transgression at the age of seventeen would entail a lifetime of punishment. Adultery, too, is ferociously punished: a first offence incurs 'the strictest form of slavery' and a second the death penalty. On the other hand, divorce by mutual consent is permitted. In part, of course, this is intended as comment on a degree of tolerance towards fornication and adultery in Europe which More deplored. But the whole passage is an entirely logical extension of the basic Utopian premise that pleasure is the ultimate end. The Utopians want to maintain the institution of marriage because the family is the basic unit in their social structure. Fornication is not just pleasurable: it carries none of the unpleasurable consequences of a permanent union. From 'promiscuous intercourse' one can gain all the pleasures of sex without incurring the responsibility of looking after one's partner in the event of illness, and without the difficulties of accommodating oneself to the needs of the other as they develop and change in the course of time. On a pleasure calculus, fornication would, to a socially unacceptable proportion of the population, score higher than marriage. Consequently, the

balance has to be so tipped by legislation that marriage scores
higher instead. Utopian law, like Utopian theology, is a means of
adjusting the calculation in the interests of the commonwealth.
The point is made with unusual explicitness: 'The reason why
they punish this offense so severely is their foreknowledge that,
unless persons are carefully restrained from promiscuous intercourse, few will unite in married love, in which state a whole life
must be spent with one companion and all the troubles incidental
to it must be patiently borne.' It is a careful statement,
emphasising tacitly that the institution of marriage does not fit
readily into the Utopian view of life and has to be forced in by
violence. It starts as a Utopian sentence and ends as a Christian
one. The phrase 'unite in married love' does not hold out a
reward, though it does carry the implication that a rich relationship may ensue; the emphasis is on the imperatives 'must be
spent' and 'must be patiently borne', and on the possibility that
the cost may be greater than the profit: 'all the troubles . . . must
be patiently borne'.

Persistent adultery, of course, would provide a means of
evading such troubles and at the same time precluding the
punishment for fornication. But it would so seriously damage the
social fabric that the punishment must be extreme. The most
significant detail is that, although automatic divorce is normal,
the injured party may, if he 'continues to feel affection for so
undeserving a mate', share the punishment of hard labour in
conditions of slavery. (The Latin phrase is in fact stronger: *in
amore persistat* implies a willed attitude rather than a lingering
sentiment.) This means that if the injured party does not forgive,
he is rewarded with a new mate; whereas if he does forgive, he is
punished as severely as the offender. This can hardly be regarded
as just; nor can it be taken satirically, that is, as representing a
more Christian treatment of the problem of divorce than current
European laxity. It encourages the individual to be unforgiving.
But the Utopians, as usual, are more concerned about the
commonwealth than about the individual. Persistent love in such
circumstances must be, according to their values, essentially mad.
To make it more mad by punishing it is of no importance
compared with securing the fabric of society. But it is impressive
and 'now and then' it moves the governor to compassion: again
there is that glimpse of something outside the Utopian scheme
which compels their respect.

The passage concerning the inspection of prospective spouses in the nude works in a broadly similar way. Its most obvious effect is general satiric reference to Europe: men take the trouble when buying horses to make sure what they are getting; in choosing wives they are, foolishly, less cautious. It also shares one of the functions of the jokes about the length of the bridge and the location of the island: More clearly does not think Europeans should adopt Utopian practices literally. Those who believe he does are mocked by such a joke. He explains the point when Hythloday adds, 'All men are not so wise as to regard only the character of the woman.' Caution about character is more important than caution about physique. But that is also the centre of the more subtle effect of this passage. In accordance with the whole accountancy basis of their thinking, Utopians select their wives in the manner appropriate to making a purchase. This is an action which 'will cause either pleasure or disgust (*aut voluptas, aut nausea*) to follow them the rest of their lives', so it is only sensible to assess carefully how much pleasure they are likely to be acquiring. 'Likely', though, is a crucial word: they have to allow for the fact that deformities may be acquired after the marriage, and such chances must simply be accepted. If we then play back the second stage of the first effect – character matters more than physique – it becomes even plainer that More is not advocating adoption of the Utopian custom. With the qualification they take into account, one can make a reasonable calculation of the quantity of pleasure a certain body is likely to provide. But when one considers character, quantification of pleasure anticipated does not seem a very promising procedure at all. Utilitarian sums are notoriously difficult to work out, and the completion of this one does not seem likely to lead to any deep form of conjugal love. Yet if one's ultimate end is pleasure, it is difficult to achieve any profounder conception of marriage than as a means to pleasure.

The constant implication is that it is an inadequate end. 'They judge it cruel that a person should be abandoned when most in need of comfort and that old age, since it both entails disease and is a disease itself, should have only an unreliable and weak fidelity.' It is cruel, but they have no valid argument against it. If a spouse is assessed as an object of 'pleasure or disgust', a diseased or old one is bound to get low marks. All they can do is apply legislative force: divorce is not allowed in such circumstances, and the laws on adultery remain to tip the balance. 'Fidelity', as that

word would be understood in a Christian context, is actually
'extreme madness'. When the source of 'disgust' is something for
which the offensive spouse can be blamed, Utopian law does not
even attempt to enforce 'fidelity': 'intolerable offensiveness of
character' is permissable grounds for divorce. So if one gets one's
sums 'intolerably' wrong, there is a safety-net. But it is the senate
that holds it. The definition of 'intolerable' is dangerously
slippery.

If marriage is a means to pleasure, then it would seem, on the
face of it, obvious that divorce will have to be permitted when both
parties find other partners with whom they think they can live
'more agreeably'. This is indeed the case in Utopia, but within the
first sentence on the subject, the qualification is added, 'but not
without the sanction of the senate'. 'They do not readily give
consent because they know that it is a very great drawback to
cementing the affection between husband and wife if they have
before them the easy hope of a fresh union.' The utilitarianism of
the Utopians, as I have said before, is not the crudest kind. The
concern expressed here is not the obvious one; it is not that, if they
grant too many divorces, there will be social chaos. The prospect
of easy divorce potentially impairs the quality of a marriage. Yet
the phrase 'cementing the affection between husband and wife'
stands out, in the same way as 'unite in married love', as one
which does not fit naturally into the Utopian conception of
marriage. As usual, they attempt to achieve by negative sanction
something which really derives from a quite different mode of
thought. In the long term, a cemented affection may prove (it
often does) more pleasurable than switching to a new partner who
seems temporarily more agreeable. So the senate adjusts the
felicific calculus by not granting divorce very readily, and its
members go carefully into each case. If a married couple find
other partners with whom they 'hope to live more agreeably', the
senate sees its role as assessing whether they are likely to be right.
The end of marriage, as of life as a whole, lies in achieving what is
most agreeable.

In the quite large area of pleasure centering around marriage,
the senate and its laws cope very well: they manipulate the
calculus adequately without having to bring God in at all.
Utopian principles cannot actually inspire persistent love, fidelity
or uniting in married love, but they do secure conditions under
which such agreeable madness can occur. Outwardly the only

difference from traditional Christian teaching about marriage is the permitting of divorce where the situation has become truly disagreeable. Yet that is not a minor detail: it is an entirely logical extension of a radically different conception of what marriage is. The underlying implication of most importance is not that European man is culpable because the Utopians can get nearer Christian practice without Christian doctrine, but that European man is culpable in so far as his basic attitude is nearer to that of the Utopians than to true Christianity. If one regards marriage as a means to pleasure, one can, with the help of a prudent administration, get an imitation of the goodies of Christian marriage without an intolerable proportion of the 'troubles'. Without the help, it seems, from the need the Utopians feel to force it onto their people through strict laws, that the chance of getting the imitation is not high; and even with it one is getting an imitation.

The difficulty, fundamentally, is that if one takes pleasure as one's ultimate end, the nature of other aspirations is crucially altered. Persistent love, for example, cannot remain in itself an ideal. Sometimes it will lead to suffering, and then, if one's end is pleasure 'first of all for [oneself]', persistent love becomes merely foolish. Divorce by mutual consent is not a detail which could be easily removed: to remove it, one would have to make persistent love, as an end in itself, more important than pleasure, that is, to overturn the whole foundation of Utopian thought. Similarly, although there may seem only slight difference between love 'for better for worse' and love for better for worse within certain limits, it actually involves a totally different conception of what love is. The centrally Christian element of self-sacrifice, which makes love absolute, has quietly disappeared from the conception of love, even though a paternalistic administration has re-introduced, by external sanction, some of its pleasurable by-products, though 'foreknowledge' that if often pays good dividends.

But the problems which arise when one denies oneself recourse to any absolutes, other than the greatest welfare of the commonwealth, are much more obvious in the discussion of Utopian attitudes towards war. They do seek other goods: they seek justice and human fellowship, for example. But since they seek them not in themselves but as means to what they consider the best distribution of the 'matter of pleasure', what they achieve is neither just nor humane, and they have to evolve the following very fishy arguments in order to pretend to themselves that it is.

'War, as an activity fit only for beasts and yet practised by no kind of beast so constantly as by man, they regard with utter loathing. Against the usage of almost all nations they count nothing so inglorious as glory sought in war . . . they do not lightly go to war. They do so only to protect their own territory or to drive an invading enemy out of their friends' lands or, in pity for a people oppressed by tyranny, to deliver them by force of arms from the yoke and slavery of the tyrant, a course prompted by human sympathy.

'They oblige their friends with help, not always indeed to defend them merely but sometimes also to requite and avenge injuries previously done to them. They act, however, only if they themselves are consulted before any step is taken and if they themselves initiate the war after they have approved the cause and demanded restitution in vain. They take the final step of war not only when a hostile inroad has carried off booty but also much more fiercely when the merchants among their friends undergo unjust persecution under the colour of justice in any other country, either on the pretext of laws in themselves unjust or by the distortion of laws in themselves good.

'Such was the origin of the war which the Utopians had waged a little before our time on behalf of the Nephelogetes against the Alaopolitans. The Nephelogetic traders suffered a wrong, as they thought, under pretence of law, but whether right or wrong, it was avenged by a fierce war. Into this war the neighboring nations brought their energies and resources to assist the power and to intensify the rancor of both sides. Most flourishing nations were either shaken to their foundations or grievously afflicted. The troubles upon troubles that arose were ended only by the enslavement and surrender of the Alaopolitans. Since the Utopians were not fighting in their own interest, they yielded them into the power of the Nephelogetes, a people who, when the Alaopolitans were prosperous, were not in the least comparable to them.'

As in the arguments to establish the pleasure philosophy itself, the Utopians juggle with the concept of human nature to suit the purpose in hand. What I have quoted here in fact follows directly the passage I have discussed before, in which the Utopians are said to think that the 'fellowship created by nature' makes written treaties superfluous. Their attitude to war is then introduced with an ironic use of the pun on the Latin words for war (*bellum*) and beast (*belua*), parallel to the pun on human and humane, which implies that human beings actually behave by nature like beasts. Despite this alarm signal, the first change that has taken place in the nature of their aspirations here is clearly desirable: to seek glory in war is not an end a Christian would wish to salvage (though the Utopians are shrewd enough to appreciate the value of honour as a negative sanction: we are told later that it 'is the greatest reproach for one spouse to return [from battle] without the other or for a son to come back having lost his parent'.) This and the generalisation which follows ('they do not lightly go to war') dispose the reader to expect that in this area their thinking may be sound. But in fact they become progressively more lost as the passage develops. With no end in view more important than their own pleasure, there is nothing to help them keep their bearings. The first reason for going to war is perfectly valid: 'They do so only to protect their own territory.' But by a gradation, which is evidently imperceptible to them, they move steadily towards the outrageous interference between the Nephelogetes and Alaopolitans. Within the same sentence they move from self-defence to driving an invader from friends' territory, and from that to overthrowing a tyrant when prompted by 'human sympathy' for the oppressed. Without pausing to consider by what calculus this 'human sympathy' will be weighed against the suffering of war, the argument curves from defence to revenge. From legitimate self-defence they have wandered into the highly dubious procedure of avenging wrongs done to their friends. And the only qualification which they feel it necessary to add is that they must be consulted before any step is taken, and that they themselves initiate the war after approving the cause. The calculation must be their own; their friends cannot be trusted to get it right. The description of the proud man in *The Four Last Things* fits them with great precision – the man who 'weeneth all is well that he doth himself, and nothing that any man doth else'.[1] The next sentence shows clearly the attempt to pursue justice: 'when merchants among their friends undergo unjust persecution', they see it as their mission to punish the injustice. Yet the crucial words are 'booty', 'more fiercely' and 'merchants': the injuries they have in mind concern seizure of the 'matter of pleasure', and what rouses them most are unjust or mal-administered laws affecting merchants, dealers in the 'matter of pleasure'. In view of their own legislation concerning the

distribution of wealth this is understandable; but it is also
potentially perilous. In their own view all laws which distribute
wealth unevenly are unjust. Theoretically, they are here justifying
themselves in going to war against any country which retains the
use of money. They are not so evil as to take full advantage of that;
but the point is, they have no means of determining where to draw
the line. All they have to guide them is their calculation of the
degree of injustice in a given mal-distribution of the *materia
voluptatis*. Their understanding of justice depends on their own
sums: they have no external standard as a check. If they get an
answer which displeases them, they wage fierce war, whether
their answer is right or wrong.

This last point is made in the third paragraph I quoted above.
The Nephelogetic traders thought they had suffered an injustice
and the Utopians evidently decided, on the basis of their own
sums, that they were right, so took revenge in the form of a 'fierce
war'. But More quietly slips in the devastating phrase 'whether
right or wrong'. The claim that it was an injustice may not have
been correct; but because the Utopians calculated that it was,
they started a war (they do not fight unless 'they themselves
initiate the war'), in which 'most flourishing nations were either
shaken to their foundations or grievously afflicted'. A heavy price
for what may have been a mistake. By the end of the passage, the
Utopians have completely lost sight of justice in any sense of the
word. When they are fighting in their own interest, they are more
likely to make reasonable calculations: at home their sums are
worked out so well that slavery in Utopia is actually sought
voluntarily by oppressed aliens. But when they are not fighting in
their own interest, the calculus is working on such inadequate
data that the results are berserk. At the end of the war the
Nephelogetes are encouraged to enslave the Alaopolitans, a
people who when 'prosperous were not in the least comparable
to them'. Apart from the doubt as to whether the Alaopolitans
have committed any wrong at all, this is not justice according to
the Utopian principle expounded earlier, by which the right of
possession goes to the people who can make best use of a territory.
They think they are fighting in pursuit of justice, but they have no
conception of justice other than the fair distribution of the *materia
voluptatis*. If they think they see an unfair distribution, they will
fight 'whether right or wrong': it is the *materia voluptatis* which
matters more than the actual justice of the case. The absence of an

ultimate end other than *voluptas* leads them from seeking justice into perpetrating gross injustice.

A similar thing happens with their means of waging war, as with their reasons for fighting. They intend to act humanely; but the principles of their thinking lead them with apparent logic to acting in ways which are inhumane by their own definitions. What seems to them the distinctively human means of fighting is 'cleverness and calculation': animals are often superior in brawn; man is best equipped to fight by clever calculation. So they begin a war by promising 'huge rewards' to anyone who will kill or capture the enemy king and his officers. In fact 'they actually offer the same rewards, with a guarantee of personal safety, to the persons proscribed, if they will turn against their fellows'. This is fully consistent with the pleasure ethic, as it reduces the possibility of extended fighting. But there are two aspects of it which are undesirable, even within the realms of their own understanding. Firstly they are using money to corrupt individuals. This conflicts directly with the basic aim of their whole social structure, which is to remove temptation by abolishing money. Secondly, by such means, the end they achieve is to create a state of disloyalty and mistrust precisely opposite to the 'fellowship' which, in the passage about treaties, they say they believe is 'created by nature'. They know precisely what they are doing here: they want to turn people 'against their fellows'; and they know that bribery will directly cause evil – 'It is well known that it has often happened that many of them [their enemies], and especially the king himself, have been betrayed by those in whom they had placed the greatest trust, so easily do bribes incite men to commit every kind of crime.' Both the means and the end are diametrically opposed to their own ideals. All that matters to them is that the calculation should work, so the only precautions they take are to make the rewards big enough to balance the dangers and to maintain their own reputation as reliable payers: 'they take care that the greatness of the peril is balanced by the extent of the rewards. In consequence they promise and faithfully (*cum fide*) pay down not only an immense amount of gold but also landed property with high income in very secure places in the territory of friends'.

The end they *intend* to achieve is, within the terms of their own thinking, good: they congratulate themselves on both their wisdom in avoiding battles and their humanity in saving innocent lives. Again the word *humanity* has undergone a silent shift in meaning: it is not being used of what man does by nature, but rather as a term of special praise reserved for the Utopians' skill in utilitarian calculus ('by the death of a few guilty people they purchase the lives of many harmless persons'). But the main point about their intentions is that they do not even intend to achieve their end by means which could possibly be regarded as good. The principle that welfare is the ultimate good provides no check at all on means: any means is justified which secures the end of maximum happiness and minimum suffering. If the bribing of traitors does not work, 'they sow the seeds of dissension broadcast and foster strife by leading a brother of the king or one of the noblemen to hope that he may obtain the throne. If internal strife dies down, then they stir up and involve the neighbors of their enemies by reviving some forgotten claims to dominion such as kings have always at their disposal'. This is superior only in its systematic efficiency to what Hythloday said of the French King's plans about England in Book I ('The Scots therefore must be posted in readiness, prepared for any opportunity to be let loose on the English if they make the slightest movement. Moreover, some exiled noble must be fostered secretly . . . to maintain a claim to the throne.'). As so often, the Utopians are behaving as European do, rather than as Christians should. It is probably the point at which the utilitarian calculus has its strongest appeal. The argument that it would be preferable to bribe traitors to assassinate Hitler, rather than fight a war causing mass civilian death, is even stronger than Hythloday's best points in Book I. But More has, as he did there, made quite clear the implications.

Even those commentators who on the whole admire Utopian thought mostly feel discomfort at their treatment of the Zapoletan mercenaries. Here they are, to the most superficial observer, obviously using an evil means to achieve the dubious good of exterminating the whole race of Zapoletans. But the most important function of the Zapoletans in the book is to serve as a critical parody of the Utopians themselves. Their moral code is less refined than the Utopians', but it is in essence the same: in them one can see in gross outline what the intelligence of the Utopians partly conceals. The Zapoletans will do whatever brings most money, as the Utopians will do what brings most pleasure. The Zapoletans accept money to fight their own kindred; the Utopians pay money to encourage men to betray their own kindred. The Zapoletans fight with 'incorruptible loyalty' for the highest bidder; the Utopians 'faithfully pay' traitors and mercenaries. (The translation blurs the point here: *incorrupta fide* is used of the Zapoletans; *bona fide* and *summa cum fide* of the Utopians). A nation which will fight without knowing for sure whether the cause is 'right or wrong' is not really justified in feeling superior to mercenaries. What seemed to the Utopians the distinctively human means of fighting, 'calculation' (*ratio*), is possessed by the Zapoletans to a high degree (*exactam habent rationem*). The Utopians are inclined to feel contempt for a people whose behaviour is controlled by small differences in pay, but not only is the 'careful account', which the Zapoletans take of such differences, remarkably similar to the careful discrimination between pleasures on which the Utopians base their ethics; we also discover, towards the end of the account of Utopian military affairs, that they expect to make a permanent profit from war. Conquered countries are made to surrender estates from which the Utopians 'may enjoy forever a large annual income' and on which some Utopian citizens live 'in great style' (*magnifice*) and 'play the part of magnates.' The important difference is that the Utopians are intelligent. The Zapoletans squander what they earn in a 'dreary sort' of debauchery (*luxus*), whereas the Utopians seek more refined and lasting pleasure (*voluptas*). Both are satisfied with the mutual trade. The Utopians pay more than any other employer, which satisfies the Zapoletans; but the Utopians have worked out the odds and deploy them with care. They like to think of themselves as benefactors to the human race in ensuring that as many Zapoletans are killed as possible; but their other reason has already been given: 'generally a large proportion never returns to claim payment'. The Utopians are shrewder accountants.

The function of the passage is to emphasise, without Hythloday noticing what is happening, the degree of evil which is involved in Utopian thought and action. But I have not so far given an entirely fair rendering. One of Swift's Houyhnhmns would have been admirably equipped to see here what Hythloday does not see. The Utopians do like to think of themselves as benefactors to mankind, and they really think it. They are not hypocrites: it is not that they try to deceive anyone, only that their thought becomes bent away from some of the goods they seek by their belief in a mistaken ultimate good. The value of any thing or any person is its or his usefulness in promoting the commonwealth, that is, the just distribution of *voluptas*. So within the terms of their own thought, it could not seem inhumane to use the Zapoletans as they do: 'just as they seek good men to use them, so [they] enlist these villains to abuse them'. It makes them lose sight of their own ideal of human fellowship; but to act differently with any consistency, they would have to make human fellowship a more important end than the commonwealth. It is the same with their notorious colonisation policies, which have attracted more adverse comment than anything else they do, because of the obvious resemblance to Nazi concepts of *Lebensraum*. 'They consider it a most just cause for war when a people which does not use its soil but keeps it idle and waste nevertheless forbids the use and possession of it to others who by the rule of nature ought to be maintained by it.' Justice and natural law are defined here by efficiency of use. More elevated definitions have been formulated, but it is the best the Utopians can do; and in this case, the argument that More would have agreed with such a 'rule of nature', if not with such a 'cause for war', are actually quite strong.

This is a doubtful case, but there are other matters, in which it is certain that More intended us to regard what the Utopians do as to some extent desirable. Even in their attitude to war they are superior to Europeans in that at least they do not regard it either as a game or as an excuse for wanton atrocity. Some of the proximate ends sought by the Utopians fit equally well into a fabric of thought in which the ultimate end is quite different from their own. An obvious example is their hospitals: More did not share their view of health, but it is unthinkable that he would not have wished to see the kind of ministration and sensible precaution described by Hythloday, in place of what was actually done in sixteenth-century England. But other things do not work in such an obvious way: the reader, as I stressed before, has to remain continuously alert. The Utopian care for the sick is not only preferable to what was happening in England; it is also quite possible to implement. More's Utopia is no scientific wonderland, such as many imitators have dreamed up: Utopian medicine is not more advanced than European. But as those final remarks in Book II make clear, there are two variables playing over this dream of the 'best state of a commonwealth', desirability and possibility. Utopian attitudes to marriage and to war, for example, are, as I have tried to show, undesirable and largely possible (Europeans share them). Very few things in Utopia are both desirable and possible; but as More's remarks at the end indicate directly, many are desirable and largely impossible.

In some cases, there is a quite complex interplay between the variables. The most obvious point about Utopian attitudes towards gold is that they are right in regarding it as an undesirable end. It is, as they say, absurd that 'a blockhead who has no more intelligence than a log and who is as dishonest as he is foolish keeps in bondage many wise men and good men merely for the reason that a great heap of gold coins happens to be his'. But although it may be possible to rectify this to some extent in a more sane society, the difficulties involved in completely eradicating the pursuit of gold as an end are registered in the details concerning what the Utopians do with it. It is not really strong enough to be a suitable metal for chaining slaves, and More is obviously not to be taken to be seriously proposing to solve the problem by using it for chamber pots. The joke points to the impossibility. (He could not have foreseen a time when chamber pots would be hoarded as antiques, but a glance into our present world will show that there is nothing magical about precious metals and stones. Man's compulsion to hoard would not be eradicated even if they were all totally destroyed.) Utopian views on gold as an end are, then, desirable but largely impossible. As for gold as a means, we have seen already that they use it to encourage treachery, pay mercenaries and finance wars of dubious justice. Undesirable and possible.

Those aspects of Utopian social organisation which are based either directly on a family structure or on an analogy with it, combine a high degree of desirability with measures of possibility which require more the information of a historian than the techniques of a literary critic to expound with any authority.

Notoriously, the most controversial aspect of Utopian life is its *communism*. Fr Surtz has convincingly undercut all the arguments that More regarded Utopian 'communism' as impossible, which were based on quotations from More's other writings on apparently the same subject. It is true that More writes elsewhere of the impossibility of re-distributing wealth equally among all; but, as Surtz argues, that is not what has happened in Utopia. Wealth is not equally distributed: no Utopian possesses anything ('Though no man has anything, yet all are rich'). Professor Hexter has argued equally convincingly that the same fact separates Utopia totally from any Marxist or socialist state in which the chief end in view is economic. More was 'not an economist at all in fact or in aspiration'.[2] The purpose of the *communism* in *Utopia* is not economic but moral. Hythloday diagnosed the three most serious sins in contemporary Europe as Pride, Greed and Sloth. The social structure he admires is aimed at the eradication of them. Hythloday says pride only thrives where rich men can contrast themselves with poor men: in Utopia that is impossible. Greed is impossible where no man can keep anything, and sloth is made impossible by a careful surveillance over a compulsory six hours' work a day. The other deadly sins, too, and many venial ones, are either impossible or very severely punished. *Communism* in Utopia is not an economic end, but a moral means.

The question whether, as a means, it is desirable or not, is, I think, deliberately left open, for each man to decide himself. As those two clues in Book I indicate, one can regard Utopia either as a kind of prison or as a kind of monastery. For some a monastic austerity would be congenial and spiritually helpful; for others it would not. More did wear a hair shirt, but he also decided, after long thought, not to become a monk. He was no hoarder, but he did not renounce all possessions.

But the question of possibility is another matter. Hythloday's definition of pride is a very limited one: I have already shown how deeply-rooted it is in other forms in both Hythloday and the Utopians. There is no gross greed in Utopia, but the ultimate end is to make all 'rich': they are not greedy for money but their ultimate end is maximum *voluptas*. The sensible objection posed by More at the end of Book I is that in such a society there is no incentive to work; sloth is overcome in Utopia, but only by means of external surveillance. It is not, to use the word Hythloday is so fond of, 'eradicated'. In short, we are back here to a fundamental difference in the conception of human nature. Hythloday and the Utopians think that in the best state of the commonwealth men will 'necessarily become good'; More shows by quietly undermining their arguments, in ways I have already analysed, that he stands by the traditional Christian belief that evil cannot be eradicated by legislation. Commentaries based on More's statements elsewhere about the impossibility of an equal distribution of wealth are not much wider of the mark than commentaries based on the assumption that, because those statements refer to a different state of affairs, More can be taken to regard Utopian *communism* as a possible ideal. Arguments that he did not regard it as an impossible economic end have no bearing on whether he regarded it as a possible moral means. To establish that he did regard it as a possible moral means, my analysis above would have to be refuted, and it would have to be proved that More ceased to believe traditional Christian teaching concerning Original Sin and Redemption for the few months he was writing *Utopia*.

Yet it will not in fact do to leave the matter here. The points I made in my last but one paragraph, about desirability, concerned individual response. There is a further question, whether More would have regarded making men in general 'necessarily become good' by legislation as desirable, even if it were possible. The answer is certainly not as clear as to the question concerning possibility, but I am strongly inclined to think he would, ultimately, not. Hythloday is very eloquent on the sense of security achieved by the Utopian system: 'what can be greater riches for a man than to live with a joyful and peaceful mind, free of all worries – not troubled about his food or harassed by the querulous demands of his wife or fearing poverty for his son or worrying about his daughter's dowry, but feeling secure about the livelihood and happiness of himself and his family: wife, sons, grandsons, great-grandsons, great-great-grandsons, and all the long line of their descendants that gentlefolk anticipate?' At one level, this is obviously highly desirable, but leaving aside questions about whether complete family concord *can* be achieved by the abolition of money, there is another word for security and happiness of such a kind: complacency. The quotation indicates very clearly how easy it is for a means to become an end: the enjoyment of welfare can become a positive obstruction to spiritual well-being. More expounds the negative correlative of this truth in his discussion of the spiritual value of tribulation in the *Dialogue of Comfort*. But it is not merely that a more insidious form of materialism can develop in a society which has eliminated the suffering caused by poverty and the evil caused by wealth. In so far as the Utopians achieve what they intend, the temptation to self-satisfaction and self-sufficiency is increased. As an end the pursuit of welfare leads away from God; even as a means it tends to do the same, in the measure to which it is successful.

This is not to say, of course, that More is therefore committed to believing that suffering and evil are good, because they may lead to God. As everyone knows, and most admit, they often lead to greater evil. The corrective point is made very forcefully in Book I. The account I gave above of Hythloday's attack on enclosure is patently inadequate. He does fail to prove his point about the futility of giving good counsel to kings; but the emotive power of his speech cannot be disregarded. It has not the tone of a persona, who has lost the point of his argument, being undermined by an author with dramatic skill. The tone is of an impassioned appeal for justice. Sheep which are kept ostensibly for the benefit of man are destroying men. The inversion of means and end is registered in the unforgettable image of sheep devouring human beings and devastating the country. Through fraud and violence the poor are driven from their homes: 'men and women, husbands and wives, orphans and widows, parents with little children . . . Away they must go, I say, from the only homes familiar and known to them, and they find no shelter to go to . . . what remains for them but to steal and be hanged'. The emotion here is clearly not undermined in any way: it is addressed directly to the reader. But to believe passionately that justice must be sought and that to create evil (stealing and, to escape capture, murder) by social injustice is an atrocity, is not the same as to believe that evil can be eradicated from man by legislation or that welfare will lead to spiritual well-being. The Utopians do achieve justice in the sense of welfare, but we have seen what happens to their sense of justice when they engage in war. If one seeks justice for the sake of welfare one may get welfare, but not justice in any profounder sense. The only hope of achieving the truly good lies in seeking the truly good, and for More the ultimate location of that is the Truly Good.

The idea that evil should be tolerated because it may lead to God is in fact a sort of grotesque utilitarian calculation which would have horrified More. Justice is the will of God, so justice is to be pursued. But to fight against injustice is not the same as to try to re-design the universe. With tact, one must act as well as one can in the play in which one finds oneself. The order of the arguments in the other passage where Hythloday speaks with more than his own passion is significant: he argues, firstly from 'the law of God', and secondly from utilitarian considerations, that punishments should be graded according to the severity of crimes and that hanging for theft encourages murder. Obedience to the will of God takes precedence over human calculations about what will work out for the best.

Although Hythloday's attack on the injustice of enclosure is not undermined in any way, there is one little phrase slipped into his speech, which shows a concern he does not really share. The order of the arguments about hanging is itself, of course, More's rather than Hythloday's: Hythloday does not notice that the law he quotes is precisely opposed to a Utopian practice he does not dissent from ('God has withdrawn from man the right to take not only another's life but his own'). In his speech against enclosure he mentions that the land-owners who devastate the villages leave 'only the church to pen the sheep in'. He says no more, and the way he does not register the full irony of it shows very clearly the distance between him and More. The building which should stand as a visible reminder of the ultimate end of man is reduced to a means of farming animals, which are kept as a means to man's prosperity. God's sheep are driven away so that man's sheep can be exploited. Hythloday and More are equally outraged by enclosure as a particularly gross example of European man's inhumanity. Both seek greater justice as a proximate end. But for Hythloday, justice in the sense of communal welfare is also the ultimate end: what needs to be done is to put man's house in order, and man can, as the men who live in No Place prove, put his own house in order. More can be allowed to reply, in words written in the close shadow of death, after long meditation on the response of Christ to human suffering, 'O timorous and weak silly sheep, think it sufficient for thee, only to walk after me, which am thy shepherd and governor, and so mistrust thyself and put they trust in me.'[3]

5   *Utopia*: Form as Discipline

I wish in this chapter to return to the discussion of the book's form, pursuing further the implications of some points I have already made in passing, but concerned primarily with suggesting why the form used by More is particularly well-suited to the intentions of *Utopia*.

The basic fictional strategy of the book lies, as in so many Renaissance works, in an interplay between fantasy and reality.[1] Utopia is nowhere, and its other nonsense names, such as Anydrus, a river without water, deliberately draw attention to the fact that it does not exist. But the discussion in Book I is very emphatically located in Antwerp, a famous European city, and two of the participants are real, well-known men. I have already indicated a difference in fictional status between More and Hythloday: the one a man busy in public office, longing to get back to his family but enjoying the company of Peter Giles, coming, significantly, out of a church full of worshippers, to see the other, a figure of almost epic appearance ('with sunburnt countenance and long beard and cloak hanging carelessly from his shoulder'), who is compared with literary characters from Homer and with Plato. A man immersed in the cares and pleasures of actual life meeting a figure who belongs more in literature than in life and who has just come from nowhere. Yet although More is well-disposed towards Hythloday first simply because he is introduced by that 'perfect friend', the real Peter Giles, 'native of Antwerp', Giles knows that More is 'always most greedy to hear' the kind of thing Hythloday will be able to tell him. Thomas More, busy diplomat, does enjoy listening at great length ('Mass being over') to a description of No Place. It is already clear that the interplay of reality and fantasy is not just a literary game (as it frequently is in minor Renaissance literature): one of the facts we learn about the real character is that he is fascinated by the unreal one.

70

The opposition of real and imaginary is carried through into details of description. The opening paragraphs give apparently irrelevant information about More's movements before reaching Antwerp. Tunstal and Themsecke are described even though they appear no more, and the whole reference to Bruges may seem a rather pedestrian explanation of how More happened to go to Antwerp at that particular time. The contrast between the Burgomaster, dismissed in a bland phrase which conceals contempt ('a figure of magnificence') and Themsecke, praised for the skill deriving from 'long experience' as well as native ability, is significant in retrospect: More and the Utopians agree about 'magnificence', but 'long experience' is something the Utopians somehow manage without.[2] But no reader could be expected to take this point at a first reading: the primary effect is to set More, at the risk of seeming pedestrian, in actual places, at identifiable times. The conversation takes place in a garden, where, by a convention ancient in More's time, the mind tends to create 'Far other Worlds, and other Seas', but on a solid bench, covered, we are told with almost Gulliverian fussiness, with turfs of grass. And after dinner, at the end of Book I, they 'returned to the same place, sat down on the same bench'. They are not in No Place; they are solidly *there*.

A related point is made by a few inconspicuous, but carefully placed, references to the unpredictability, the precariousness of actual life. More says in the prefatory letter to Giles: 'one must take care to be as agreeable as possible to those whom nature has supplied, or chance has made, or you yourself have chosen, to be the companions of your life'. The order of the phrasing here is important: a large proportion of actual life is decided by nature or by chance, rather than by human choice. Peter Giles slips a remark into his introductory description of Hythloday indicating that Hythloday's deliberate isolation is more conditioned than he would care to acknowledge: 'This attitude of his, but for the favor of God, would have cost him dear.' Morton's achievement is partly the result of gift and of endeavour, but also partly of chance: he 'had sustained numerous and varied vicissitudes of fortune, so that by many and great dangers he had acquired a statesman's sagacity, which, when thus learned, is not easily forgotten'. Hythloday likes to think of himself as a man in control of his own life, so we only discover through a parenthesis in a sentence explaining why the Utopians had no priest, that, of the five Europeans who accompanied him to Utopia, two had 'succumbed to fate'.

In the fantasy world, this sort of inconvenience, like most other sorts, is largely circumvented. If nature slips up, families are re-distributed, and forests are 'uprooted' to be replanted nearer the sea. Sensible diet and sensible pursuit of pleasure, including the pleasure of health, reduce the danger of sudden death; but the Utopians have other means of insuring themselves against chance. They themselves avoid fighting as long as they can use others; when they do have to fight, they have two substitute leaders ready to take over, 'the fortunes of war being always incalculable', and they keep one division in reserve even when pursuing a beaten enemy, just in case the 'whole fortune of the battle' suddenly changes. Harvests are not always predictable, so 'though they are more than sure how much food the city with its adjacent territory consumes, they produce far more grain and cattle than they require for their own use'. The rocks across the mouth of their bay, a potential danger, are in fact exploited to their advantage: they guide themselves by landmarks; if an enemy comes the landmarks are moved. A list of such details would be very lengthy. It extends to the level of the seating arrangements: the women sit on the outside in case they are pregnant and have any 'sudden pain or sickness'. The Utopians think they have a commonwealth which will 'last forever, as far as human prescience can forecast', and they have very systematically insured against everything that human prescience can forecast. They have efficiently insulated themselves from the toils and troubles of a recalcitrant external world.

As for that recalcitrant inner world, the old Adam, he is either tamed or forgotten. I have showed before how a considerable degree of cheating in the form of juggling with the term *human nature* is necessary to arrive at the desired equation pleasure = virtue. There is a similar kind of cheating, which the reader is again expected to notice, with the nature of the Utopians themselves. I have analysed passages where they are, by nature, like Europeans; there are others where they are morally superior in quite implausible ways, where they clearly belong to a fantasy world, which the actual world could never become because men are simply not like that. As they are so much more equitably employed, the Utopians need only work six hours a day. So the question naturally arises, what do they do with the rest of their waking hours? Most of them, says Hythloday, spend them listening to lectures: an academic's dream, but scarcely probable. The rest, says Hythloday, fill in the time by voluntarily doing more of the work they have been trained to do in their compulsory six hours. A politician's dream: workers actually wanting to do more than they have to, for no personal gain. But that is the point: this could only happen in a fantasy world. The same point is made in the form of a joke, in the game the Utopians are fond of playing. Nothing so frivolous as chess could appeal to them: they have instead a game in which the 'vices fight a pitched battle with the virtues' and the sober Utopians imbibe, as they play, instruction on how such battles are conducted. (The other game they like is one which would particularly appeal to a people whose moral thought is a calculus: 'a battle of numbers in which one number plunders another').

Elsewhere, human naughtiness is not completely ignored, but so tamed that it becomes quite innocuous. At the end, Hythloday says that ambition is one of the things which has its roots 'extirpated' in the Utopian commonwealth. In its vicious forms, it is, by rigorous laws; but Utopus was shrewd enough to find an outlet for it in the gardens attached to the blocks of houses. The pleasure the Utopians derive from these gardens is partly direct, but also partly from a harmless form of ambition – 'the keen competition between blocks as to which will have the best kept garden'. As usual, More is making more than one point at a time. The passage concludes: 'There is nothing which their founder seems to have cared so much for as these gardens.' More would have dissociated himself from the degree of their concern, but he was well known to be unusually fond of gardens. It is another reminder that although it is Hythloday, not More, who describes Utopia, the More outside the book created Hythloday and everything he describes, and the More inside the book is attracted by him.

The final clearly fantastic element of Utopia I want to emphasise affects both outer and inner worlds: its totally static nature. Utopian civilisation has lasted for 1760 years, an ironic length of time as R. J. Schoeck has pointed out,[3] with a change only in the construction of the houses (the ground-plan of the city having been sketched by Utopus himself). No barbarian hordes have overrun it; no desire for change among its inhabitants has disturbed the structure of its constitution. It is frequently said that such monotony would be undesirable to the point of oppressiveness. This seems to me probably one of the areas left open for individual response. I do not think More would have been as upset about it as post-Romantic critics: self-expression, self-fulfilment were not among his ideals. On the other hand, he does emphasise the physical monotony of the cities with the possible intention of indicating that inflexibility can be undesirable. But the main point here concerns possibility rather than desirability: by nature man is a changeable animal. It simply is not possible to contain his desire for change by issuing travel permits at the governor's discretion. Utopia has the static character of human concepts as opposed to human behaviour. It belongs in the country of the mind, not in any geographical or historical location.

Yet, as I have already suggested, it is a country which More, caught up as he is in the affairs of very real geographical and historical locations, enjoys visiting. Hythloday may be a distributor of nonsense, but even the sober Utopians 'are very fond of fools': 'there is no prohibition against deriving pleasure from their foolery'. Similarly, Cardinal Morton gives free rein, for a limited time, to the hanger-on who wants 'to give the impression of imitating a jester but whose imitation was too close to the real thing'. Or as More himself puts it, making the point more directly, 'in the private conversation of close friends this academic philosophy is not without its charm'.

But that last phrase is in fact an understatement; he is opposing Hythloday's argument when he uses it. Actually he is strongly drawn to the fantasy world. The best commentary on the relation between fantasy and reality in *Utopia* is More's description of a day-dream about Utopia in a letter to Erasmus, which I will quote at some length.

'You have no idea how thrilled I am; I feel so expanded, and I hold my head high. For in my daydreams I have been marked out by my Utopians to be their king forever; I can see myself now marching along, crowned with a diadem of wheat, very striking in my Franciscan frock, carrying a handful of wheat as my sacred scepter, thronged by a distinguished retinue of Amaurotians, and, with this huge entourage, giving audience to foreign ambassadors and sovereigns; wretched creatures they are, in comparison with us, as they stupidly pride themselves on appearing in childish garb and feminine finery, laced with that despicable gold, and ludicrous in their purple and jewels and other baubles. Yet, I would not want either you or our friend, Tunstal, to judge me by other men, whose character shifts with fortune. Even if heaven has decreed to waft me from my lowly estate to this soaring pinnacle, which, I think, defies comparison with that of kings, still you will never find me forgetful of that old friendship I had with you when I was but a private citizen. And if you do not mind making the short trip to visit me in Utopia, I shall definitely see to it that all mortals governed by my kindly rule will show you the honor due to those who, they know, are very dear to the heart of their king.

'I was going to continue with this fascinating vision. But the rising Dawn has shattered my dream – poor me! – and shaken me off my throne and summons me back to the drudgery of the courts. But at least this thought gives me consolation: real kingdoms do not last much longer.'[4]

Poor naive Hythloday: he really thought Utopian institutions could uproot pride from human nature.

In this letter More is showing more baldly what the fictional structure of *Utopia* is designed to convey. His enjoyment of the dream is very strong: it is very pleasant, very 'fascinating' to let the mind roam far from the 'drudgery of the courts', specifically to let it wander into a land where the most obvious follies of the present world are removed, where magnificent robes can be seen for what they really are ('childish garb') and where men of real wisdom will be honoured as they think they should be. But at the same time he knows it is only a dream, that he, like Morton, has to return after his temporary diversion to the quotidian reality of his legal chores. The initial reaction is like Hythloday's ('poor me') and the secondary reaction is to let the dream play back on the reality, illuminating it indirectly: the kingdom in which he is a drudge is almost as temporary as the one in which he was king. Utopia, so far from existing forever, is a momentary dream inside a reality itself transient. Berger[5] has an excellent phrase for what is happening: More is having 'an attack of Hythloday' – or rather he has had an attack, for the form in which the dream is related, like the form of *Utopia*, shows that at the time of writing he is standing back and looking at it with a steadiness which makes the shape of the island ('like a new moon') appear an apt metaphor for the attack itself.

For, within the dream, although the obvious follies of the world are removed, radical folly remains in the eye of the beholder. In his account of the dream in the letter, More is making himself ridiculously proud: proud of being made king, proud of the figure he cuts in his diadem of wheat (the Utopian governors carry a sheaf, but have no crown), 'striking' in a garment meant to signify poverty and humility, surrounded, like any European king, with a 'huge entourage', proud of his superiority to the 'stupid pride' of ambassadors and kings; yet not wanting to be judged as if he were an ordinary man whose character might change if his fortunes suddenly rose. And then, arising directly out of the pride, corruption: in this land where factionalism has been extirpated and favouritism and bribery made impossible, More's friend will get special treatment. The whole vision is in fact a way of drawing attention to a deliberate omission in *Utopia* which is seldom noticed. We are told how city governors are elected, and about the relation between them and the lower officials and the senate; but there is no reference to a king. More was not a forgetful man. The Utopians think it prudent to bear in mind the lower conception of *human nature* when it comes to precautions about the office for governor ('The governor holds office for life, unless ousted on suspicion of aiming at tyranny'). The ousting of a tyrannical city governor could be managed easily enough, if necessary, by the power of the remaining 53 cities. But where would the power come from (and who would control it?) which could oust a king of all Utopia? The fantasy-mind can ignore such inconvenient problems, but those who do not keep fantasy and reality distinct may find that pride, so far from being uprooted, may spring up unexpectedly in the most obvious places. More knew that he was not exempt from human pride; he had the wit to mock himself for his pride in 'my Utopians' and all the fantasy-life which his creation tempted him to indulge in. A land which had such a king would have little to fear; but pride is seldom accompanied by such a moral intelligence as More's.

In *Utopia*, as I have shown before, the pride is manifested not by More, but by Hythloday and by the Utopians, who are held distinct from the actual world by More, but not by Hythloday. There are three extremely important fictional strategies involved here, which, in their total effect, correspond to that of the argument between the two characters in Book I. The attraction of the dream world is very powerful, as are the best of Hythloday's arguments. Almost all people with a social conscience feel the desire to seek a Utopia, a commonwealth in which the most obvious evils of their own society have been removed. What More has done in Hythloday's account is to carry through that dream, and in such a way that intelligent people can be really stirred by it. His is not a gross utopia: it is not a totally naive dream like *News from Nowhere*, in which men have mysteriously ceased by nature to feel sexual jealousy or to engage in political strife, and so have no need for a system of legal punishment, no need for any coercion at all; nor does it lead to a materialist or sensualist indulgence. It could be really attractive to an austere, intelligent man, outraged by the injustices drawn daily to his attention in the courts and later at Court. As a matter of fact, it has attracted readers for four and a half centuries. Almost all people dream of earthly paradises and, specifically, almost all humane people feel at times the desire to re-write the conditions of existence, to create a world radically more just than the one in which they find themselves.

Yet More has also seen what really carrying it through involves. He has posited, within the dream, the 'best state of a commonwealth' as his ultimate end, and although he has not been deflected into vulgarising that end, he has rigorously pursued it. The commonwealth, the real mental as well as physical welfare of the people in this life is his end, so intelligent pleasure necessarily becomes the *summum bonum*. But that, for More, was not really the *summum bonum*. Although the best state of the commonwealth was profoundly desirable, the pursuit of it as an ultimate end leads at important points, even if by no means at all points, to radical conflicts with his deepest beliefs. So although, as a first fictional strategy, the fantasy has been put into the mouth of a man of considerable intelligence and of very strong social concern, the second strategy is to introduce other characters (that is, Morton and himself) in order to distance the fantasy. Hythloday lives totally in the dream world: he wants positively to cut himself off from the real world. More and Morton enjoy the dream for a while, but have reservations about what it leads to, and return to their responsibilities in the real world. This second strategy is reinforced by making Hythloday in some respects foolish. He is unable to see the implications of what he describes: none of the irony in the description of Utopian military practices, for example, is apparent to him, and the only reservation he expresses about Utopian customs is a solemn laugh at the exhibition of spouses to each other before marriage. Like Gulliver he is generally, unlike his creator, lacking in a sense of humour, that very fundamental means of distancing oneself from what one observes. He is not, of course, as foolish as Gulliver frequently is: he has to be intelligent for the first strategy to work properly. But he is foolish enough to register the point that there is a fundamental naivety, a radical folly, in the idea that a man, Utopus or Hythloday, can re-design the world according to a more convenient pattern.

Broadly speaking, of his two names, the first, Raphael, represents what he would like to be, and the second what he is; though that is not wholly true, for his intelligence and his love of justice are strong enough for him and his Utopians to be in some respects as admirable as they would like. What he and his Utopians lack most fundamentally is an external frame of reference. The Utopians can absorb selected aspects of European thought into their own system, but they have no external check on the mind's desire to bring everything within its own field of calculation: God becomes a step in their own arguments and the external world of chance is tamed. Similarly, Hythloday can look critically from the fantasy world at Europe, but he cannot step outside the fantasy world and look back critically at that. 'I was not quite certain that he could brook any opposition to his views, particularly when I recalled his censure of others on account of their fear that they might not appear wise enough, unless they found some fault to criticize in other men's discoveries.' Hythloday would do away with enclosure, but he is enclosed within his own dream. Physically he has returned to Europe, but mentally he is still living in Utopia. There is no hope of containing European savagery within the safe rules of the fantasy world, so he clings desperately to the fantasy. 'I am fully persuaded that . . . no happiness can be found in human affairs unless private property is utterly abolished.' A man who can say that is so trapped inside his dream that the only possibility is to return to a No Place which resembles a new moon.

The third fictional strategy is closely related to the second. In so far as he cannot step outside fantasy, Hythloday is foolish; in so far as he will not, he is proud. I have already drawn attention to the pride in both Hythloday and his Utopians. The attribution of pride to the character who is to some degree a dupe is an extremely important rhetorical move. A wise man is very strongly tempted to feel superior to the fools who surround him. More, meeting the 'magnificent' Burgomaster of Bruges, must have felt very like the Utopians, who are so unimpressed by the idiotic Anemolian ambassadors dressed up in parti-coloured robes and as much gold as they can fit on (though the Utopians characteristically do not laugh, as More might have done: the mother tries to quiet her boy who thinks it is childish, but she is 'in earnest'). But pride is the first of the Deadly Sins: to feel superior to those who dress up for show is potentially to share the vice and folly of those one condemns. Through his fictional structure, More, unlike Hythloday, can stand back from that initial reaction: he can be self-critical as well as critical of others. Form becomes a means of self-discipline. By standing outside the fantasy, unlike Hythloday, he can be critical both of the dream (its dangers and its follies) and of the dreamer (his folly and pride). So he can use the dream to make criticisms of European society; but since the dream is not his ultimate frame of reference, he can make further criticisms by criticising the dream and the dreamer.

The effect is, as I said above, closely similar to that of the argument between Hythloday and More in Book I. The argument is finely balanced because there is much to be said on both sides, but a careful analysis will, I think, show that Hythloday definitely loses it. In Book II the fictional strategies are in themselves demanding on the reader's critical sense, and the precise nature of the criticism registered through them are (notoriously) difficult to determine. But the intention is not the kind of self-protective withdrawal of the writer from responsibility for what is written, which is common in twentieth-century writing. Quite the reverse is the fact. More is not dissociated from Hythloday in order to insulate himself from criticism; the form is a means of criticising an aspect of himself, as he shows so baldly in that letter to Erasmus. He is no god paring his fingernails, no Tiresias who has seen all and stands outside all; he is a man who is trying hard to be more like Morton than like Hythloday. The purpose of accumulating difficulty is, as in the argument about counselling princes, to emphasise that the questions at issue are extremely difficult ones. It is very easy to dream up utopias; it is very hard to think through what it would really be desirable and possible to attempt. The intention is not strategic withdrawal, but strategic involvement of the reader and of the writer. To More, as an austere and profound Christian, the truth was in essence extremely clear, painfully clear; but in practice extremely difficult to apply and to hold clearly in mind. The more complex the political situation and the more fertile the mind, the greater the difficulty becomes. For a peasant it is relatively easy to know what is truly courageous; for a statesman it is extremely hard. The form More has chosen emphasises both the external and the internal difficulty. The difficulty of solving human problems can be registered very directly by making the relationship between Utopian and European highly unstable, by constantly shifting the variables of possibility and desirability; and the internal difficulty can be registered by the separation of Hythloday and More, in the two different ways in which the separation is exploited in the two Books, dialogue and tacit distancing. By simply engaging the reader in the difficulty, provoking him, through his literary art, to think, More is already providing him with an alternative to a return to unself-critical fantasy. But the alternative might seem, if he went no further than this, to be a highly sophisticated equivocation, the sort of equivocation which was so popular among some of the New Critics, in which literary art draws a dialogue with reality into itself, but remains ultimately autotelic.

In fact, in one of the most memorable passages in the book, More makes it clear that his thought moves in the opposite direction: that he is not subsuming reality into art, but using art to express appropriate responses to reality. In replying to Hythloday in Book I he uses the image of life as a play, in order to make the point that one must respond to the situation in which one finds oneself, rather than shut one's eyes and live out fantasies. 'Otherwise we have the situation in which a comedy of Plautus is being performed and the household slaves are making trivial jokes at one another and then you come on the stage in a philosopher's attire and recite the passage from the *Octavia* where Seneca is disputing with Nero. Would it not have been preferable to take a part without words than by reciting something inappropriate to make a hodgepodge of comedy and tragedy? You would have spoiled and upset the actual play by bringing in irrelevant matter – even if your contribution would have been superior in itself. Whatever play is being performed, perform it as best you can, and do not upset it all simply because you think of another which has more interest.' (The translation here is a little defective: the last word is one of the synonyms of pleasant or agreeable, and 'spoiled and upset' are not quite strong enough: the Latin words have a range of meanings extending to destroyed and overthrown). What is at issue is whether the philosopher will bide his time and perform his role as well as possible, or whether he will, through self-indulgence, make things worse than ever. The image concedes Hythloday's point that the 'play in hand' is a trivial affair, but implies that the appropriate response to external restraints which are not agreeable is to work within them, not to pretend they do not exist. A man who acts as if he were in a play more to his own taste will cut that perennial comic figure of a solemn moralist preaching to buffoons.

The image of life as a play had, of course, been used by Erasmus a few years before, in *The Praise of Folly*, and the implications of Erasmus's use of it also lie behind More's. 'If someone should unmask the actors in the middle of a scene on the stage and show their real faces to the audience, would he not spoil the whole play? . . . Now what else is our whole life but a kind of stage play through which men pass in various disguises, each one going on to play his part until he is led off by the director? And often the same actor is ordered back in a different costume, so that he who played the king in purple, now acts the slave in rags. Thus everything is pretense; yet this play is performed in no other way.'[6] More is relying on what Erasmus makes more explicit, that life is *only* a play, and a comedy at that. Ultimately the 'director' will see that all is well, that the deceptions are exposed and the irregularities of life resolved. To spoil the play before it is complete is to interfere with the intentions of the 'director'. More compresses these implications into the phrases about the obligation to perform one's allotted role 'neatly and appropriately', because he wishes to emphasise, more strongly than Erasmus, that although some sorts of action are absurd, others are required. His image makes simultaneously the points that this life is ultimately unimportant and that it is temporarily important, that it is a trivial comedy, about which it is absurd to become too outraged, yet that it is also a play in which the obligation to perform one's role as well and as appropriately as one can is of the utmost seriousness and importance.

The appropriate responses are shown in Morton, a man who enjoys a limited 'attack of Hythloday', who enjoys a jest, and who returns, when the time comes, to his duties. If life itself is ultimately a comedy, laughter will clearly, at times, be what is most appropriate: in fact a sense of humour is very important in maintaining that crucial distance between Hythloday and More, the dreamer and the man who both acts and sees the relative insignificance of the play. It is humour which makes the difference between seeing the external reality of European politics as a hopeless depravity, from which one can only run away, and seeing it as a trivial comedy, in which one must nonetheless play one's part. It is humour which makes it possible to control the internal propensity to pride, which is inherent in fantasies about re-writing the conditions of nature. Hythloday is so busy uprooting pride in Europe that he does not notice it sprouting in himself and in his new world. The best hope of freedom from the evils, which are inside him as well as outside, lies not in the dream of Utopia, but in the action of such a man as Morton. The most immediate response to a corrupt world is to dream up a better one; but in the form of *Utopia* More has disciplined the primitive aspiration towards an ideal society into the freedom within service which a more profound aspiration has revealed to him.

6   *Rasselas*: Form as Model

Critical response to *Rasselas* has not extended to the lunatic extremes of interpretation to which *Utopia* has been subjected, but it is surprisingly wide for a work clearly intended as a moral fable or apologue. Some have found the tone anguished; others serene. Some think it a profoundly gloomy book; others a very comic one. Some think it is about a fruitless search for happiness in this life, culminating in a decision to hope for it in the next; others think it is more about the nature of the human mind, that its concerns are psychological rather than metaphysical. Some read it as if it were by a satirist like Swift; others (inevitably) as if it were an absurd comedy by a precursor of Beckett. All these views (even the last) have been expressed by critics of considerable sophistication: I am not groping in the critical detritus to dredge up Aunt Sallies. With a work as unexplicit as, say, *King Lear*, such variety is obviously to be expected, but although its fictional mode is crucial to its meaning, *Rasselas* also has a degree of affinity to Johnson's periodical essays which might incline one to suppose that the room for doubt would be small.

The reason, I think, is similar to what I suggested in relation to *Utopia*: the process of reading is deliberately made difficult, in order to educate the reader. In many respects, which I hope to clarify, *Rasselas* belongs with the work of Erasmus, More and Swift. The philosopher of chapter 18 tells Rasselas *what* to think, but by the end of the chapter what Rasselas is most conscious of having learnt is 'the inefficacy of polished periods and studied sentences'. His real education lies in learning *how* to think. Yet the differences from the three earlier writers are equally important: in ways which I shall also examine, Johnson draws on expectations derived from familiarity with them and with other writers, in order to jolt the reader by not fulfilling them.

I have in fact already indicated a major difference, namely the inclusion of characters who learn. *Rasselas* is clearly not a novel, and it is perhaps preferable to refer to the figures in it as personas rather than characters: we seldom become emotionally concerned about their individual predicaments, and consistency of characterisation is readily sacrificed to development of theme. Yet there are crucial changes in them which can only come about through the passage of time. In *Utopia* there is a spatial contrast, corresponding to moods appropriate to different occasions: More enjoys listening to Hythloday on the day of rest, and on most days there is a litigation, diplomacy and family responsibility. There is no reason why he should not revisit Utopia for a mental holiday, provided he returns in due course; the letter to Erasmus which I quoted shows he did so. But despite the long-lasting naivety which afflicts all men in ways often apparent to others and occasionally to themselves, Rasselas will never return to the state of immaturity in which he could ask Imlac, 'Is there such depravity in man, as that he should injure another without benefit to himself?' His geographical journey, like Hythloday's, leads, in itself, to nowhere. Imlac, talking about pilgrimage, indicates before it starts that he need not scour the earth to find truth: 'Truth, such as is necessary to the regulation of life, is always found where it is honestly sought.' Yet his honest search leads to an irreversible change. I shall return later to Johnson's understanding of the significance of time, and later still to George Eliot's. But as a journey, Rasselas's search is of that peculiar kind described by T. S. Eliot:

> We shall not cease from exploration
> And the end of all our exploring
> Will be to arrive where we started
> And know the place for the first time.[1]

Ultimately it will not end until his death, and it will not end in unknown 'regions of speculation and tranquility' (to borrow a phrase which Rasselas in a precocious moment applies to the inventor who tries to fly). At best, it may end in knowledge of his own place and knowledge which many have recovered before him. But it may not, for 'end' can mean intention, and intentions are not always fulfilled. It does not end where he expected it to end, but at least he has learnt how it should end. In moral terms, Johnson is in More's world: truth is static, not evolving. In psychological terms, he is nearly in George Eliot's: individual grasp of truth develops through time. I shall discuss later the way in which he differs from most other users of a journey as an image of this developing grasp, since this is part of his technique of unfulfilled expectation. In formal terms, *Rasselas* is *sui generis*: I do not wish to imply, by my selection of the four fictions discussed here, that it is in formal terms to be seen as a mid-way stage in some putative history of the novel from More to George Eliot, for obviously the novel as a study of an individual's grasp of truth through time had already been developed further than Johnson chose to go.

Yet in terms of the effect on the reader, it can be seen as interestingly mid-way. More's form dramatises an attitude towards fantasy, but beyond that readers are thrown almost wholly on their own resources: they must be critical of the dream world, but with that warning they must shift for themselves. George Eliot's form is much more specific in its educative effective: as she said in famous phrases, she intended to enlarge men's sympathies, or to use language she avoided, she taught charity by so arranging her fiction as to demand its exercise in the process of reading. Johnson does not educate a particular virtue in this way, but his form does communicate a more developed attitude than More's. To express it with a clumsiness appropriate to critical gropings after subtle aesthetic achievements: 'Keep going: you won't find what you expect, but you will not be left with nothing.' The form itself conveys this attitude independently of explicit statements, though of course it coincides with Johnson's theme, as I shall try to clarify in the next chapter. The form is an integral part of the intention. The traditional Christian Humanist concern is with the question, 'How to live?' In Erasmus, More and Swift this becomes to a large extent, 'How to think?' (by forcing the reader to do it), since they saw clear thinking as necessary to good action. With Johnson's particular form of pessimism, the question implicit in most of his periodical writing shifts in emphasis towards 'How to face life?' The form of *Rasselas* repeatedly enacts a pattern which the mind can adopt in response to that question.

The most direct way in which it does this is in what may be termed the broken antithesis.[2] Eighteenth-century writing proceeds so generally by means of antithesis that it may be regarded as a convention which a contemporary reader would expect normally to be fulfilled. Sometimes readers are expected to opt for one of the alternatives offered in the antithetical structure; more often they are steered towards a middle choice which will avoid the disadvantages of both extremes. The patterns are so common in Pope that particular examples need not be quoted: either a desirable ideal will be set against a satirised aberration, or opposite extremes will be satirised to leave open a desirable middle. In Swift there is frequently a variant which he might well have learnt from Erasmus and More: a persona will argue that because one proposition is false the opposite must be true; the reader is expected to perceive the logical fallacy and to see that the real truth lies somewhere between.[3]

Johnson's modification of this convention can be seen in clear outline in the sequence of chapters 17–23. Chapter 17 is the first of Rasselas's 'experiments upon life', in which he associates with 'young men whose only business it is to gratify their desires'. In one way it is an obvious place to begin a search for happiness, but its naivety is quickly realised, and Rasselas swings in the following chapter to the antithetical choice of the philosopher who teaches complete control of the 'lower faculties' by reason. When the futility of this choice is crushingly demonstrated, Rasselas is left not merely with destroyed opposites, but with no clear hope that there may be a possible middle. The next three chapters take the procedure a step further. Having tried two opposites in the city of Cairo, Rasselas attempts a different sort of opposite and inspects the life of those who live in rural retreat from 'public life'. The intention of his party is to visit the Hermit, but Johnson delays the climax of that meeting by making them first chance on two other variants of rural life. In Chapter 19 he rudely shatters the ancient poetic convention, which always irritated him, that happiness is to be found in 'pastoral simplicity': shepherds in fields, as opposed to those in poems, have hearts 'cankered with discontent' and look up 'with stupid malevolence' to their social superiors. Yet in the following chapter, the rich man living in a large rural estate is also found to be unhappy, because his wealth attracts envy which will soon lead to the plunder and destruction of his home. So when Rasselas and his party finally arrive at the Hermit's cell 'on the third day', the Hermit is to be seen as in a middle state between the shepherds and the prosperous man, which by established convention might be expected to be the rational and possible compromise. He is not poor – he has books, paper and 'mechanical instruments' to stimulate him – nor is he visibly rich (his hidden treasure is an insurance against a future change of mind, not for present use); but he is not consequently happy. 'The life of a solitary man will be certainly miserable, but not certainly devout.' His chapter closes with a return to Cairo, on which he gazes 'with rapture', anticipating the happiness Rasselas has already failed to find there.

As Professor Wasserman has pointed out, another traditional pattern is invoked at this point as a possible resolution of the broken antithesis of city and country. It is proposed by one of the learned men who discuss the Hermit in Chapter 22: 'there was a time when the claims of the publick were satisfied, and when a man might properly sequester himself, to review his life, and purify his heart'. Public life in youth and maturity; rural retreat in old age: it seems there can be chronological resolution to the antithesis. But he is answered by another man who has been 'more affected' by the actual pattern of the Hermit's history (active life, retreat, return to the city): instead of diachronic compromise, there may be only perpetual oscillation. 'Of the present state, whatever it be, we feel, and are forced to confess, the misery, yet, when the same state is again at a distance, imagination paints it as desirable.'

The sequence seems complete, and in fact Johnson has broken even more expectations than the main framework presents. The precise lesson Rasselas learns from his experience with the rational philosopher is 'the emptiness of rhetorical sound and the inefficacy of polished periods and studied sentences'. The Hermit seems to offer a detailed alternative to this, as well as the major alternative of rural life: he is famous as a man 'whose age and virtue made him venerable', that is, as one who might be expected to have the wisdom of experience, not just an impressive oratorical style. Yet when he is asked the crucial question about the 'choice of life', his reply has toppled over the edge of that line where truism remains importantly true, into sententious vacuity and comic banality: 'To him that lives well, answered the hermit, every form of life is good; nor can I give any other rule for choice, than to remove from all apparent evil.' Similarly, the retreat of the prosperous man includes enough resemblance to the inanity of the Happy Valley ('they heard the sound of musick, and saw youths and virgins dancing in the grove') for us to hope in contrast for something intellectually superior at the Hermit's cell. The hope is momentarily fed: 'When the pleasure of novelty went away, I employed my hours in examining the plants which grow in the valley, and the minerals which I collected from the rocks.' Then broken in the next sentence: 'But that enquiry is now grown tasteless and irksome.'

But the main sequence itself is not in fact closed: Johnson does not leave us simply with all the alternatives and compromises of this second stage broken. Chapter 22 ends with the interview with the philosopher who advocates living according to nature. In a sense this draws the whole sequence together. Rasselas has tried men who seek sensual pleasures and a philosopher who rejects them, and country life of various ranks as well as city life. Here, finally, is a philosopher, lecturing in a city about living according to nature ('observe the hind of the forest, and the linnet of the grove', says he, in Cairo), advocating a way of life less rational than the young men of Chapter 17 ('consider the life of animals, whose motions are regulated by instinct'). Rasselas was wiser than this in his early adolescent stage back in the Happy Valley. 'Nor do I', he declaims to the animals there, 'envy your felicity; for it is not the felicity of man. I have many distresses from which ye are free; I fear pain when I do not feel it; I sometimes shrink at evils recollected, and sometimes start at evils anticipated.' Every separate choice and every compromise is inadequate. Rasselas has apparently completed a circle representing a total and rather ludicrous failure. But chapter 23 then continues with further hope and a new impetus gained through closer collaboration with Nekayah. So Johnson seems to conclude a sequence of broken expectation at chapter 21 (on the Hermit); re-opens and concludes it even more emphatically in chapter 22; and breaks it open again in chapter 23 with a whole new vista of possible alternatives ('We will divide the task between us', says Nekayah).

Some readers have naturally taken this to indicate a certain stupidity or, at the very least, comic naivety in Rasselas; but although he has got nowhere in his search for a 'choice of life', his time has not been as completely wasted as in his day-dreaming phase in the Valley. His persistence does include a degree of sheer inability to take a point. This is registered most clearly in Nekayah's response to the shepherds of chapter 19: she 'could not believe that all the accounts of primeval pleasures were fabulous . . . She hoped that the time would come, when with a few virtuous and elegant companions, she should gather flowers planted by her own hand, fondle the lambs of her own ewe, and listen, without care, among brooks and breezes, to one of her maidens reading in the shade'. On the other hand, even Nekayah is a little more perceptive two chapters later: she observes before they speak to him that the Hermit has not 'the countenance of a man that had found, or could teach, the way to happiness'. As for Rasselas, whereas he will not credit Imlac's scepticism about the philosopher of chapter 18, he sees through the philosopher of chapter 22 after one question. Whereas Rasselas naively lectures the young men in chapter 17, and Nekayah's response to the fears of the prosperous country-dweller is to retire to her own room, their reaction to the Hermit's sudden decision to return to public life is tactful and kind: 'They heard his resolution with surprise, but, after a short pause, offered to conduct him to Cairo.' It is left to 'one of the youngest' of the disputatious philosophers of the next chapter to pronounce the Hermit a hypocrite. One of the others in fact draws an inference from his statement about human mutability (quoted on p. 87 above), which Rasselas is not yet ready to register, but which is beginning to shape itself out of his experience: 'But the time will surely come, when desire will be no longer a torment, and no man shall be wretched but by his own fault.' Rasselas does not yet take the point, but it is there for the reader to anticipate what to expect.

In addition to a small growth in maturity, they have gained a considerable degree of pleasure, though it is recorded for them by the narrator, since they are as yet too intent upon the failure of their search to notice how much they are enjoying it. Back in the Happy Valley, Rasselas had concluded his declamation to the animals, 'surely the equity of providence has ballanced peculiar sufferings with peculiar enjoyments'. In the first stage of his search he sees some suffering, but he does some enjoying.

The pattern, then, forces the reader to go through a sequence of expectation and disappointment very like Rasselas's, even though he knows what will happen. The reader is unlikely to be as naive as Rasselas, but his literary experience continually tempts him to expect an alternative or compromise, which is then negated. When his experience leads him to believe the sequence of negation has closed, Johnson reopens, recloses and reopens it, continually drawing him on. Yet it is as if another hand were occasionally putting a grape into Tantalus's mouth while his whole attention goes on hopelessly trying to grasp the bunch. The important difference between the reader and the Rasselas of this stage of the book is that the reader can see Rasselas but Rasselas cannot see himself.

The range of variations on the patterns of broken antithesis is considerable, and I shall glance only at a few examples. For instance, in chapter 23, in which 'the prince and his sister divide between them the work of observation', Nekayah attempts to forestall the pattern. She sends Rasselas to inspect the 'splendour of courts', and does not herself go to the opposite, but to the middle: 'perhaps, what this world can give may be found in the modest habitations of middle fortune; too low for great designs, and too high for penury and distress'. Rasselas, of course, finds the obvious, but Nekayah, who expected to avoid the opposite end of the antithesis, finds that it extends to the area she thought safe: 'I saw many poor whom I had supposed to live in affluence. . . . It is the care of a very great part of mankind to conceal their indigence from the rest: they support themselves by temporary expedients, and every day is lost in contriving for the morrow.' Yet the chapter concludes with an unexpected consolation. Many of the people she tried to help rejected or resented gifts through pride; 'Many, however, have been sincerely grateful without the ostentation of gratitude, or the hope of other favours.'

A few chapters further into this section, in which the prince and Nekayah divide the task between them, Rasselas, having shown that happiness is not to be found in the highest social ranks, argues, like Moria or like one of Swift's personas, that it must therefore exist in 'seats of humble privacy and placid obscurity'. Nekayah does not trouble to point out the obvious fallacy and instead, by taking up his last remark ('Surely [the humble private citizen] has nothing to do but to love and to be loved, to be virtuous and to be happy'), demolishes an apparent means of sidestepping the antithesis: 'we do not always find visible happiness in proportion to visible virtue. . . . All that virtue can afford is quietness of conscience, a steady prospect of a happier state; this may enable us to endure calamity with patience; but remember that patience must suppose pain'. Her emphasis is negative, and to a large degree rightly so: Johnson very frequently insists, with unflinching honesty, that misfortune always afflicts good and evil men without any apparent discrimination at all. But even so, what Nekayah has admitted 'virtue can afford' is much.

The whole section, of course, in its division of labour is very clearly built on the principle of broken antithesis. It reaches its natural conclusion at the end of chapter 29, where Nekayah states explicitly that the middle way is not the obvious solution it might seem: 'Every hour, answered the princess, confirms my prejudice in favour of the position so often uttered by the mouth of Imlac, 'That nature sets her gifts on the right hand and on the left.'. . . There are goods so opposed that we cannot seize both, but, by too much prudence, may pass between them at too great a distance to reach either.' The reference to Imlac and her word 'prejudice' are highly ironic. Rasselas has been kept going in this section precisely because Nekayah would not, at the start of it in chapter 23, accept Imlac's pessimistic doubts. Nekayah says there: 'Imlac favours not our search, lest we should in time find him mistaken.' The impetus was provided by another antithesis: Rasselas 'was yet young' and from the older Imlac, who added new doubts to the doubts raised by his own searches, he turned to the sister who is also still young. By the end of the section, the young princess, by the structure she herself set up, is reduced to total agreement with the man she expected to prove mistaken. On the other hand, to adapt the words of the title of chapter 25, although she has not achieved the success she anticipated, her diligence has led her to recover some scraps of wisdom which she would never have accepted merely from the lips of Imlac. The most important are reserved till the end: 'he does nothing who endeavours to do more than is allowed to humanity. . . . Of the blessings set before you make your choice, and be content'. The last phrase as it stands is of course a hopeless wish, but Imlac refines the point at the beginning of the next chapter: 'while you are making the choice of life, you neglect to live.' It would seem again that we have reached a conclusion: there is no perfect choice, therefore stop looking for it, make the inevitably imperfect choice, and get on with the business of life.

But, as before, Johnson breaks open the apparent conclusion, concludes more emphatically and then reopens. Imlac does not actually mean what one expects him to mean in the context. What he says after the remark I have quoted is that Rasselas and Nekayah must not restrict themselves to a single city of the present day: they must extend their enquiries to the antiquities of Egyptian civilisation. Rasselas is, with some justification, unimpressed: 'My curiosity, said Rasselas, does not very strongly lead me to survey piles of stone, or mounds of earth; my business is with man.' But Imlac replies with great cogency, using arguments frequently found in Johnson's essays, that it is a moral duty to study history, to enlarge one's comprehension, to understand what caused mistakes and successes, to acquire means of seeing the present in perspective, and so on. Nekayah adds that it is a pleasure as well – 'I, said the princess, shall rejoice to learn something of the manners of antiquity' – an important remark for it shows that she is becoming conscious of enjoyment. They do enjoy the excursion to the Pyramid which ensues, but this new vista of enquiry, which Imlac opened, is closed by him, in a way which translates Nekayah's deductions in chapter 29 into wholly negative terms: 'It seems to have been erected only in compliance with that hunger of imagination which preys incessantly upon life, and must be always appeased by some employment. . . . I consider this mighty structure as a monument of the insufficiency of human enjoyments.' There it stands, a choice made, majestic in its dominion over humanly foreseeable time ('a fabrick intended to co-extend its duration with that of the world'), yet the central symbol in the book of the futility of merely filling time, built 'to amuse the tediousness of declining life, by seeing thousands labouring without end, and one stone, for no purpose, laid upon another'. The life of active endeavour is certainly preferable to the torpor of the shepherds, of the young men of Cairo, of the girls Nekayah meets in chapter 25, and of the women in the Arab's harem; it will lead incidentally to much important wisdom; but in itself, the utmost it can achieve is the world's largest pile of stones.

There seems no more to say; yet when they emerge from the Pyramid, in chapter 33, they are faced with a quite new beginning, the nature of which I shall discuss in my chapter 8.

The aspect of form in *Rasselas* I have been concerned with so far has been that which takes us nearest to what happens in the minds of the characters themselves, and which is also furthest from the procedures of Erasmus, More and Swift. I wish now to examine three principles of form which can be related clearly to the work of the three earlier writers, even though they include important differences. By the means which I have already analysed, Johnson encourages the reader to approach the subject thinking in terms of 'either (a) or (b)', and, when that clearly fails, 'neither (a) nor (c) therefore (b)'; and when that also fails, he will be found to have substituted, 'none, but something else'. In the three ways which I shall discuss next, he does to some extent educate the reader into a particular pattern of thought, but is more concerned simply to alert him to the existence of complexity where it might not be expected.

Firstly there is a very considerable variety of tone, which to a large extent accounts for the variety of critical response I have referred to above. The book is sometimes solemn, sometimes satirical, sometimes comic, depending on the context, and it is not easy to sustain the flexibility of reaction which it demands. To demonstrate the variety, it will be convenient to analyse the first chapter, since it is there that Johnson intends to alert the reader to what he may tend to forget as his attention becomes more occupied.

The title-page (*The History of Rasselas, Prince of Abissinia*) provokes expectations of a narrative (Fielding's full title, for example, was *The History of Tom Jones, A Foundling*) about royalty in an exotic country – in short an oriental romance. Beside it, the title of the first chapter ('Description of a palace in a valley') seems oddly flat and cursory. Then, in contrast to both, comes the famous first sentence, which actually sets the dominant tone, destroying totally any possibility that what follows will be a romance or a cursory narrative, couched in language which could by only a slight intensification become pompous, but moving with a relentless dignity which will permit no escape into mockery except by the irredeemably trivial: 'Ye who listen with credulity to the whispers of fancy, and persue with eagerness the phantoms of hope; who expect that age will perform the promises of youth, and that the deficiencies of the present day will be supplied by the morrow; attend to the history of Rasselas prince of Abissinia.' The second sentence reverts to the flat tone – 'Rasselas was the fourth son of the mighty emperour' – to register for the observant the fact that the likelihood of his ever succeeding to the throne is actually very small; but then shifts, via the word 'mighty', into something quite different: 'in whose dominions the Father of waters begins his course; whose bounty pours down the streams of plenty, and scatters over half the world the harvests of Egypt'. To call the Nile 'the Father of waters' is to establish traditional symbolism as an available convention, and the phrasing of the last part of the sentence suggests, very naturally in such a context, the possibility of a richness and fruitfulness on earth which the first sentence has seemed to exclude, though the source of it is not the man who pursues but 'the Father of waters' who pours.

Alarm signals are built into the first two sentences which describe the Valley: '. . . Rasselas was confined . . . till the order of succession should call him to the throne' – that is, for a fourth son, probably for life. 'The place, which the wisdom or policy of antiquity had destined for the residence of the Abissinian princes' – when policy is distinguished from wisdom it is potentially ugly. But the dominant impression at first is of a secure haven, indeed a womb-like refuge. (The passage has been trampled by amateur Freudians, but the analogy seems explicit enough to be intentional). Mountains overhang it, but it is 'spacious', so they do not yet seem oppressive. The 'dreadful noise' of the falling water is safely outside the Valley. But as the suggestions of a resemblance to paradise accumulate, so do further alarm signals. The first half of a sentence seems harmless ('The sides of the mountains were covered with trees, the banks of the brooks were diversified with flowers'); the second becomes cloying and decadent ('every blast shook spices from the rocks, and every month dropped fruits upon the ground'). The summarising sentence is seen to contain a quiet irony, as one looks back over the preceding two. 'All the diversities of the world were brought together, the blessings of nature were collected, and its evils extracted and excluded.' 'Nature' is referring here only to the world outside man, for whereas the 'beasts of prey' are excluded, the 'beasts of chase' are there for man to continue to kill. One of Johnson's sources[4] reports the same without irony, but Johnson seems, from his choice of specific animals, to have wished to recall Book IV of *Paradise Lost*, in which the beasts are 'since . . . of chase'. Here a touch of comedy is appropriate: Johnson's 'solemn elephant reposing in the shade' is comically recovering the dignity he lost in Milton by wreathing his 'lithe proboscis' to amuse the other animals. And after the heaping of alls upon everys, the air thick with spices and the ground littered with fruits, Johnson laconically adds that the Valley provides the 'necessaries of life' but 'all delights and superfluities' are brought in at the annual visit of the emperor.

Yet the very sentence in which he says that also contains the first clarification of the darker hints already given, the first precise indication that the pleasing security of the Valley necessarily involves coercion: 'everyone . . . was *required* to propose whatever might contribute to make seclusion pleasant' (my italics). Temporarily the tone hovers: after the alarming final phrases of the same sentence ('vacancies of attention' and 'tediousness of time') there comes a short, emphatic, apparent reassurance: 'Every desire was immediately granted.' But from 'seclusion', the emphasis shifts steadily via 'blissful captivity' to the blunt, unqualified final word of the paragraph, 'imprisonment'. Clues have been distributed, hinting at what is wrong ('vacancies', 'tediousness', 'those only were admitted whose performance was thought able to add novelty to luxury'), but an element of mystery is retained: 'appearance of security and delight', 'the effect of longer experience could not be known'. And there is something permanently attractive about the Valley, for the 'artificers of pleasure' hope to be allowed to remain there, and 'every year produced . . . new competitors for imprisonment'.

The chapter concludes with the most unambiguously human contribution to the Valley and the most unambiguously sinister, the palace. The chapter title indicated the emphasis it should carry. Unlike the Valley itself, its 'magnificence' is immediately oppressive: 'The roofs were turned into arches of massy stone joined with a cement that grew harder by time'. The Valley is cloyingly synthetic; the palace is proudly unnatural: 'the building stood from century to century, deriding the solstitial rains and equinoctial hurricanes, without need of reparation'. With hindsight we will see here a competitor for the eminence of the Pyramid. It is too large to be 'fully known' by those who use it for its ostensible purpose (to live in); it can only be fully known by some officers whose job it is to guard its secrets. There is no danger of the Valley being invaded, yet it is 'built as if suspicion herself had dictated the plan': the iron gate may exclude the 'evils of nature', but has evidently not excluded the evils of man. Every room has 'an open and secret passage'; many columns have 'unsuspected cavities, in which a long race of monarchs had reposited their treasures', and the book in which these secret hoards are recorded is 'itself concealed in a tower'. All this in a place where 'every desire was immediately granted': the tone is very dark by the end of the chapter, and in a characteristic way, Johnson shifts abruptly at the beginning of the next to satirical naivety. 'Here the sons and daughters of Abissinia lived only to know the soft vicissitudes of pleasure and repose.'

No practised reader now takes Johnson to be writing in the naturalistic mode of most English prose fiction: such description as he provides is there to make conceptual points in the development of his argument, not as background or to provide any illusion of realism. (In a later chapter, when a maid breaks a porcelain cup, the intention is not to remind us that Rasselas is in a situation which requires the employment of servants who are sometimes careless, but to suggest to Rasselas that 'what cannot be repaired is not to be regretted'). But a chapter which carries a title advertising it as the sort of introductory description which can be quickly skipped through, so that one can get to the story promised by the title of the book, actually requires, without the fireworks of Erasmus or Swift, the kind of mental agility which they demand.

In fact the difference can be stated more positively than by pointing to the absence of fireworks: unlike his predecessors in this tradition, Johnson establishes very firmly a stylistic norm or, to adopt Yvor Winters's use of the word, convention.[5] Despite a general flexibility, which includes broader comedy than anything in the first chapter, the convention of style, creating a convention of feeling, is one of profound direct seriousness, befitting a search for the best end of human endeavour. The shifts away from the convention, into satire and even farce, do not bring its appropriateness into question; on the contrary, one of the effects is to forestall and disarm any questioning which might come from outside. A book written wholly in the style of the first sentence of chapter 1 might well attract mockery as the lucubrations of a 'solemn elephant'. Johnson's control over his style is such that, despite a would-be languishing mourner who gradually forgets 'the duty of periodical affliction', and a would-be aviator who spends a year making wings and falls 'in an instant' into a lake, the tone of that sentence remains dominant. By isolating certain series of tones it is naturally easy for critical accounts of the book to arrive at different conclusions; but as well as merited discomfort and wilfully self-imposed unhappiness, there is real and inevitable suffering in the book, and Johnson was not one (to paraphrase the end of chapter 18) whose humanity would suffer him to insult misery with mockery. The effect of the convention established by the dominant tone is to guide the reader towards an appropriate mode of feeling and a frame of mind, in which a failure to recur to moods of the deepest seriousness will convict him of the purblindness of the characters themselves at their weakest moments.

The second means of communicating complexity I wish to discuss is the use of dialogue. The different forms in which Johnson used it can be compared respectively to Swift's and to More's. In Swift, actual or implied dialogue is almost invariably between a naive character and one who is permanently or temporarily wise. Johnson uses this form particularly in the chapters on Imlac's history. When Imlac refers to his father's intention to make him become the richest man in Abissinia, Rasselas asks, 'Why . . . did thy father desire the increase of his wealth, when it was already greater than he durst discover or enjoy?' The question exposes the lunacy of the pursuit of wealth as an ultimate end; and at the same time, through its manifest naivety, it affirms that, despite the lunacy, men quite commonly do take wealth as their ultimate end. Later, as the experience of the characters accumulates, this degree of naivety becomes unavailable, but variations of the form become possible. Nekayah says to Pekuah, referring to the women in the Arab's fortress, 'why did you not make them your companions, enjoy their conversation, and partake their diversions? In a place where they found business or amusement, why should you alone sit corroded with idle melancholy?' No one feels it necessary to comment on the irony of this from the lady who, advised by Imlac not to 'suffer life to stagnate', nonetheless for some weeks retired constantly at a fixed time of the day 'and returned with her eyes swollen and her countenance clouded'. On the contrary, Pekuah actually affirms her solidarity with Nekayah's human weakness: 'you know that the mind will easily straggle from the fingers, nor will you suspect that captivity and absence from Nekayah could receive solace from silken flowers'. It is ironic that men can perceive a folly in the behaviour of others which they cannot or will not perceive in their own; but it is a fact, and a fact to which irony is not always the most appropriate response.

The dialogue between Rasselas and Nekayah, in the sequence of chapters in which they divide 'the work of observation' between them, is at first a straightforward version of this first form. In chapter 26, Rasselas plays the role of naif to draw out the successive stages of Nekayah's report on domestic life which culminates in the aphorism 'Marriage has many pains, but celibacy has no pleasures.' The chapter closes with Rasselas still trying to refute observed fact with verbal logic: 'Surely he is most likely to please himself that has no other inclination [i.e. no spouse's] to regard.' In the following chapter (27) Nekayah is in turn naive, as Rasselas demonstrates the impossibility of avoiding discontent in public life. Yet the see-saw is not evenly balanced, for chapter 27 opens with a 'short pause' after which Rasselas tells Nekayah she is prejudiced and has 'supposed misery where she did not find it' – and immediately proceeds to a totally black picture of public life based more on supposition and less on observation than Nekayah's version of domestic life. And at the end it is he who is again the naif, proposing the foolish argument I quoted before, that since happiness does not exist in the 'highest stations' it must exist in humbler ones. In the more equal and more heated discussion which follows, Rasselas generally comes off worse. But each of Nekayah's victories over him is at the same time a defeat of her own attempt to prove Imlac mistaken. Both enjoy the battle of wits; both lose their sense of direction; both make incidental discoveries. Several critics have pointed out that Nekayah's analysis of discord in domestic life is supported by the quarrel, which develops as she continues it, between herself and Rasselas. But Rasselas, noting the bitterness which has arisen, argues, like More, from fact to imperative rather than to dream: 'We are employed in a search, of which both are equally to enjoy the success, or suffer by the miscarriage. It is therefore fit that we assist each other.' It does not stop the argument, but he has hit on a truth more important than what they are conscious of looking for.

The form of this stage of the dialogue is more like Book I of *Utopia* than anything in Swift. Rasselas usually loses, but the arguments both put forward are often extremely strong. Nekayah does not stoop to answer Rasselas's silly proposition that happiness must exist in humble stations, but instead makes a profound statement about the indiscriminate nature of affliction and its relation to virtue. Rasselas tries to trivialise it by misrepresentation (having just used that very word to attack Nekayah's speech): she did not, as he pretends, suppose that 'national calamities' are common. But having laboriously refuted what she did not say, he suddenly lights on one of the most important truths in the book: 'We will not endeavour to modify the motions of the elements, or to fix the destiny of kingdoms. It is our business to consider what beings like us may perform; each labouring for his own happiness, by promoting within his circle, however narrow, the happiness of others.' It leads very naturally to an argument in favour of marriage. When Nekayah voices doubts based on her observations of the dismaying variety of causes of discord in marriage, Rasselas pounces, with all the pleasure of victory in dispute, on the inconsistency with her aphorism at the end of chapter 6 ('Marriage has many pains, but celibacy has no pleasure'). 'Thus it happens,' he says, 'when wrong opinions are entertained, that they mutually destroy each other, and leave the mind open to truth.' What kind of truth this process leaves is analysed by Nekayah at the end of chapter 29 ('There are goods so opposed that we cannot seize both, but . . . may pass between them at too great a distance to reach either'): the attempt to avoid extremes by means of compromise may leave one in possession not of truth but of nothing at all. Rasselas's victory is in fact already more apparent than real: there is an equal inconsistency between his last remark in chapter 26, where he favours celibacy ('Surely he is most likely to please himself that has no other inclination to regard') and his argument in favour of marriage in chapter 28 ('I cannot be persuaded but that marriage is one of the means of happiness'). But Nekayah again refrains from this obvious retort, and instead universalises her inconsistency into a truth about human limitation, which goes much deeper than the main subject of their argument: 'of two systems, of which neither can be surveyed by any human being in its full compass of magnitude and multiplicity of complication, where is the wonder, that judging of the whole by parts, I am alternately affected by one and the other. . . . We differ from ourselves just as we differ from each other, when we see only part of the question.' Yet when Rasselas in turn puts forward an argument of real power, moving from 'It is therefore fit that we assist each other', to a point which undercuts all the facts concerning unhappiness ('You surely conclude too hastily from the infelicity of marriage against its institution; will not the misery of life prove equally that life cannot be the gift of heaven?' – in other words, marriage is a divine, not a human institution, and so incidental unhappiness cannot count as an argument against it), it is Nekayah's turn to be petty, throwing Rasselas's earlier point back at him: 'we are not now enquiring for the world, but for ourselves.'

The last chapter on the subject, chapter 29, is concerned with the question of time. Rasselas argues, with considerable power, that early marriages, based usually on romantic dreams, are subject to potentially disastrous disillusion through the passage of time: 'They marry, and discover what nothing but voluntary blindness had before concealed.' They also lead to rivalry between parents and children as the gap in ages is too small. Nekayah replies, with equal power, that late marriages are made difficult by the very maturity of the partners. Time has confirmed fixed opinions and established habits which it is difficult to accommodate to those of a partner whose experience has been different: 'even though mutual esteem produces mutual desire to please, time itself, as it modifies unchangeably the external mien, determines likewise the direction of the passions, and gives an inflexible rigidity to the manners. Long customs are not easily broken'. There is also the danger that the parents will die before the children are mature. The alternatives are so equally balanced that Rasselas attempts to propose a diachronic middle way. Nekayah closes this final option with her classic statement of the dangers of compromise: the man who tries to elude opposites will probably be left with nothing.

This section of the book is often regarded as the least successful because the most abstract and least fictionalised. But in fact the argument is more highly dramatised than in the previous section of successive vignettes. By making the two characters argue, with human inconsistency and partiality, but also with power, Johnson is able to demonstrate dramatically the difficulties of the questions involved, and at the same time the limitations of human ability to cope with them. At the moments when the characters feel most sure they have the answer, they usually look most foolish: no perfect solution exists. Yet when all the negatives have been registered and pondered, the view which remains least vulnerable is a guarded positive. 'To live without feeling or exciting sympathy, to be fortunate without adding to the felicity of others, or afflicted without tasting the balm of pity, is a state more gloomy than solitude.' Characteristically the form of the statement is cautious: there is no guarantee of happiness; but the alternatives are worse.

The third means of emphasising complexity I wish to define is partly implicit in the analysis already made. In *Utopia*, Hythloday argues a very powerful case, which in some particulars More concedes; but he argues from a consistent point of view, from which More consistently dissents. In *Rasselas*, the characters are deliberately made inconsistent, but each one of them is capable, at different times, of perceiving important truths. In other ways also, they behave more like persons than personas. They do not have the substance of characters in a novel, but on the other hand they do demand a fuller emotive response than the personas of More or of Swift.

Imlac obviously expresses more wisdom than any of the others, but there is now general critical agreement that he is not to be taken simply as Johnson's spokesman. When he is carried away into fantastic claims about the learning required by a poet, Rasselas, young as he is, can see his folly: 'Thou hast convinced me, that no human being can ever be a poet.' As I shall argue later, his behaviour in the last chapter is not wiser than that of the younger generation. All the main characters, on occasion, make remarks which clearly carry the full approval of the author. Even the Arab can tell Pekuah, 'the angels of affliction spread their toils alike for the virtuous and the wicked, for the mighty and the mean'. One of the effects is to require the kind of constant vigilance in reading which More has other means of demanding. The convention of style which I discussed above usually makes it clear (as it is not often in Erasmus, More or Swift) which statements carry such authority; but Johnson has a skill in parodying his own best style which can nonetheless leave an unwary reader looking as foolish as a naive persona.

The point, that the characters in *Rasselas* lie somewhere between the conventions of the main traditions of the novel and those of works in which *persona* is an unquestionably preferable word to *character*, can be made quickly by contrasting the would-be aviator and the Astronomer. The aviator is clearly no more than a persona: even though he is drawn to land after his bathetic fall into the lake 'half dead with terrour and vexation', no emotional response is expected from the reader. The pettiness of 'vexation' limits 'terrour' to part of the satirical effect. In contrast, the seriousness and the tactful charity with which Imlac responds to the Astronomer (and much else, to which I shall return later) requires the reader to regard him as a suffering individual, as well as an important factor in the rhetorical structure of the book. In *Utopia* the figures are given characteristics only for the purpose of establishing their relative reliability and of providing clues for assessing what they say. No more would be relevant, since the questions More is concerned with are posed in intellectual terms. Johnson requires a greater complexity in this respect, since he is also concerned to define appropriate emotional responses to similar, but slightly different questions.

Even where his intention is, like More's, to contrast idealism with realism, dream with fact, he does not always use the immediate deflationary procedure of the chapters on the aviator. At the beginning of chapter 12, Rasselas outlines at some length

what he would do if he had the 'choice of life': 'I would injure no
man, and should provoke no resentment: I would relieve every
distress, and should enjoy the benedictions of gratitude. I would
choose my friends among the wise, and my wife among the
virtuous; and therefore should be in no danger from treachery, or
unkindness . . .'. Whereas in *Gulliver's Travels* a similar fantasy,
put into the mouth of Gulliver, is immediately shattered by seeing
the real state of the Struldbruggs, who have the immortal life
Gulliver thought he would like, nothing at all is said or seen to
destroy Rasselas's dream. Imlac merely continues, without
comment, the narration of his travels. Deflation is not only
delayed for fifteen chapters (that is, about one-third of the total
length of the book), but when it comes is put into the mouth of
Rasselas himself: 'It is evident, that as any man acts in a wider
compass, he must be more exposed to opposition from enmity or
miscarriage from chance; whoever has many to please or to
govern, must use the ministry of many agents, some of whom will
be wicked, and some ignorant; by some he will be misled, and by
others betrayed.' This is not a new discovery made by Rasselas,
for it is actually a paraphrase of something Imlac had said to him
back in chapter 8: 'Subordination supposes power on one part and
subjection on the other; and if power be in the hands of men, it will
sometimes be abused. The vigilance of the supreme magistrate
may do much, but much will still remain undone.' The implication of this procedure is not fully clear until the very last chapter,
where Rasselas recurs to his dream: 'The prince desired a little
kingdom, in which he might administer justice in his own person,
and see all the parts of government with his own eyes; but he could
never fix the limits of his dominion, and was always adding to the
number of his subjects.' This is not a case of the comic
inconsistency of a persona: Rasselas still knows perfectly well, as
the penultimate sentence informs us, that this dream could not be
realised. It is a human inconsistency and the persistence of a
human dream, to which a response of laughter alone would be
callow.

What we have here is an instance of a generally characteristic
procedure of the book, which is manifested in numerous different
ways throughout. W. J. Bate, in a very penetrating essay, has
defined it in the term *satire manqué*.[6] The effect is closely analogous
to that of the broken antithesis which I discussed earlier. Again
and again Johnson sets up all the machinery of a satirical

situation, and then refrains from delivering the deflationary punch. Even where he allows the satire to take its course, he normally complicates the final response. The chapter on the Hermit ends satirically, with the references to the treasure he had reserved as an insurance and the 'rapture' with which he gazes on Cairo. But those who think this makes him a hypocrite soon find themselves in the company of the 'youngest' of the men who discuss his experience. Even the aviator is not wholly a fool. It is ironic that the wings he designed for use in the air only sustain him in the water, but if he had not developed so 'many ingenious contrivances to facilitate motion and unite levity with strength', he would have drowned. It validates his authority to make a point which remains important throughout the book: 'Nothing . . . will ever be attempted, if all possible objections must be first overcome.'

The philosopher of chapter 22, who advocates living according to nature, is subjected to unqualified satire: the end of that chapter is the moment of purest comedy in the whole book. But in chapter 18, where the other philosopher advocates living according to the dictates of reason, the expectations of a satirical structure, which are carefully accumulated, are, to the reader's shock, glaringly unfulfilled. He is 'raised above the rest' and Rasselas's phrase about him looking 'down on the scenes of life changing beneath him' should remind the reader of the aviator and his fall.[7] His teaching about the conquest of passion is ironically delivered 'with great energy', and he accepts Rasselas's gold with a 'mixture of joy and wonder'. Rasselas naively cannot 'conceive how any man could reason so forcibly without *feeling* the cogency of his own arguments' (my italics), and Imlac explicitly warns him not to be hasty in his admiration. The irony even continues after the philosopher's affliction: money is again required to gain access to him; the man who spoke of reason as resembling the 'sun, of which the light is constant, uniform, and lasting' is found 'in a room half darkened, with his eyes misty, and his face pale'; and he who thought man should not allow himself to be 'emasculated by tenderness' is reduced to saying that he looked for all the comforts of his age from his daughter's 'tenderness'. Yet any reader inclined to an attitude of satirical superiority to the philosopher is convicted of the callowness of 'one who has never felt the pangs of separation'. And any reader inclined to mock the naivety of Rasselas will have learnt less than Rasselas himself,

'whose humanity would not suffer him to insult misery with
reproof'. We do not find the satire on rationalism which we
expect; we do find that 'humanity' is a more adequate response to
human suffering than either rational or satirical aloofness. It is,
again, almost the procedure of a novel, but in a crucial way not
quite. We are made to appreciate that the suffering of the
philosopher is, in a very important sense, real: we cannot respond
to a man, who speaks in the phrases and cadences of 'you are come
at a time when all human friendship is useless; what I suffer
cannot be remedied, what I have lost cannot be supplied', as if to
Gulliver half-drowning in a bowl of cream. On the other hand, we
are not being made to feel in order that our feelings should be
educated. The purely intellectual point, that 'rhetorical sound'
will not provide a means of rising above the human condition, is
an important component in what is happening; the rest lies in
outlining an attitude by embodying it in a literary pattern. We do
not feel enough for the philosopher to have our sympathies
enlarged, to use George Eliot's words: we do feel enough, here and
on many other occasions, to take the point that without sympathy
there is no humanity.

Few readers have regarded laughter as an adequate response to
chapter 18, but it remains not uncommon to read it as satire on
stoicism, seeing the philosopher's suffering merely as part of a
demonstration of the inadequacy of his teaching. Taken out of
context and read through the spectacles of Swift or Voltaire it
could easily seem so, but in Johnson one very commonly finds the
opposite, that is, the inclusion of a satirical response in order to
undercut it. In Juvenal's tenth Satire, men who have been granted
the desire for longevity are subjected to mockery for what it
actually brings them, in pain from disease and loss of faculties. In
the parallel passage of *The Vanity of Human Wishes*, Johnson places
the 'sneer' on the lips of legacy-hunters (line 277), as a means of
actually increasing sympathy for the wholly isolated and vulnerable dotard. But he does not merely rely on the reader's general
acquaintance with his cast of mind. The pattern is included so
often in *Rasselas* that it becomes a convention, established within
the work itself as a means of sustaining the dominant mode of
feeling.

Chapter 17, in which Rasselas 'associates with young men of
spirit and gaiety', might more readily seem comic than what
follows in the next. To look for the 'choice of life' in such company

is obviously naive in the extreme, and giving nearly half the chapter to a solemn lecture, addressed to the cynical ('they laughed at order and at law') debauchees ('their pleasures were gross and sensual') raises preliminary expectations that we shall be laughing at the inexperience of a serious young man who still thinks all men are reasonable. The tone of the first part of the lecture in fact encourages such expectations: 'I have seriously considered our manners and our prospects.' This almost calls for yellow stockings and cross garters, and it is followed by glib aphorisms which merit the impatience Rasselas felt towards his old instructor in the Happy Valley: 'The first years of man must make provision for the last. He that never thinks never can be wise.' But as he goes on, the tone gradually modulates into the direct, unmockable seriousness of the first sentence of the book: 'let us live as men who are sometime to grow old, and to whom it will be the most dreadful of all evils not to count their past years but by follies, and to be reminded of their former luxuriance of health only by the maladies which riot has produced'. This is met with laughter, of course, 'a general chorus of continued laughter' from the young men. So anyone inclined to mock the end of Rasselas's lecture will find himself in unintelligent company. As usual, a partially satirical effect is working in the other direction as well. The word 'continued' is ironic: for how many years can these men, now young, continue to find what Rasselas has said comic? And this also is complicated: 'They stared a while in silence one upon another, and, at last, drove him away by a general chorus of continued laughter.' They do experience a repressed recognition of the real seriousness of what Rasselas has said, a response for which we were in fact prepared before the beginning of his lecture ('the eye of wisdom abashed them'). These men merit satire more than Rasselas, but they are men. They take 'a while' to engender between them the confidence to laugh.

This is not a novel: we have no further interest in the young men, and Rasselas soon 'recovered his tranquility'. But his moment of pain is important: 'The consciousness that his sentiments were just, and his intentions kind, was scarcely sufficient to support him against the horrour of derision.' That is strong language. What is in question is not whether mockery is effective, but what effect it has. Throughout the book, Imlac maintains a careful balance between helping the prince and his sister to recognise that their quest is futile and preventing the despair which would result from premature or unqualified recognition. Mere derision of serious intention would be merely paralysing. By complicating the response in even such an apparently lightweight chapter, Johnson creates a convention of feeling which leads beyond the paralysis of merited satire.

To place the emphasis as I have is to run the risk of under-estimating the comedy which has, to some extent rightly, received much attention from critics in the last twenty years. The sententiousness of Rasselas in chapter 17 is comic in a man of his age, and an important stage of Johnson's rhetoric (as well as much of the enjoyment of the book) is lost if the reader does not register it. Not many readers are likely to split their sides over it, but there is a wide range of humour in *Rasselas*, extending even to farce in the chapter on the aviator. Laughter is, after all, one of the means of enjoyment where much is to be endured. It is also one of the means of seeing clearly the futility of easy answers to impossible questions. It is, in itself, more searching than the rationalism of the philosophers of chapters 18 and 22. As Niebuhr has written, 'Insofar as the sense of humour is a recognition of incongruity, it is more profound than any philosophy which seeks to devour incongruity in reason.'[8] Yet its limitations are equally important. He continues, 'But the sense of humour remains healthy only when it deals with immediate issues and faces the obvious and surface irrationalities. It must move toward faith or sink into despair when the ultimate issues are raised.' In Johnson, of course, it moved towards faith; for some of his recent critics the only escape from despair, in the face of what he shows, is to exaggerate the comedy.

The penalty, in terms of reading *Rasselas*, is inevitably simplification. The characters in *Rasselas* do not make jokes: the comedy is at their expense. In so far as we laugh, it is at them rather than with them. Usually it points to the incongruity between dream and reality, the distancing sort of comedy which puts things into perspective that the human mind habitually gets out of perspective. Its function is crucial, as I shall attempt to show in more detail in the following chapters; but it is only one phase of a characteristically two-phase rhetoric. Rasselas will not set the world to rights by delivering lectures; but even though his 'sentiments *were* just, and his intentions kind' (my italics), they could only just support him against the 'horrour of derision'. He is very immature; but growing up is painful. It is a minor case ('he recovered his tranquility'), but so characteristic that I need not list the major ones. At one moment we are looking down at a character; at another through his eyes. It is the same in *The Vanity of Human Wishes*:

> Let observation with extensive view . . . (1. 1)
> Where-e'er he turns he meets a stranger's eye. (1. 111)

George Eliot does something very similar in her different medium, for her own purposes. In Johnson it seems to me a radically Christian art: comedy sees an incongruity which a character does not; charity and humility cut short the implied sense of superiority. But whatever the source of it, the effect is to complicate response. One can always see folly more clearly in other people, and by increasing distance, comedy and satire make it clearer still. But life cannot always be held at a distance, and it is not always others who are foolish.

7   *Rasselas*: Ends

Of the four books I have chosen to analyse in this study, *Rasselas* is the one most directly and explicitly concerned with human ends and their adequacy. Its most obvious subject is Rasselas's search for a choice of life which will secure him happiness in this life. Given quite exceptional opportunity, first in a secluded utopia, and later with abnormal freedom of access to other possibilities of choice, no human end he can envisage brings him the happiness which is his end-in-view. Yet by a process never explicit, though always implicit, he is steered towards a transcendent end (which Nekayah calls the 'choice of eternity'), and although he does not find what he seeks where he expected, he is often incidentally in possession of it (the company of Imlac and the others brings much real pleasure).

The divergence of critical opinion I referred to at the beginning of chapter 6 results largely from partial responses to the formal complexities already discussed, but to a lesser extent also from a duality in the theme. Johnson is concerned partly with a willed, chiefly rational search for happiness and the impossibility of securing it on earth, and partly with an involuntary habit of the human mind, reaching always for what it does not have, often merely because it does not have it, a habit which Johnson himself expresses most vividly as a 'hunger of imagination'. Emphasis on the first naturally leads to a sombre reading of the book; the second is largely, though not wholly, comic. The first effects a metaphysical-religious statement about the limitations of the human condition; the second a psychological observation on the human mind. My argument here will be that both are equally important, and that they are continuous. They are both separated and held together by the syntax of the first sentence, by which they are introduced ('Ye who listen with credulity to the whispers of fancy, and persue with eagerness the phantoms of hope'). There is crucial difference, but also continuity, between eager pursuit and credulous fancy. Both concern man as an animal needing by

108

nature to propose purposes to himself; the one is a semi-rational
sophistication, itself misdirected, of the other, a basically irrational urge liable to degenerate into disease; but without either,
life is insupportable or subhuman.

There are recorded in the book several attempts to deny or to
escape the human need for purpose. The young men of Cairo live
wholly in aimless self-gratification, but Rasselas finds their way of
life inadequate so quickly that his recognition is reported in the
second sentence of the chapter. When we are told, a few sentences
further on, that 'He thought it unsuitable to a reasonable being to
act without a plan, and to be sad or chearful only by chance', an
irony can be perceived in retrospect, for his own plan gets him
nowhere, and his happiness derives more from chance than from
anything he plans; but, as I have showed above, the truth in what
he says is half-recognised even by the wilfully blind young men
themselves. The women in the Arab's seraglio have a similarly
purposeless existence forced upon them and are represented,
through transparent metaphor, as subhuman: 'They ran from
room to room as a bird hops from wire to wire in his cage. They
danced for the sake of motion, as lambs frisk in a meadow.' Their
restricted life radically incapacitates them for specifically human
experience: 'That which he gave, and they received, as love, was
only a careless distribution of superfluous time, such love as man
can bestow upon that which he despises, such as has neither hope
nor fear, neither joy nor sorrow.' They have nothing to hope for,
nothing to fear; consequently they are neither fully human nor
happy.

The Hermit makes a wholly voluntary and (as he thinks)
wholly informed decision to withdraw from the world of purposive
activity, 'having found the world full of snares, discord, and
misery'. But the language in which he expresses it already begins
to place it in ironic perspective: 'I had once escaped from the
persuit of the enemy by the shelter of this cavern, and therefore
chose it for my final residence.' The word first used of the Hermit's
withdrawal in chapter 19 was 'retreat'; 'escaped' has a crucially
damaging effect on its connotations. 'Final residence', of course,
prepares us for the ironic end to the chapter, where the Hermit is
returning eagerly to Cairo. The language of the next sentence
clearly recalls the Happy Valley: 'I employed artificers to form it
into chambers, and stored it with all that I was likely to want.'
And as he goes on, he describes the inescapable boredom,

experienced back in chapter 2 by a young man who 'began to withdraw himself' from the activities afforded by the Valley and discovered the 'wants of him that wants nothing'. His escape becomes dangerously similar to that of the young men of Cairo – 'My fancy riots in scenes of folly' – though unlike them he is intelligent enough to act on the half-truth he has recognised, and returns to purposive life in the city.

It is the Happy Valley itself which represents the most important effort in the book to remove purposive activity from human life: 'revelry and merriment was the business of every hour from the dawn of morning to the close of even'. Through the gratification of every predictable desire and through extensive propaganda ('To heighten their opinion of their own felicity, they were daily entertained with songs, the subject of which was the *happy valley*'), it is intended to remove the wish for change which is a precondition of purposive activity. 'Every art was practised to make them pleased with their own condition.' Imlac tells Rasselas that he decided to enter the Valley for much the same reason as the Hermit gives for his retreat: 'Wearied at last with solicitation and repulses, I resolved to hide myself for ever from the world, and depend no longer on the opinion or caprice of others.' His declared wish is ironically similar to what is forced on the Arab's women – to 'bid farewell to hope and fear'. So although propaganda and force are required to keep the inhabitants inside the Valley once they have entered it, it does include something which makes it an attractive alternative to active life when viewed from outside. Even Rasselas, having only just escaped from it, speaks to the young men of Cairo in language which shows attraction towards what Imlac mistook it to be. 'Happiness, said he, must be something solid and permanent, without fear and without uncertainty.'

Yet it is built, as Rasselas had discovered, on a fundamental misunderstanding of human nature. The satisfaction of desires will not lead to human happiness. This is one of Johnson's most penetrating contributions to the criticism of utopian idealism, which had been initiated, as I have emphasised, by the father of Utopia: give a man a utopia and he will want something different. Rasselas makes the point, in a suitably elementary, but nonetheless unanswerable way, as early as chapter 2: 'I am, like [a beast], pained with want, but I am not, like him, satisfied with fulness.' Utopian preference for the static sense of well-being over the

perpetual disturbance of desire, rational though it is, will not
satisfy human nature. 'I long again to be hungry that I may again
quicken my attention.' The sages of the Valley already know this
and take care to stimulate new desires: '[The inhabitants']
appetites were excited by frequent enumerations of different
enjoyments'. Yet despite their efforts and the gratification of every
appetite they excite, Rasselas is not content and Imlac tells him in
chapter 12 that his discontent is shared by all: 'I know not one of
all your attendants who does not lament the hour when he entered
this retreat.'[1] The Valley is inferior to Utopia in an important
respect: the understanding of pleasure there is limited largely to
the pleasures of the senses, whereas most Utopians put more
emphasis on the pleasures of the mind. But even when Imlac
furnishes Rasselas with the pleasures of contact with a mind
'replete with images', they both still wish to escape from the
Valley. When Rasselas naively supposes that human evil can be
excluded by the removal of the possibility of competitive purpose
('We are in a place where impotence precludes malice, and where
all envy is repressed by community of enjoyments'), Imlac replies
in a way which unanswerably destroys all hope of an earthly
utopia inhabited by recognisably human beings: 'There may be
community, said Imlac, of material possessions, but there can
never be community of love or of esteem. It must happen that one
will please more than another; he that knows himself despised will
always be envious; and still more envious and malevolent, if he is
condemned to live in the presence of those who despise him.' In
fact the possession of the utopia in itself removes the real hope of
substantive change which is a precondition of both endeavour and
happiness: most of the inhabitants of the Valley live in the
'natural malignity of hopeless misery'. Even Imlac, whose
abnormal humanity enables him to resist the temptation to
malignity, is reduced to living off his memories of the past. To a
man of intelligence, life in the Valley is in the long term
insupportable because purposeless.

Rasselas's recognition, in the early chapters of the book, of the
inadequacy of the Valley to meet human need, is represented
primarily with the comedy which is sometimes appropriate to the
'hunger of imagination'. He is unable to prevent his perception of
really important truths about human happiness from becoming
entangled with the self-dramatisations of adolescent imagination.
As he lifts his head towards the moon, he cuts a very comic figure,

addressing animals in a tone approaching that of the first sentence of chapter 1, but contaminated with self-pity: 'Ye, said he, are happy, and need not envy me that walk thus among you, burthened with myself.' In fact, fantasy temporarily goes far in supplying what the Valley fails to give him: consciousness of the delicacy of his feelings and of the eloquence with which he has expressed them provides such 'complacence' that he cheerfully joins the usual diversions of an evening in the Valley.

In the following chapter, with its punning title, 'The wants of him that wants nothing', where the meanings of 'wants' (lacks, needs and desires) interchange to include the most important points made, Rasselas is at first seen in a rather better light. The humanity we find in him throughout ('unwilling to offend a man whom he had once reverenced and still loved') is contrasted with the tactless officiousness of the 'old instructor'; and the latter's pedestrian exposition of the false premise of the Valley ('Look round and tell me which of your wants is without supply: if you want nothing, how are you unhappy?') is intelligently exploded by Rasselas ('That I want nothing, said the prince, or that I know not what I want, is the cause of my complaint; if I had any known want, I should have a certain wish; that wish would excite endeavour'). The old man looks even more foolish at the end of the chapter when his arguments produce the very effect they were intended to prevent. But the remark through which Rasselas exposes his folly ('I shall long to see the miseries of the world, since the sight of them is necessary to happiness') has the ring of a callow debating-point. To win an argument against an old fool is not necessarily to discover the route to happiness, but in the next chapter his success has propelled Rasselas into the illusion that it is.

The hope which it has engendered brings a form of happiness, even though it has no clear object. Desire in itself creates a degree of pleasure which fulfilment of desire cannot. 'He was fired with the desire of doing something, though he knew not yet with distinctness, either end or means.' But objectless desire in fact merely replaces the external prison of the Valley with the internal one of introverted imagination. 'Considering himself as master of a secret stock of happiness, which he could enjoy only by concealing it, he . . . endeavoured to make others pleased with the state of which he himself was weary.' The language is intended to recall the hiding of the treasure in the pillars of the palace:

Rasselas is more burdened with himself than before. His own remark to Nekayah in chapter 28 completes the criticism ('each labouring for his own happiness, by promoting within his circle, however narrow, the happiness of others'). The duplicity and selfishness of his new endeavour contrasts ironically with the universal benevolence he likes to fancy himself distributing in his day-dreams. 'His chief amusement was to picture to himself that world which he had never seen; to place himself in various conditions; to be entangled in imaginary difficulties, and to be engaged in wild adventures: but his benevolence always terminated his projects in the relief of distress, the detection of fraud, the defeat of oppression, and the diffusion of happiness.' Fantasy can obviously take worse forms: these are the dreams of a well-meaning adolescent. But he is indeed 'entangled in imaginary difficulties'.

It is a fundamentally comic state of mind, which comes to an appropriate climax in the pursuit of the imaginary oppressor of an orphan virgin, interrupted by the brute fact of the mountain that forms part of his external prison. Rasselas himself is able to smile at his own folly, though at first he still believes that the only obstacle to 'the enjoyment of pleasure and the exercise of virtue' is the external mountain. What follows is a peculiarly Johnsonian mixture of comedy and solemnity. It would take a fool to laugh at Rasselas's calculation of the proportion of his life which he has squandered in adolescent fantasy, or at the accent of 'I have lost that which can never be restored.' Yet the tone of the declamation which follows, about the birds which have left the nest and so on, is at some mid-way stage between the seriousness of the first sentence and the comic pomposity of his earlier speech to the animals. Its sheer length has already begun to remind us of the pleasure he takes in his own eloquence, when the tone shifts wholly into comedy: 'he past four months in resolving to lose no more time in idle resolves'. Then as usual, Johnson breaks the expected conclusion ('This was obvious . . .') and concludes more emphatically ('He, for a few hours, regretted his regret'). The 'hunger of imagination', which persistently builds internal prisons, is to be seen here as primarily comic. On the other hand, we have seen a young man pass, through a process of self-reproach, however immature, from adolescent moping to a settled determination of purpose: at the end of chapter 5, he has abandoned fruitless searches for non-existent escape routes, but is 'determined to keep his design always in view'. Laughter dominates here; but in *Rasselas* it is never a wholly adequate response.

In the central chapters of the book, Johnson's concern is more with Rasselas's determined purpose, to which I shall turn shortly, but he keeps the subject of fancy continuously available. The philosopher of chapter 18 has almost invariably been taken to be a stoic. What he says about the conquest of passion and about indifference to pain, pleasure and misfortune is certainly what Johnson elsewhere finds most unsatisfactory in stoic thought. But the first stage of his lecture is on a topic Johnson did not associate with stoicism, the need to keep *fancy* under the dominion of reason. Just as his views on the conquest of passion are quietly placed in ironic perspective by the information that he delivered them 'with great energy'; so are his views on the conquest of fancy by reporting them in the tired metaphorical language of rebellion in the 'fortresses of the intellect'. He compares reason to the constant light of the sun, and fancy to the transitory light of a meteor; after the death of his daughter he is found in a half-darkened room speaking in entirely non-metaphorical language. Such a way of learning how to achieve true control of fancy is not comic at all, but one of the many things the chapter is doing is to show how easy is the illusion of control and how difficult and rare the reality.

In the chapters concerning Nekayah's grief for Pekuah, Johnson explores the operation of fancy upon grief with a degree of comedy which, without the convention of seriousness which I discussed in my chapter 6, could very easily become bad taste. Nekayah is clearly imprisoned in fantasy. The repeated word 'treasured' recalls Rasselas's first response to the idea of escape, with its reference to the literal treasure of the palace: she 'treasured up with care every trifle on which Pekuah had set an accidental value. . . . The sentiments of her, whom she now expected to see no more, were treasured in her memory as rules of life'. Her self-pity has the ring of Rasselas's invocation to the animals: 'The time is at hand, when none shall be disturbed any longer by the sighs of Nekayah: my search after happiness is now at an end.' She wants to make the prison literal by hiding herself in solitude, and Imlac replies with a word used of Rasselas's earlier condition – 'Do not entangle your mind . . .'. In chapter 36, the irony directed at her self-dramatised grief, the grief wilfully maintained by a fanciful exaggeration of what Pekuah really meant to her, builds up to a fiercely satirical climax in 'wholly released herself from the duty of periodical affliction'. But the qualification of the satire, registered throughout by the patience of Imlac and the assiduous kindness of Rasselas, is also brought to a climax in the following sentences, which make it plain that grief is not reducible to mere 'hunger of imagination': 'Her real love of Pekuah was yet not diminished . . .'.

The phrase 'hunger of imagination' comes from chapter 32, Imlac's speech about the Pyramid, and his argument is not only that the Pyramid may stand as the ultimate symbol of its folly, but that it is endemic in human nature: 'It seems to have been erected only in compliance with that hunger of imagination which preys incessantly upon life.' The hunger is in itself ultimately purposeless: 'A king, whose . . . treasures surmount all real and imaginary wants' is driven to fill time by watching 'thousands labouring without end, and one stone, for no purpose, laid upon another'. But any reader inclined to an attitude of comic or satiric superiority is directly challenged by the continuation of Imlac's argument, in chapter 44. 'There is no man whose imagination does not sometimes predominate over his reason. . . . No man will be found in whose mind airy notions do not sometimes tyrannise, and force him to hope or fear beyond the limits of sober probability.' It is the definitive answer, characteristically delayed, to the philosopher of chapter 18. It does not merely contradict him, in a way which events have proved correct, but includes him, for the phrase 'airy notions' picks up the language in chapter 18 ('from the unshaken throne of rational fortitude, [he] looks down on the scenes of life changing beneath him'), which was satirised by analogy with the ridiculous aspirations of the aviator. But it goes beyond an answer to an inadequate philosophy, to a profound summary of a psychological truth. A mind undisciplined by constant exposure to what lies outside itself is necessarily driven to the creation of fantasy: 'He who has nothing external that can divert him, must find pleasure in his own thoughts, and must conceive himself what he is not; for who is pleased with what he is?' Not *may* but 'must'. The 'hunger of imagination' is insatiable, 'preys incessantly upon life'. The whole context of Imlac's analysis represents it as a disease, and words such as 'malady', 'insanity' and 'madness' recur throughout; but to become radically afflicted by it, it is enough to do nothing.

The saddest example of it in the book is the Astronomer, a man mature enough to subject himself to a self-criticism beyond the capacity of young Rasselas and Nekayah ('I reasoned long against my own conviction, and laboured against truth with the utmost obstinacy. I sometimes suspected myself of madness . . .'), but who can only be freed from his lunatic delusion through his growing contact with and trust in the views of minds other than his own. Again, Johnson does not flinch from recording the absurdity of a man who can think he controls the weather. The Johnsonian orotundity merely increases the comedy potentially in the claim itself: 'the sun has listened to my dictates, and passed from tropick to tropick by my direction; the clouds, at my call, have poured their waters, and the Nile has overflowed at my command; I have restrained the rage of the dog-star, and mitigated the fervours of the crab'. 'Dictates', 'direction', 'call', 'command': the elegant variation compounds the ridiculous arrogance; and this lunatic talks particularly of mitigating the effect of the sun on two days traditionally associated with madness. All Johnson's mastery of parody goes into that sudden descent from latinity: what man in his senses could talk solemnly of mitigating the fervours of the crab? But Imlac's quiet tact, which proceeds from profound charity, acts as a continuous check on the temptation to laugh, and for those who do not observe it, Johnson includes an unusually direct reproof, by forestalling inadequate responses and juxtaposing them with appropriate ones in the characters' own reactions: 'The prince heard this narration with very serious regard, but the princess smiled, and Pekuah convulsed herself with laughter. "Ladies, said Imlac, to mock the heaviest of human afflictions is neither charitable nor wise." ' It would be misleading to call this *dark comedy*. From a certain perspective, such as that of the grotesque beings who mock human suffering in a famous passage of Johnson's Review of Soame Jenyns's *Free Enquiry*, it is light comedy; but that is shown unequivocally to be an inadequate perspective. The Astronomer is not in his senses, and to see his plight as actual (as opposed to potential) comedy, of any kind, is to put oneself in the company of those who find it amusing 'to see a man tumble with an epilepsy, and revive and tumble again, and all this he knows not why'.[2] Any such being would be inhumanly cruel; any such being who was also by nature liable to the same disease would be a fool. Or as Imlac puts it with characteristic restraint, he would be neither charitable nor wise.

Those who listen to the 'whispers of fancy' more often merit

laughter than those who pursue the 'phantoms of hope'. It is here
that the tone becomes more dominantly sombre.

The two primary 'phantoms of hope' pursued by Rasselas are
his dream of becoming a perfect ruler and his search for a 'choice
of life' which will bring him happiness. The first is so almost
entirely a dream that it is barely distinguishable from a whisper of
fancy. He is a prince, but we know from the start that he is a fourth
son, so it is not surprising that he makes no positive attempt to
pursue it. All the eagerness of his youth is channelled into the
second, which he makes a willed decision to pursue: 'Whatever be
the consequence of my experiment, I am resolved to judge with
my own eyes of the various conditions of men, and then to make
deliberately my *choice of life*.' During the period of escape and
acclimatisation, Imlac is 'unwilling to crush the hope of inexperience', but just before the experiments begin, at the end of chapter
16, he throws out a remark which so completely undermines the
possibility of making a definitive choice that, if adequately
pondered, it would have the same effect as 'fourth son': 'The
causes of good and evil, answered Imlac, are so various and
uncertain, so often entangled with each other, so diversified by
various relations, and so much subject to accidents which cannot
be foreseen, that he who would fix his condition upon incontest-
able reasons of preference, must live and die inquiring and
deliberating.' When Rasselas evades the point by saying that his
birth gives him a degree of freedom other men do not have, we are
given in effect a paradigm of this aspect of the book. Each time the
search appears to have ended in a final negative, another path is
found, providing no answer but a new hope of escape. I have
analysed the pattern in formal terms in the preceding chapter.
What it means to Rasselas is that, however often he finds evidence
that his search is hopeless, he continues to hope, or to pretend to
hope. The steady demonstration that no choice will guarantee
happiness is met constantly, even if less steadily, with the
semi-rational sophistication of fancy which Rasselas has reached
before he starts – 'surely happiness is somewhere to be found'.
The wisest of those who comment on the history of the Hermit
states both the obstinacy of hope and its continuity with
imagination: 'the hope of happiness, said he, is so strongly
impressed, that the longest experience is not able to efface it. Of
the present state, whatever it be, we feel, and are forced to confess,
the misery, yet, when the same state is again at a distance,

imagination paints it as desirable'. It is a careful statement: the unhappiness is both felt and, to the eye of honesty, known; yet despite the knowledge, the hope which lends to perpetual unrest will not be destroyed. This is virtually the condition of the man with epilepsy.

The famous distinction made by Gabriel Marcel, between problem and mystery, helps to clarify what is being said here.[3] A problem concerns something external to man, to which there is always the possibility of solution, when the relevant information and techniques have been found. A mystery concerns something in the nature of man himself, to which no solution can be possible, so long as he remains recognisably human. The most obvious conclusion of Rasselas's search is that it is a mistake to hope that happiness can be secured anywhere; yet those who have abandoned hope are reduced to the 'natural malignity of hopeless misery', to transforming what purports to be an earthly paradise into an actual hell, in which the only room for relief lies in tempting others into the same prison. It is no matter of naivety in Rasselas, for Imlac too says 'some desire is necessary to keep life in motion', and the statement about the Hermit's history is more precisely relevant to Imlac's than to Rasselas's. Between them the characters explore the possible evasions of the dilemma so comprehensively that to continue to believe that 'surely happiness is somewhere to be found' must be admitted to be a forlorn hope; yet it is a hope essential to humanity. If the knowledge that the hope is vain destroys hope, it reduces humanity to passive malignity. So the man who strives to channel the aimless hunger of imagination into a purposive search for happiness has compounded his difficulty: to the degree that he is successful, he will find that his search has no end, but if he therefore ceases his activity he returns himself to the purposelessness he sought to escape. It does not seem to me wholly mistaken to use the word *tragic* of this situation.

The last possible evasion is to perpetuate the search, to make searching an end in itself. If no way of life can secure happiness and man is 'condemned to hope',[4] perhaps a solution may lie in perpetual change. As Nekayah says, close to the end, 'Such . . . is the state of life, that none are happy but by the anticipation of change: the change itself is nothing; when we have made it, the next wish is to change again. The world is not yet exhausted; let me see something tomorrow which I never saw before.' Of course it will not serve. The Astronomer points out (after the characteristic delay) that they have searched so widely that it is now getting very hard to find new ground, and Rasselas is clearly becoming bored with the search ('since nothing else is offered, I am resolved to view [the catacombs], and shall place this with many other things which I have done, because I would do something'). In fact Johnson has forestalled this possibility of solution almost throughout, by the constant reminder that security is a condition of happiness. The word 'security' recurs in the book almost as frequently as 'happiness'. As Rasselas says during the very first of his 'experiments', 'Happiness . . . must be something solid and permanent, without fear and without uncertainty.' Nekayah thinks similarly in chapter 36: 'Why should we endeavour to attain that [i.e. happiness], of which the possession cannot be secured?' Happiness certainly is found, not often where it is sought, but actually almost continuously in the book. But man cannot be content with it until it is secured; and with what he has secured he becomes bored. No evasion will survive a pondering of the full structure of the book.

Those who seek to reduce the mystery to a problem are either brusquely or tactfully demonstrated to be misguided. The philosopher of chapter 22 is so comfortably padded inside his verbal world that he can be dismissed with a laugh. 'He looked round him with a placid air, and enjoyed the consciousness of his own beneficence.' As Rasselas soon finds, he can only maintain his placidity because there is no relation between what he says and what is. Any question can be answered if words are emptied of content. Rasselas responds with profound appropriateness: 'He therefore bowed and was silent.'

The philosopher of chapter 18 believes he has found the solution to life in the rational isolation of complete patience. If passion is conquered, man is no longer 'the fool of hope', and 'invulnerable patience' is the route to a permanent happiness which is available to all. These are not the views of a fool, but of many of the wisest men of antiquity, so it is fitting that their inadequacy should be shown not through comedy, but through the mystery of natural evil. Despite what he thought, he, like all men, felt hope – 'My daughter, my only daughter, from whose tenderness I *expected* all the comforts of my age, died last night of a fever. My views, my purposes, my *hopes* are at an end' (my italics) – and feared isolation – 'I am now a lonely being disunited from society.' So far from arming him with patience, truth and reason can only clarify the reality of his pain: 'What comfort, said the mourner, can truth and reason afford me? of what effect are they now, but to tell me, that my daughter will not be restored?' A philosophy which solves grief by maintaining that it is irrational is no help to a man whose daughter has just died.

The completion of the main demonstration, that happiness cannot be secured, comes in chapter 45, the conversation with the old man who might be presumed to have acquired through age the detachment desiderated by the philosopher. It begins inauspiciously with the younger people admiring the reflection of the moon, so although he has ostensibly achieved what the philosopher desired ('years have calmed his passions, but not clouded his reason'), we are not sanguine about Rasselas's wish to discover 'whether youth alone is to struggle with vexation, and whether hope remains for the latter part of life'. A direct hint about the nature of the disillusionment impending is placed in the next paragraph, when the information that he was 'chearful and talkative' is explained: 'He was pleased to find himself not disregarded'. But a major subsidiary theme of the book, which I shall discuss shortly, is that despite the ubiquity of unhappiness there is a really substantial pleasure to be gained from knowledge, and it is this which is shot down in his first reply: 'I rest against a tree, and consider, that in the same shade I once disputed upon the annual overflow of the Nile with a friend who is now silent in the grave.' The princess thought that 'everything must supply [him] with contemplation'. She is right: the moon is not merely a source of visual delight to him. 'I cast my eyes upwards, fix them on the changing moon, and think with pain on the vicissitudes of life.' The other major subsidiary theme is that although virtue will not guarantee happiness, it will in retrospect provide some peace of mind. Imlac himself proposes this to him. It means little when it cannot be shared: 'I have neither mother to be delighted with the reputation of her son, nor wife to partake the honours of her husband.' And there is in any case another side to the coin: 'My retrospect of life recalls to my view many opportunities of good neglected, much time squandered upon trifles, and more lost in idleness and vacancy.' Now that he has nonetheless achieved through endeavour all that man may hope to achieve, the mere passage of time has built him another prison: 'I cannot extend my interest beyond myself.' And even that enforced isolation has not brought him the expected compensation of tranquillity. He has still to 'endeavour to abstract my thoughts from hopes and cares, which, though reason knows them to be vain, still try to keep their old possession of the heart'. Even at his age the knowledge that hope is vain will not serve to eradicate it. The best course lies in re-channelling it: '[I] hope to possess in a better state that happiness which here I could not find, and that virtue which here I have not attained.' This is not a picture of old age which places any emphasis at all on its most obvious disadvantages: there is no mention of physical disability, of pain, or of mental incapacity. This is how it is at best.

The three young people, of course, cannot face the implications of what he has said. Rasselas is reduced to direct contradiction of what he hoped at the beginning, a very crude form of argument by antithesis which betrays the futility of trying once again to evade. If a man of his age can be calm, 'it was likely that the days of vigour and alacrity might be happy'. Nekayah tries an even more desperate way of discounting what he said. 'She had seen the possessors of estates look with envy on their heirs, and known many who enjoy pleasure no longer than they can confine it to themselves.' His point was actually opposite: he is saddened because time has left him with no one who can share pleasure with him. And Pekuah can only think him either delirious or over-subjective. 'For nothing, said she, is more common than to call our own condition, the condition of life.' But as Imlac had told Rasselas in chapter 16, as he began to emerge from the blind subjectivism of youth, 'Every man . . . may, by examining his own mind, guess what passes in the minds of others'; and when all the subjective views they have encountered coincide, it is scarcely logical to hope that objectivity will reveal what she would prefer. Imlac's own response is mixed: he can smile at the fertility of hope, but he has the charity not to destroy it by mockery: 'He forbore to force upon them unwelcome knowledge, which time itself would too soon impress.'

Time is in fact a crucial factor in the search, which it is folly to ignore. Reminders of the passage of time are scattered throughout the book, not only in direct statements – the aviator takes a year to make his wings, Rasselas spends two years in Cairo before beginning the 'experiments upon life', Nekayah mourns Pekuah for seven months, and so on – but also in apparently casual references to the close of day or, especially, to the flooding of the Nile. Even the end of the chapter I have just discussed, where the main point is that Nekayah and Pekuah have remained insensi-

tive enough to regard the Astronomer's affliction, even after
Imlac's reproof, as material for pleasantry ('the madness of the
astronomer hung upon their minds, and they desired Imlac to
enter upon his office, and delay next morning the rising of the
sun'), carries a very gentle reminder that time cannot actually be
halted, that they too are 'sometime to grow old'.

Johnson's treatment of time is characteristically complex. I
have already discussed the early phase of Rasselas's experience, in
which the discovery of the inexorable passage of time is handled
with a mixture of deep seriousness and comedy. The comedy
dominates, for Rasselas is then still in early manhood, but the
more solemn note is picked up in the words of the philosopher who
has irremediably lost what he failed to value fully while he had it
(the philosopher's 'what I have lost cannot be supplied' directly
recalls Rasselas's 'I have lost that which can never be restored').
But time is seen in chapter 35, where Imlac helps Nekayah in her
grief, to have a beneficient effect in certain situations. 'While we
glide along the stream of time, whatever we leave behind us is
always lessening.' To try to stop time is certainly foolish and can
become comic: by living in the past, hoarding her memories of
Pekuah, Nekayah is compounding her own suffering, and when
that lessens despite her efforts, merely making herself ridiculous.
To accept its natural effect in this instance will actually reduce the
pain.

The relation of the Pyramid to time is ambivalent. In a sense, it
represents a victory by human endeavour over the worst time can
do; yet according to Imlac's account, it was only built to escape
the tedium of unfilled time, 'to amuse the tediousness of declining
life'. It is a victory over time in that it has stood through all
recorded history: yet it is also a monument to the futility of filling
time to no purpose. But it is as an enemy to human endeavour that
time is most frequently seen in the book. It has primarily the effect
of adding another dimension to the tragic dilemma. Not only is
man caught between the need to hope and the knowledge that
hope is vain, but as he hesitates between the need and the
knowledge, he is continuously approaching the moment when
choice will no longer be possible. Nekayah begins to make the
point when, in reference to that visible 'stream of time', the Nile,
she says that there is a wholly inevitable limitation to man's
freedom of choice: 'No man can taste the fruits of autumn while he
is delighting his scent with the flowers of the spring: no man can,

at the same time, fill his cup from the source and from the mouth of the Nile.' And it is completed by Rasselas as they contemplate the bodies in the catacombs: 'they were, perhaps, snatched away while they were busy, like us, in the choice of life'. Even before it puts an end to the possibility of choice, time drains the natural energy of youth. Without the enthusiasm of Rasselas, Imlac would not have attempted escape from the Valley. Time acting on intelligence moves inevitably towards the knowledge which means paralysis; the commonest defence against it is stupidity.

Johnson frequently varies the tone even of the part of *Rasselas* which is concerned with the 'phantoms of hope'. Near the beginning of his search, Rasselas starts to think that it is pointless for precisely the wrong reason: 'For some time he thought choice needless, because all apppeared to him equally happy.' His naivety can be funny: 'Whenever I shall seek a wife, it shall be my first question, whether she be willing to be led by reason?' And in this instance Nekayah's reply is also comic: 'Wretched would be the pair above all names of wretchedness, who should be doomed to adjust by reason every morning all the minute detail of a domestick day.' But the prevailing mood is very black. The picture of man, trapped between hope and knowledge, and pursued by time, is very nearly pure tragedy.

What holds it just short of tragedy is no element of comedy: Johnson controls very carefully the range of what we may properly find comic. What actually holds it short of tragedy is the accumulating undercurrent of an argument of the book, which comes briefly to the surface in Nekayah's remark, 'I hope hereafter to think only on the choice of eternity.' We have seen that, despite apparently overwhelming grounds for abandoning it, the hope of an intelligent man is infinite. Ultimately, the only sensible object of infinite hope is infinity.

I am aware that those who regard such hope as necessarily vain will be devolved back upon laughter if they are to evade despair. An infinite hope which has no absolute end can only be either comic or Absurd. But Johnson believed it did have such an end. He devotes one of his last chapters to a pedantic argument about the nature of the soul in order to demonstrate that to his mind the most important answers lie beyond finite view, in the realm of faith. The long discussion about the 'immateriality' of the soul seeming to 'imply a natural power of perpetual duration', which is within the reach of philosophy, is quite irrelevant to the crucial point made at the end of it by Nekayah: 'the Being which made the soul, can destroy it'. Imlac has to snap out of his new 'enthusiastic fit' and admit that only faith can teach whether the creator of the soul will exercise his power to destroy it regardless of its 'natural power' or to extend its life through eternity. It has been suggested by a number of critics, that Nekayah's remark about the 'choice of eternity' is so casually made and so little emphasised, that it can be ignored as a cursory nod of respect towards religion in a book which analyses the human condition in non-religious terms. Explicit reference to Christian belief is not frequent, but it is in fact spread throughout the book. The words of the man discussing the Hermit (quoted on p. 89), the final remark of the old man (quoted on p. 121) and Imlac's statement in chapter 47 ('In the state of future perfection, to which we all aspire, there will be pleasure without danger, and security without restraint') all directly anticipate Nekayah's reference to eternity; and there are also many incidental recourses to Christian belief, such as Imlac's important advice to Nekayah in chapter 34, which includes reference to 'Him . . . who will suffer none to be finally punished for obedience.' In the course of a later reply to Nekayah, about the value of mortification, Imlac casually drops a deeply Christian remark which explodes the whole enterprise of the 'choice of life': 'Pleasure, in itself harmless, may become mischievous, by endearing to us a state which we know to be transient and probatory, and withdrawing our thoughts from that, of which every hour brings us nearer to the beginning, and of which no length of time will bring us to the end.' This is in effect Christian criticism of Utopian complacency. If Rasselas did find a way of life which secured happiness, the price, within a Christian context, might well be his soul.

The whole structure of the book, in which man persistently seeks as an ultimate end a 'choice of life' that will bring certain happiness on earth, and finds, after exhaustive search, that although the end is illusory the urge to seek remains, must be making either a religious or an anti-religious point. It cannot be neutral or indifferent: either this situation is Absurd or it constitutes an informal kind of religious proof. In *Adventurer* 120, Johnson makes more explicit what this aspect of the structure of *Rasselas* means to him. The incongruity between suffering and desert in this life affords 'some proof' of a just retribution in another. In particular, 'It is scarcely to be imagined, that Infinite

Benevolence would create a being capable of enjoying so much more than is here to be enjoyed' unless there will come 'a time, when every capacity of happiness shall be filled, and none shall be wretched but by his own fault'.[5] Man is doomed to chase 'phantoms of hope', but if he is both honest and persistent, he will find, wherever he starts, that hope has ultimately only one sensible location. The very thwarting of man's self-proposed ends leads him, if he will admit it, to a more adequate one.

The possibility of tragedy remains: men very often do not admit defeat. Johnson does not explore the possibility in *Rasselas*, though he does so at length in *The Vanity of Human Wishes*. The worst defeat is ostensible victory (satisfaction with an end which is inevitably temporary), and Johnson clearly chooses not to dwell on it when he makes the old man, who largely has what he sought, aware of its inadequacy. Instead he brings out a form of comedy which does not reduce in any way the fundamental seriousness, but which is not at all 'dark'. In fact, it is very like the Christian comedy implicit in *Utopia*. The young people have become adequately aware of truths long known, yet obscured by their own immediate purposes; but such awareness cannot be continuous in recognisably human beings. So there is a benign humour in the form of Nekayah's remark, 'I hope hereafter to think only on the choice of eternity.' It is not an answer to human nature; it can only be a hope. As such, within a Christian context, it has divine support, but it cannot ever be 'secure' while life lasts. Rasselas and the others face a fundamental truth as they contemplate the bodies of the dead, but they continue to be humanly attached to the life which remains: 'They then hastened out of the caverns, and, under the protection of their guard, returned to Cairo.' They hasten away, and they protect themselves against attack, and they return to the city of the living. Yet they have taken the point, so we only smile at the human weakness we share. So long as the point is taken, there is light comedy in human frailty. If it were not taken, there could, for Johnson, be no comedy at all.

Laughter brings relief to the picture of life recorded in *Rasselas* only within certain limits. But Rasselas and his companions are left with three other discoveries, apart from the importance of the 'choice of eternity', which act as palliatives. No pretence is made that virtue will lead to happiness; indeed the Arab states explicitly that 'the angels of affliction spread their toils alike for the virtuous and the wicked'. On the other hand it is shown or stated in a number of places that virtue can bring a certain peace of mind, which vice can destroy. Such limited tranquillity as the old man has depends on there being 'no heavy crime' burdening his mind. Rasselas foreshadows the point in his lecture to the young men. Nekayah is a little more positive in chapter 26: 'he that lives well cannot be despised'. Pekuah achieves a certain peace during her period of captivity through a willed resignation which is a positive virtue also in less obvious forms of affliction: 'I endeavoured to appear contented where sullenness and resentment would have been of no use, and that endeavour conduced much to the calmness of my mind.' The endeavour does not bring content, but it does conduce much to tranquillity of mind.

It is Imlac who puts the idea in its most important form, in chapter 34, when he is reducing the degree of real grief suffered by Nekayah. His remarks constitute Johnson's most direct rejection of utilitarian ethics, a rejection which links him with both More and George Eliot. 'When we act according to our duty, we commit the event to him by whose laws our actions are governed, and who will suffer none to be finally punished for obedience. When, in prospect of some good, whether natural or moral, we break the rules prescribed us, we withdraw from the direction of superior wisdom, and take all consequences upon ourselves. Man cannot so far know the connexion of causes and events, as that he may venture to do wrong in order to do right. . . . This at least . . . is the present reward of virtuous conduct, that no unlucky consequence can oblige us to repent it.' He makes a related point when trying to help the Astronomer: a sense of guilt immensely increases the affliction caused by the 'hunger of imagination'. Here his understanding of human psychology is as profound as the moral intelligence of his remarks to Nekayah. 'No disease of the imagination . . . is so difficult of cure, as that which is complicated with the dread of guilt: fancy and conscience then act interchangeably upon us, and so often shift their places, that the illusions of one are not distinguished from the dictates of the other.'

A second palliative is knowledge. However it is gained, whether through personal instruction, books or travel, knowledge brings a certain degree of natural pleasure. Imlac states the fact in chapter 11: 'Knowledge is certainly one of the means of pleasure, as is confessed by the natural desire which every mind feels of increasing its ideas. Ignorance is mere privation, by which nothing can be produced: it is a vacuity in which the soul sits motionless and torpid for want of attraction; and, without knowing why, we always rejoice when we learn, and grieve when we forget. I am therefore inclined to conclude, that, if nothing counteracts the natural consequence of learning, we grow more happy as our minds take a wider range.' But Imlac is having a small 'enthusiastic fit' here. The point about ignorance is true, but that 'if' in the last sentence quoted covers too much for the last clause to be more than a vague hope. When he goes on to say that Europeans are less unhappy than Abyssinians because they have more 'engines', roads and bridges, and their possessions 'are more secure', we have only to remember the aviator ('what would be the security of the good, if the bad could at pleasure invade them from the sky?') to see that he is dreaming: technology is abused as much as used. He has already told us that his knowledge of western Europe is second-hand.

In itself, knowledge is seen to provide a real but a limited pleasure. After his day-dreaming phase, the first substantial happiness Rasselas experiences derives from the enquiries necessitated by his intention to escape. 'He met a thousand amusements which beguiled his labour, and diversified his thoughts . . . rejoicing that his endeavours . . . had supplied him with a source of inexhaustible enquiry.' A little later he is so enthralled by the knowledge Imlac can furnish him with that he 'regretted the necessity of sleep'. But by the time Imlac proposes the excursion to the Pyramid, a lecture on the value of historical knowledge is necessary to stir Rasselas into wishing to go, and he can summon no enthusiasm at all for the catacombs. The old man has 'ceased to take much delight in physical truth', the Hermit's study of plants and minerals eventually became 'tasteless and irksome', and the solitary pursuit of knowledge has led to the Astronomer's madness. Imlac's pursuit of knowledge has been insatiable, but at best he has to put its result in negative terms: 'I am less unhappy than the rest, because I have a mind replete with images, which I can vary and combine at pleasure.' Pekuah gains much pleasure from the new knowledge acquired through travel after her capture, despite her fear and grief. But Imlac, who spent a large part of his life travelling, began to long for his native country and his old companions. The word used most frequently

about the pleasure of knowledge is 'divert' or one of its derivatives.
It is used with precision. The first definition of 'diversion' in
Johnson's Dictionary is 'The act of turning anything off from its
course', and the third is 'Sport; something that unbends the mind
by turning it off from care.' 'Amuse' is used in the same way; and
'diversify' can mean both broaden and scatter. The first sentence
I quoted in this paragraph includes three words which prepare us
for the conjunction at the beginning of the next: '*But* his original
curiosity was not yet abated' (my italics). Johnson was fully aware
of the value of knowledge and the importance of its pursuit; but in
relation to the 'choice of eternity', the accuracy of the word
'diversion' must be registered.

Within the context of *Rasselas*, the most important value of
knowledge would seem to be that the sharing of it leads to human
companionship. The women in the Arab's seraglio cannot offer
either him or Pekuah any relationship of value, 'for of what could
they be expected to talk? . . . They had no ideas but of the few
things that were within their view . . . As they had no knowledge,
their talk could take nothing from the tediousness of life'. In
contrast, the company of Pekuah is 'such a banquet' to him that
for a long time he postpones sending for the ransom, even though,
as he says, 'the purpose of my incursions is to encrease my riches'.
He enjoys teaching her astronomy; and she learns it, though she
'had no great inclination to this study', to please him. Earlier, her
enjoyment of the travelling depended on his ability to explain to
her what she was seeing. Later, it is her knowledge of astronomy
that provides her and Nekayah with legitimate means of access to
the company of the Astronomer; and the development of that
relationship, based for a considerable time on the exchange of
knowledge, not only brings great pleasure to all, but is the
primary cause of his recovery. It is the extent of his knowledge
which attracts Rasselas to Imlac: 'he thought himself happy in
having found a man who knew the world so well, and could so
skilfully paint the scenes of life'. But it is primarily as a friend that
he comes later to value him: 'He had a friend to whom he could
impart his thoughts, and whose experience could assist him in his
designs. His heart was no longer condemned to swell with silent
vexation.' The one advantage Imlac says is possessed by Europeans, which is not subject to the irony I have indicated, is that
communications are such that 'one friend can hardly be said to be
absent from another'. Rasselas replies that he envies nothing of

what Imlac has mentioned 'so much as the facility with which separated friends interchange their thoughts'.

So much emphasis is laid upon human companionship, that it constitutes in itself a third palliative. With their priorities re-ordered by the experience of losing and recovering Pekuah, the party loses interest in travel: 'They returned to Cairo, and were so well pleased at finding themselves together, that none of them went much abroad.' When Rasselas indicates in the next sentence that 'he intended to devote himself to science, and pass the rest of his days in literary solitude', Imlac warms him to observe first what happens to those 'who are grown old in the company of themselves', and goes on to describe the Astronomer. In the general discussion of imagination which is provoked by the history of the Astronomer, Imlac argues that the disease he suffers from is 'one of the dangers of solitude'. 'To indulge the power of fiction, and send imagination out upon the wing, is often the sport of those who delight too much in silent speculation.' As the Astronomer begins to recover, he tells Imlac that, since he has 'divided his hours by a succession of amusements', he has begun 'to trust less to an opinion which he never could prove to others'. Two effects of company are distinguished as the means of curing his disease. Imlac states the first: it is a means of remembering 'that you are only one atom of the mass of humanity, and have neither such virtue nor such vice, as that you should be singled out for supernatural favours or afflictions'. It curtails an individual's proclivity to self-pity and pride by putting his self-image in perspective. The Astronomer himself indicates the second: 'I never found a man before, to whom I could impart my troubles.' When he told Imlac about his illusion he prefaced his remarks with, 'Imlac, I have long considered thy friendship as the greatest blessing of my life.' The chapters which follow prove him right.

The experience of others confirms what is shown most fully in the Astronomer. Rasselas wasted two years in protracted adolescent fantasy because he had met no one he felt able to talk to about his aspirations. The Hermit finds solitude does not necessarily lead to devotion; indeed 'My fancy riots in scenes of folly. . . . In solitude, if I escape the example of bad men, I want likewise the counsel and conversation of the good.' But Johnson has, as always, included a corrective balance which should forestall an exaggerated deduction. Company does not in itself lead to what the Hermit has seen he needs: the society in which Rasselas spends

time in Cairo before his search begins is held together by
'reciprocal' envy and deceit. Company can be mere diversion
from the 'tyranny of reflection'.

The imbalance of Nekayah after the loss of Pekuah is partly
caused by solitude. At first she is in no way to blame. Her female
attendants utter only transparently egocentric clichés: 'her
women attempted to comfort her, by telling her that all had their
troubles. . . . They hoped that some good would befall her
wheresoever she was, and that their mistress would find another
friend who might supply her place'. Consequently 'she could not
talk to them but with caution and reserve'. Similarly, when Imlac
is repeatedly unable to give her the answer she wants about his
attempts to find Pekuah, 'he was less and less willing to come into
her presence'. But later the solitude becomes voluntary, with the
effects I have discussed above. Imlac's advice has eventually to
resemble that of her women, though his motive is different: 'you
will meet in your way some other favourite, or learn to diffuse
yourself in general conversation'. The experience of Pekuah
makes in positive terms the point which that of Nekayah makes in
negative. She notices quickly that her maids are very distressed
and look to her for succour. She recognises the danger of her own
position but thinks more of them: 'I, however, kissed my maids,
and endeavoured to pacify them . . . I eat [supper] rather to
encourage my maids than to comply with any appetite of my
own.' When their minds are more at ease, the effect on Pekuah
herself repays the effort of sympathy: 'I was pleased with their
pleasure, and animated with their confidence.' Intellectually and
morally she is less of a prisoner than Nekayah. She suffers more
when restricted to the company of the seraglio than when her
prison is only literal. Even when she 'grew at last hopeless and
dejected, and cared so little to entertain [the Arab], that he for a
while more frequently talked with my maids', she quickly pulls
herself together: 'as I recovered some degree of cheerfulness, he
returned to me, and I could not forbear to despise my former
uneasiness'.

Pursued as ends in themselves, both knowledge and company
can be merely 'diversions' from the pursuit of the 'choice of
eternity'. But Johnson was aware that the human mind, even
when rightly orientated, remains in some need of diversion, and
that to discover a right orientation, it needs expansion. 'Ignorance

is mere privation, by which nothing can be produced.' Imlac speaks of knowledge as 'certainly one of the means of pleasure'; it is also (not certainly but possibly) a means to virtue – ignorance can lead only to 'stupid malevolence'. A mind not diverted by company becomes morbidly introverted. 'He who has nothing external that can divert him, must find pleasure in his own thoughts', and that way lies insanity. The human mind by nature seeks diversion, and if it does not turn to knowledge and company, the alternatives are worse. But in fact knowledge and company are seen more positively than merely as means of avoiding stupor and madness. The pleasure of learning is very vivid to both Rasselas and Imlac, and as Nekayah says in the discussion of marriage, 'to live without feeling or exciting sympathy' is to lose a large part of what happiness life can afford. Knowledge and company can be legitimate proximate ends.

By the time Rasselas has re-phrased this in more positive terms – 'each labouring for his own happiness, by promoting within his circle, however narrow, the happiness of others' – we have reached a point where it can be regarded more emphatically as an end, though, within the context of Johnson's Christian thought, still an end secondary to the 'choice of eternity'. As Rasselas has little opportunity for such action, this is seen most clearly in Imlac. His sense of pity, and the tact which proceeds from it, are clearly goods in their own right, and not in any sense 'diversions'. He learns to despise money and so cannot follow the kind of life his father wanted him to and become a merchant, but 'his grossness of conception raised my pity'. Unlike the other inhabitants of the Valley, he looks 'with pity', not envy, on would-be new-comers. He shows compassionate tact in his unwillingness to crush Rasselas's hopes too rapidly. When Nekayah is grieving for Pekuah he, like Rasselas responding to the philosopher, does not 'insult misery with reproof', but he does talk her out of the part of grief it is possible to remove, her unjustified feelings of guilt. Later, he carefully controls the treatment of her, giving the stiffer advice himself, to lose herself in activity and company, but getting Rasselas to mitigate it by promising to continue the search for Pekuah. His assiduous tact is not only opposed to the unfeeling attempts of Nekayah and Pekuah to 'bring [the Astronomer] to an open declaration' of his illusion, but in the course of time so changes their attitude that all contribute together to the

Astronomer's cure. Such a man has earned the right to consider
that 'He that lives well in the world is better than he that lives well
in a monastery.'

The end which Rasselas proposed to himself proved illusory.
But because he pursued it with such determined vigour, he has
perceived not only an ultimate End, but also proximate ends
which incidentally provide him with a reasonable degree of what
he sought. There is no guarantee of happiness in any 'choice of
life', but there are some things which the fortunate can enjoy, and
others which they can do for the unfortunate.

8 *Rasselas*: Fiction and Acceptance

In this chapter I shall return, as in my last on *Utopia*, to wider questions of form than I was concerned with in the first, in particular to the relation between human aspiration and recalcitrant reality, in so far as that relation is represented within the fictional strategies of the book. Firstly, I want to discuss the structure of the whole. I have already emphasised the recurring pattern of broken expectation and also suggested that, despite the sequence of failures which seems to say only that happiness is nowhere, there is a development within the book which is registered in certain important changes in Rasselas – in short, he matures. When the book is looked at as a whole, these two observations will be seen to be closely associated.

In the first chapter, the palace in the Valley is represented as oppressive, something from which it will seem reasonable to seek to escape, and in those that immediately follow, this intention takes shape in Rasselas's mind and is eventually acted on. He and a carefully chosen companion make a secret attempt to escape from enforced confinement, to what Rasselas conceives to be freedom to choose his own way of life, and we are encouraged to expect they will succeed in escaping, whatever doubts we have formed about Rasselas's hopes. Yet despite their efforts at concealment, Nekayah discovers their attempt shortly before they leave, not as a result of the envy or policy which they feared, but through a combination of affection and chance. 'Do not imagine, said the princess, that I . . . followed you with any other design than to partake of your conversation . . . not suspicion but fondness has detected you.' The expected form, of a man escaping from an imposed utopia, which he does not want, to a personal utopia he will select for himself, has already been disrupted.

In the next sequence of chapters, culminating in the chapter (22) concerning the philosopher of nature, the plan envisaged by

133

Rasselas is largely followed. The reactions of Nekayah and
Pekuah are occasionally reported, but their importance is minor
compared with the discoveries made through a systematic search
by Rasselas, with some assistance and commentary by his chosen
mentor. When this carefully planned attempt reaches a dead end,
it is followed by the series of chapters in which 'the prince and his
sister divide between them the work of observation'. The
individual deliberate search for a utopia has failed, but it is
quickly replaced with a new form, a collaborative effort in which
the elusive utopia will be systematically hunted down from two
directions simultaneously. The relationship between brother and
sister is being used as a necessary extension of a still fully
deliberate search.

The Happy Valley clearly represents a quite unrealistic
situation. Some aspects of it are directly fantastic; others can only
be achieved by forms of restraint which no intelligent human
being could regard as compatible with true happiness. But the
two stages of the following phase of the book are in a different way
equally unrealistic. I have already quoted the dialogue with Imlac
which Rasselas concludes by saying that his rank gives him an
advantage in freedom of choice, which Imlac has told him cannot
exist for men in general. There are some minor means of
extending his advantages, which are afforded by the fictional
form: for example, 'the laws of eastern hospitality' allow the party
to enter the property of the man of prosperity who lives in the
country. But a laconic paragraph in chapter 16, when they first
establish themselves in Cairo, indicates the main means: 'the
ladies could not, for a long time, comprehend what the merchants
did with small pieces of gold and silver, or why things of so little
use should be received as equivalent to the necessaries of life'. The
last part of the sentence seems to put this in the tradition of the
Utopian attitude towards gold; but in fact they quickly find that
money is of very great use. The preceding paragraph has already
described Imlac's sale of some of their jewels, so as to furnish a
house with 'such magnificence' as will draw 'men of every nation'
to visit them. Money gains Rasselas access to the first philosopher
('He had now learned the power of money'). 'Small presents' are
necessary to elicit such information from the shepherds as they are
capable of expressing; 'presents and civilities' provide Rasselas
with means of closely examining the behaviour of men in 'high
stations'; and Nekayah finds among humbler households that

'there are few doors, through which liberality, joined with good humour, cannot find its way'. Johnson is not generous with factual information in this book: the emphasis on money is a quite deliberate, though quiet, means of indicating that Rasselas and his party exist, in this stage of the book, in a state of freedom as abnormal as their state of confinement in the first.

To some extent, this is a further dimension in the general argument concerning the impossibility of securing happiness. The main characters meet many who live in normal circumstances, but even granted the alternative possibilities of abnormal security and abnormal freedom, what they seek cannot be found. But it also has a place in the total structure of the book, in which the argument concerning the impossibility of securing happiness is only a part. One of the most important consequences of Rasselas and Nekayah working together is that they can each check the fantasies of the other. The relationship between Rasselas and Imlac is almost wholly of pupil to tutor: Rasselas only brings Imlac back to reality once, with little success, when he interrupts his 'enthusiastic fit' about the qualifications of a poet. With Nekayah, Rasselas has a more balanced, and to that extent more normal, relationship, each acting as an external discipline on the propensity of the solitary human mind to convert hope into assumption. Equally important is the fact I have already noted: Rasselas is engaged on a search for the 'choice of life', but he did not choose to be accompanied by the sister who turns out to be so helpful to him.

The final phase of the book opens with an event which is wholly a matter of chance.[1] Just after Imlac has delivered his oration on the Pyramid, which would seem finally to have completed the search with a conclusive negative, they discover that Pekuah has been abducted by the Arabs. This in itself is a surprise to the reader: Rasselas and his party have been inspecting the world essentially as spectators; now they are suddenly involved in it. It is also generally agreed to be the most notable instance of breaking the expectation, set up by the title, that *Rasselas* is an oriental romance: the whole incident, from the point of view of the rest of the party as well as of Pekuah, is treated in as realistic a manner as the conventions of the book will allow. Rasselas brandishing his sabre 'in the first heat of his resentment' forms the exception which emphasises the mundane realism of ineffectual policing and corrupt 'private agents' who extort money with false reports.

Imlac has, of course, already told us, before the search began, how it is: 'every man is placed in his present condition by causes which acted without his foresight, and with which he did not always willingly co-operate'. But now it has happened, unexpectedly. Abnormal confinement and abnormal freedom are replaced by normal subjection to quite arbitrary external event. This is not the fantastic Fortune of romance; it is the mundane chance of human existence.

The effect of Nekayah's chance discovery of the intention to escape was a companionship which proved helpful, though only in a fruitless search. The effect of this more disturbing chance is that the characters are drawn much further into a relationship which is in itself a good, and to some extent away from the pursuit of illusions. They are drawn together by the loss of Pekuah, even though Nekayah's wilful grieving is a serious obstruction, and when she is found they are 'so well pleased at finding themselves together, that none of them went much abroad'. The same process is continued when they meet the Astronomer and, through collaborative effort, effect the cure which increases the circle of companionship. As I emphasised at the end of the last chapter, it is specifically companionship that destroys the Astronomer's illusion. Seen in these broad structural terms, the book is about a rather different form of escape than what Rasselas envisaged, namely an escape from the restrictions created by the human mind's desire to impose its own order on reality, an escape from both the fantasy of an enforced utopia and the fantasy of an impossible freedom and power, into the real pleasure and real freedom of relationship; an escape which has to be willed, but cannot be merely willed; an escape which cannot be as complete as the mind would wish, for Nekayah suffers 'real grief' as well, and the Astronomer's illness remains potentially in all men; and an escape which must not become escapism, for the 'choice of eternity' approaches as time passes.

Looking back at the earlier parts of the book with the knowledge provided by hindsight about the importance of chance, one can see that it has, throughout, played a very much greater role than we were encouraged to notice while our primary attention was held by developments in Rasselas's plans, first to escape from the Valley and then to make his 'choice'. Chance has both limited and assisted choice. That laconic second sentence tells us that Rasselas was a 'fourth son', but the idea of escaping from the Valley only begins to take shape in his mind when he is drawn, despite his deliberate attempt to avoid it, into conversation with his rather foolish old instructor in chapter 3. The image which Rasselas has in his mind and which we are allowed, for the rhetorical purposes of the book, to share, until we reflect with hindsight, is of himself desiring freedom and restricted by external obstructions. But in fact at certain crucial stages external facts which impinge upon his consciousness lead, by chance, to a freedom which his chosen course of action is failing to attain and sometimes positively obstructing. When he is pursuing his imaginary orphan virgin, it is the real, external mountain which happens to free him from the self-imposed prison of fantasy. At first, of course, the comedy is extended as he makes an almost precisely mistaken deduction: 'This [mountain] is the fatal obstacle that hinders at once the enjoyment of pleasure, and the exercise of virtue.' But when he sits down to muse about it, he is led into the calculation of the time he has wasted which culminates in an important stage in his growth towards maturity. The latter part of this stage in his growth is precipitated by another chance event, the breaking of a porcelain cup by a maid. From the cliché which is her response, Rasselas extracts an important truth, and on this occasion Johnson explicitly directs the reader's attention to the general implication. Rasselas had 'not considered, how many useful hints are obtained by chance, and how often the mind, hurried by her own ardour to distant views, neglects the truths that lie open before her'. Chance will frequently expose truths invisible to a mind focused only on its own projections.

In chapter 7, the 'rainy season', which is potentially one of those natural evils which cannot be excluded from the Valley, 'continued longer and with more violence than had been ever known'. It demonstrates the limitations of human power ('all the level of the valley was covered with the inundation'), but it is also the accidental cause of Rasselas's first being drawn into the company of Imlac. It comes at a very crucial moment, when the energy of deliberate effort is about to fail: 'notwithstanding all his endeavours to support himself, discontent by degrees preyed upon him, and he began again to lose his thoughts in sadness'. Chance on this occasion leads to the external human contact which provides escape from what is essentially a diseased state of mind ('preyed upon him'). His own inclination at the time is to 'wander in the woods'; the rain which keeps him indoors causes him by chance to meet the man who both brings immediate pleasure ('the prince regretted the necessity of sleep') and later effectually helps him to escape from the Valley. Another major inundation occurs in the last chapter, but I shall discuss that later.

The means of escape itself derives from a mature combination of chance observation and applied intelligence. Rasselas has already combed the perimeters of the Valley for ten months in an unsuccessful attempt to find a way out. But the rain has driven the conies from their burrows, forcing them to take shelter among the bushes in holes dug behind them 'tending upwards in an oblique line'. In itself this chance is of no help, but reflection on it suggests to Imlac the best way of digging through the mountain. A little later, a piece of good fortune ('a fissure in the rock . . . enabled them to pass far with very little obstruction') prompts Imlac to make a corrective point. Intelligence can make good use of chance; but a false reverence towards chance can lead to a condition of fantasy as damaging as a pretence that life is not subject to it. 'If you are pleased with prognosticks of good, you will be terrified likewise with tokens of evil, and your whole life will be a prey to superstition. What facilitates our work is more than an omen, it is a cause of success. This is one of those pleasing surprises which often happen to active resolution.' The word 'prey' has been used again, to emphasise that diseased fantasy, which can be cured by an intelligent acceptance of chance, can be caused by an unintelligent veneration of it. 'Active resolution' which is undisciplined by the recognition of external restraints, of which chance is one of the most obvious, ends in impotent fantasy; but 'active resolution' nevertheless remains a condition of success. A related point is made by Nekayah's wilful grieving. Imlac has already reduced her distress by convincing her she is in no way to blame for a chance side-effect of a good intention ('do not . . . consider that as blameable by which evil has accidentally been caused. Your tenderness for the timidity of Pekuah was generous and kind'); to allow what is known to be mere chance, however distressing, to dominate one's life, completely and permanently, is analogous to superstition. When Nekayah talks of permanent withdrawal from a world in which she lacks Pekuah, Imlac replies with a sharp metaphor: 'they who restrain themselves from receiving comfort, do as the savages would have done, had they put out their eyes when it was dark'. Maturity requires acceptance of a recalcitrant reality represented by chance, but submission to chance is superstitious folly.

The final reminder of the fact of chance, before the last chapter completes a larger sequence of thought, is appropriately found in the catacombs. 'Those that lie here stretched before us . . . were, perhaps, snatched away while they were busy, like us, in the choice of life.' It is always possible that chance may very rudely interrupt human choice. It is appropriate that the final reflection should place the emphasis on the most humiliating fact. 'I have here the world before me; I will review it at leisure', says Rasselas at the start of his search, putting at its most literal what is represented metaphorically in the plans of the aviator and the philosopher to survey the world from a position of super-human security. He has abnormal leisure; but even for him the world is neither passive nor static. But it is not merely the final fact that is humiliating. Between them, the characters try every means they can devise to track down a choice of life which will bring happiness. It eludes them; yet they are frequently happy. Fantasy brings Rasselas a 'secret stock of happiness', but the cost, in terms of regret for lost time, is high. The most unqualified happiness they experience almost all arises more from chance than from choice. Rasselas meets Imlac because of bad weather; Nekayah joins them not knowing what they are doing; they value each other's company more after chance has separated them; even in the relationship with the Astronomer, the actual motive of Pekuah and Nekayah is initially curiosity, and they fail to 'bring him to an open declaration' but gain instead a 'familiar friendship' which is mutual. The psychological effect of chance is the breaking of restrictive fantasy; the moral effect is a check on pride. Happiness cannot be secured; it may be granted.

Before moving on to the second part of this chapter, it is necessary to dwell briefly on the aesthetic implications of Johnson's use of chance, as in the light of modern experiments in fiction and the criticism which derives from them, it is in danger of appearing naive, though such appearance would be, I believe, false. Chance is introduced into the formal structure, at moments chosen by the author, to depict the relationship between human will and non-human, indifferent, reality. In other words, Johnson's use of chance is deliberate, and that might seem to involve a naive inconsistency. The argument which would underlie such a view is widely current: that is, that the only logical way to embody in fiction (which is necessarily man-made) the recalcitrance of brute reality to human will is in the opposition of formlessness to form. Form must be broken to express the formlessness of *reality*. This procedure is not logical: I have commented in my Introduction on its extension into true logicality. Its only effect is to limit what the writer can say. Form is his only means of expressing relationships of any kind; formlessness cannot express anything except formlessness. So to write with any complexity about the relationship between human will and formlessness, it is necessary to subsume the formlessness within the form. If formlessness is represented purely mimetically, that is, if the writer represents it merely by breaking out of his form, rather than by including it within his form, all he can say in effect is, 'There is human will and there is chance'. Johnson did not wish to say merely, 'There is human will and there is chance'; he wished to relate them in several interesting ways. To do so he used a complex form, which includes broken form and chance within a deliberated structural whole.

My argument so far in this chapter has, I hope, made clear an interesting similarity (which includes considerable difference) between Johnson's treatment of the relation between fantasy and reality and More's. In what follows, I shall be concerned with what might almost be termed utopian elements in *Rasselas*. In fictions of this kind, in which the realism of nineteenth-century novels is not sought, it is common for several characters to be largely projections of one single character. This is clearly the case in *Pilgrim's Progress*. In *Utopia*, the difference between More and Hythloday is in some ways absolute, but at the same time Hythloday represents the dream-world More would in some moods temporarily enjoy inhabiting. Morton more obviously represents what he would like to be – and in fact subsequently became. In *Rasselas*, it is important that the characters should remain for some purposes wholly distinct, since Johnson wishes to represent the value of companionship between them; but they too, for other purposes, should at times be seen as different projections of one.

The aviator is the first, relatively simple, instance of a projection of Rasselas. In the chapter preceding the one about the aviator, Rasselas is described as being 'impatient as an eagle in a grate'. In the episode which follows, the aviator to a large extent projects this image of him, while Rasselas himself acts out the voice of common sense which questions it. When Rasselas says, with his own recent experience in mind, 'your imagination prevails over your skill', the aviator replies (as Rasselas felt in the preceding chapter) that all that is needed is more determined effort: 'We are only to proportion our power of resistance to the different density of the matter through which we are to pass.' When Rasselas says the physical effort required is more than man possesses, the aviator moves rapidly from speculative science to total fantasy: 'man will float in the air without any tendency to fall. . . . To survey with equal security the marts of trade, and the fields of battle'. This is a metaphorical version of what Rasselas intends to do when making his choice of life. The aviator attempts a solo flight; Rasselas is at this stage seeking to escape alone. Rasselas considered himself 'as master of a secret stock of happiness, which he could enjoy only by concealing it'. When he asks the aviator why he does the same ('Why, said Rasselas, should you envy others so great an advantage?'), the pride, which is as inherent in the vision of a private utopia as selfishness, is diagnosed in the reply. 'If men were all virtuous, returned the artist, I should with great alacrity teach them all to fly. But what would be the security of the good, if the bad could at pleasure invade them from the sky?' Like Rasselas in his earlier fantasies, he is certain of his own virtues – so certain that he has forgotten he does not yet actually know how to fly. This is essentially 'hunger of imagination' ('the contagion of his confidence seized upon the prince') and as pure fantasy its comic destruction is no serious affliction. Rasselas had 'suffered himself to hope for a happier event, only because he had no other means of escape in view'.

A very much more important projection of Rasselas's hopes is provided by the history of Imlac. Its major function, as several critics have noted, is to anticipate the subsequent search, to demonstrate fully what Imlac explicitly says several times, that objectively speaking the search is pointless: Rasselas could have learnt almost all he discovers himself from what Imlac describes. A second function is closely related, but more specific. The aviator offers simply the hope of escape from the Valley, which is what Rasselas first wants. But in the chapter before he meets the aviator, having become more doubtful of the possibilities of physical escape, he becomes more interested in the pursuit of knowledge. He still wants to escape, since the knowledge he desires most concerns men in the world outside, but he gains much pleasure from extending his knowledge of natural history inside the Valley. Imlac is attractive because he 'knew the world' and could describe the 'various conditions of humanity', and Imlac's own life-history represents in fact an exaggeration of this phase of the development in Rasselas, a search for knowledge of the ways of men as a primary end. In other words, it is an escape from an imposed utopia into a chosen personal utopia, a city in the solitary mind.

That Imlac's history represents a kind of dream-like projection of Rasselas's desires is hinted by the time at which it is told: the compulsory diversions of the Valley continue until midnight, and Imlac begins after they have ceased. The earlier stages of his narration bear a very close relationship to Rasselas's own history, despite the obvious circumstantial differences. During his first twenty years, before his father would allow him to travel, he 'lived in a continual course of gratifications', and towards the end of them he 'lost much of the reverence with which [he] had been used to look on [his] instructors'. At the end of this Happy Valley stage of his life, when he began his travels, his 'heart bounded like that of a prisoner escaped' and he 'felt an unextinguishable curiosity kindle in [his] mind'. During his long sea voyage, when he is in a state of physical confinement and mental excitement, he goes through something like Rasselas's day-dreaming phase, 'forming schemes for my conduct in different situations, in not one of which I have been ever placed'. His general experience of the outside world, is, like Rasselas's, ambivalent. There is partly an anti-climactic sense of uniformity. His initial hopeful response to the sight of the sea ('thinking my soul enlarged by the boundless prospect, imagined that I could gaze round for ever without satiety') is rapidly crushed ('in a short time, I grew weary of looking on barren uniformity, where I could only see again what I had already seen'). But he does find a moral variety in human nature: he finds some of the learned men at Agra 'morose and reserved, and others easy and communicative; some were unwilling to teach another what they had with difficulty learned themselves; and some shewed that the end of their studies was to gain the dignity of instructing'. At one point, the development of Rasselas is almost synchronised with Imlac's autobiography. In the same chapter as Imlac answers Rasselas's question about motiveless depravity in man ('Is there such depravity in man, as that he should injure another without benefit to himself?'), he narrates his own experience of it, when he met the Arab tribe which has carried on 'through all ages, an hereditary war with all mankind, though they neither covet nor envy their possessions'.

In so far as they differ, Imlac's travels are an inferior variant of Rasselas's search, and this is registered briefly by a Gulliverian trait in Imlac. Gulliver always prides himself on his speed in learning the languages of the lands he visits, whereas it takes Rasselas two years to learn the language in Cairo. Imlac tells him that in Agra 'I applied myself to the language of the country, and in a few months was able to converse with the learned men.' A little later, the resemblance to Gulliver is extended: 'The emperour asked me many questions concerning my country and my travels; and though I cannot now recollect any thing that he uttered above the power of a common man, he dismissed me astonished at his wisdom, and enamoured of his goodness.' But really Imlac, as well as Rasselas, is morally superior to Gulliver: only two paragraphs later he describes his refusal to help his merchant companions obtain introductions to the ladies at Court 'not because they had injured me, but because I would not enable them to injure others'. In general, there is a difference between Johnson and Swift parallel to that between More and Erasmus: Johnson and More can emphasise the difficulty of some of the problems they raise by using characters who are much more intelligent, and specifically more intelligent morally.

Imlac's escape is essentially from the pursuit of wealth, which his father tried to impose on him (he 'originally intended that I should have no other education, than such as might qualify me for commerce'), to a free pursuit of knowledge. A major argument of the book clearly justifies him, but there is an element of indulgence which suggests that the two pursuits are not so wholly different as they seem to Imlac. He was, he says, 'determined to gratify my predominant desire, and by drinking at the fountains of knowledge, to quench the thirst of curiosity'. And despite his 'thirst' he has less than Rasselas's sense of purpose: 'I had no motives of choice to regulate my voyage.' His travels are at first quite aimless: he merely enjoys learning the varieties of human nature at his father's expense. When he does finally make a choice, it is of a profession which will rationalise his indulgence. 'I found that Poetry was considered as the highest learning.' He fairly quickly finds that the most obvious method of acquiring the knowledge needed will not do: 'I soon found that no man was ever great by imitation.' But equally rapidly, he finds an alternative which at once focuses and justifies (in his own eyes) his basic desire: 'Being now resolved to be a poet, I saw every thing with a new purpose . . . no kind of knowledge was to be overlooked.'

Discussion of Imlac's conception of the qualifications of a poet has tended to centre on a sterile debate about how far it was shared by Johnson. Of course Johnson allows him to use ideas he agreed with, and of course he makes him exaggerate some of them to the point of absurdity; but the important point is how they relate to the development of Imlac's pursuit. Johnson first makes it with one of those characteristic modulations from literal language into metaphorical, for which he has still not been accorded adequate fame. 'Sometimes I wandered along the mazes of the rivulet, and sometimes watched the changes of the summer clouds.' Rasselas tries very gently to clarify the visionary scheme: 'In so wide a survey . . . you must surely have left much unobserved.' But Imlac can easily defend the possibility of his dream with neoclassical clichés about examining the species rather than the individual. The 'streaks of the tulip' phrase has become so notorious that the last part of the sentence, in which it is used, seldom registers. '[The poet] does not number the streaks of the tulip, or describe the different shades in the verdure of the forest.' The point is that, in his anxiety to answer the threat to his vision which Rasselas has naively voiced, Imlac is directly contradicting what he has just said. Then 'I . . . pictured upon my mind every tree of the forest'; now he is unconcerned even with the difference in their colours. That point settled to his satisfaction, he can sweep on through progressively dizzier heights of human and transcendental knowledge until he is, with total and dismaying seriousness, speaking of the poet, that is, himself, as a 'being superiour to time and place' – in short as a metaphorical aviator.

The thud with which Rasselas brings him to earth at the beginning of the next chapter (11) has now been noted often enough to be well known. But its purely comic effect is very importantly qualified by the second deflation, which has attracted almost no comment. Chapter 12, in which it occurs, begins significantly with Rasselas's dream about a kingdom of perfect justice and security. The young man who can see the absurdity of Imlac's 'enthusiastic fit' cannot do so because of superior wisdom: the capacity for fantasy, which he can see in Imlac, lies also within himself. Imlac's travels have been (like Hythloday's) essentially solitary: the merchants who accompanied him were only interested in exploiting his ignorance of commerce. Now that much of his life has passed, the stimulus even of his specific purpose is not enough to motivate continuation of the accumulation of knowledge. He feels the need to share it with his 'old companions'. Utopia is no place for an ageing man. 'Often did I figure to myself those, with whom I had sported away the gay hours of dawning life, sitting round me in its evening, wondering at my tales, and listening to my counsels.' It is a sort of vision, couched in a sort of language, that makes the reader anticipate a comic deflation, and such expectations are encouraged by the ten-month delay contemplating the relics of Egypt, which seems to cast doubt on the force of the nostalgia drawing him home. But the clipped tone of the sentences which expresses the brutal facts conveys a very real repressed pain. 'Of my companions the greater part was in the grave, of the rest some could with difficulty remember me, and some considered me as one corrupted by foreign manners.' It is to this that his pursuit of knowledge has brought him. The man who has projected the dream of escape into the freedom of knowledge, so far as to conceive of himself as a being 'superiour to time and place', is not superior to time.

The pattern I have emphasised before is again enacted. Imlac does not repine over the breaking of his vision of returning as the great national poet: he is better able to 'contemn the applause of his own time' than a reader who expected his failure might suppose. He tries to find a patron, to open a school, to marry. When each attempt fails, the closure seems more complete. The man who felt superior to time and place now wants 'perpetual confinement'. And of course when he has it, he no longer wants it. No iron gate can shut out the 'hope and fear' to which he wished to bid farewell.

Before he left the Valley, which Imlac willingly took refuge in, Rasselas wanted three things in addition to want itself: escape, knowledge and to act benevolently on a large scale. The first two of these desires are expanded in the experience of the aviator and of Imlac. The third is isolated and enlarged for fuller analysis in the Astronomer. It remains with Rasselas himself in the form of a dream of a perfect state in which justice will be ensured – the fully utopian dream, which is ostensibly altruistic, but which is persistently bedevilled with pride. The Astronomer believes he distributes justice not just to a single nation but to the whole world, by maintaining a fair balance of weather. Potentially it is the most comic of the three projections of Rasselas's desires; in treatment it is actually the least comic. Of all the characters in the book, he is the nearest to the conventions of a novel and furthest from a mere persona in an apologue. His reluctance to speak even to Imlac about his belief in his powers proceeds not merely from a secretiveness, making a moral point, but from a human embarrassment which is one of the many ways in which sympathy is drawn towards him.

He is introduced in terms which might lead us to expect, despite the convention of broken expectation, that he might be happier than most. He has both learning and charity. It has been argued that he is too concerned with the stars, that he should be seen in the context of Raphael's advice to Adam in *Paradise Lost*: the practice of virtue is more proper to man than the study of astronomy.[2] But in fact his 'most favourite studies are willingly interrupted for any opportunity of doing good by his counsel or his riches'. Imlac, as well as Rasselas, expected him to be happy, though as he narrates his story Imlac is already using the past tense of his own expectation. The story itself, like Imlac's, is told at night: Imlac and the Astronomer are hoping to observe one of the moons of Jupiter. The image of cloud is used again, as chance creates the opportunity for the leap into trust ('A sudden tempest clouded the sky, and disappointed our observation') – an ironic chance for a man who controls the weather, and one which leaves them 'in the dark'.

From the start of his exposition, the analogy with Rasselas's utopian state is emphasised: 'I have administered this great office with exact justice, and made to the different nations of the earth an impartial dividend of rain and sunshine.' The dream is not contaminated with any vulgar delight in power or any self-interested abuse of it. In fact it has made him 'far less happy than before'. As he explains later, his integrity increases his misery: 'If I . . . am determined by my own ease in a doubtful question of this importance, how dreadful is my crime!' Yet there is a staggering, even if unconscious, pride implicit in it: 'I am, probably, the first of human beings to whom this trust has been imparted.' As he goes on to describe the process of its growth, it becomes clearer how far along it Rasselas had already gone. At first it was a wholly conscious hypothesis – 'whether, *if* I had the power of the seasons, I could confer greater plenty' (my italics). But the dream becomes, in the course of time, so habitual an indulgence in 'imaginary dominion', that it requires only a chance coincidence of his wish for rain and an actual inundation to precipitate a complete subjection to his own fantasy. That wish arose essentially out of benevolence: he saw fields withering in the heat. As he explains to Imlac the responsibilities he proposes to bequeath to him, this point receives more emphasis than any other. He has tried various means of general improvement, such as changing the axis of the earth, but any gain to one region is always offset by a loss to another, so the best means of administering the justice, which he profoundly intends, is to leave things as they are. He warns Imlac specifically against the pride of innovation and the injustice of self-interest or concern for his own country at the expense of others. It is very precisely a utopian vision: the word 'welfare' circumscribes the limits of his concern. 'Hear therefore . . . what . . . the welfare of a world requires.' The major difference is one of scale, which emphasises the pride. 'If the task of a king be considered difficult, who has the care only of a few millions . . . .'.

But the procedure of exposing the danger and folly by means of exaggeration is balanced by the discourse in which Imlac stresses that the tendency is by nature inherent in all men. 'No man will be found in whose mind airy notions do not sometimes tyrannise.' His point is confirmed by the structure of the chapter, which concludes with each of the other characters confessing to a utopian dream. Nekayah's is merely silly, an indulgence in a sugary land of impossible pastoral. Pekuah's includes pride: the dream of being queen almost makes her forget to bow to Nekayah. But in Rasselas's attempt to eradicate external evil ('all wrong should be restrained, all vice reformed, and all the subjects preserved in tranquility and innocence'), evil has fully sprouted in the dreamer's own mind: 'I start, when I think with how little anguish I once supposed the death of my father and my brothers.'

When the Astronomer has recovered sufficiently for the others to ask his opinion on the 'choice of life', what he specifies as the most important loss incurred by his own choice combines with a general argument of the book to foreshadow the means of escape from the airy notion which has tyrannised him: 'I have missed the endearing elegance of female friendship, and the happy commerce of domestick tenderness.' He has pursued knowledge and dreamt of dispensing benevolence at the expense, not of virtuous action, but of companionship. When he speaks of his cure, the imagery of imprisonment recurs: 'If I am accidentally left alone for a few hours, said he, my inveterate persuasion rushes upon my soul, and my thoughts are chained down by some irresistible violence, but they are soon disentangled by the prince's conversation, and instantaneously released at the entrance of Pekuah.' The mind is certainly free to create utopias; but utopias seem to have a way of destroying freedom. The Astronomer is deeply grateful at being released from his, into the genuine freedom of human relationship.

The close of the book is, in large part, an extension of the implications of the Astronomer's experience. Imagery of imprisonment is used frequently throughout with pejorative connotations, but as I have pointed out above, one of those who suffers most literal loss of freedom is able to make to some extent a positive reaction to it. Through sustained endeavour to keep her attention directed outwards, towards knowledge and towards the needs of her maids, Pekuah is in metaphorical terms less of a prisoner than Nekayah, self-committed to the restraint of her dramatised grief. The chapter concerning monastic life, which comes near the end, is a means of extending the point. As a literal pssibility, it seems, according to Imlac's account, of limited value. He sees it as a refuge for those who cannot 'stem the temptations of publick life', rather than as a positive ideal. His last remark – 'there is scarcely one that does not purpose to close his life in pious abstraction with a few associates serious as himself' – would seem, from the harshness with which Pekuah's misunderstanding reduces it to spiritual snobbery ('I have heard the princess declare, that she should not willingly die in a croud'), to be a personal dream of no very great emotional importance to him. It leaves the emphasis on: 'In monasteries the weak and timorous may be happily sheltered, the weary may repose, and the penitent may meditate.' But regarded as an image of a pattern of life more rewarding than any of the utopias in the book, its function is more positive. At the beginning of the chapter Rasselas sees the life of the monks of St Anthony as a reproach to himself, and in his reply Imlac contrasts it not only with the 'prison of pleasure' in the Happy Valley, but also with the kind of freedom which Rasselas was in his earlier reactions driven to prefer, the 'distraction of unguided choice', as he puts it. The monks' labour has meaning, since it provides them with the 'necessaries' of life; their devotion has meaning, since it 'prepares them for another state, and

reminds them of its approach, while it fits them for it'; consequently, restraint provides them with protection rather than
confinement and has positive value: 'they are not left open to the
distraction of unguided choice, nor lost in the shades of listless
inactivity'. The reproach to Rasselas becomes even more direct,
towards the end of the chapter, as Imlac turns to the more general
subject of mortification. If Rasselas achieved the choice of life he
thought all-important, it might be the means of losing sight of the
end which the monks have so directly in view.

Again, it might seem as if an answer to the search has been
found. To paraphrase the philosopher of chapter 22, 'consider the
life of monks, whose motions are regulated by the best possible
balance of instinct, reason and religion; they obey their guides and
are happy. Adapt their ways to life in the world outside and you
will be happier still'. Imlac does in fact become enthusiastic
enough to say, 'their toils are cheerful'. Johnson, however, very
quietly indicates that it is an ideal and not an answer, by putting
both Rasselas and Nekayah through complete reversals of opinion
in the course of the chapter. At the beginning, Nekayah thinks
happiness lies in 'the anticipation of change' and wants to
continue viewing the world, and Rasselas feels self-reproach when
he thinks of the monks. At the end, Nekayah is evidently thinking
of withdrawal to a convent, and Rasselas asks the Astronomer if
he can 'delay her retreat, by shewing her something which she had
not seen before'. To Johnson, as to More, the truth was very
simple, very easy to see, but very difficult to hold completely and
continuously in mind.

This, of course, is one of the main points of the final chapter, the
famous 'conclusion in which nothing is concluded'. A major line
of thought has already been brought to a conclusion in Nekayah's
remark, at the end of the preceding chapter, about the 'choice of
eternity'. From the displeasing utopia of the Happy Valley, we
have passed, through Rasselas's search for a freely chosen
personal utopia and the demonstration that his search is vain, to a
recognition of the only possible location of an aspiration towards
infinite good. But neither she nor we yet inhabit it.

The opening of the chapter quietly draws together some of the
remaining threads. 'It was now the time of the inundation of the
Nile: a few days after their visit to the catacombs, the river began
to rise. They were confined to their house.' Time is still passing:
this is the sixth time that the Nile has risen in the course of the

book. An external fact over which they have no control has again drawn them together. They are 'confined', as the human mind has seemed to be throughout, either by something external or by itself; and the reference back to the catacombs introduces the dimension of time to the condition of confinement: their present confinement is only relative, but another is impending.

What they do in their confinement seems, in relation to the ideals which have been discovered, very depressing. They behave in no way like the monks, and they do not think about the 'choice of eternity'; they continue instead in a dreary round of utopian fantasy. The ironies are quite fierce. 'Pekuah was never so much charmed with any place as the convent of St Anthony . . . and wished only to fill it with pious maidens, and to be made prioress of the order: she was weary of expectation and disgust, and would gladly be fixed in some unvariable state.' 'Charmed' with a convent: the triviality of response already destroys the possibility of taking her dream to contain any serious religious aspiration. She still has the pride she recognised in her dream of being queen, but now she seems to recognise it no longer: the 'unvariable state' must include scope for the promotion of Pekuah to prioress. Nekayah's dream includes a Gulliverian stupidity.[3] In order to educate young people into 'models of prudence and patterns of piety', her modest intentions are first 'to learn all sciences' and then to found a 'college of learned women, in which she would preside'. Prudence and piety will somehow emanate from pride. Rasselas still wants his utopian kingdom of perfect justice. He has taken the point, at last, that to achieve the justice, the kingdom would need to be small enough for him to administer wholly by himself, since (as Imlac told him back in the Valley) 'if power be in the hands of men, it will sometimes be abused' and only Rasselas is immune from corruption; but he has a little difficulty in reconciling this with the ambition for larger territory, 'and was always adding to the number of his subjects'.

In fact when the three dreams are seen in sequence, the prospect seems even more depressing than when they are seen individually. Between them they re-enact the phases of utopian enterprise which the book as a whole has moved through and, one hoped, beyond. Pekuah feels a weariness which leads to a desire for security and freedom from 'expectation and disgust', just as Imlac was drawn to the Happy Valley because he was 'wearied at last' and wanted to 'bid farewell to hope and fear'. Nekayah is at one stage of Rasselas's reaction against the Valley, thinking that 'of all sublunary things, knowledge was the best'. And Rasselas is at another, the stage one would have hoped demolished by exaggeration in the Astronomer's delusion, in which the dream is to practise the virtue Nekayah aims to teach, in the particular form of administering perfect justice. That stage, we have seen before, is followed by weariness. They seem trapped in a dreary cycle of perpetual fantasy.

To some readers, Imlac and the Astronomer have seemed excluded from this condition, at a stage of maturity where resignation has replaced dream. 'Imlac and the astronomer were contented to be driven along the stream of life without directing their course to any particular port.' To me they seem wholly included, reserved till the last since they appear to have reached a conclusion, which, like most conclusions in the book, is false. The 'stream of life' flows only in one direction, and to men of their age its final port cannot be distant. To be 'contented to be driven' along it entirely by chance is not maturity but apathy, an apathy which has throughout been associated both with age and with failure. Only through willed endeavour and deliberate activity, however misguided, has anything been discovered at all. Imlac himself has already analysed the crucial difference between acceptance of chance and submission to it. Nekayah, in the context of the river image, has already diagnosed another implicit fallacy: 'There are goods so opposed that we cannot seize both, but, by too much prudence, may pass between them at too great a distance to reach either.' In fact, their particular 'scheme of happiness' is only an extension of the aimless travelling of Imlac's history before he entered the Valley. He has not abandoned his dream any more than Rasselas has his. But when one is travelling in time it is not wise merely to enjoy the journey without envisaging its end. Taken together, the dreams of the young people and of the old have an effect analogous to that of the chapters in which Rasselas and Nekayah work from opposite directions. The young are full of futile hopes; the old are reduced to aimless passivity. No 'scheme of happiness' will provide an answer: as always the argument by antithesis fails.

It is a very black picture to place at the end of even a sombre book. But then it is followed by a sentence which yet again breaks expectation. 'Of these wishes that they had formed they well knew that none could be obtained.' By itself this could still be extreme pessimism: to know the truth and continue to live in fantasy is not significantly better than merely living in fantasy. But all the utopian dreaming in this chapter has been introduced by the sentence following those I quoted on p. 149: 'The whole region being under water gave them no invitation to any excursions, and, being well supplied with materials for talk, they diverted themselves with comparisons of the different forms of life which they had observed, and with various schemes of happiness which each of them had formed.' In its constituent parts, this is an extension of what we have seen before. Chance has thrown them into each other's company, instead of into further excursions which would only repeat what they now know. The knowledge they have gained through their deliberate activity enables them to make use of the chance to 'divert' themselves. And 'talk', human company, enables them to keep the diversion within the acceptable limits of sanity, in particular from allowing any of their private fantasies to exert the power of the Astronomer's delusion, which company destroyed. Taken as a whole that sentence fully validates the one I quoted at the beginning of this paragraph. A utopia shared is a utopia controlled.

To control, of course, is not to eradicate. To summarise more fully Johnson's extensions of More's criticism of utopian dreaming: give a man a utopia and he will want something different; but however often it is repeated that no utopia on earth can succeed, man will go on seeking one. He cannot help it, because the 'hunger of imagination' is both part of his nature and inextricably related to what drives him towards ultimate Purpose, even though it is permanently vulnerable to disease. The best that can be done is to contain the illusion within conversation, and to try to keep the more important hope as much in mind as possible, fitfully as that is bound to be.

Since this is a process, there can, in one way, be no conclusion. There will be no conclusion until life concludes. Hence the merely provisional last sentence. 'They deliberated a while what was to be done, and resolved, when the inundation should cease, to return to Abissinia.' It is a willed, purposive action ('deliberated', 'resolved'), subject to external restraint (the end of the inundation), but is no answer to the widest interpretation of a question about 'what was to be done'. Yet in this book of repeatedly broken expectation, Johnson has in fact broken the final expectation raised by his chapter title. There is a conclusion to the book, even though no man can keep it permanently focused in his mind. Every time we expect a conclusion there is none; when we expect none, there is one, even though the last sentence does not package it for us. Johnson has finally subsumed formlessness within form. The characters have glimpsed the real End, have enjoyed some secondary ends, and have found means of disciplining the fantasy ends which constitute the most powerful distractions from the real End. They return home, since they now know that No Place is no alternative. To that extent they have got nowhere. But they have learnt much about the needs for, and limitations of, human purpose, even though they remain human in their inability to hold it all continuously in mind. What they seek is not encapsulated in an answer analogous to the single choice Rasselas thought he could make, for in life the search is more like a journey which to the traveller will afford only fitful glimpses of the truth. But in literary art it can be rendered and, 'while the music lasts', held still within a complex form.

9 *The Mill on the Floss*: Purpose without Purpose

The Mill on the Floss is unlikely to seem as obvious a choice as the other three fictions I have selected for the present study. In this chapter I shall try to clarify, at the cost of some simplification, what I take to be the most radical purpose in the novel, that is the search for some ultimate meaning for human life in a world which in the author's view has no transcendent Purpose. In a famous letter to Dr Payne, written in 1876, she claims explicitly that this was a general intention in her fiction: 'my writing is simply a set of experiments in life – an endeavour to see what our thought and emotion may be capable of – what stores of motive, actual or hinted as possible, give promise of a better after which we may strive – what gains from past revelations and discipline we must strive to keep hold of as something more sure than shifting theory. I become more and more timid – with less daring to adopt any formula which does not get itself clothed for me in some human figure and individual experience, and perhaps that is a sign that if I help others to see at all it must be through that medium of art'.[1] In chapter 10 I shall discuss those aspects of the book which are most clearly highlighted by thinking of it in unaccustomed relation to *Utopia* and *Rasselas*; and in the following two chapters I shall pursue some of the underlying questions of form and of philosophy raised by this kind of fiction and by my account of it.

It is well known that George Eliot was an agnostic. Not only did she have intellectual objections to the bases of Christian belief, but when mature she felt an antipathy towards the legalistic restrictiveness of the form of Christianity she had believed in during her youth. Yet it is clear from the letter to Payne I have just quoted that she sought in her fiction to establish a sense of purpose in human life based on moral endeavour, drawing on 'past revelations' but not tied by any 'theory'. Thus it is common to refer to her essay in the *Westminster Review* of January 1857:

. . . in proportion as morality is emotional, *i.e.*, has affinity with Art, it will exhibit itself in direct sympathetic feeling and action, and not as the recognition of a rule. Love does not say, 'I ought to love' – it loves. Pity does not say, 'It is right to be pitiful' – it pities. Justice does not say, 'I am bound to be just' – it feels justly. It is only where moral emotion is comparatively weak that the contemplation of a rule or theory habitually mingles with its action . . .[2]

and then to put forward as the moral basis of her art the narrator's remark in chapter 61 of *Middlemarch*:

There is no general doctrine which is not capable of eating out our morality if unchecked by the deep-seated habit of direct fellow-feeling with individual fellow-men.

Clearly her art does have moral effect by enlarging men's sympathies, forcing the reader to 'direct fellow-feeling'. But one must not assume from this that she thought of moral action as proceding only from impulsive sympathetic response to particular predicaments, or that she was moving towards an existentialist theory of the novel. She says 'unchecked', not uncancelled, and the 'direct fellow-feeling' is to be a 'deep-seated habit'. One has, too, to take into account that curious nostalgia for attending church, which she expressed in a letter to John Cross (19 October 1873): '. . . the very nature of such assemblies being the recognition of a binding belief or spiritual law which is to lift us into willing obedience and save us from the slavery of unregulated passion or impulse'. She wants a 'law' which can be set against 'impulse'; yet what, for an agnostic, can be the status of such a law? 'Binding belief or spiritual law' is not a phrase which suggests a willingness to ground it ultimately in the principle of utility. Nietzshe remarked of George Eliot in *Twilight of the Idols*: 'When one gives up Christian belief one thereby deprives oneself of the *right* to Christian morality. For the latter is absolutely *not* self-evident: one must make this point clear again and again, in spite of English shallowpates. Christianity is a system, a consistently thought out and *complete* view of things. If one breaks out of it a fundamental idea, the belief in God, one thereby breaks the whole thing to pieces. . . . Christian morality is a command . . . it stands or falls with the belief in God.'[3] To clarify George Eliot's position in relation to these difficulties, I want to introduce the word *virtue*, by which I mean *a cultivated disposition such that one can reasonably say that a man who possesses it, and acts accordingly, is more fully human than a man who does not.* Whether Nietzsche was right, or whether it is logically possible to have an ethic based on virtue (rather than 'command' or law) without bringing God in, I shall not attempt to discuss until a later chapter; in the present chapter I want to show that the concept of virtue is central to George Eliot's moral thought and her art as a novelist, and that it resolves the apparent contradiction of rejecting 'rules' and yet wanting something equivalent to a 'spiritual law' – in short that it crystallises her sense of purpose in human life.

In all her fiction, George Eliot normally sees character in terms of a developing process. Character is not static, but evolved through time by the gradual unfolding of genetic traits and by the gradual formation of habit resulting from the repetition of similar moral choices in changing situations. As she puts it in *Romola* (chapter 39), 'Our lives make a moral tradition for our individual selves.' This is, of course, related to a very wide-ranging characteristic of nineteenth-century thought, but it is also a basic constituent of ethics based on the concept of *virtue*. As Aristotle puts it, 'people's characters take their bias from the steady direction of their activities', and similarly Aquinas, in the discussion of habit which leads up to his definition of virtue, 'repeated acts cause a habit to grow'. In *The Mill on the Floss* it is put in the language of nineteenth-century determinism, in the reference to 'irreversible laws within and without [Maggie], which, governing the habits, becomes morality'.

That last quotation indicates quietly that George Eliot was aware that not only the repeated choices which become habit, but also wholly external events, influence the development of character. The point is noted explicitly in Book 6 chapter 6: ' "Character," says Novalis, in one of his questionable aphorisms – "character is destiny". But not the whole of our destiny.' I shall discuss the implications of this more fully in the next chapter but one.

It is made very clear from the beginning that by nature, before anything comprehensible begins to influence them, Tom and Maggie are very different. Maggie is highly intelligent and impulsive; Tom is much less intelligent and very self-controlled.

But at the beginning especially, it is important to notice what else
there is, so that we can trace the history of the individual choices
which constitute life, as they gradually form the nature of the
adults. The moral atmosphere of the Tulliver household is
strongly tainted by Mrs Tulliver's family, the Dodsons, who
express and consistently stand by a sense of duty and propriety,
which as an ethic is hopelessly tangled with pride, materialism
and pitilessness, but which does represent the way countless
people think, even, George Eliot suggests through her irony, in
our present 'advanced state of morality'. One aspect of it is
expressed by Mrs Glegg at the family council after Tulliver has
lost his law suit. She is speaking to Mrs Tulliver, her sister: 'it's
right you should feel what your state is, and what disgrace your
husband's brought on your own family, as you've got to look to for
everything – and be humble in your mind'. Similarly, at the end of
the book, when she offers to take Maggie in after Tom has rejected
her, she adds, 'an' she must be humble'. At the end there, one does
not easily associate this with the Maggie we have come to know.
Yet in the description of the wooden doll which is her fetish at the
beginning, there is a clear streak not only of Tulliver blood in the
phrase 'luxury of vengeance' but of Dodson blood in the reflection
that 'even aunt Glegg would be pitiable when she had been hurt
very much, and thoroughly humiliated, so as to beg her niece's
pardon'. Maggie has Tulliver blood and Dodson blood, even
though she grows out of it.

The difference, of course, is pointed in the word 'pitiable'.
When Mrs Glegg offers to take Maggie in, she thinks not in terms
of pity but of family pride; whereas in Maggie that basic pattern,
given in the description of the fetish, of impulsive revenge turning
on reflection towards pity, gradually shifts further towards the
pity. Tom clearly has more of the Dodsons in him than Maggie: in
the discussion over whether Aunt Moss should be made to repay
her brother, Mrs Glegg rightly feels 'that the Dodson blood was
certainly speaking in him'. When he buys Maggie the fishing-line,
he has to draw attention to his own righteousness: 'Wasn't I a
good brother, now, to buy you a line all to yourself? You know, I
needn't have bought it, if I hadn't liked.' When his father sends
him up to release Maggie from her retreat to the attic after the
disgrace of starving Tom's rabbits, he is reluctant to obey: 'he was
particularly clear and positive on one point – namely, that he

would punish everybody who deserved it: why, he wouldn't have minded being punished himself, if he deserved it; but, then, he never *did* deserve it'.

Unlike the mature Dickens, George Eliot does not often use highly prominent symbolism to indicate where significance lies, and instead establishes as a convention in her novels a web of relatively subdued metaphor, such as the imagery of seeing, which she uses in *The Mill* and, more famously, in *Middlemarch*. Consequently, when she does use heavy symbolism, many readers feel a certain unease or aesthetic dissatisfaction. In *The Mill on the Floss*, this is the case with the flooding of the river and with the embrace in which Maggie and Tom are eventually drowned. I have not found any of the current critical accounts of the flooding convincing, so I share the unease when, particularly towards the end, she keeps referring to it. But the embrace, usually referred to as a clinging, is more carefully used at the major crises in the relationship between Tom and Maggie. That just a little of the pejorative connotation of 'clinging' is intended, is clear at the beginning of the chapter concerning the fishing-line and the rabbits: when Tom returns from his school, 'Maggie hung on his neck in rather a strangling fashion.' Later it is clear that it represents an unsatisfied need for love, unsatisfied by Tom's indifference. Her behaviour after Tom says he will punish her for starving the rabbits follows the pattern with the fetish, though already the fetish has ceased to provide adequate release. She will take a proud vengeance (the phrasing of the first sentence takes us deep into the child's mind): 'Well, then, she would stay up there and starve herself – hide herself behind the tub, and stay there all night; and then they would all be frightened, and Tom would be sorry . . . but then the need of being loved, the strongest need in poor Maggie's nature, began to wrestle with her pride, and soon threw it.' When Tom comes up, coldly, to release her, at his father's command, 'she rushed to him and clung round his neck'; and in response to this begging for love and forgiveness, Tom can break out of his Dodson shell: 'there were tender fibres in the lad that had been used to answer to Maggie's fondling; so that he behaved with a weakness quite inconsistent with his resolution to punish her as much as she deserved'. He calls her 'Magsie', the form he uses only when he is pleased with her, and offers her a bit of the cake he is still clutching. The shared eating is clearly a quasi-sacramental act, but we do not lose sight of the two undignified children, the one subdued by her hunger for love, the other going to administer justice, plumcake in hand, both eating 'with a humiliating resemblance to two friendly ponies'. But although the 'weakness' and humiliation temporarily give Tom a real dignity, the next day his feelings have settled back to: 'Still he was very fond of his sister, and meant always to take care of her, make her his housekeeper, and punish her when she did wrong.' And this is the fundamental pattern into which he moulds *his* experience.

We see the same pattern, for example, in the episode with Bob Jakin. When Bob pours scorn on Tom's dog, Yap, as no good for rat-catching, Tom's first reaction is pity. He feels 'a little hurt' for the dog, even though he has not the courage to say so. But when the dog fails to go for a water-rat they see, Tom 'kicked him over, feeling humiliated as a sportsman to possess so poor-spirited an animal'. Some time later, at the school with Philip, it is made clear that this pride expressed in cruelty is only the worst side of a character capable of acting better. When he is frightened by Mr Poulter's sword, he runs to fetch Philip, knowing that Mr Poulter and the drilling-lessons painfully remind Philip of his deformity; but 'Tom would never have done so inconsiderate a thing except under the severe stress of his personal pride.' Yet this is the pattern he adopts, and when he follows it through to the rejection of Maggie near the end, it becomes hideous: 'I will sanction no such character as yours: the world shall know that *I* feel the difference between right and wrong.' Rejection of what is loved because of failure and the humiliation of being associated with the failure in the eyes of others: it is the same as kicking the dog. If we look back to the end of the chapter with Bob Jakin, after Tom has punished him for cheating with the halfpenny, we see why: 'If Tom had told his strongest feeling at that moment, he would have said, "I'd do just the same again." That was his usual mode of viewing his past actions; whereas Maggie was always wishing she had done something different.' When Maggie, to cut short an unfruitful contention, eats the larger part of the jam puff, she regrets it immediately; whereas when Tom says, with a cruelty which clearly foreshadows his adult behaviour, 'I like Lucy better than you: *I* wish Lucy was *my* sister', he will not accept Maggie's apology for knocking over his card-house, and only continues to assert his dominance and indifference by flicking hard peas at a dying blue-bottle. The same contrast is made years later when

Maggie asks Tom to free her from the promise not to see Philip. 'Maggie had hardly finished speaking in that chill, defiant manner, before she repented . . .'. Two paragraphs later Tom is saying, 'There is no need for my repeating anything I said a year ago.' The quite deliberate refusal to reconsider moral decisions makes development largely impossible to him.

Yet although we must register this degree to which he was responsible for what he became, we must also note that external as well as internal causes are seen to be decisive. When he is first at school the insecurity he feels, faced with an alien world of learning, is channelled into pity for his teacher's daughter: 'If Tom had had a worse disposition, he would certainly have hated the little cherub Laura, but he was too kind-hearted a lad for that – there was too much in him of the fibre that turns to true manliness, and to protecting pity for the weak.' The influence lasts long enough for his first reaction to Philip to include, against his own expectations, a degree of pity (for his girlish looks). But when Philip feels a need to assert his intellectual superiority by parading his knowledge of heroes, Tom's sense of justice takes hold again: 'Tom, in his turn, wished to make the balance dip in his favour. This hunchback must not suppose that his acquaintance with fighting stories put him on a par with an actual fighting hero, like Tom Tulliver.' The pattern is then repeated soon after in the episode with Mr Poulter's sword.

But the most decisive external event is the failure of Mr Tulliver. Our first impression is that it matures Maggie more than Tom. The tact she has learnt through her own experience of criticism, and shows, on meeting Philip, by behaving as if unconscious of his deformity, is evident in the way she tells Tom the news. Chapter 2 of Book 3 is one of the finest in the whole book. Our attitude towards Mrs Tulliver's lament over her linen and silver should be delicately balanced. Clearly there is a mean materialism in the degree of her concern, and an egoism which repels us in the emphasis on her own suffering: 'to think as your father should ha' married me to bring me to this!' Yet the title of the chapter, 'Household Gods', far from being ironic, reminds us of the several other places in the book where George Eliot expresses the sanctity with which familiar places and things are invested by minds capable of deep feeling. For example, in Book 2 chapter 1, she expresses the preference for a familiar elderberry bush over an exotic shrub: 'there is no better reason for preferring

this elderberry bush than that it stirs an early memory – that it is
. . . the long companion of my existence, that wove itself into my
joys when joys were vivid'. Just before that, in fact, she says that it
is only (paradoxically) the materialist-minded who will not have
such feelings. Maggie's distress, when she discovers that the 'dear
old' copy of *Pilgrim's Progress*, which Tom had coloured, was sold
at the auction, has nothing to do with possessiveness. So our own
attitude must be delicately poised as we watch the responses of
Tom and of Maggie to Mrs Tulliver's outbursts. Tom's is to
fellow-feeling in resentment. His 'natural inclination to blame'
makes him for the first time think of his father with reproach.
Maggie's counter-response is an outburst of anger in defence of
her father. We note that it 'was heightened by some egoistic
resentment at Tom's silent concurrence with her mother in
shutting her out from the common calamity'. Yet she has also
clearly matured through reflection on her experience. 'Maggie
hated blame: she had been blamed all her life, and nothing had
come of it but evil tempers. Her father had always defended and
excused her, and her loving remembrance of his tenderness was a
force within her that would enable her to do or bear anything for
his sake.' The word 'force' in that last sentence is important: it is
not a matter of returning tit for tat; it is that her father's love has
created in her a *force* which she feels as sacred. The chapter closes
with one of Tom's impulses of pity, which enables Maggie to unite
them by putting her arms round his neck.

But in the following chapter, the Family Council, it is clearly
Tom who in one way has matured faster. Whereas Maggie makes
a futile outburst of anger which reminds us of her father's folly at
the previous family gathering, Tom's simple conception of justice
enables him to hold a firm course, which not only impresses the
Dodsons with their narrow idea of family honour, but commands
our respect too, in the honouring of his father's wishes about the
money lent by Luke and the money owed by Aunt Moss. He has
even remembered the reason for the latter – Tulliver's anxiety to
behave to his own sister as he hopes Tom will behave to Maggie –
though when we later recall this, it is because Tom forgets it.
Qualifications have to be registered: his duty towards his father is
mixed with stronger blame for the obstinacy in going to law, and
his success in his new role encourages the attitude of superiority
towards Maggie which tends to self-righteousness. Yet the new
self-assurance enables him to rise above any petty memories and

recognise the real generosity of Bob Jakin's offer of his ten
sovereigns: 'Tom was touched keenly enough to forget his pride
and suspicion.' In fact, he is capable of resisting the pressure of his
own 'moral tradition' to the extent of cancelling the 'slight air of
patronage', which he shows towards Bob at the beginning of the
episode, by actually offering his hand, a gesture which would not
come easily to such a nature as Tom's. Although we later feel
them as limitations (in Book 6, end of chapter 12) his qualities are
precisely right for the new situation, and he becomes integrated in
his new role: 'Tom's strong will bound together his integrity, his
pride, his family regrets, and his personal ambition, and made
them one force, concentrating his efforts and surmounting
discouragements.'

This absorption both emphasises by contrast and actually
helps to increase Maggie's disorientation. When she tries to help
the family economy by taking in plain-sewing, Tom tells her not to
lower herself. There is kindness as well as self-reliance in his
action; yet it would have been more kind to let her too find a little
role for herself. The decisive influence on her at this stage is
Thomas à Kempis, who represents to her the idea that if
gratification of personal desire is not the supreme good, the
renunciation of it must be. What she does not see at first is that
renunciation on such terms is itself an egocentric impulse. For
example, when Tom tells her not to do the sewing, she sees not the
kindness in his blundering attempt, but the hardness of her own
lot, the crosses she takes on herself: 'That is the path we all like
when we set out on our abandonment of egoism – the path of
martyrdom and endurance, where the palm-trees grow, rather
than the steep highway of tolerance, just allowance, and self-
blame.' Yet despite the immaturity she has begun to see the
ground in which her own nature is rooted – ground which the
mature Tom can only glimpse when in her presence, and seldom
even then.

Up to this point in the discussion, it has not been necessary to
use the word *virtue*, though the way in which George Eliot has
represented repeated moral choice becoming habit, and thence a
kind of second nature, is central to any ethic based on *virtue*. But in
order to understand Maggie's relationships with Philip and with
Stephen, one does, I think, need to introduce the word, even
though George Eliot does not. She sees clearly inadequacies in two
kinds of moral thought: in an ethic of external rules, which applied

rigidly might be repressive and even lead to hypocrisy; and in an
ethic based on the calculation of consequences, which in practice
can too easily become a matter of rationalising one's selfish desire.
But there is some confusion about what she offers instead, because
she uses the words 'feeling', 'impulse' and 'emotion' in two quite
different ways. On the one hand they represent the selfish desires
of the ego, which, as is particularly clear in the case of Tito in
Romola, she sees as amoral, tending by natural process to become
immoral; and on the other hand these words are used of
aspirations which she wants to carry all the force of obligation and
even sanctity. One can see her casting about, for example, at the
end of chapter 2 of the last book, where Dr Kenn is deliberating
over what advice to give Maggie after the elopement with
Stephen. The 'man of maxims' is dismissed with some asperity at
the end with his 'ready-made patent method'; so also is the
consequentialist: 'The principle on which [Maggie] had acted was
a safer guide than any balancing of consequences.' Yet what
status had the 'principle' if it was neither a 'maxim' nor a
utilitarian calculation? Kenn and George Eliot confuse the issue
by simply emphasising that much must depend on the individual
case: 'moral judgements must remain false and hollow, unless
they are checked and enlightened by a perpetual reference to the
special circumstances that mark the individual lot'. This is one of
George Eliot's commonest and most important themes, but it
does not help sufficiently here: looking as closely as one can at the
individual lot, does one decide, ruling out selfish impulse, by
external rule or by calculation of consequences? Both have been
dismissed.

The basis of Maggie's actual decisions, in fact, lies elsewhere,
namely in what George Eliot calls her 'moral tradition', which one
might paraphrase as the virtues she has cultivated. To understand an ethic based on *virtue*, it is necessary to make a distinction
between two senses of the word *natural*, a distinction related to one
which I have made in discussing *Utopia*. On the one hand, being
natural can mean following impulse; on the other, it can mean
acquiring and standing by the virtues which make one more fully
human. The exercise of a virtue can legitimately take on at least
something of the status of a 'spiritual law'; it is something *to be
done*, since it is a fulfillment of human nature. It can also be clearly
distinguished from the *being natural* signified by the word *impulse*,
since it has to be cultivated, to be made into what George Eliot

calls a 'moral tradition', sustained, for example by the 'force' which Tulliver's tenderness towards her had created in Maggie.

I have used the expression, 'something *to be done*', in deliberate distinction from 'something which ought to be done'. Since George Eliot does not want external rules, her moral imperative needs to be not something which is done because one is commanded to do it, but something which it is reasonable to do because it is reasonable to aim at being as fully human as possible. This, of course, gives the word 'law' in George Eliot's phrase 'spiritual law', a special and potentially misleading sense; but this is precisely why I want to introduce the word *virtue*, even though she does not use it in the sense I have defined. It is more like a natural law, such as that by which an acorn strives to grow into an oak; but in the case of human beings, who have minds, individual intention is an essential part of the striving. The completion of human nature becomes the most inclusive end of human purpose.

One of the most demanding questions the book puts is, why do we feel Maggie is right to meet Philip and wrong to elope with Stephen? Ostensibly the same issues are involved: the secret betrayal of a prior obligation for the sake of what seems more natural. In the case of meeting Philip, I think we have to recognise that we look through two distinct perspectives. In *our* eyes it is fortunate because it develops Maggie's mind and (because Tom finds out before their father does) there are no collateral disasters. Through Maggie's eyes, on the other hand, it is *wrong* because it involves a betrayal of that 'tradition', that *virtue*, which is what is most human in her. She feels it as wrong throughout the relationship, with more maturity than she showed in the earlier response to Thomas à Kempis. At the first meeting, 'it seemed to her inclination, that to see Philip now and then, and keep up the bond of friendship with him, was something not only innocent, but good: perhaps she might really help him to find contentment as she had found it. The voice that said this made sweet music to Maggie; but athwart it there came an urgent monotonous warning from another voice which she had been learning to obey: the warning that such interviews implied secrecy – implied doing something she would dread to be discovered in – something that, if discovered, must cause anger and pain; and that the admission of anything so near doubleness would act as a spiritual blight.' And in the last meeting before Tom finds out, she says to Philip, 'I have never felt I was right in giving way about seeing you.' This view is not only Maggie's: in George Eliot's own voice it is described as a 'true prompting against a concealment that would introduce doubleness into her own mind, and might cause new misery to those who had the primary natural claim on her.' It is one thing for *us* to approve the meetings because of the consequences; it would be quite another if Maggie herself thought in those terms. She is right to see it as wrong, because it is a denial of the pity and fidelity towards her father, which have prior claims on her.

When Philip expresses exasperation that she will not look on her situation in terms of consequences to herself ('you are shutting yourself up in a narrow self-delusive fanaticism, which is only a way of escaping pain by starving into dullness all the highest powers of your nature'), it is made quite clear by George Eliot herself that it would be wrong for Maggie and is wrong (selfish) of Philip to think in such terms: 'she felt there was some truth in what Philip said, and yet there was a deeper consciousness that . . . it was no better than falsity. Her double impression corresponded to the double impulse of the speaker'. Towards the end of the chapter (Book 5, chapter 3), George Eliot more generally challenges the whole basis of Philip's consequentialist thinking: 'If we only look far enough off for the consequences of our actions, we can always find some point in the combination of results by which those actions can be justified: by adopting the point of view of a Providence who arranges results, or of a philosopher who traces them, we shall find it possible to obtain perfect complacency in choosing to do what is most agreeable to us in the present moment.' Another justification for their meeting might be that Maggie should not respect her father's narrow feelings of revenge against her own more Christian wish for reconciliation. Philip puts this argument too: 'it is not right to sacrifice everything to other people's unreasonable feelings'. But Maggie knows where it terminates: 'Often, when I have been angry and discontented, it has seemed to me that I was not bound to give up anything; and I have gone on thinking till it has seemed to me that I could think away all my duty. But no good has ever come of that – it was an evil state of mind.'

Until Tom finds out, Maggie is able, by what is referred to as 'doubleness', 'sophistry' and 'subterfuge', to indulge her pity for Philip without openly denying her prior obligation to her father, though she sees this as wrong. As soon as Tom does find out and the duplicity ceases to be possible, she acknowledges the prior obligation and gives up Philip, with a feeling which includes relief at freedom from the concealment. So although there was some duplicity in her seeing Philip, it never drove her to a total denial of her basic virtues of pity and fidelity, and the duplicity itself arose largely out of the virtue of pity – pity for Philip. The apparent contradiction here (that a virtue leads to a wrong) arises from the fact, noted by most writers on *virtue* ethics, that the misuse of one virtue affects the exercise of others. Maggie's dishonesty ('doubleness') maims her pity.

That pity as well as selfish inclination was involved, is clarified in the scene with Tom after he has discovered the secret meetings: 'it was wrong of me – but I was so lonely – and I was sorry for Philip'. Tom utterly fails to understand her: he has developed to some extent the virtue of justice, but it is a justice maimed by the absence of pity: 'Your duty was clear enough.' So the clutch between them now is not one of union, but Tom's 'terrible clutch' on a virtue Maggie also possesses but temporarily betrayed. Tom cannot here rise to Maggie as he did in the past, and instead, like his father, produces the Bible to bind her to an external obligation. In her outburst after Tom has insulted Philip, Maggie, although she does not use the terms I have been using, summarises the present state of the difference between them in a similar way. Initially, her pity was an innate gift: 'sometimes when I have done wrong, it has been because I have feelings that you would be the better for, if you had them'; whereas Tom has 'always enjoyed punishing'. But with Maggie's recent development in mind, we see the degree to which virtue is cultivated by reflection and is distinguishable from impulse: 'You have no pity: you have no sense of your own imperfection and your own sins.'

The difference between impulse and virtue is driven home by the dying Mr Tulliver. Tulliver has the impulse to pity: again he explains his generosity to his sister Aunt Moss in terms of a feeling that somehow it will influence Tom's treatment of Maggie after his own death. Yet he cannot reflect enough on that impulse to see that it is wholly inconsistent with his refusal to forgive Wakem. 'I don't forgive him. . . . What's forgiving to do? I can't love a raskill. . . .' and he dies bewildered. This crisis, like the bankruptcy, brings Tom and Maggie temporarily together – Book 5 ends: 'they clung and wept together' – but that failure of Mr Tulliver to cultivate charity presents Tom with precisely the conflict which must divide them. Tom has conflicting obligations thrust upon him: the obligation to pity (to look after Maggie) and the obligation to justice (which is his rather nobler interpretation of Tulliver's more personal desire for revenge). Unlike Maggie he chooses justice. We see clearly that it is the wrong choice, yet we are not allowed to reject him too easily: 'if you are inclined to be severe on his severity, remember that the responsibility of tolerance lies with those who have the wider vision'. Near the end, his justice is that of the Pharisee, but before he is pushed to that point, he does his best to interpret it liberally. In response to Maggie's appeal, when she tells him she is going to meet Philip at Lucy's house, he can even soften far enough to justify a reference to the cake-eating episode: 'Maggie's ready affection came back with as sudden a glow as when they were children, and bit their cake together as a sacrament of conciliation. She rose and laid her hand on Tom's shoulder.'

The treatment of Stephen Guest has always been felt to be a weakness in the book. One reason, of course, is that, the conventions of her age being what they were, George Eliot was unable to represent convincingly enough the power of purely sexual attraction. She is able to portray the early stages with some delicacy, as Maggie and Stephen begin to become aware of each other ('Each was oppressively conscious of the other's presence, even to the finger-ends'), but later one feels the need for a more Lawrentian vocabulary. That is only an excuse: it remains a weakness in the book. But I think another major reason for dissatisfaction with Stephen is often the reader's fault, not the author's. The relationship between Maggie and Stephen only takes on its full significance when it is seen as part of the pattern of the whole book, and in particular in conjunction with the relationship between Maggie and Philip. The dual obligation put on Tom by his dying father was the hardest problem *he* could be faced with; the relationship with Stephen confronts Maggie with *her* greatest problem. Writing of Sophocles' *Antigone*, George Eliot refers to the pull of two incompatible obligations as an important ingredient of tragedy.[4] In the relationship with Philip Maggie was shielded most of the time from the most profound conflict (pity for her father against pity for Philip) by the good fortune that Tulliver did not find out about it. In the relationship with Stephen she has to face the conflict not only more openly, but, after the elopement, seemingly committed to the side her nature rejects.

Stephen uses three arguments in his attempts to keep her with him, each of which Philip had used, though in a different form. Firstly, he uses an ostensibly altruistic consequentialist argument: 'there may be misery in it for *them* as well as for us'. Philip had argued in Book 5, chapter 1 that his friendship with Maggie might heal the breach between the fathers. Maggie later opposes Stephen with a statement of a fundamental weakness of consequentialism: 'We can't choose happiness either for ourselves or for another: we can't tell where that will lie.' Secondly, he uses the version of consequentialism which more obviously represents a rationalisation of selfish impulse. This centres round the word *natural* and the distinction I made earlier, between following one's nature in the sense of obeying one's impulses, and fulfilling one's nature in the sense of acquiring those virtues which make one more fully human. Stephen, like Lawrence, uses a consequentialist argument based on the first sense of *natural*: 'It is unnatural: we can only pretend to give ourselves to anyone else.' The alternatives to Stephen, as to Lawrence, are following nature or making oneself a hypocrite. Philip's form of the argument was more intelligent and less directly selfish: 'It makes me wretched to see you benumbing and cramping your nature in this way.' As I said earlier, there is a degree of selfishness in this rationalising to justify his own inclinations, which George Eliot immediately draws our attention to, though it requires only slight re-statement to constitute our own grounds for finding the relationship fortunate. Thus we can see Stephen's inferiority; but at the same time we can see that Maggie has to reject *both* forms of the argument: 'Love is natural; but surely pity and faithfulness and memory are natural too.'

The third appeal both Philip and Stephen make on Maggie is to her pity, and this is where the greatest conflict lies. At the first meeting in the Red Deeps, Maggie excused her father by saying he was not happy. Philip replied, 'No more am I . . . *I* am not happy.' Similarly, Stephen writes in the letter Maggie reads before the flood: 'whose pain can have been like mine? Whose injury is like mine?' The crude egoism of Stephen here makes one wonder why Maggie does not see through it, why she feels, in fact, 'as if her real temptation had only just begun'. It is often seen as a contrived part of an ending which is contrived as a whole. But if we see Maggie's pity as a virtue in the sense I have defined, as something so part of her nature in the non-Lawrentian sense, as to constitute that which *is to be* acted on (a 'spiritual law'), it will be clear that when *Stephen* appeals to her pity the very foundations of her moral life are shaken. As I have said, George Eliot does not use the word *virtue*, which causes some confusion, but it is obvious from a passage where Maggie is reflecting just before the elopement, that she conceived of Maggie's pity in this way. Maggie toys with the Lawrentian form of the consequentialist argument: 'when something like that fulness of existence – love, wealth, ease, refinement, all that her nature craved – was brought within her reach, why was she to forego it that another might have it – another, who perhaps needed it less?' But she has to reject it: 'Where, then, would be all the memories of early striving – all the deep pity for another's pain, which had been nurtured in her through years of affection and hardship – all the divine presentiment of something higher than mere personal enjoyment, which had made the sacredness of life? She might as well hope to enjoy walking by maiming her feet, as hope to enjoy an existence in which she set out by maiming the faith and sympathy that were the best organs of her soul.'

Pity is clearly seen here as part of her nature; to deny it would be like maiming her feet. She is forced by the situation to deny pity as impulse (towards Stephen), which would involve injustice, in order to stand by pity as *virtue* (her obligation to Philip, Lucy and Tom). It is *virtue* in this sense which George Eliot sees as 'binding', rather than the accepted senses of the words *duty*, *law* and *conscience*, which she somewhat confusingly uses. In so far as she drifts with Stephen (here the river image *is* finely used) Maggie betrays that which is most deeply human in her, but she has the stature to recognise her mistake, so Lucy and Philip are right to believe in her. The 'law' (if the word can be used at all) which is involved is not one which restricts, but one which fulfils human nature – even though the conditions of life make its exercise potentially tragic. *Virtue* provides man with an ultimate purpose, irrespective of the accidents of existence.

10 *The Mill on the Floss*: Fiction and Fantasy

During the first meeting with Philip at the Red Deeps, Maggie, under the influence of Thomas à Kempis, talks of the desirability of giving up wishing. Philip's reply points directly to an important connection between George Eliot's book and *Utopia* and *Rasselas*. ' "But I can't give up wishing," said Philip, impatiently. "It seems to me we can never give up longing and wishing while we are thoroughly alive. There are certain things we feel to be beautiful and good, and we *must* hunger after them. How can we ever be satisfied without them until our feelings are deadened?" ' The last sentence here is part of Philip's subjectively biased argument with Maggie, and the preceding one, moving from feelings to an imperative which carries the narrator's as well as Philip's italics, could not have been written by More or by Johnson. But the basic paradox, that wishing for what one does not have is simultaneously of questionable value and an inescapable condition of human life, is in different forms central to this as much as to the two earlier books. The difference I wish to emphasise most in the present chapter is that George Eliot is more optimistic about the possibility of development in the individual (though not, in her novels, in mankind generally) through the interaction of desire and disappointment.

The kind of tension between dreaming and waking, which George Eliot sustains throughout the book, is indicated by the introductory chapter, 'Outside Dorlcote Mill'. Partly because the narrator is standing here *outside* the mill, this opening description forms a little dream-world, impossibly complete in its beauty and richness for a late February afternoon. The noises of the mill in fact provide the characteristically utopian insulation from the outside world: 'They are like a great curtain of sound, shutting one out from the world beyond.' As in *Utopia*, a return has to be made from this temporary enjoyment of the dream-world: 'It is

170

time, too, for me to leave off resting my arms on the cold stone of this bridge.' The phrase 'it is time', however, also points to an interesting difference. It is a repeated phrase, the preceding sentence also beginning with the same words: this dream-world, like most nineteenth- and twentieth-century utopias, is located in a chronologically rather than geographically distant setting. A large part of the feeling here is nostalgia, a desire to return to the past, now become through the passage of time a dream-world, and a reluctance to come back to the present, inevitable as that is. In a parallel way, when Maggie is faced with the more complicated problems of later years, she often longs for the simplicity of her childhood relationship with her brother. But the opposition of dream-world to present reality is not so clear-cut as the word nostalgia would suggest. The 'cold stone' of the bridge is inside the dream, even though it marks the transition out of it to the present situation of the narrator ('pressing my elbows on the arms of my chair'); and although most of the first sentence beginning 'It is time' is nostalgic, the 'deepening grey of the sky' starts the progression which is continued through 'cold stone': 'It is time the little playfellow went in, I think; and there is a very bright fire to tempt her: the red light shines out under the deepening grey of the sky.' The preceding paragraph has quietly indicated that the dream-world is not only itself subject to time but not all beauty and richness. The waggoner's dinner is getting 'sadly dry in the oven', and his horses' necks are 'bowed under the heavy collar' as they strain towards their 'hardly-earned feed' and a drink from the 'muddy pond'. Analogously, Maggie's childhood relationship with Tom was not as simply happy as she later likes to think of it.

Thus far the relationship between dream and waking reality resembles that of *Utopia*: the dream seems preferable, but on closer inspection proves less completely so; the conditions of life are not so easily transformed as the fancy wills. The most important difference lies in the positive value of the imagination in George Eliot. In both *Utopia* and *Rasselas* the imagination is an inevitable part of human nature, which a responsible individual should discipline as intelligently as he can, so that it can be both enjoyed and used creatively. In *The Mill on the Floss* the opposition of fantasy and reality is retained with similar complications; but the imagination has taken on the additional important function of sympathy. When one looks more closely at the dream world, one not only finds it to be less completely preferable than the fancy likes to suppose it; specifically one finds objects of sympathy which put a restraint on the naturally subjective proclivity of dream. We are made to feel the hunger of the waggoner and the exhaustion of his horses. So the narrator does not have to repeat on a larger scale the return from dream to reality which is set as a clue in this opening chapter. The subjectivism tending towards egoism, which More disciplines by separating his own name from Hythloday's, Utopia from Antwerp, is controlled in George Eliot by the capacity of the imagination itself to enter into the minds and feelings of other people. The possibility of imagination degenerating into fantasy remains: in this first chapter there is some indulgence in fantasy, from which, as a rhetorical man-oeuvre, the narrator awakes to set about his business of telling the less rose-tinted history of the Tulliver family. But the same faculty as can become a selfish indulgence can also be the very means of overcoming subjectivity. It is through disciplined imagination that Maggie achieves the moral advance which George Eliot regarded as more important than any other, that is, the realisation that other people have what is called in *Middlemarch* 'an equivalent centre of self', a consciousness with needs as great as one's own.

The first chapter stands as a kind of definition of the author's attitude to fiction and an indication of the attitude she wants the reader to share. In so far as that differs from More's and Johnson's, it is summarised more directly in *Scenes of Clerical Life*[1]: 'I wish to stir your sympathy with commonplace troubles – to win your tears for real sorrow: sorrow such as may live next door to you.' I shall discuss the implications of this conception of the purpose of fiction in my next chapter (11). Here I wish to examine George Eliot's view of the human importance of imagination in its various forms, as shown through her treatment of individual characters.

The members of the older generation in the book, Mr and Mrs Tulliver, the Dodson sisters and their husbands, have little innate capacity for imagination, and what measure they do have more often takes the form of fantasy than of sympathy. Mrs Tulliver's inability to see from any perspective but her own is rendered in the comic image of a goldfish which 'retains to the last its youthful illusion that it can swim in a straight line beyond the encircling glass. Mrs Tulliver was an amiable fish of this kind, and, after running her head against the same resisting medium [her husband's mind] for fourteen years, would go at it again today with undulled alacrity'. The image of a fish is used again later, when by asking Wakem not to buy the mill, she achieves, through her inability to move beyond the confines of her own point of view, precisely the opposite of what she intends: 'fly-fishers fail in preparing their bait so as to make it alluring in the right quarter, for want of a due acquaintance with the subjectivity of fishes'. In so far as she is aware of the views of other people, they have the ironic effect of confirming her egocentricity. 'Her imagination was not easily acted on, but she could not help thinking that her case was a hard one, since it appeared that other people [her sisters] thought it hard.' In the preceding chapter (Book 1, chapter 8), the same point is made of Mr Tulliver: 'as we are all apt to believe what the world believes about us, it was his habit to think of failure and ruin with the same sort of remote pity with which a spare long-necked man hears that his plethoric short-necked neighbour is striken with apoplexy'. The criticism of Tulliver here is very sharp: his ignorance about himself is being confirmed by the means which could, to a man of moral imagination, expose it, and he is selfish as well as stupid. But the characteristically George Eliot generalisation warns the reader not to believe this observation leaves him in a necessarily superior position: 'as we are all apt to believe . . .'.

When the limited imaginations of the older generations do operate, they normally create fantasy. Mrs Tulliver and her relations are treated with a more consistently comic tone than Mr Tulliver. Their fantasies revolve round the preservation of possessions for use at a time when in fact it will no longer be possible to enjoy them. During Tulliver's exposition of his plans for Tom's schooling in chapter 2, his wife is carried away into a comically irrelevant fantasy about her best Holland sheets: 'An' if you was to die tomorrow, Mr Tulliver, they're mangled beautiful, an' all ready, an' smell o' lavender as it 'ud be a pleasure to lay 'em out . . .'. Fortunately Tulliver is following his own train of thought exclusively and, having acquired 'the marital habit of not listening very closely', does not notice this part of her speech or the production of the key to the linen-chest which the vivacity of her imagination in this direction has fired her to. In Mrs Glegg the fantasy is similarly focused on what will be thought of her possessions after her death: 'when Mrs Glegg died, it would be found that she had better lace laid by in the right-hand drawer of her wardrobe, in the Spotted Chamber, than ever Mrs Wooll of St Ogg's had bought in her life'.

The households of the Pullets and the Gleggs provide more extended images of the same habit of mind. In the Pullet house there are elaborate precautions against the present use of possessions in order to preserve them for a time which will clearly never come. The polished oak stairs are treacherous to climb as the 'very handsome carpets' are 'laid by in a spare bedroom'. 'Mrs Pullet's front-door mats were by no means intended to wipe shoes on: the very scraper had a deputy to do its dirty work.' The comedy reaches a climax in the production, from a locked wardrobe in the unused 'best room', of the magnificent bonnet which, as Mrs Pullet acknowledges, may never be worn, though if it were it would be the best in Garum church. But the association with death qualifies the comedy for a reader who has more imagination than the characters. Mrs Pullet leads the 'procession' to a 'darkened room' where they see 'what looked like the corpses of furniture in white shrouds', and unlocks the wardrobe 'with a melancholy deliberateness which was quite in keeping with the funereal solemnity of the scene'. The sisters know that this elaborate ceremony surrounds an object of transient fashion – Mrs Tulliver points out that the fashion in 'crowns' is never alike two summers in succession – and they are aware of death – Mrs Pullet fears that a death in the family may make the necessity of wearing mourning remove the hope of using the bonnet altogether. But neither has the moral imagination to draw any inference from these facts which could discipline their fantasy; and that inadequacy is not altogether comic.

The Glegg household is also a semi-metaphorical projection of fantasy. Mrs Glegg's illusion about 'her own exceptional strength of mind' is both fostered by and metaphorically rendered in her two parlours, which provide her with two 'points of view from which she could observe the weakness of her fellow-beings': from the front she can see the degenerate society of St Ogg's; from the back the foolish hobby of her husband. Neither point of view can offer any challenge to the subjectivity of the lady who sits complacently in the middle. Mr Glegg too has a 'double source of mental occupation, which gave every promise of being inexhaustible' – fantasies about the relation between slugs and contemporary national events, and about his wife's 'contrairiness'.

The garden in which he can economise on the wages of two gardeners becomes for him a tangible fantasy-world, where the 'inalienable habit of saving, as an end in itself', which he shares with the Dodson sisters, can be indefinitely enacted. Glegg fantasy further resembles Pullet fantasy in the way death can be assimilated into the dream, without in any way disrupting it by morally imaginative reflection on transience. 'To survive Mr Glegg, and talk eulogistically of him as a man who might have his weaknesses, but who had done the right thing by her . . . made a flattering and conciliatory view of the future.' Death does not suggest to Mrs Glegg any limitation to her subjective fantasies. From the sentence I last quoted, I have omitted the rambling, parenthetical centre which enacts at appropriate length the way her imagination is released into uncustomary vivacity by the prospect of increased subjective freedom after her husband's death.

Unlike most of his contemporaries in the book, Mr Tulliver does have a degree of moral imagination, though it operates only in one direction, towards Maggie. Just before he demands the repayment of the money he lent to his sister and her husband, he becomes aware of a connection which makes him hesitate. 'He had not a rapid imagination, but the thought of Maggie was very near to him, and he was not long in seeing his relation to his own sister side by side with Tom's relation to Maggie. Would the little wench ever be poorly off, and Tom rather hard upon her?' He is not a man accustomed to changing his mind, but on this occasion he does so, not only after resolving but even after acting. The sentence describing the change of mind emphasises, through its phrasing, that what is involved is specifically the ability, under this stimulus, to see the matter from more than his own point of view – 'he turned his head from side to side in a melancholy way, as if he were looking at some painful object on more sides than one'. To see clearly from the side of his sister and her husband is to challenge crucially his subjective point of view, and he returns to withdraw his demand. The sentence which concludes the chapter emphasises that Tulliver has not the intellectual equipment to recognise what has happened, but the fact remains, that through imagination he has achieved a growth of real moral importance: 'simple people, like our friend Mr Tulliver, are apt to clothe unimpeachable feelings in erroneous ideas, and this was his confused way of explaining to himself that his love and anxiety for "the little wench" had given him a new sensibility towards his sister'.

This is not, however, the way in which Mr Tulliver's imagination most commonly works. When we first meet him, in chapter 2, he is expounding his vision of Tom's future, an education which will make more than a miller or farmer of him. 'I should like Tom to be a bit of a scholard, so as he might be up to the tricks o' these fellows as talk fine and write with a flourish.' Tulliver himself is fitfully aware that this is largely fantasy: as he admits later, 'what I'm a bit afraid on is, as Tom hasn't got the right sort o' brains for a smart fellow. I doubt he's a bit slowish'. But he is not aware at all that the fantasy has a subjective basis. The form of the sentence first quoted in the present paragraph is a recurrent one. The opening words of the chapter are his, 'What I want', and they are repeated in various forms through the conversation. 'I want Tom to be . . .' 'I mean him to set up . . .'. Clearly he intends to benefit his son; but fantasy which comprises so little sympathy sways from an early stage towards the egocentric: 'It 'ud be a help to me wi' these law-suits, and arbitrations, and things.' By the next chapter, in the conversation with Riley, this element of the fantasy has become more definitely ugly: 'if I made him a miller an' farmer, he'd be expecting' to take to the Mill an' the land . . . I shall give Tom an eddication an' put him to a business, as he may make a nest for himself, an' not want to push me out o' mine'. Maggie, who overhears this, is rightly indignant at the unjust judgement of Tom it implies. As the conversation continues, it becomes clear that the matter of Tom's education is not an isolated fantasy. As Tulliver explains the grounds of his choice of marriage partner, it becomes evident that he is a man who likes to see himself habitually as the centre of his world, the master of the circle around him: 'I picked her from her sisters o' purpose, 'cause she was a bit weak, like; for I wasn't agoin' to be told the rights o' things by my own fireside.' It is his refusal to concede any form of dominance to others that leads him persistently into law-suits and the related financial difficulties.

To such a man, the effect of a challenge to the subjective view of himself, by an external event beyond his control is unlikely to be morally helpful. When he loses the law-suit against Pivart and Wakem he is only driven further into fantasy. He has the illusion, fed as usual by the opinions of others, that he takes the news well, since there is no outburst of temper; but in fact the only change is that, because he can no longer assert himself in the actual world, he asserts himself all the more vigorously in his imagination. 'All the obstinacy and defiance of his nature, driven out of their old channel, found a vent for themselves in the immediate formation of plans by which he would meet his difficulties.' A 'rush of projects' passes through his mind, based on fantasies that the world will arrange itself around his own desires. 'There was no doubt (in the miller's mind) that Furley [who has a mortgage on the land] would do just what was desirable.' The most obvious implication of the blatant facts of his situation simply cannot be assimilated into his view of himself. 'There are certain human beings to whom predominance is a law of life – they can only sustain humiliation so long as they can refuse to believe in it, and, in their own conception, predominate still.' When the letter informing him that Furley has sold the mortgage to Wakem removes all possibility of such belief, Tulliver has the physical collapse into unconsciousness which is both psychologically probable and metaphorically apt.

From then on, his fantasy focuses itself more intensely and more specifically on revenge against Wakem. Tom, over whom he can still exercise power, is made to write in the family Bible that he will perpetuate Tulliver's fantasies of hatred; and even when Tom has told him of his success in earning enough to pay off the creditors, thus restoring the family honour, Tulliver's mind remains more intent on the possibility of triumph over Wakem than on his son's achievement. He wakes at five the next morning, shouting, and explains to his alarmed wife, 'I was dreaming. . . . I thought I'd got hold of him.' His death is finally accelerated, ironically, by a fortuitous coincidence of fantasy and fact. Riding back after the meeting with his creditors at St Ogg's, he longs to meet Wakem. 'Why did he not happen to meet Wakem? The want of that coincidence vexed him, and set his mind at work in an irritating way.' But when the coincidence does occur, the fulfilment of his fantasy, in the whipping of Wakem, destroys not his dream but himself. As he dies, 'his hands moved uneasily, as if he wanted them to remove some obstruction that weighed upon him'. The obstruction is never removed, and he dies in the words of the last sentence referring to him, a 'dimly-lighted soul'.

In the characters of the younger generation, Maggie and Tom, George Eliot is able to analyse the relationship between fantasy and external fact over a more extended and morally crucial period

of time. The desire to constrain the recalcitrant external world
within the tidier boundaries of one's individual perspective is
endemic in the human mind. In the older generation, habit has so
limited the ability to discipline that desire, that even in Mr
Tulliver, the least hardened among them, there is no very real
possibility of change. Of the younger characters, Lucy seems
equally unlikely to develop. She is extremely good-natured, but
her 'cunning projects' to influence events for what she takes to be
the better are (except for the rather incredible moral intelligence
she shows in her last visit to Maggie) crucially disabled by
inability to imagine what is truly happening in the minds of
others. But in Maggie and Tom we can see the development from
childhood to maturity of their potential for imagination, as of their
moral characters in general. They are, of course, contrasted in
strength of imagination. When Maggie chatters about what Tom
would do if they were in Africa and a lion were coming for them,
Tom enters only very briefly into the fantasy – 'I should get a gun
and shoot him' – and quickly dismisses the subject with contempt
– 'the lion *isn't* coming.' Whereas Maggie finds 'boundless scope'
for her imagination in isolated sentences from a Latin Grammar,
Tom loses interest in the *Iliad* on finding that it is mere fiction. But
it is the direction of imagination that matters more than strength:
the richness of Maggie's often leads her near to disaster, and the
poverty of Tom's leads him at an important time to a major
success.

Such fantasy-life as Tom does have as a boy is similar to his
father's. Indeed, like most boys, he bases the image of his future
life upon what he takes to be his father's present life, 'which he had
always thought extremely pleasant, for it was nothing but riding
about, giving orders, and going to market', and he is dismayed at
the prospect of a stuffy education probably leading to a stuffy way
of life. But it includes an ominous element of his father's own
fantasy: 'when he was a man, he should be master of everything,
and do just as he liked'. The most extended flight of imagination
in his boyhood is borrowing Mr Poulter's sword and pretending
he is going to become a soldier. It is significant that he needs the
collaboration of Maggie in the fantasy, as a means of overcoming
the sense of seeming foolish himself. ('There was nobody but
Maggie who would be silly enough to believe him'). But even
more significant is the dramatisation of a role of dominance over
Maggie: when she is insufficiently over-awed by the terrible

aspect of a Tom made up with black cork and red kerchief, the drawing of the sword and the exhibition of cut and thrust quickly reduces her to a satisfactory degree of terror. To relate the sword to Tom's sense of justice would, I think, be to move outside the idiom of George Eliot's symbolism; but the injury Tom does to his foot *is* to be related to the image used in Maggie's reflections about pity and fidelity quoted on p. 169 above. Tom's humanity is maimed by the total lack of pity he has here, as on a more important later occasion, for his sister.

It is to some extent the very limitation of Tom's imagination, that enables him to come to terms so rapidly and so successfully with the change in family circumstances and his personal prospects, caused by the bankruptcy. By the end of his time at Mr Stelling's he is dreaming of himself as more than his father ever was, a 'fine young man' who would 'make a figure in the world' (of St Ogg's). But when Maggie brings him the news, he has already, before leaving the Stelling house, shifted his utopia from the future to the inaccessible past: 'his school-years seemed like a holiday that had come to an end'. No languishing after visions of the future now out of his reach complicates the 'practical sagacity', which contrasts with Maggie's 'dreamy weariness' and enables him to impress everyone with a sudden 'manliness of tone', 'self-command and practical judgement'. 'At sixteen, the mind that has the strongest affinity for fact cannot escape illusion and self-flattery', and when he comes to think of getting work, he anticipates an impossibly rapid time-scale for his success in regaining the family honour. But his response to the depressing realisation that 'the first step towards getting on in the world was a chill, dusty, noisy affair, and implied going without one's tea in order to stay in St Ogg's and have an evening lesson from a one-armed elderly clerk, in a room smelling strongly of bad tobacco', is to set himself, with a rather grim and forbidding determination, to make that step. His life takes on a settled singleness of purpose which leaves no scope for unproductive fantasy. 'Tom's interest in life, driven back and crushed on every other side, was concentrating itself into the one channel of ambitious resistance to misfortune. . . . Tom had very clear prosaic eyes, not apt to be dimmed by mists of feeling or imagination.' Clear, daylight purpose leaves no room for the vague dreams which complicate the life of his more imaginative sister, and the result is more than material success. Faced by no problem except the persistent difficulty of dreary perseverance, he achieves and sustains a real moral strength. 'A character at unity with itself – that performs what it intends, subdues every counteracting impulse, and has no visions beyond the distinctly possible – is strong by its very negations.'

But although imagination does not distract Tom from his strong singleness of purpose, neither does it liberate him. When Maggie wishes she had learnt double-entry book-keeping so that she could now teach it to Tom, he becomes resentful and she justifiably calls him harsh. ' "No, I'm not harsh", said Tom, with severe decision.' The harshness has always been present in the relationship; the shared suffering has not softened Tom. Nor has he gained in self-knowledge through having his earlier dreams thwarted: he says severely he is not being harsh, and does not notice that his manner contradicts his words. Severity towards him by the reader has been forestalled: we have been told he had just been 'made to feel his inferiority' at work, so all we have here is the understandable 'reaction of his strong, self-asserting nature'. But it remains his nature, from which he is not liberated by imaginative understanding of Maggie's feelings. In fact the horizons of his life have diminished. When Maggie visits his lodgings, her mind is 'crowded' by sad reflections on the small parlour which now constitutes his 'home', a word which had once 'meant for both of them the same sum of dear familiar objects'. The one object he has kept by him is the Bible which stands as the outward representation of the reduction, of all that 'home' meant, to a singleness of purpose too closely approaching what his father made him write in it.

Tom, then, achieves a victory over fantasy which had lain beyond the reach of the older generation; but his life can hardly be said to have been enhanced by it. Maggie is more deeply plagued by imagination, but works, through an extended series of painful collisions with external reality, to a humanity enriched by it. Her imagination is neither hardened into sterile fantasy, nor destroyed to make way for single daylight purpose; it is disciplined through time by a creative response to the challenges of the recalcitrant external world.

Already in her early childhood, imagination provides Maggie with both a fruitful extension of emotion and a morally helpful release for it. In chapter 4, George Eliot takes us with extraordinary penetration into the childlike imagination of Maggie's response to the mill. It becomes for her 'a little world apart from her outside everyday life', and the reader is made to share the range of her sensitivity, the 'dim delicious awe' evoked by the constant motion of the massive grinding stones, the simple pleasure of sliding down the heaps of grain, which any child would love, and the fantasies about the private lives of the flour-dusted spiders, which are characteristic only of highly gifted children. But the spiders already show the working of a more important aspect of imagination than fantasy. The paragraph I am referring to concludes with a sentence demonstrating in the pomposity of its phrasing that this child is in danger of too arrogant a view of her own abilities: 'She was in the habit of taking this recreation as she conversed with Luke, to whom she was very communicative, wishing him to think well of her understanding, as her father did.' She then goes on to quiz Luke about the extent of his reading. The potential insensitivity of a self-centred attitude in the outside world is counteracted on this occasion, and on others, by the sympathy included in the 'little world apart' created by the imagination. The quietly comic phrasing here keeps us within the ambit of the child's mind, but the implications for Maggie's potential character of her ability to imagine the spiders' 'painful difficulty' are very important. 'There must be a painful difficulty in their family intercourse – a fat and floury spider, accustomed to take his fly well dusted with meal, must suffer a little at a cousin's table where the fly was *au naturel*, and the lady-spiders must be mutually shocked at each other's appearance.' Towards the end of the following chapter, the fishing episode forms a utopian moment of related moral value. 'Maggie thought it would make a very nice heaven to sit by the pool in that way'; but it is essentially a shared utopia, uniting brother and sister to a rare degree. 'They trotted along and sat down together, with no thought that life would ever change much for them: they would only get bigger and not go to school, and it would always be like the holidays; they would always live together and be fond of each other.' The middle of the sentence is mainly Tom's thought, the last part mainly Maggie's; but they are fundamentally 'together' in this little world of childhood imagination. She includes Tom in it, and he can consequently meet her there.

The wooden doll, which is Maggie's fetish, provides the focus for an emotional release through imagination that is morally as valuable to her development as emotional extension. It becomes the object on to which she can project feelings it would be either impossible or undesirable to express directly to the people who actually arouse them. During Tom's absence it has many kisses lavished on it. When she overhears the plans to send Tom away to Mr Stelling's, it becomes the focus of her anxiety and disorientation – 'she held her doll topsy-turvy, and crushed its nose against the wood of the chair'. When she is scolded, she does not foster resentment, but transfers the punishment to the doll, driving nails into its head or beating it against the wall, 'with a passion that expelled every other form of consciousness – even the memory of the grievance that had caused it'. Since that becomes an habitual pattern of experience, even on the occasion (after the scolding about the death of the rabbits) when she feels too miserable to find relief through the doll, her fantasies of revenge ('she would stay up there and starve herself') do not last long. The episode with the jam puffs is similar. Maggie retreats from Tom's obstinacy into a private world, 'lost to almost everything except a vague sense of jam and idleness'; but her response to the more severe pain of unmerited reproach which follows is an indulgence in the 'superior power of misery' that lasts only ten minutes before 'resentment began to give way to the desire of reconciliation'.

The effect of Maggie's imagination is not, however, always morally salutary. Some of her fantasy is mere escapism. When Tom deserts her on one occasion, she can find no comfort other than 'refashioning her little world into just what she should like it to be. Maggie's was a troublous life, and this was the form in which she took her opium'. Lucy becomes for her a fantasy-self: 'She was fond of fancying a world where the people never got any larger than children of their own age, and she made the queen of it just like Lucy, with a little crown on her head, and a little sceptre in her hand . . . only the queen was Maggie herself in Lucy's form.' It is not far, from the characteristic egocentricity of fantasy included here, to the positive jealousy towards Lucy when Tom seems to prefer her company – a jealousy expressed in a cruelty which represents a potentially dangerous version of the use of the fetish: 'she was actually beginning to think that she should like to make Lucy cry, by slapping or pinching her, especially as it might vex Tom, whom it was of no use to slap, even if she dared, because he didn't mind it'.

The most extended instance of sterile and potentially dangerous fantasy in Maggie's childhood is her attempt to join the gypsies, the chapter in which 'Maggie tries to run away from her shadow'. Her concept of life with the gypsies is typically utopian: she sees it as a way of life 'entirely in harmony with circumstances', in which respect will be paid to herself 'on account of her superior knowledge'. It is 'to be her refuge from all the blighting obloquy that had pursued her in civilised life'. In accordance with the tradition, she has to go on a journey to reach it, a journey experienced in literary terms, with references to Apollyon, Jack the Giantkiller, St George and Leonore. Intrusions of fact, such as the dirt of the gypsies and their mercenary intentions, can for a long while be kept at bay by fantasy. 'It was just like a story', and Maggie wishes she had brought her books with her. As dream, it reaches its climax in the extension of the fantasy about Lucy: 'If I was a queen, I'd be a very good queen, and kind to everybody.' As dream, it turns, in itself, towards the terror of nightmare, the powerless desire to return home from characters who have come to seem diabolic. On this occasion, external fact rescues her from the misery of indulged fantasy – the pecuniary good sense of the gypsies in taking her home, and the love of her father which silences the expected reproaches from her mother and Tom. Maggie cannot escape the shadow thrown by lights other than her own consciousness, even though on this occasion none of the credit is hers, the desire to return home from the fantasy world being beyond her power to effect.

For Maggie, as for Tom, the retrospectively idealised world of childhood ends abruptly with the bankruptcy of their father. 'They had entered the thorny wilderness, and the golden gates of their childhood had for ever closed behind them.' But Maggie's more imaginative nature cannot so quickly adapt itself to the transformation of the external world. She suffers from the egocentricity of fantasy: 'everybody in the world seemed so hard and unkind to Maggie: there was no indulgence, no fondness, such as she imagined when she fashioned the world afresh in her own thoughts'. Her consciousness becomes dominated by the contrast between the reality of her situation – a girl in a brown frock looking at the 'dull walls of [the] sad chamber' where her father lies – and her inner life of 'eager, passionate longings', 'straining after dreamy music'. The narrator comments, 'No wonder, when there is this contrast between the outward and the inward, that painful collisions come of it.' The rest of her life is a series of such collisions.

The major analysis of her failure at this stage of her life to adapt inner world to outer comes in the central part of chapter 3 of Book 4. The first part of the chapter concerns Bob Jakin's gift of books to her, an episode which sets up Bob as a foil to Maggie, in that his own adaptation to difficult circumstances leads him on this, as on other occasions, very rapidly and without complication to sympathetic generosity. After Bob has gone, Maggie does not even look at the books but sinks directly into self-pity: 'She leaned her cheek against the window-frame, and thought that the light-hearted Bob had a lot much happier than hers.' Complete retreat into the inner world, where romance can dominate, no longer seems adequate to her: 'if she could have had all Scott's novels and all Byron's poems! . . . And yet . . . they were hardly what she wanted. She could make dream-worlds of her own – but no dream-world would satisfy her now'. There is a certain irony here: pure romance will no longer satisfy since it is self-evidently remote from reality, but she does continue to inhabit more sophisticated dream-worlds. So the next sentence continues, 'She wanted some explanation of this hard, real life', but she seeks it in Latin Grammar, Geometry and Logic, and with the characteristic vanity of fantasy ('a certain mirage would now and then rise on the desert of the future, in which she seemed to see herself honoured for her surprising attainments'). The diet is too dreary for her, and within a few weeks concentration on such books gives way to dreamy gazing at the sky. The failure propels her into a more irrational and uglier egocentricity: 'She rebelled against her lot, she fainted under its loneliness, and fits even of anger and hatred towards her father and mother, who were so unlike what she would have them to be . . . would flow out over her affections.' And the swing continues further into the kind of romance she thought now beneath her: 'Then her brain would be busy with wild romances of a flight from home in search of something less sordid and dreary: she would go to some great man – Walter Scott, perhaps' – as she had gone before to the gypsies. Imagination in its morally valuable form occasionally impinges on the fantasy: the voice of her father asking for his slippers reminds her that 'there was another sadness besides her own'. But on the whole her imagination seems to her to be merely a burden to herself: 'She thought it was part of the hardship of her life that there was laid upon her the burthen of larger wants than others seemed to feel – that she had to endure this wide hopeless yearning for that something, whatever it was, that was greatest and best on this earth.' It is through that yearning that she achieves a larger humanity than her parents or brother; but its effect at this stage is to keep her trapped in self-pity.

The route out of self-pity is Thomas à Kempis, whose book seems in no way, like the others she has encountered, an extension of any desire to romanticise the world, reshaping it to her own desires. The book was brought from the outside, by Bob, and her reaction to it is guided by the ancient pen-markings of another reader. But the simplicity of Bob's moral life, shown in the first third of the chapter, still stands as an opposite to Maggie's response to Thomas à Kempis, which is the main subject of the last third. The first sentence following the extended quotation from the book includes an ominous reference to music, a metaphor used frequently of Maggie's romantic yearnings, but blends it with the image of waking from a dream, a recurrent image of returning from fantasy to reality: 'A strange thrill of awe passed through Maggie while she read, as if she had been wakened in the night by a strain of solemn music, telling of beings whose souls had been astir while hers was in stupor.' The duality of response remains clear in the analysis which follows. Thomas's book importantly confirms her intuitive exercise of imagination in the sense of sympathy: 'for the first time she saw the possibility of shifting the position from which she looked at the gratification of her own desires – of taking her stand out of herself, and looking at her own life as an insignificant part of a divinely-guided whole'. But at the same time, imagination as fantasy is also continuing to obstruct her growing clarity of vision: 'With all the hurry of an imagination that could never rest . . . renunciation seemed to her the entrance into that satisfaction which she had so long been craving in vain.' Renunciation as the satisfaction of her cravings: poor Maggie still cannot see very clearly. But the superior reader is, as usual, checked in his own self-satisfaction: 'That is the path we all like when we set out on our abandonment of egoism.' There is in fact a real development in Maggie here, despite its incompleteness. She does discipline her self-pity and replace it with sensitive concern for her mother and father; and the effect on herself is manifest: 'That new inward life of hers . . . yet shone out in her face with a tender soft light that mingled itself as added loveliness with the gradually enriched colour and outline of her blossoming youth.' Her growth in stature of all kinds is empha-

sised by the contrasting reference at the end of the chapter to Mr
Tulliver, wholly static in his concentration on revenge. On the
other hand, one of the most important realities her newly
developed self has failed to take adequate account of is indicated
in the phrase I omitted from my last quotation: 'notwithstanding
some volcanic upheavings of imprisoned passions'.

The implied reaction takes place, of course, in the series of
meetings with Philip in the Red Deeps. But Maggie's state of
mind at this stage is complicated, and she remains confused in her
response to the desires of imagination. Most immediately, Philip
provides for her, in this romantically named place, an escape from
the mundane dreariness of renunciation. They discuss the
emotive power of music, and at their first meeting there Philip
tries to give her a volume of Scott. Through Philip her longings for
expansion of her intellectual and aesthetic horizons can be
fulfilled: she tells him 'your mind is a sort of world to me' – a
world, that is, of liberation and indefinite growth ('I think I
should never be tired of being with you,' she continues). The
meetings also provide an outlet for more intimate pent-up
emotions. At an early stage, Philip becomes a kind of fantasy
substitute for Tom: 'You would have loved me well enough to
bear with me, and forgive me everything. That was what I always
longed that Tom should do.' In the last of their meetings, he has
become the fulfilment of a romantic dream of even greater
attraction to an adolescent girl: 'It seemed so far off – like a dream
– only like one of the stories one imagines – that I should ever have
a lover.' But imagination in the other sense is also operative
throughout the relationship: the desires to make Philip happy and
to compensate for the emnity of their fathers are genuinely
altruistic and develop her capacity for moral sympathy. And more
radically confusing for her is her continued belief in what she
learnt from Thomas à Kempis; so that all the time she is divided
between attraction to the variety of things Philip can offer her and
the belief that they must be renounced. For a year the Red Deeps
remain for her simultaneously a refuge 'from all that was harsh
and unlovely' and an indulgence in selfish enjoyment which it is
her clear duty to give up for the sake of her father.

It is external conditions which make it possible to continue in
such confusion for so long (the existence of the Red Deeps, where
meetings can remain so long undiscovered); and it is external event
(Tom's discovery of the meetings) that releases Maggie from it.

Immediately after the event, she naturally sees it as disastrous, as having thrown her back 'in the thick of a hot strife with her own and others' passions' after the 'clearness and simplicity' of her life under the uncomplicated influence of Thomas à Kempis. But as her mind clears, she becomes aware primarily of two things, of the rightness of her sympathy for Philip, and of relief at the 'deliverance from concealment'. The following chapter concerns Tom's achievement of the money to pay off the debts and is called 'The Hard-won Triumph'. Ostensibly there is a one-sided contrast between Tom at a moment of high success, and Maggie beating the floor in impotent sympathy for the pain Philip must have felt at Tom's insults. But Maggie's pain has taught her more than Tom will ever know. This time, external factors have only brought about, at the cost of much pain, what she most deeply wished from the start, but did not adequately know.

Maggie's final extended excursion into fantasy is with Stephen. The chapter which opens this part of the book is called 'A Duet in Paradise', but the relationship between Stephen and Lucy portrayed in it is a rather saccharine paradise, parallel but inferior to the paradise which Maggie and Tom left at the end of their childhood. Our view of it is directed explicitly by Philip's reported comment on the kind of music which sets the tone of the courtship: 'He says it has a sort of sugared complacency and flattering make-believe.' But Maggie is still young enough to be attracted by sugar. From the interwoven responses to Thomas à Kempis and to Philip she developed her power of control over her imagination; but to sustain control over long periods of time is another matter. 'After her years of contented renunciation, she had slipped back into desire and longing' – specifically the old longing for the 'image of intense and varied life' she now takes Lucy's drawing-room to embody. George Eliot makes it quite clear from the start that the attraction of Stephen is based more on fantasy than on what he actually is: 'It was not that she thought distinctly of Mr Stephen Guest, or dwelt on the indications that he looked on her with admiration; it was rather that she felt the half-remote presence of a world of love and beauty and delight, made up of vague, mingled images from all the poetry and romance she had ever read, or had ever woven in her dreamy reveries.' The imagery which recurs at every stage in the development of the relationship is of music, of dream and of drifting on water – imagery of surrender to feeling and fantasy in forgetfulness of external

reality. 'The new abundance of music, and lingering strolls in the
sunshine, and delicious dreaminess of gliding on the river – could
hardly be without some intoxicating effect on her, after her years
of privation.' The word 'dreamy' is used repeatedly to describe
the state of mind of both Maggie and Stephen, and on one
occasion there is reference to the word George Eliot habitually
associated with escapism, opium.

In this new situation Philip has in effect the same role as
Thomas à Kempis had had during the phase of the Red Deeps,
becoming a 'sort of outward conscience to her'. The most
important difference is simply that the experience with Philip has
taught her to think of renunciation more as a step to active
sympathy, less as a subtle form of self-satisfaction: 'I do always
think too much of my own feelings, and not enough of others' – not
enough of yours. I had need have you always to find fault with me
and teach me.' But more comprehensively, her affection for him
becomes the focus of all that makes sense of her life, both the
positive and the negative feelings which make for stability and
against chaos. 'Her tranquil, tender affection for Philip, with its
root deep down in her childhood, and its memories of long quiet
talk confirming by distinct successive impressions the first
instinctive bias – the fact that in him the appeal was more strongly
to her pity and womanly devotedness than to her vanity or other
egoistic excitability of her nature, seemed now to make a sort of
sacred place, a sanctuary where she could find refuge from an
alluring influence which the best part of herself must resist, which
must bring horrible tumult within, wretchedness without.' In a
way, this resembles that early desire to return home from the
gypsies; but at that stage her fear was only for herself.

She does, again, disobey her 'outward conscience', but there
remains important difference. The active word 'resolution' is used
of her decision to run away to the gypsies. Agreement to meet
Philip required the pretence that some element of chance was
involved: Maggie jumps at Philip's 'subterfuge' – 'If I meet you by
chance, there is no concealment in that?' In going away with
Stephen there is not even active pretence: she is, in the words of
the chapter title, 'Borne along by the Tide', 'without any act of her
own will' and only 'dimly conscious' of the 'dreamy gliding' of the
boat. It is, of course, a fulfilment of her dreams 'there was . . .
then, a life for mortals here below which was not hard and chill –
in which affection would no longer be self-sacrifice . . . and the

vision for the time excluded all realities'. But the next chapter is called, starkly, 'Waking'.

There is in fact a double awakening as Maggie moves upwards through the levels of consciousness. The first is to a dream dearer to her best self than the pure romance of the drift with Stephen, a dream of the legend of St Ogg in which the Virgin becomes Lucy and the boatman a mixture of Philip and Tom – a Tom who is not really angry with her. But 'from the soothed sense of that false waking she passed to the real waking', the recognition that she has brought 'sorrow into the lives of others' who are most close to her, and that she has made herself 'an outlawed soul, with no guide but the wayward choice of her own passion'. The only comfort is that her action was not truly deliberate: 'There was at least this fruit from all her years of striving after the highest and best – that her soul, though betrayed, beguiled, ensnared, could never deliberately consent to a choice of the lower.' But the pain for others is what is most vivid to her waking imagination – the 'murdered trust and hopes' of Philip and Lucy. As before, she longs to return home, but in consciousness that it is not only a refuge, but will entail greater pain for herself than staying with Stephen – 'Home – where her mother and brother were – Philip – Lucy – the scene of her very cares and trials – was the haven towards which her mind tended.' As before, there is a contrast between the end of this chapter and the beginning of the next. Here Maggie is left wrestling with the pains of her complex imagination – the tormenting mixture of pity for Stephen ('she saw Stephen's face turned towards her in passionate, reproachful misery') and continued tempting dream ('an easy floating in a stream of joy'), which is the cost of the choice that most fully reconciles the self-sacrifice learnt from Thomas à Kempis with the sympathy developed in her relationship with Philip. In the first paragraph of the next chapter we see Tom in possession of the mill, having regained it through 'years of steady self-government and energetic work'. But the relative worth of his form of self-possession is already hinted at in the same sentence – 'he had half-fulfilled his father's dying wish'. What he makes of the other half is painfully clear from the first words he speaks here: to the sister Tulliver asked him to take care of, he says, 'You will find no home with me', and he stands by them. He has not the slightest imagination of what she is feeling.

I do not wish to consider until the next chapter the ending of the book, though that is Maggie's last collision with reality, the last enactment of her desire to return home from excursion into fantasy. But in the preceding chapter I have already suggested ways of seeing her experience before the ending as essentially tragic in form, and I am now in a position to propose another. Both the internal and the external conditions of her life are beyond her control; but if she had less imagination she would be a smaller person (such as Tom); and without the sensitivity to external conditions which disciplines her imagination she would also be smaller (like her father). So the collison between imagination and fact, which causes repeated pain, is both inevitable and necessary to her stature. In other words, George Eliot has, through her own imaginative power, elevated her fiction from the idiom of nineteenth-century determinism to that of classical tragic necessity.

11   *The Mill on the Floss*: Naturalism and Purpose

The roots of naturalism in the mid-nineteenth-century English novel obviously ante-date the accelerated agnosticism of that period, which had removed for George Eliot the belief in a transcendent purpose shared by More and Johnson. But I want to examine in this chapter some of the particular values which the form held for a writer in search of a secular substitute. Some of what seem to me the most important of these have already been discussed in the preceding two chapters, but certain aspects of them require further clarification.

Although there is some duplicity involved, which I shall draw attention to in the next chapter, there is not in *The Mill on the Floss* an external End, towards which the characters may be seen to be striving with varying degrees of adequacy – there is no 'choice of eternity'. Consequently the 'choice of life' has to be something generated to a much greater extent from within. Purpose is not revealed, but has to be evolved. So the kind of satirical structure found in *Utopia* and *Rasselas* becomes impossible – that is, a structure in which the aspirations most extensively followed through – towards maximum pleasure for all and towards personal happiness – are put in ironic perspective by reference to a more important final aspiration assumed to be as obvious to reader as to writer. In so far as life is taken, in a fiction of George Eliot's kind, to be on the largest possible scale purposeful, the aspirations of the characters are turned, more or less adequately, directly towards the most important purposes conceived by the author. This does not, of course, imply that the characters themselves have to be consistently conscious of those purposes; indeed, because the purposes are evolved, not revealed, most of the characters seldom or never glimpse them, and the most successful of them, Maggie, is only intermittently conscious of them, for periods of increasing length. But because the author *is*

conscious of them throughout as purposes of universal, not merely
personal value, the form can be clearly distinguished from that of
an existentialist novel. The values are not entirely self-generated
by the characters: the author has already decided what values are,
universally, most important. So Maggie's development is
properly to be described in a vocabulary which includes the word
maturity, as opposed to one which includes *authenticity*. Vocabulary
based on the metaphor of growth is in fact most apt, for George
Eliot's thinking, like that of so many nineteenth-century writers,
is profoundly influenced by contemporary developments in
biology. Individual lives are seen characteristically in the imagery
of the physical growth of an organism, and that growth is seen
within the context of a general evolution of the human species. I
shall return to the metaphysical implications of this in Chapter
12, but at present I want to discuss further the effect on form.

In the terms of a quotation I made towards the end of my first
chapter about *The Mill on the Floss*, Maggie's growth towards a
mature virtue of pity is analogous to the development of a pair of
adult human feet. I have already traced the stages of that and of
the parallel growth in her capacity to discipline her imagination.
But growth may be stunted or twisted. So the general form, a
vision of character shaping itself through persistent patterns of
behaviour over a lengthy period of time, is given in the epigraph to
Chapter 70 of *Middlemarch* –

> Our deeds still travel with us from afar
> And what we have been makes us what we are.[1]

But that chapter concerns Bulstrode, who has crucially maimed
part of his humanity, as Tom maims a different part of his.
Farebrother makes the qualifying point in chapter 72 of *Middlemarch*: 'character is not cut in marble – it is not something solid
and unalterable. It is something living and changing, and may
become diseased as our bodies do'. In an intelligent naturalistic
form, history becomes not merely the naive attempt to mimic the
world of reality, which its detractors take it to be, but a means of
tracing the adequacy of an individual's orientation, an orientation
which may lead to proper or to more or less stunted human
growth. If purpose has to be evolved within the frame of the book,
history of some kind is in fact inevitable. The use of a historical
form in fiction was, of course, not new: the author of *The History of*

Tom Jones was highly conscious of a relation between the form of his work and history; and there is a more highly developed sense of the moral significance of time to be found in the works of the next generation, for example in Crabbe and Jane Austen and Wordsworth; and there is an even more obvious relationship between *The Mill on the Floss* and the novel Dickens wrote almost exactly at the same time, *Great Expectations*. But the agnostic George Eliot is more heavily dependent on the form which she adapted: in the world of her beliefs, there is no access to higher values except through a growth which must take time, and can therefore be rendered only through history.

The important characters in her novels are always seen in terms of process. Of Lydgate she says perhaps most famously, 'character too is a process and an unfolding. The man was still in the making, as much as the Middlemarch doctor and immortal discoverer, and there were both virtues and faults capable of shrinking or expanding'. In the phrasing here, one can see also how George Eliot exploits the form necessary to her vision in a way which maintains an aesthetic interest: we do not, at this stage, know which way Lydgate's character will unfold, and to sustain our suspense the narrator pretends not to know either. Similarly, in an early chapter of *The Mill on the Floss*, there is a proleptic comment, which we can correctly decode in retrospect, but which at a first encounter merely stimulates curiosity: 'Under these average boyish physiognomies that [Nature] seems to turn off by the gross, she conceals some of her most rigid, inflexible purposes, some of her most unmodifiable characters; and the dark-eyed, demonstrative, rebellious girl may after all turn out to be a passive being compared with this pink-and-white bit of masculinity with the indeterminate features.' In her greatest novel, George Eliot begins at a moment crucial in the lives of her major characters, when the general bias of them is already formed, but before the decisive experiences of adult life have precisely shaped them. This gives her scope to trace, in much more extended detail, the effect on individual development of relationship with other adults. The most important changes in Dorothea and Lydgate come in response, less to the events of marriage, death, financial difficulty, than to relationship with other people, primarily their spouses. The structure of *The Mill on the Floss* leaves much less room for exploration of that process; but on the other hand, it does reach back much further into the early stages of the lives of Tom and Maggie. In an early chapter, George Eliot refers explicitly to the importance of childhood experience in the development of the individual: 'Every one of those keen moments has left its trace, and lives in us still, but such traces have blent themselves irrecoverably with the firmer texture of our youth and manhood.' In the detailed account of those 'keen moments', and of their relation to the growth of character, the book is, I think, unequalled by any English writer, including Wordsworth, of whose influence George Eliot was probably conscious.

The naturalistic form, then, allows George Eliot to show individual human beings growing through time into a fully developed humanity (Maggie) or into a deformed humanity (Tom). Tom roughhews an end for himself, but the end of human life, as embodied in George Eliot's model of a properly developed human being, is shaped with obviously greater adequacy by Maggie. I shall return later to the fact that no divinity is presumed to do the shaping. But this development of the individual is very explicitly seen by George Eliot in the context of a development of the human species as a whole. In the first chapter of Book 4, she offers a lengthy defence of her decision to spend a large proportion of the book on the apparently drab characters of the older generation. 'I share with you this sense of oppressive narrowness; but it is necessary that we should feel it, if we care to understand how it acted on the lives of Tom and Maggie – how it has acted on young natures in many generations, that in the onward tendency of human things have risen above the mental level of the generation before them, to which they have been nevertheless tied by the strongest fibres of their hearts.' The lives of Tom and Maggie are crucially influenced by the lives of their elders; but the belief in an 'onward tendency of human things' is quite explicit here. The purpose embodied in an individual's cultivation of virtue is part of the general evolutionary purpose of humanity. The form of the novel allows George Eliot to portray both.

The basic characteristics of the two families, the Dodsons and the Tullivers, are set up at the opening of Book 4. 'The Dodsons were a very proud race, and their pride lay in the utter frustration of all desire to tax them with a breach of traditional duty or propriety. . . . To live respected, and have the proper bearers at your funeral, was an achievement of the ends of existence. . . . The right thing must always be done towards kindred. The right thing was to correct them severely . . . but . . . never forsake or ignore them.' 'The same sort of traditional belief ran in the Tulliver veins, but it was carried in richer blood, having elements of generous imprudence, warm affection, and hot-tempered rashness.' The phrasing here points in rather too polarised terms to a resemblance in Tom to the Dodsons and in Maggie to the Tullivers; in fact the blood of both families is in the veins of both children.

It is true that elements of Dodson remain in Tom. For example, after the drama of the bankruptcy has died down, 'he felt the humiliation as well as the prospective hardships of his lot with all the keenness of a proud nature . . . his father was really blamable, as his aunts and uncles had always said he was'; and more positively a little later, 'Tom felt intensely that common cause with his father which springs from family pride, and was bent on being irreproachable as a son.' But during the same period, the Dodson in him is valuably qualified by the Tulliver. The manliness of his behaviour owes much to what he has inherited from his father – 'the double stimulus of resentment against his aunts, and the sense that he must behave like a man and take care of his mother'. When he says he will honour his father's wishes about the money owed by Aunt Moss, Mrs Glegg 'felt that the Dodson blood was certainly speaking in him'; but the generosity of it is more from Tulliver blood – she continues, 'though, if his father had been a Dodson, there would never have been this wicked alienation of money'. The course which Tom steers at this stage of his development is superior to what the older members of both families would have done. He goes beyond his father's crude concept of revenge against Wakem in restoring the family honour; but his concept of justice is also wider than mere Dodson protection of family interests. On the other hand, in his later situation, the amalgamation of inherited traits brings him morally lower than either side. When Aunt Glegg, who offers, unlike Tom, to take Maggie in after her disgrace, finds a 'stronger nature than her own' in Tom at this stage, the nature is one which has reverted to a lower moral level – 'a nature in which family feeling had lost the character of clanship by taking on a doubly deep dye of personal pride'. In an evolutionary process, individual regression always remains a possibility.

It is Maggie, of course, who most fully represents in the book what George Eliot calls the 'onward tendency of human things'.

In temperament she is more Tulliver than Dodson: that very early chapter which opens with Mr Tulliver's 'What I want . . .' ends with Maggie saying, 'I don't *want* to do my patchwork . . . I don't want to do anything for my aunt Glegg.' Her impulsiveness is clearly from him; but as I showed above, she, unlike him, cultivates her impulsive affection into virtue. Her Dodson traits are largely left behind as she matures; but an important part of her moral strength in fact represents a refinement of a basically Dodson characteristic. When Aunt Glegg is reflecting about Tom's rejection of Maggie, she thinks, 'If you were not to stand by your "kin" as long as there was a shred of honour attributable to them, pray what were you to stand by?' That is, in George Eliot's word, a 'narrow' belief; but one can see in it the seed of Maggie's fidelity in standing by her obligations to her father (with Philip) and to Philip (with Stephen). In this respect Maggie is not a Tulliver: her father takes pleasure in defying the views of his wife's family, and his sense of obligation to his own sister, Aunt Moss, is comparatively fitful. Maggie interprets words like *bonds* and *ties* more intelligently than her aunt, but the broader understanding has clearly evolved from the narrower. The naturalistic form allows George Eliot to show the process of evolution while keeping the characters individually credible. In schematic terms one might say that Maggie's more advanced moral nature evolves from a mixture of the better qualities of both sides of the family – from the Dodson allegiance to kin mixed with the impulsive kindness of the Tullivers (and a degree of obstinacy from both). But in reading, one is more conscious of the difference of the individuals than of a schematic evolution.

We have, then, the apparently paradoxical situation of the morally most advanced character in the book being the most strongly and consciously bound by the obligations of the past. But the paradox is only apparent, since George Eliot sees moral progress most fundamentally as a movement away from egoism towards altruism, and heightened awareness of obligations towards others, incurred in the past, is clearly a particular form of that general progress. In fact, because there is no external End that can become the object of the yearnings towards the good which characterise the most advanced moral type, the past tends naturally to become the focus for otherwise unattached feelings of something sacred. Maggie often expresses this strongly, and not even Philip can understand her. In the first meeting in the Red

Deeps she says, 'The old books went; and Tom is different – and my father. It is like death.' The implications of this attachment to the past, the sacredness it confers on her responsibilities to her father, are completely lost on Philip, who replies, 'I would give up a great deal for *my* father; but I would not give up a friendship . . . in obedience to any wish of his that I didn't recognize as right.' At the last meeting the contrast remains the same. Maggie says, '. . . it cuts me to the heart afterwards, that I should ever have felt weary of my father and mother'; and Philip replies, 'Don't think of the past now, Maggie; think only of our love.' The past, or rather what her moral imagination has shaped out of the past, becomes, since there is none other outside herself, the location of ultimate value and stability for her. She tells Stephen that to give way to her present feelings of love for him 'would rend me away from all that my past life has made dear and holy to me. I can't set out on a fresh life, and forget that: I must go back to it, and cling to it, else I shall feel as if there were nothing firm beneath my feet'.

A statement of that kind would clearly have little force for a reader who had not been taken, through the naturalistic form, into those moments of Maggie's past life which have made it 'holy' to her. But the use of an omniscient narrator within that form allows George Eliot to generalise beyond Maggie's personal situation and write about the past as a universal source of moral value in a godless world. The writing on such occasions owes much to Wordsworth. 'Our delight in the sunshine on the deep-bladed grass today, might be no more than the faint perception of wearied souls, if it were not for the sunshine and the grass in the far-off years which still live in us, and transform our perception into love.' The 'striving after something better and better in our surroundings', characteristic of man at an advanced stage of materialist civilisation, is quite clearly distinguished from the moral effort which leads to real human progress: 'heaven knows where that striving might lead us, if our affections had not a trick of twining round those old inferior things – if the loves and sanctities of our life had no deep immoveable roots in memory'. The St Ogg's of the time of the narrative is not contrasted with nature and home, but seen as an extension of them, 'as a continuation and outgrowth of nature', 'a town which carries the traces of its long growth and history like a millennial tree'. The effect of this character of the town on the lives of its inhabitants is to give a stability and a source of real, even if narrow, moral order.

There are no plate-glass windows or 'other fallacious attempt to make fine old red St Ogg's wear the air of a town that sprang up yesterday . . . for the farmers' wives and daughters who came to do their shopping on market-days were not to be withdrawn from their regular, well-known shops; and the tradesmen had no wares intended for customers who would go on their way and be seen no more'.

For Mr Tulliver, the Mill itself provides a far more than merely material centre of stability, and the prospect of losing it is profoundly disorientating to him. After the bankruptcy, 'It was when he got able to walk about and look at all the old objects, that he felt the strain of this clinging affection for the old home as part of his life, part of himself.' Its atmosphere is radically salutary: 'just now he was living in that freshened memory of the far-off time which comes to us in the passive hours of recovery from sickness'. When he goes on, in the next paragraph, to talk to Luke about his orchard, the direction of his thought puts one in mind more of Wordsworth than of, say, Hardy: he associates the trees with his father who enjoyed planting them and with his younger self who enjoyed helping him, even in the cold weather. The place is loved for its connection with the human relationships formed there, but the place is important in focusing the relationships. George Eliot learnt much from the Wordsworth of 'Michael' and 'The Ruined Cottage'. The underlying and often explicit metaphorical language of my quotations in this and the preceding paragraphs is of growth, but a growth rooted in the stability of the past. The growth is not away from, but out of the past: its strength derives from its roots. The old hall of St Ogg's is a muddle of architectural styles, but its achievement is that its past has been integrated into its present form: the past has not been sacrificed to present caprice, and those who built in Gothic stone did not 'sacrilegiously pull down the ancient half-timbered body'. The naturalistic form allows George Eliot to write extensive passages of descriptive prose which clearly imply that it is no quirk of Maggie's character that confers on the past the status of something sacred, something upon which the richness of man's humanity is radically and permanently dependent.

But although the naturalistic form importantly aids George Eliot in the representation of her particular visions of purpose and meaning in human life, it is also a form which facilitates acknowledgement of the recalcitrance of brute fact to human will.

I have already emphasised the importance of such recalcitrance to human development, in the preceding chapter. One of the major values of this form of novel is that it can render faithfully the degree of importance of external forces and events relative to the total significant history of the individual. To take a minor instance, when Tulliver wishes the mortgage bond to be to no client of Wakem's, events turn out to the contrary within a fortnight – 'not because Mr Tulliver's will was feeble, but because external fact was stronger'. But this recalcitrance extends beyond the kind of dialectic between desire and external fact which I have traced at more length in relation to Maggie: it is possible also to include apparently quite random events. Tom would clearly not have become the kind of man he did, if it had not been for the mistakes of his father in bankrupting himself and in forcing Tom to write the declaration of revenge in the Bible, and those events are not part of any consistent pattern: with respect to Tom they are random. Obviously there is an aesthetic illusion involved in this: the author has selected the external events in order to bring to bear influences of a significant nature. But it only makes sense to challenge that aesthetic privilege in a world which is assumed to have no purpose at all. George Eliot does not assume such a world. To deny that privilege in her work would be to make not a critical but a metaphysical point – a point which would logically entail on the critic a rejection of all literature which assumes purpose of some kind – that is, a rather limiting situation.

George Eliot makes explicit her awareness of the importance of wholly external events in a famous passage in Book 6 chapter 6, which I have quoted earlier (' "character is destiny". But not the whole of our destiny'), and in which she goes on to imagine a Hamlet whose father was never murdered – a Hamlet who would probably have married Ophelia and lived relatively happily ever after. In other words, Maggie's history cannot possibly be accurately inferred from a knowledge only of her own characteristics, however detailed. This is one of the chief qualifications to be registered to that epigraph from chapter 70 of *Middlemarch* which I quoted early in this chapter ('what we have been makes us what we are'); the other chief qualification is that the independent wills of other characters can be as crucial as external events.[1] The naturalistic form of this kind of novel, in which characters cannot be regarded as various projections of a single human type, since they have wholly independent consciousness, makes it possible to

register with great sensitivity the limitations imposed on individual human purpose by its human as well as non-human
environment. A Maggie without Tom would not be the Maggie
we know. A Rasselas without Nekayah would not be significantly
different, even though *Rasselas* would be.

So far in this chapter, I have been concerned with the
relationship between form and the possibilities envisaged by
George Eliot of shaping human purpose and of finding human
meaning in a world without transcendent purpose. I want now to
consider the relations between her form and her own literary
purposes. She herself very firmly distinguished between her own
form and what she took to be utopian form. In a letter of 15 August
1866 to Frederick Harrison, she wrote, 'Avowed Utopias are not
offensive, because they are understood to have a scientific and
expository character: they do not pretend to work on the
emotions, or couldn't do it if they did pretend.'[2] She seems to have
had in mind here nineteenth-century programmatic utopias,
rather than More's book, but the main point, that her own form
works on the emotions, whereas the utopian form does not, is
clearly broadly true. Fully as much as More, she wished to
educate the reader, but to educate him primarily by stretching
and refining his capacity for sympathetic feeling. The difference
can be related to the difference of human purpose envisaged,
though I do not wish to imply that the relation can be regarded as
a historical generalisation. The reader to whom *Utopia* and
Rasselas were directed was one who needed to tighten his
intellectual grip on truths well known but not known well; the
reader addressed by *The Mill on the Floss* is one who needs to
become as much like Maggie and as little like her father or brother
as possible. For More and Johnson, the ultimate purpose was
known: the reader needed to re-assess his relation to it. For
George Eliot, the ultimate purpose has to be shaped: so a function
of the book becomes to contribute to the reader's own process of
shaping, to help him, like Maggie, develop towards a fuller
humanity. This could, of course, be said of many great literary
works of previous centuries, but as a deliberate artistic intention it
certainly became more common in the nineteenth century.
George Eliot seems to me in this, as in other respects, to owe much
to Wordsworth in particular. In the famous letter to John Wilson,
Wordsworth said, '. . . a great Poet . . . ought, to a certain degree,
to rectify men's feelings, to give them new compositions of feeling,

to render their feelings more sane, pure, and permanent . . . It is not enough for me as a Poet, to delineate merely such feelings as all men *do* sympathise with; but it is also highly desirable to add to these others, such as all men *may* sympathise with, and such as there is reason to believe they would be better and more moral beings if they did sympathise with'. Of the very large number of places in which George Eliot says much the same, the best-known is the letter to Charles Bray of 5 July 1859: 'If Art does not enlarge men's sympathies, it does nothing morally.'[3] In accordance with the evolutionary conception of human nature which I have referred to above, her meliorism as it is generally called, this extension of an individual's humanity through reading becomes part of the moral growth of mankind in general: in other words, the novel becomes a direct contribution to the moral evolution which is the highest human purpose defined in it.

The most obvious extension of the reader's sympathies in this book is towards childhood experience. In chapter 7 of Book 1, George Eliot asks of her readers, 'Is there any one who can recover the experience of his childhood not merely with a memory of what he did and what happened to him . . . but with an intimate penetration, a revived consciousness of what he felt then?' In this book she has recovered that experience with a penetration exceeding even Wordsworth's, not only as a means of understanding the development of the children towards the adults they become, but in order to sharpen the reader's sensitivity to the consciousness of children – the 'strangely perspectiveless conception of life' which gives an intensity to experiences that from an adult point of view seem trivial. In some of the early episodes, we enter so sensitively into the minds of both Maggie and Tom, that I do not think childhood consciousness is so accurately registered by any other English writer. And although that degree of acclaim cannot be accorded to the representation of adolescent experience, the same intention is followed through with major success. As Maggie and Tom begin the dreary process of long-term adaptation to the effects of the bankruptcy, George Eliot writes, 'There is no hopelessness so sad as that of early youth, when the soul is made up of wants, and has no long memories, no superadded life in the life of others; though we who look on think lightly of such premature despair, as if our vision of the future lightened the blind sufferer's present.' As in all George Eliot's fiction, a central purpose is to extend the reader's sympathies towards very ordinary people, as opposed to the intense individuals of a more customary art, the 'experience of a human soul that looks out through dull grey eyes', as she puts it in *Scenes of Clerical Life*. Of Mr Tulliver she writes, much as she was later to write of Casaubon, 'The pride and obstinacy of millers, and other insignificant people, whom you pass unnoticingly on the road every day, have their tragedy too.' Even the very minor character, Mr Riley, is to be understood sympathetically – 'If you blame Mr Riley very severely for giving a recommendation on such slight grounds, I must say you are rather hard upon him.' We are told equally explicitly not to be too hard on Philip, when his arguments with Maggie are clearly self-interested, and on Tom, when he frequently seems severe himself.

But the real achievement here obviously lies not so much in this sort of explicit demand, as in actually provoking sympathy, and the means by which George Eliot does this are essentially functions of her naturalistic form. In a form which allows multiplicity of centres of consciousness, some centres will be morally inadequate, and their very inadequacy stimulates a responsive reader to supply the deficiency. This mode is particularly manifest in the chapter concerning the response of St Ogg's society to the news of Maggie's disgrace (Book 7, chapter 2). Like Johnson, George Eliot has a capacity for extremely powerful satire which is normally held in check, in accordance with a more inclusive purpose. But in this chapter, the satire against 'the world's wife' and its radically uncharitable attitude, masquerading under a grotesquely narrow interpretation of Christian respectability, is allowed full rein. We have already, of course, sympathised with Maggie through being made to share her experiences and emotional conflicts which have led up to the situation; but the sympathy is greatly increased by reaction against the travesty of her motivation and that of the other people involved, which forms the substance of the gossip circulated by the 'world's wife'. The same sort of thing is happening less obviously throughout the book. For example, we know why Mr Tulliver sends Tom to Mr Stelling's and why he keeps going to law, and we also know the opinion of the Dodson sisters about his behaviour. Their view is reductive and we do not share it, but it helps to focus ours. In this case, in fact, the mode is slightly more complicated: there is something to be said for their view, whereas the satire against the 'world's wife' is unqualified. When Tom blames his father for his obstinacy in going to law with the consequence of bankruptcy, there is much to be said for his judgement, though he should be more reluctant than he is to make it of his own father. So in the more sophisticated instances of this mode, there is a complicated inter-play between judgement and sympathy. We partly accept Tom's judgement, but qualify it with the sympathy induced by broader understanding; and as a result we partly judge Tom's inadequacy, but qualify that in turn, through our accumulated understanding of him. Ultimately, the result for the reader is both an enlargement of sympathy and a sharpening of discernment (to sympathise with a character, we have to know what it is to look through his eyes, to have his limitation of vision) with a continuous challenge to potential arrogance – one can scarcely read in this convention without seeing that all visions, including one's own, are limited.

The full effect of this form of naturalism can only be achieved, again, through the use of an omniscient narrator: we have a view of what truly occurs in the minds of individual characters – often a more adequate view than they have themselves – against which we can measure the more or less adequate comprehensions of them by other characters. As a convention this has, of course, been challenged, and in the world of certain other novelists legitimately so. But in George Eliot's world, it cannot be reasonably challenged: it is a frankly fictional, final extension of that sympathy which she sees as the highest manifestation of human purpose and as her own aesthetic purpose. She is not, as has been argued by some, illogically in the position of a god whose existence she has denied. She uses the literary convention of omniscience to show the reader that in life no man is omniscient, that because no man actually knows infallibly, as the reader is temporarily privileged to know through fiction, what is in the mind of another, he must strive endlessly, through sympathy, to see as much as he can. To the extent that he does not, he will be culpably unjust.

The other primary means of extending the reader's sympathies in this novel has already been discussed at length from other perspectives – that is, the tracing of the history of the characters over a long period of time, with the effect of fully explaining the reasons for behaviour, which a more cursory summary of facts might lead one to condemn. George Eliot has this in mind when, at the beginning of the chapter concerning the 'world's wife', she says, 'We judge others according to results; how else? – not knowing the process by which results are arrived at.' The 'world's wife' judges Maggie harshly, partly because it does not understand her to the extent the reader does from having lived vicariously through her development. As I suggested in my earlier discussion, this historical understanding of the individual is also set in the context of a more general historical understanding of the moral development of a society. In the terms of the present argument, our sympathies are extended back into the moral life of St Ogg's society in the generation older than Maggie. As George Eliot emphasises at length in the opening chapter of Book 4, it is a narrow society, but it does represent a real phase of popular English civilisation, which at one point she sets briefly in the context of a continuous past, running back, via Puritans and Loyalists, to Danes, Saxons and Romans. As such, the extension into it of the sympathies of the relatively deracinated modern reader is of human importance in itself.

Taken together, these various means of extending the reader's sympathies have the effect of encouraging a respect for other persons, even where more or less severe moral criticisms have simultaneously to be registered. In the strict sense of the words, George Eliot is a moral determinist[4] – that is, she believes that all moral decisions can be traced to specific causes (that they are not arbitrary). But this by no means entails on her any lack of belief in human responsibility, since the individual can choose, in a complex situation, which of the causes operative on him become decisive. What it does entail on her literary art is a meticulous effort to lay before the reader the fullest possible account of the causes operative on her characters (while keeping within the aesthetic restraint of potential tediousness). To make the point briefly, Tom is a lesser person than Maggie, but he is only partly, not wholly, responsible for what he becomes. So the obligation on the novelist is to provide the fullest possible account of relevant causes; and the obligation on the reader is to respect, as far as he can, what Tom made of possibilities far less rich than are at the disposal of Maggie. Or even more briefly, in the words of the young Maggie, even Aunt Glegg is pitiable. If one understands the full difficulties, the full limitations which particular people have to cope with, one not only perceives the countless mundane tragedies of which George Eliot writes, but also develops a true respect for other persons. It is, of course, possible to achieve this effect in other forms, but the naturalistic form of the novel is one in which it can be achieved with abnormal power by a mind as capacious as George Eliot's.

Potentially, the form is one which is highly vulnerable to diverse interpretation: the quantity of information, which may be assembled by individual readers in ways not intended by the writer, is unusually large. To the chagrin of certain sorts of critic, George Eliot avoids this problem by employing a wholly authoritative narrator. There is a healthy variety of perspectives available in modern criticism of the book, but the only radical variants have risen either through failure to note the repetition of the word 'dream', and its implications, in the account of the affair with Stephen, or through coming completely outside George Eliot's explicit value-system and arguing that Maggie should have opted for what she calls (borrowing Philip's language) 'fullness of existence' instead of self-sacrifice. The scope for critical fantasy is not so extensive as with the other fictions I discuss in this book.

Finally in this chapter, I wish to consider the form of *The Mill on the Floss* in relation to authorial fantasy. In her moral thought, George Eliot always regarded abstraction as potentially dangerous. She expresses this most powerfully in chapter 61 of *Middlemarch*, writing of Bulstrode: 'There is no general doctrine which is not capable of eating out our morality if unchecked by the deep-seated habit of direct fellow-feeling with individual fellow-men.' The same point is made less clearly at the end of the chapter in *The Mill on the Floss* concerning Dr Kenn's advice to Maggie: 'to lace ourselves up in formulas of that sort is to repress all the divine promptings and inspirations that spring from growing insight and sympathy'. The effect on her art can be seen in the letter to Payne quoted above (p. 154): 'I become more and more timid – with less daring to adopt any formula which does not get itself clothed for me in some human figure and individual experience, and perhaps that is a sign that if I help others to see at all it must be through that medium of art.'[5] Another letter I have quoted from earlier provides further clarification, the letter to Harrison of 15 August 1866, in which she writes of 'the severe effort of trying to make certain ideas thoroughly incarnate, as if they had revealed themselves to me first in the flesh and not in the spirit'.[6] In other words, her moral thought is initially in abstract terms, but then checked through embodiment in her naturalistic art.

For a writer who does not believe in a transcendent purpose, which will ultimately be worked out independently of human action, the temptation to regard fiction as a means of re-shaping the brute world according to his own desires is particularly strong. The advantage here of the naturalistic form is that the writer's fantasy is to some extent disciplined by the independent life of his characters. Clearly the traits of the characters are selected by the writer in accordance with his general purpose; but once those characters are set in motion they cannot, without causing the reader aesthetic dissatisfaction, be manipulated in a way inconsistent with their natures to make the writer's points. There is what I would call *resistance* in the medium. There are of course, many forms of resistance in different aesthetic media. In the hands of an intelligent poet, metre, for example, can provide the resistance to self-indulgence which can constitute a crucial discipline. But the novel, with its very few generic formal constraints, can offer dangerously little resistance to authorial fantasy: the author can become like a god creating his own world, which may be pleasant enough to inhabit, but bear no valuable relationship to the greater one outside it. George Eliot makes a related point, in a remark directed obliquely at the innumerable minor novels about education written in the late eighteenth and early nineteenth centuries. She is referring to Tom at Mr Stelling's: 'he was not a boy in the abstract, existing solely to illustrate the evils of a mistaken education, but a boy made of flesh and blood, with dispositions not entirely at the mercy of circumstances'. Tom clearly forms part of the over-all design of the book, but he cannot be reduced to the status of a mere example. He does not merely illustrate the thesis that the absence of pity reduces man's humanity: his independence as a centre of consciousness offers resistance to the thesis, and so forces George Eliot to refine it. Specifically, we see the elements of pity in the boy Tom, which are gradually reduced as he follows the path of development charted partly by himself, partly by external events; so he does not appear to us as a monster, but as a well-intentioned, limited man, for whom we can feel the sympathy, which George Eliot wished to provoke, more than she wished to prove any thesis. The *resistance* works within the general purpose of the author, but has the effect of refining it.

But although it does include this resistance to an over-theoretic account of life, George Eliot's naturalistic form is, as I have said above, not a naively literal attempt to mimic the untidiness of quotidian actuality. Her fiction is, quite consciously, fiction – deliberately fashioning an artefact, making a model. Many novelists, conscious of the paucity of known conventions operative in their medium, have included within their own novels instructions to the reader on how he should read. This seems to me what Dickens is doing, for example, when in chapter 5 of *Bleak House* he very explicitly draws the parallel between Krook and the Lord Chancellor – giving an example of the kind of parodic relationship which an informed reader will then find between various sets of almost all the characters in the book. George Eliot is, I think, teaching the reader in a similar way when, in response to Tulliver's figurative expression of exasperation, 'You'd want me not to hire a good waggoner, 'cause he'd got a mole on his face', Mrs Tulliver expounds at some length her general opinion of moles. Tulliver replies, 'No, no, Bessy; I didn't mean justly the mole; I meant it to stand for summat else.' George Eliot's book requires a reader more intelligent than Bessy: the literal facts of it are not 'justly' all there is to it; it is a model with implications.

I have already traced the patterning of the divergent developments of Maggie and Tom and of Maggie's relationships with Philip and with Stephen; the point can be made here by reference to more minor examples of the structure of George Eliot's model. There is a short passage on Mr Stelling which seems on first encounter to have no real relevance to the development of the book: 'Perhaps it is, that high achievements demand some other unusual qualification besides an unusual desire for high prizes . . .'. But it is in fact set up as a foil to the ambitions of his pupil, Tom, which are at first equally illusory but within a short space of time transformed by diligent application. A slightly more extended instance centres on Wakem. His concept of revenge is more sophisticated and calculated than Tulliver's – 'To see an enemy humiliated gives a certain contentment, but this is jejune compared with the highly blent satisfaction of seeing him humiliated by your benevolent action or concession on his behalf.' But Philip manages to persuade him out of a self-defeating perpetuation of rancour towards the younger Tullivers; and he succeeds primarily because he makes Wakem feel 'you're the only fellow that knows the best of me', as Tulliver felt of his favourite child. Then Wakem's willingness to let Philip marry Maggie, despite the whipping he received from her father, is finally to be contrasted with the refusal of Tom to sanction the marriage, even when Lucy, speaking like Philip to Wakem, assumes he will be more magnanimous than his previous behaviour suggests. This sort of patterning is obviously much more extensively spread through *Middlemarch*, but to a lesser extent it is also in *The Mill on the Floss* one of George Eliot's means of pursuing her purposes within the limits imposed by the *resistance* of the naturalistic form.

A more obvious instruction issued to the reader, about the idiom of the book, is the opening of the first chapter of Book 4, the contrasted descriptions of the banks of the Rhine, lined with romantic castles, and those of the Rhone, lined with sordid ruined villages. It is quite clearly a means of indicating the position of the book in relation to the customary contrast, extending well back into the eighteenth century, between novels and romances. The Rhine scene suggests to the imagination 'a day of romance' with robber barons and drunken ogres; the Rhone 'a narrow, ugly, grovelling existence', which prepares us for the following extended discussion of the 'sordid life . . . irradiated by . . . no romantic visions' of the Tulliver and Dodson families. A related signal is given mid-way through Book 6 by Lucy, whose intelligence is not much greater than Mrs Tulliver's. She says to Maggie, 'I shall puzzle my small brain to contrive some plot that will bring everybody into the right mind, so that you may marry Philip, when I marry – somebody else' [i.e. Stephen]. The plot her small brain has conceived here is the traditional crossed-pairs-resolving-into-double-pairs pattern of commonplace love romances of the late eighteenth and early nineteenth centuries. *The Mill on the Floss*, of course, dislocates that wish-fulfillment pattern completely: Maggie's relationship with Stephen ruins his engagement to Lucy and cannot, given Maggie's nature, conclude in marriage, and the two paries injured by it, Lucy and Philip, could not conceivably pair off as even a partial romance conclusion.

The distinction implied here, between romance and realism, can be defined a little more precisely by extending the terms of reference beyond the prose fiction of the period George Eliot had in mind. Taking a slightly wider perspective, I should want to distinguish four versions of the relation between fiction and reality. Firstly, fiction may be offered as an escape from reality – the wish-fulfilment of a low order of romance. Secondly, it may be offered as a means of access to a higher reality than is normally experienced in mundane life; this is the form of the high romance of much medieval literature, of *Sir Gawain and the Green Knight*, for example. Thirdly, fiction may be regarded as the only reality, apart from the brute chaos of things permanently incomprehensible to the incorrigibly pattern-making habits of the human mind; this is a form of fiction offered by certain modern writers of rather desperate philosophical persuasions. Fourthly, fiction may act as a means of articulating a relationship between desire and reality. On my account, *Utopia* and *Rasselas* belong in the fourth of these categories. But when one thinks of *The Mill on the Floss* in relation to them, only a Lucy-like critic could be content with cramping it into one. In my second chapter on it, I tried to show that to some extent it also is largely concerned with relationships between fantasy and reality, of various forms in minds of various casts. But although there is no pre-existent higher reality as there is in medieval romance, I have also emphasised the ways in which the development of Maggie and of a responsive reader can be seen as a route to higher values than those of the Tullivers and Dodsons, the shallow Stephen and the well-intentioned but unimaginative Lucy: fiction has to some extent become the means of fashioning the higher values. There is no revealed model of the best form of human nature, which for More and Johnson could be an implied reality, superior to the models projected by human dream: the model of the best has to be created by man. Since that is so, George Eliot's fiction, as opposed to her characters' fantasy, becomes the means of access to the best available reality. In fact, since the possibility of objective validation is removed by the rejection of Revelation, the subjective persuasion of the novel becomes a highly important means of access. 'I think', said George Eliot, in the letter to Harrison I have quoted before, 'aesthetic teaching is the highest of all teaching.'

Unfortunately I have to conclude this chapter with an argument that the end of *The Mill on the Floss* is largely fiction of the form defined in my first category above. The ending has frequently been criticised as a very crude piece of authorial fantasy. I think it involves much fantasy but that it is not altogether crude. As Barbara Hardy has pointed out, it is not unprepared: the river-images and the references to death by drowning are actually rather oppressively multiplied throughout the book.[7] In addition one might add that it is a culmination of the pattern of reconciliation with Tom which I referred to in Chapter

9 above (brother and sister drown in an embrace), and a culmination of the pattern of return home which can be traced, from the gypsy episode, through compliance with Tom's demand to stop the meetings with Philip, to return to St Ogg's from Stephen at Mudport. 'Which is the way home?' asks Maggie in the flood. But both culminations exist on the level of fantasy as well as of deliberated fictional completion.

The reconciliation with Tom, as represented by a final embrace, necessitates a change from the Tom we last saw (his last words to Maggie were: 'the sight of you is hateful to me', and we are told by the narrator, two chapters later, that 'the sight of her, as he had told her, was hateful to him'). So we are informed that when he is rescued by Maggie there was 'a new revelation to his spirit, of the depths in life, that had lain beyond his vision which he had fancied so keen and clear'. If we are thinking only of Maggie here, this is potentially credible. We have seen the gradual growth of Maggie's virtues, and it is possible for a profoundly virtuous action by one person to give another person a sense of what it is to be more fully human than he is able to become unaided. That happens credibly in *Middlemarch* when Dorothea visits Rosamond. But here the outward drama leaves no time for sufficient dialogue, or sufficient analysis of what passes through Tom's mind, for us to believe Tom could be so changed. The author's fantasy has ignored the *resistance* offered by the character of Tom.

On each of the previous occasions, the return home has been in effect a return from romance to reality, a return which has been accompanied by some sense of relief, but which Maggie has made progressively less for the sake of that relief, progressively more for the sake of obedience to her growing virtues. In this last instance, that progression is broken. Just before the flood, Maggie has faced the full dreary reality entailed by her virtuous choice not to rejoin Stephen. At the parallel moment with Philip, she fell. 'After hours of clear reasoning and firm conviction, we snatch at any sophistry that will nullify our long struggles, and bring us the defeat that we love better than victory,' and Maggie jumps at Philip's sophistry. The only sophistry which can make her waver towards Stephen is his appeal to her pity: she resists it, knowing full well that she is not making a grand dramatic gesture, but a choice which will entail on herself very lengthy, very unromantic suffering ('I am so young, so healthy . . .'). From this suffering, the return home is no return to reality but to a fantasy version of her childhood with Tom. Ostensibly the flood is the final action of external reality, but it does not work, as such reality works elsewhere, as a discipline on Maggie's fantasy. On the contrary, it induces in her (as the drift with Stephen had done) a state which is described as 'dreamlike', and as that gives way to full consciousness, 'there rushed in the vision of the old home – and Tom' (and then comes the cry 'Which is the way home?') In the parallel dream, in the chapter called 'Waking', on the boat to Mudport, there were two wakings – a 'false waking' to a dream that 'she was a child again in the parlour at evening twilight, and Tom was not really angry', and then the real waking to the facts of adult life she actually confronts. At the conclusion there is no second waking, and Maggie's life ends in the sugar-plum world of a surrogate heaven – 'living through again in one supreme moment the days when they had clasped their little hands in love, and roamed the daisied fields together'.

The romance Lucy would like to have written does not seem much cruder than this fantasy of a return from the complexities of adult life to a dream-version of childhood. There is no way of shifting responsibility for it onto Maggie: the Maggie we see in the last chapters before the flood has more than adequate maturity to reject such a fantasy; the very success of George Eliot's form to the time of the flood makes painfully obvious this lapse from naturalistic novel to low romance. Yet as I suggested above, the ending is not unprepared and even seems the deliberate culmination of large-scale patterns in the book's structure: it cannot be regarded as a sudden abberration. Various biographical explanations have been put forward, including, very plausibly, George Eliot's undesired estrangement from her own brother. But I think the problem lies rather deeper than that. The return home is clearly to a large extent reconciliation with Tom – the inscription on their tomb which ends the book emphasises it ('In their death they were not divided') – but home means more to Maggie, and to George Eliot, than Tom alone: home and the past life focused there have always been the ultimate location of value for Maggie, the place where the relationship with her father grew into a 'force' in her moral life, a place, as I have shown in this chapter, in itself effectually sacred. In terms of the fiction, home has in George Eliot's book the status of both the 'choice of eternity' in Johnson's and the world of daily life (as opposed to Utopia) in More's: it is the location both of ultimate value and of the responsibilities to which one must return. But for George Eliot there was no eternity, no final location of value. She certainly yearned to go there, as much as Maggie whom she allows to go; but for her it was No Place. One can return to the past metaphorically as a source of value, but one cannot return to the past literally, finally. So at the end we have in effect a final break-down of form. Until the last moment, the attraction of utopia is resisted and disciplined; at the last moment, the return home, which was to have been a return to responsibility, is actually an excursion into fantasy, to utopia. Of course it spoils the book; of course it betrays George Eliot's personal needs in a most unbecoming way. But I am inclined to think that the needs demand more sympathy than the failure reproof. I shall discuss them further in the next chapter.

12 *The Mill on the Floss*: 'Which is the way home?'

In this conclusion of my discussion of *The Mill on the Floss*, I want to comment on the adequacy of George Eliot's concept of human purpose as I take it to be embodied in her novel. This is to stray into an area regarded as taboo by 'sensitive' critics; but not to meet at that level a great novelist, who in Leslie Stephen's words 'ventured to speculate on human life and its meaning', seems to me failure of nerve rather than observance of professional discipline.

As I have already shown, I take her concept of purpose to be that of the nurture of a full humanity by an individual, within the framework of a more general evolution of the human race towards such humanity. This can be expressed either as the cultivation of virtues or (less adequately in my view) as the discipline of imagination away from fantasy towards sympathy. According to both ways of expressing it, the human quality of most importance is morally intelligent pity.

Of the other dominant models of social and individual purpose current in her time, it can certainly be said that she had no time for utilitarianism. Her fable 'Brother Jacob' is largely directed against the calculation of consequences which is central to utilitarian ethics. 'David was by no means impetuous; he was a young man greatly given to calculate consequences, a habit which has been held to be the foundation of virtue. But somehow it had not precisely that effect in David: he calculated whether an action would harm himself, or whether it would only harm other people. In the former case he was very timid about satisfying his immediate desires, but in the latter he would risk the result with much courage.' By chapter 72 of *Middlemarch* there is no doubt that the reader is expected to share the views of Dorothea, who is 'discontented with Mr Farebrother. She disliked this cautious weighing of consequences, instead of an ardent faith in efforts of

213

justice and mercy, which would conquer by their emotional force'.
The rejection, by the narrator of *The Mill on the Floss*, of Philip's
consequentialist arguments ('If we only look far enough off for the
consequences of our actions, we can always find some point in the
combination of results by which those actions can be justified') is
not over-influenced by the consciousness of Maggie; similar views
are commonly explicit elsewhere in George Eliot's works.

In very conscious opposition to some aspects of utilitarianism,
Mill put forward in the third chapter of his essay *On Liberty* a
concept of individual self-development clearly derived from
Romantic thought. I have no scope here to do justice to the
complexity of Mill's thought on this matter, but I take his as a
particularly intelligent form of the idea, expressed almost con-
temporaneously with *The Mill on the Floss* (1859). He quotes
Wilhelm von Humboldt, whose thinking derived most immediately from Goethe: 'the end of man . . . is the highest and most
harmonious development of his powers to a complete and
consistent whole'.[1] In Mill's mind, this takes a form in some ways
close to George Eliot's. 'To say that one person's desires and
feelings are stronger and more various than those of another, is
merely to say that he has more of the raw material of human
nature, and is therefore capable, perhaps of more evil, but
certainly of more good'; whereas if people follow what Mill calls
the 'Calvinistic theory' of mere conformity, they reach a condition
such that 'by dint of not following their own nature they have no
nature to follow: their human capacities are withered and
starved'. The metaphor underlying his thought, like George
Eliot's, is organic. 'Human nature is not a machine to be built
after a model, and set to do exactly the work prescribed for it, but a
tree, which requires to grow and develop itself on all sides,
according to the tendency of the inward forces which make it a
living thing.' Those who constrain growth within preconceived
frames inhibit proper human development, 'just as many have
thought that trees are a much finer thing when clipped into
pollards, or cut out into figures of animals, than as nature made
them'. The difference between Mill and George Eliot becomes
clearer when he leaves metaphor and becomes more explicit:
' "Pagan self-assertion" is one of the elements of human worth, as
well as "Christian self-denial".' But they are alike in their
rejection of 'general rules of conduct' as an adequate basis for
moral behaviour – the effect of such rules, says Mill, is 'to maim by

compression, like a Chinese lady's foot, every part of nature which stands out prominently, and tends to make the person markedly dissimilar in outline to commonplace humanity'.

In *The Mill on the Floss* there are two forms of the argument that it is natural for the individual self to develop freely, unrestrained by external models, put forward, as I said in chapter 9, by Philip and by Stephen. Philip's form is not qualified as intelligently as Mill's, by the recognition of the rights of others, but is clearly superior to Stephen's. As Maggie approaches the Red Deeps before the first meeting with Philip there, a description of the trees, with which she is said to have 'a sort of kinship', provides an image of her which contrasts with Mill's tree: 'She was calmly enjoying the free air, while she looked up at the old fir-trees, and thought that those broken ends of branches were the record of past storms, which had only made the red stems soar higher.' The way the image develops in Philip's mind associates him with Mill's form of thought: 'the pity of it, that a mind like hers should be withering in its very youth, like a young forest-tree, for want of the light and space it was formed to flourish in!' Philip puts the argument implied here into very direct terms when he speaks to her: her way of renunciation based on Thomas à Kempis, he says, 'is only a way of escaping pain by starving into dulness all the highest powers of your nature. . . . It makes me wretched to see you benumbing and cramping your nature in this way'. Maggie's subsequent history makes it plain that there is something to be said for Philip's view. He says years later at Lucy's house, 'You want to find out a mode of renunciation that will be an escape from pain. I tell you again, there is no such escape possible except by perverting or mutilating one's nature.' As an escape from pain, which it partly is (though only partly), Maggie's renunciation does have a stunting effect; and also it does not fully work, as Maggie herself admits a few pages further on: 'You used to say I should feel the effect of my starved life, as you called it, and I do. I am too eager in my enjoyment of music and all luxuries, now they are come to me.' Yet this element of truth in what Philip says does not affect the major implication of the fir-tree image: the breaking of the lower branches sends all the vigour of the tree into a growth upwards. Maggie gives explicit answers to Philip, which I quoted in Chapter 9 and will not repeat; but to be fair to Philip, he does develop himself. In his letter to Maggie near the end, he shows he has finally learnt from her what renunciation may mean, and achieved the more important sort of growth which may result from self-restraint. 'The new life I have found in caring for your joy and sorrow more than for what is directly my own, has transformed the spirit of rebellious murmuring into that willing endurance which is the birth of strong sympathy. I think nothing but such complete and intense love could have initiated me into that enlarged life which grows and grows by appropriating the life of others; for before, I was always dragged back from it by ever-present painful self-consciousness.'

Like Philip, Stephen makes frequent appeals to a concept of natural freedom as opposed to artificial restraint. But he has nothing like the image of a fully developed tree at the back of his mind; his image is more of bending before an uncontrollable force. 'It has come upon us without our seeking: it is natural – it has taken hold of me in spite of every effort I have made to resist it. . . . We have proved that the feeling which draws us towards each other is too strong to be overcome: that natural law surmounts every other; we can't help what it clashes with.' Maggie's answer is that such a force would uproot her whole life if she did not resist it. 'It is not the force that ought to rule us – this that we feel for each other; it would rend me away from all that my past life has made dear and holy to me.' In the more abstract language of the sentence I quoted in Chapter 9, she had made the same point earlier: 'Love is natural; but surely pity and faithfulness and memory are natural too.' But it is not merely that the crude form of 'pagan self-assertion' represented by Stephen conflicts with the image of growth and has no exclusive claim on the word *natural*. So far from developing the self, it is actually a restriction. Maggie says to Stephen, when it is clear they have drifted too far, 'You have wanted to deprive me of any choice.' That is not quite fair to Stephen, but it has been the effect of the episode. Surrender to the natural force, which Stephen argues should over-ride all other considerations, leads not to a fuller humanity, but specifically to a loss of properly human autonomy. 'All yielding is attended with a less vivid consciousness than resistance; it is the partial sleep of thought; it is the submergence of our own personality by another.'

In contrast to this, Maggie's general human growth may be seen to some extent as a growth in autonomy. The older generation behaves in a way which could be said to be more determined, in the sense that there is less individual choice involved in specific situations, more automatic reflex. When Mrs

Tulliver asks her sister, Aunt Pullet, to approach Aunt Glegg about the five hundred pounds, she is said to be acting in the hope that 'similar causes may at any time produce different results'. With her husband, as we see repeatedly, this is quite deluded. The Dodsons are equally determined in their behaviour. The extreme case is Mr Pullet with his habitually produced musical box (he knows in advance which tune it is going to play): 'Uncle Pullet had a programme for all great social occasions, and in this way fenced himself in from much painful confusion and perplexing freedom of will.' When the older Dodsons do take moral action, it is normally not against circumstance but in confirmation of it. After the bankruptcy, 'there was a general family sense that a judgement had fallen on Mr Tulliver, which it would be an impiety to counteract by too much kindness'. Similarly, in Tom's opposite situation, Aunt Pullet says, 'now Tom's so lucky, it's nothing but right his friends should look on him and help him'. Tom develops a little towards greater autonomy: his feelings at the time of the bankruptcy are recognised to be Dodson, but his behaviour surprises everyone, and he resists the 'judgement' of circumstance by sustained individual endeavour. But as I have shown before, that sustained endeavour helps also to increase the natural rigidity of his character. The flexibility in Maggie which allows her to grow can only appear to a man such as Tom as inconsistency; 'I never feel certain about anything with *you*. At one time you take pleasure in a sort of perverse self-denial, and at another you have not resolution to resist a thing that you know to be wrong.'

Maggie is fully aware that there is 'a terrible cutting truth' in these words, but she is also aware that the ability to utter them proceeds from an innate narrowness in Tom: 'he was below feeling those mental needs which were often the source of the wrong-doing or absurdity that made her life a planless riddle to him'. What makes Maggie a more fully human individual is partly the innate pity I have discussed before – the sentence following the one I quoted in the last paragraph concerning the 'judgement' on Tulliver is: 'Maggie heard little of this, scarcely ever leaving her father's bedside, where she sat opposite him with her hand on his.' But uncultivated pity is potentially chaotic: 'yielding to the idea of Stephen's suffering was more fatal than the other yielding [to romance], because it was less distinguishable from that sense of others' claims which was the moral basis of her resistance'. What she has to do, as the complications of life unfold, is to develop an understanding of where pity *should* operate and where it should not. Like all organic growth, the process is to a close observer uneven but in a broad perspective steady. From that rather misleading chapter in which Dr Kenn deliberates, it might seem that the ideal which Maggie represents is near the complete autonomy of the existentialist individual or the advocate of what modern Protestant theologians call *situation ethics*. 'Moral judgements must remain false and hollow, unless they are checked and enlightened by a perpetual reference to the special circumstances that mark the individual lot.' This is said to be a 'truth' by the narrator; but the words 'checked and enlightened' are crucial. The morally mature person will *check* his judgements in relation to the circumstances of a specific situation, judgements rooted in a cultivated understanding of the general issues involved. Maggie becomes an autonomous moral being not in the sense that each moral decision is made *ab initio*, but, in the image of the fir-tree, rooted in her past and reaching continuously upwards towards a higher manifestation of her nature. In a more abstract language, I think the word *virtue*, as I defined it in Chapter 9, best makes the point. Maggie does grow morally in a way analogous to organic growth; but George Eliot does have a preconceived image of what it is desirable for her to grow into: the virtues develop from within Maggie, but they have also the status of desiderata which exist independently of her, towards which she grows. Like Mill, George Eliot regards 'general rules' as an inadequate basis for full moral development, but she has an image of completed humanity nearer to a model than what he has in mind in the essay *On Liberty*.

In the rest of this chapter, what I want to argue is that the source and authority of that model are more specifically Christian than George Eliot wished to believe, and that independently of actual Christian faith its status is very precarious.

The first stage of this argument is that there is a crucial duplicity involved in the use of a Christian heroine. George Eliot believed in no transcendent End, but Maggie did. This has, of course, been frequently noted; so has the fact that it is common not only in other George Eliot novels but also in novels by other nineteenth-century writers. But the usual view is that the belief of the character is levelled down to a sort of liberal humanism not dependent on actual Christianity – in George Eliot's case specifically to the demythologised translation of Christian values by Feuerbach. A full treatment of this matter would involve a more extended discussion of Feuerbach than I have scope for here. I shall merely argue from the novel that Maggie uses a specifically Christian language, which in her own person her creator could not have used; and that the development of Maggie's virtues, which constitutes George Eliot's purpose without Purpose, depends on that language.

The first relevant stage of her development is the reading of Thomas à Kempis. It is true that the chief thing Maggie learns from Thomas is simply to shift her focal point from her own desires to the needs of others, through self denial. It is also true that Maggie's reading is guided by the ink markings in her copy – a human hand pointing her attention towards the most general, least specifically Christian thoughts in the book. But even the quotations thus edited cannot exclude explicit articles of faith: 'Both above and below, which way soever thou dost turn thee, everywhere thou shalt find the Cross: and everywhere of necessity thou must have patience, if thou wilt have inward peace, and enjoy an everlasting crown. . . . In heaven ought to be thy dwelling, and all earthly things are to be looked on as they forward thy journey thither.' A little later the narrator is assuring us that the book is a 'lasting record of . . . human consolations.' From her own quotations that can be seen to be clearly untrue: its consolations, in so far as it is concerned with consolation, are actually of a kind George Eliot rejected as 'opium'.[2] She clearly perceived that there was a problem here: the narrator proceeds to confront the difficulty of finding a sense of purpose which might lighten the lives of that portion of society 'condensed in unfragrant deafening factories, cramping itself in mines, sweating at furnaces, grinding, hammering, weaving under more or less oppression of carbonic acid' – 'life in this unpleasurable shape demanding some solution even to unspeculative minds'. And what she offers are explicitly 'motives in an entire absence of high prizes . . . something, clearly, that lies outside personal desires, that includes resignation for ourselves and active love for what is not ourselves'. One might want to challenge that 'clearly' as a rhetorical, not logical, step in the argument; but this is not a philosophical essay. The central point is that George Eliot's own creed is being expressed here in what she called 'formula';[3] the 'human figure' in her novel is motivated by a crucially different creed. At this stage, of course, Maggie is explicitly represented as immature: 'She had not perceived – how could she until she had lived longer? – the inmost truth of the old monk's outpourings, that renunciation remains sorrow, though a sorrow borne willingly.' As she grows up, Maggie does gradually perceive this; but she does so in the terms of 'the old monk', not of the agnostic George Eliot.

What is involved here is the problem of validating a concept of Duty without the other two 'trumpet-calls', God and Immortality, from which she separated it in her famous conversation with F. W. H. Myers. It arises very clearly in one of the dialogues with Philip. Maggie says, 'Our life is determined for us – and it makes the mind very free when we give up wishing, and only think of bearing what is laid upon us, and doing what is given us to do.' Philip replies, in words I have quoted before, 'It seems to me we can never give up longing and wishing while we are thoroughly alive. There are certain things we feel to be beautiful and good and we *must* hunger after them.' Maggie's language here is radically ambiguous. To George Eliot it is merely the language of nineteenth-century determinism – 'determined' refers to the concatenation of internal and external causes operating on individual life, and 'is laid' and 'is given' are metaphorical variants. But for Maggie there is a God who has done the laying and giving. So what Philip says to her is, in her language, literally temptation (at one of the meetings in the Red Deeps she actually says, 'You are a tempter'). George Eliot herself would have countered Philip's *'must'* with her concept of Duty without religious sanction. How adequately she could have answered him is not at the moment in question: the point here is that Maggie does not use her agnostic language. To persuade us that a warm impulsive girl like Maggie could be motivated by her own austere version of Duty, George Eliot would have to have written a different novel. This Maggie can sustain her point of view against Philip by recourse to such thoughts as 'I think we are only like children, that some one who is wiser is taking care of' – a sentence which can, in a way George Eliot could not herself imitate, be followed immediately by, 'Is it not right to resign ourselves entirely, whatever may be denied us?' In her fiction at least, the values she wished to sever from dogmatic Christianity are not so severed.

In the interesting essay I have referred to before,[4] Barbara Hardy touches on the role of religion in the book, and like most modern critics she thinks it small. Maggie's 'God can merge into the God of our anguished cries to no God' and what turns the book suddenly into a 'Providence novel at the end' is the removal of the protracted ordeal of undramatic renunciation by the flood which effectually substitutes a form of 'opium'. It is true that George Eliot had a particular distaste for the Christian use of ultimate reward or punishment as a motive for moral behaviour, and the ending, among its other faults, rewards Maggie in a way which conflicts with that distaste. But the last quotation in my penultimate paragraph ('the inmost truth of the old monk's outpourings [is], that renunciation remains sorrow, though a sorrow borne willingly') shows that George Eliot was aware that not all Christian action is motivated by a crude conception of providence. Maggie does not learn an ultra-Christian form of renunciation; she learns to understand Thomas better. This is explicit in the chapter called 'Waking': 'she had thought [renunciation] was quiet ecstasy; she saw it face to face now – that sad patient loving strength which holds the clue of life, and saw that the thorns were for ever pressing on its brow'. The phrase 'clue of life', picked up from a preceding sentence, refers to what she learnt from Thomas. Again just before the flood, Thomas comes to her mind: 'I have received the Cross, I have received it from Thy hand; I will bear it, and bear it till death, as Thou hast laid it upon me.' The ending is as untrue to Maggie's mature understanding of Christian submission as it is to George Eliot's concept of 'clear-eyed endurance'.

As for Maggie's attitude to God, it is true that she does invoke Him occasionally in the manner suggested by Professor Hardy. When she says on Lucy's last visit, 'God bless you for coming, Lucy', she might well not mean it literally. But when she says a page later, 'I pray to God continually that I may never be the cause of sorrow to you any more,' the word 'continually' makes it more likely to be a true prayer than mere exclamation. Elsewhere there are instances where there can be no doubt at all. 'I couldn't live in peace if I put the shadow of a wilful sin between myself and God.' An agnostic could not speak like that. A page later Maggie speaks of Philip in the language I analysed above: 'He was given to me that I might make his lot less hard.' Just before the flood, the language becomes more evasive ('Her soul went out to the Unseen Pity that would be with her to the end'). But the reason is an unease in George Eliot. Maggie has just been remembering a quotation from Thomas à Kempis; it is George Eliot who is trying to translate the Holy Ghost into Feuerbachian love. The character with whom we are asked to sympathise does not think in demythologised terms. When she speaks of 'the divine voice within us', she, unlike George Eliot, means it quite literally. George Eliot believed that human pity could be fully cultivated without recourse to more than a metaphorical Unseen Pity; but that is not what she has shown in this novel, or in her other novels dealing with Christian characters.

It is perhaps a partial recognition of the difficulties she was in here that is responsible for the unsatisfactory treatment of Dr Kenn. As a man, he is represented as being of abnormal sympathetic understanding: at the bazaar he shows 'penetrating kindness' and 'helpful pity'. As a priest, he is represented as the advocate of a sort of demythologised Church acting in the role which George Eliot herself found most sympathetic: 'the Church ought to represent the feeling of the community, so that every parish should be a family knit together by Christian brotherhood under a spiritual father'. But at the same time, George Eliot wants to use him to show the failure of the contemporary Church to fulfil such a role. So in the deliberations which follow his longest talk with Maggie (Book 6, chapter 2), he is made first to regard 'the idea of an ultimate marriage between Stephen and Maggie as the least evil' – an idea which would cause least friction in the community, but which involves incredible imperceptiveness about Maggie's character. Against that he has to be made aware, since he is not to be a moral blockhead, that 'the principle on which she had acted was a safer guide than any balancing of consequences'. But on the other hand, he has to be made impotent, since the Church, in George Eliot's view, was failing, and Kenn seems to have no guide other than her concept of 'community' – 'intervention was too dubious a responsibility to be lightly incurred'. When he finally gives way under the pressure of public opinion and begs Maggie to move to another parish, he is actually made to think in the consequentialist terms he had previously rejected: continued support of Maggie 'was likely to obstruct his usefulness as a clergyman'. To fit George Eliot's dogma, Kenn has rather resolutely to be made a failed Feuerbachian. The incoherence of that with his supposed sensitivity is a real but minor blemish in the book. It is much more damaging to George Eliot's general views that Maggie coherently follows not

Feuerbach but the very specific Christian teaching of Thomas à Kempis.

George Eliot's alternative to specific Christianity may be described as christianity with a small 'c' (Christian values without belief in Christian dogma); in the second stage of my argument here, I want to consider the adequacy of that as a human end, independently of the fact that it is not what we have in the case of Maggie Tulliver. As I have said before, this is seen as an individual end within the context of a general social end, which in turn is seen as the extension of biological evolution. I shall discuss the social end first, then the individual end.

The general relationship between social development and natural evolution is hinted at a number of times – for example in the opening chapter of Book 4: 'I have a cruel conviction that the lives these ruins [on the banks of the Rhone] are the traces of . . . will be swept into the same oblivion with the generations of ants and beavers.' A page later the Dodsons and Tullivers are referred to as 'emmet-like'. As man is a higher order of animal than literal ants, so Maggie is a higher order of human being than the metaphorical ants of the earlier generation. In the ways I have shown before, she develops her humanity out of an understanding of her past and of the influences it has on her, an understanding intelligent enough for her to shape the effect of her past deliberately: she is profoundly affected by it, rather than unconsciously determined in her behaviour, like an ant. The concepts underlying this have been traced best by Bernard Paris. I will not try to summarise his findings, but merely borrow from his reference to G. H. Lewes's *Study of Psychology*, an area of Lewes's work which George Eliot referred to as 'the supremely interesting element in the thinking of our time'. Lewes argues that the specifically human stage in the evolutionary process was the appearance of consciousness, in particular the consciousness of others, as distinct from but like oneself – the social consciousness which is the basis of moral action. 'The law of animal action is Individualism; its motto is "Each for himself against all." The ideal of human action is Altruism; its motto is "Each *with* others, all for each." '[5] This seems to me to be a particularly important formulation of the significance George Eliot attached, for many other reasons and following many other contemporary thinkers, to altruism, since it offers a scientific authority, rather than one which derives from any conscious secularisation of Christian

values. It offers, in effect, a quite independent argument for the
superiority of altruism to egoism: specifically human social
structures depend on altruism, in the sense that without it
mankind would degenerate to a lower order of evolution. Small 'c'
christianity seems to be entailed on any human being who wishes
to remain superior to the apes.

I will not comment on the adequacy of this argument any
further than is relevant to *The Mill on the Floss* – the general
answers are too obvious to need making. Firstly, large 'C'
Christianity had existed at St Ogg's for at least several centuries,
and yet in the generation preceding Maggie's 'one sees little trace
of religion, still less of a distinctively Christian creed. Their belief
in the Unseen, so far as it manifests itself at all, seems to be rather
of a pagan kind; their moral notions, though held with strong
tenacity, seem to have no standard beyond hereditary custom'.
This is what has developed out of generations 'when people could
be greatly wrought upon by their faith'. It is not easy to imagine
how small 'c' christianity could take more permanent hold on the
imagination of ordinary people. The honesty of the tale belies the
meliorism of the teller.

Secondly, Maggie is by any account a very extraordinary
person. Very few human individuals have both that degree of
imagination and that degree of intelligence. Yet she has a difficult
and protracted struggle to achieve a mature altruism. It is not
easy to believe that for more ordinary individuals there can be
more than Mrs Tulliver's leap of motherly love for a rejected
daughter, or Philip's belated, and perhaps impermanent, understanding of what Maggie had said about endurance. It is true that
Maggie had far to go, that the morality of her parents and their
siblings was narrow; but for a latter-day Maggie to have a less
difficult path, the ethic of her society would have to be more
advanced; and on the showing of George Eliot's novels, the only
hope of advance is through individuals like Maggie.

Thirdly, there is in *The Mill on the Floss*, explicitly at several
points and implicitly almost throughout, a kind of nostalgia which
is not reconcilable with the meliorism based on evolutionary
thought. The ethics of the Dodsons and Tullivers may be narrow,
but they have an integrity of which the honesty of George Eliot's
irony exposes the absence in a later generation: 'These narrow
notions about debt, held by the old-fashioned Tullivers, may
perhaps excite a smile on the faces of many readers in these days of

wide commercial views and wide philosophy, according to which everything rights itself without any trouble of ours.' After a similar sentence I have quoted before (p. 198), the nostalgia is even more directly expressed: 'Ah! even Mrs Glegg's day seems far back in the past now, separated from us by changes that widen the years.' In analysing the first chapter (p. 170ff above), I emphasised the qualifications, but the dominant tone is very obviously nostalgic, and that tone then resonates throughout the book. As the waggoner was hungry and his horses over-worked, so the life that centres on Dorlcote Mill is hard and sometimes harsh; but it has a strong sort of simplicity, beside which the more 'advanced' society of Lucy's house is very superficial; and the life of Mudport seems unlikely to be superior. We do not see the world the narrator inhabits, but irony such as, 'All this, you remember, happened in those dark ages when there were no schools of design – before schoolmasters were invariably men of scrupulous integrity, and before the clergy were all men of enlarged minds and varied culture', does not encourage us to believe it better. The ending of the book, with all its faults, has a Maggie returning to an earlier stage of moral development, a stage of impulsive love rather than complicated moral decision, which is deeply analogous to the return of the book to a point in English history when a girl of outstanding intelligence would not, like Marian Evans, have been disposed to question Christian dogma, a point when no difficult justification for renunciation was required, since it was truly a matter of 'binding belief', to use the phrase from the 1873 letter to Cross about attending church.[6] 'Which is the way home?' is more than Maggie's question. The chapter describing St Ogg's (Book 1, chapter 12), like the Prelude of *Middlemarch*, sets the age of heroism in the distant past; the present of the novel concerns a comparatively narrow, restricting world; but the present of the narrator seems superior, on the evidence of the novel, only in the commercial greed which is nearer to Lewes's law of animal action than his ideal of human action. The only sign of the 'growing good of the world' referred to at the end of *Middlemarch* lies in the individual growth of Maggie, to which I shall now turn.

The word *virtue* as I defined it in an earlier chapter and the thinking subsumed within that word, seem to me an adequate solution at the level of the individual to the problem of developing sympathy into consistently altruistic behaviour. *Mere* sympathy is not adequate: sympathy for Stephen leads potentially to chaos, even after the romance aspect of the episode has given way to protracted mundane difficulty. The refining of sympathetic imagination, away from imagination as fantasy, is only effective while the drift with Stephen is a romance; it does not help at the very last in her sequence of choices, the point when it seems that sympathy for Stephen's 'pain' might over-ride the other obligations ('It was Stephen's tone of misery [in his letter] . . . that made the balance tremble'). But *virtue*, with its language of what *is to be* done, can with real cogency prevail over impulse: 'she should feel again what she had felt when Lucy stood by her, when Philip's letter had stirred again all the fibres that bound her to the calmer past'.

There are, however, grave difficulties involved in basing a non-religious ethic on what is essentially a model of ideal humanity. This is not, of course, to say that there are not safer bases for non-religious ethics (very few modern philosophers would share Nietzsche's view quoted above, p. 155); but I do not recall any which have the emotive power of George Eliot's (or of Conrad's, which are similar, though less confident). What satisfies philosophers does not necessarily much move men. I have come back here to a point which arose in discussing *Utopia*: there are problems in the usage of a word like *human*, a word which can be both descriptive and normative. I defined *virtue* as 'a cultivated disposition such that one can reasonably say that a man who possesses it, and acts accordingly, is more fully human than a man who does not'. That is really an attempt to turn a normative model of human nature into a descriptive one. To lack pity, for example, is in this view to be an incomplete human being in essentially the same way as to lack feet is to be incomplete. I think that is true, and I have tried to show George Eliot's moral thought is based on that assumption. But Nietzsche would reply that pity is only *human* in a normative sense (and as such he would reject it), not in a descriptive sense: men obviously need feet; they do not obviously need pity – we merely desiderate a model which includes pity because we have been conditioned by centuries of Christian perversion. His own normative model is notoriously opposite: 'At the risk of annoying innocent ears I set it down that egoism pertains to the essence of the noble soul, I mean the immovable faith that to a being such as "we are" other beings have to be subordinate by their nature, and sacrifice themselves to us.'[7] My own recourse at this point is to a revealed model I regard as objectively true; but I do not know what answer George Eliot could give to Nietzsche's objection. Her model of normative humanity, upon which her concept of human purpose depends, is derived from a supernatural belief she rejected: in that sense it is parasitic and hollow.

The difficulties in fact seem to compound as one tries to envisage a possible answer. The whole framework of George Eliot's thought is, as I have stressed repeatedly, based on concepts of growth and evolution. She could, then, perhaps, say that pity is a quality which is *becoming* human in the descriptive sense. It is not descriptively human in the generation of the older Dodsons and Tullivers; but one can see it becoming so in Maggie, as the representative of a larger humanity evolving through the meliorist process. Yet it is formidably difficult to fit a static model into an evolutionary framework. Maggie grows, but the desiderated model towards which she grows is itself static. The structure of the book shows clearly that George Eliot regarded Tom's justice as morally more advanced than Tulliver's revenge, and less advanced than Maggie's just pity. But it is equally clear that George Eliot has no conception of the evolution of a virtue greater than pity. So the question arises – on whose authority did the evolution of the moral nature of man stop at a point which Maggie found Thomas à Kempis defining in relation to a life which George Eliot believed ended two thousand years earlier? It is easy enough to fit an evolutionary model into the framework of an evolutionary conception of moral life. Just as in the history of art, man has developed new ways of seeing, so in the history of moral thought new models of man can emerge which will pass from the normative to the descriptive as men in general gradually catch up with their intellectual leaders. The art and the moral norm which are revolutionary in one generation become accepted and so widely imitated as to be a descriptive model in the next. That is relatively logical, even though rather comically incongruous with the recorded history of man if the evolution is supposed to be a progress. But it is not what George Eliot offers. Like Maggie, she wants not to reject the past and its beliefs, nor even just to incorporate them, but to derive her binding authority from them. The model she offers the future is a static one drawn from the past. More fundamentally than evolution, the end she desires is a return. But the framework of her thought is one in which return is illogical. 'Which is the way home?' That is where she wants to go, but meliorism is not a helpful route.

As to the cogency of the model independently of the Christian beliefs from which it is derived, some blunt reservations cannot, in honesty to the book itself, be suppressed. Maggie is really the only person who grows through the suffering entailed by her large humanity; and on herself the humanity entails far more suffering than anything else. Tom drowns almost immediately after his (incredible) expansion of vision; Stephen would never understand Maggie; Philip, on the report of the Conclusion, remains in a state of nostalgia for the days of the Red Deeps. The Conclusion itself projects a fitting image of a largely static nature – 'Nature repairs her ravages – repairs them with her sunshine, and with human labour.' In so far as it has changed, it has not evolved, but has been scarred: 'Nature repairs her ravages – but not all. . . . To the eyes that have dwelt on the past, there is no thorough repair.' With respect to Maggie, the protracted ordeal of her life is very like that of the old woman in the picture she describes in her childhood: 'they've put her in to find out whether she's a witch or no, and if she swims she's a witch, and if she's drowned – and killed, you know – she's innocent, and not a witch, but only a poor silly old woman. But what good would it do her then, you know, when she was drowned? Only, I suppose, she'd go to heaven, and God would make it up to her'. For George Eliot there was, of course, no heaven, and the sugar-plum surrogate paradise of Maggie's last 'supreme moment' is no alternative answer to the question I have just quoted. Unless the world of the reader is to be believed superior to that of the book – and the whole convention of the book implies that the worlds are much the same – there would seem nothing to be gained by choosing the way of Maggie's virtues, and much to be lost. If there's no God, what good is virtue when no one gains by it?

I put that question with deliberate vulgarity, because that is not how a reader, of any persuasion, who has any sensitivity to George Eliot, actually responds. George Eliot herself had a very austere conception of duty as an end of human endeavour independently of any personal benefit to be derived from it. She had many objections to specific Christian belief, but the one most frequently expressed in her letters and essays is that it debased moral action by introducing as a motive the expectation of personal reward or punishment in an after-life, so that good is not pursued because it is good but because it brings reward. (As I have argued above, More – like most Christians – would regard this as a debased understanding of Christian teaching: that motive is put forward by the Utopians). To some extent, the meliorism became for her a vicarious alternative: the point of virtuous action is, to borrow a phrase from *Middlemarch*, to widen the skirts of light, and in that book the 'incalculably diffusive' effect of virtuous action is certainly greater than in *The Mill on the Floss*. But there too the effect we see is short-lived: Rosamond does credibly respond to Dorothea, but it does not lastingly affect her attitude to her husband; Mrs Bulstrode, through that most moving demonstration of solidarity with her husband in chapter 74, does profoundly help him, but even after that his pride continues to cut him off from the full love she could offer him. Meliorism may have been a personal opiate for George Eliot, but on the evidence of the novels the 'growing good of mankind' seems a remote prospect. Yet, curiously perhaps, that makes the virtue more moving. In any utilitarian perspective it is more or less futile, more or less foolish. Lydgate's pitying fidelity towards his worthless wife, quite unappreciated by her, unperceived by anyone else except Dorothea, who does not need to learn from it, is really, in an atheist world, very foolish. So in Conrad's *Secret Agent* the most innocent person is literally an idiot, and the only heroism is shown by the two least intelligent normal people, Mrs Verloc and her mother, who each remain ignorant of the true nature of the other's self-sacrifice. But it is not only Christian readers who feel compelled to use words such as *noble* and *heroic* of Mrs Bulstrode, Lydgate, Mrs Verloc's mother, Mrs Gould, Maggie. Foolish as they may be, such models remain profoundly moving: in defiance of any pedantic distinction between *normative* and *descriptive*, they continue to compel the response, *'That* is what it means to be truly human.'

Perhaps for many, certainly for some, they point the way to a more secure home than their creators found. But for those who can go no further, they stand as the embodiment of an aspiration, which seems to have no ultimate end, but which undeniably continues to exist. Maggie's virtue, in particular, incorporates a respect both for her individual past and for the wider human past. For those who, like George Eliot, delight more in 'emotional agreement' with men of past ages than in 'intellectual difference' from them, the book exists as a meeting-place; and those who live by trying to make sense of their past rather than by rejecting it, find 'emotional agreement' with Maggie's individual history. In those respects the book itself represents a way home. But 'emotional agreement' is sadly volatile.[8] Bernard Paris, who wrote what is probably the best exposition of George Eliot's structure of values because at that time he virtually shared it, had within four years swung to a quite alien structure which made him reject both George Eliot's moral understanding of Maggie and the whole theory of her fiction as 'experiments in life' which underlies it.[9] Yet for those who both refuse to deny that the characters I named at the end of my last paragraph (for example) embody what they wish to call most deeply human, and have no recourse to ultimate validation, 'emotional agreement' has to serve. The alternatives are to adopt a new model of man which can act as the focus of a different conception of ultimate purpose, or to give up hope of such a purpose. In Chapters 13 to 16 I shall discuss a great novel by a man who would not give up, but who I think shows, through his own combination of honesty and self-deception, that the human pursuit of new models is even more precarious than 'emotional agreement' with foolish old ones.

13   *Women in Love*: Dead Ends

The fact that *Women in Love* was written during the First World War clearly influenced some of the attitudes it includes, as I shall show later, but Lawrence's belief, that the human ideals of the past were dead, was no temporary reaction to the upheaval of that time. In 1927 he expressed very clearly his rejection of the old models of man, which he thought could mean rejecting models altogether: 'All our education is but the elaborating of the picture. "A good little girl" – "a brave boy" – "a noble woman" – "a strong man" – "a productive society" – "a progressive humanity" – it is all the picture. It is all living from the outside to the inside. It is all the death of spontaneity. . . . If we could once get into our heads – or if we once dare to admit to one another – that we are *not* the picture, and the picture is not what we are, then we might lay a new hold on life. For the picture is really the death, and certainly the neurosis of us all.'[1] Some of the characters in *Women in Love* live according to the old pictures; many react against them in a merely mechanical way, which Lawrence regards as equally destructive of life; only Birkin and Ursula gradually learn to 'lay a new hold on life'. I shall discuss Birkin and Ursula in the next chapter; in this I want to examine Lawrence's attitude to the dead ends of the other characters.

The treatment of the old ideals is comparatively brief. One of the functions of the opening chapter is to imply that the traditional understanding of marriage is no longer possible to the intelligent. Ursula is, as always, more tentative than Gudrun, but to her question, 'Do you hope to get anywhere by just marrying?' the answer they largely agree on is that marriage is 'impossible'. Similarly the relationship with home and father is dead. When Ursula asks about Gudrun's feelings for her father, Gudrun replies, 'I haven't thought about him: I've refrained.' – ' "Yes," wavered Ursula.'

The episode at the wedding they witness, at the end of the chapter, constitutes an early example of ostensible spontaneity being subsumed within convention. This is the fundamental pattern of most ostensible rebels in the book: their action is actually as predictable as the conventions they seem to flout. When the groom is late, the bride runs from him in a way which seems to breach decorum; but as the groom pursues her, we have in effect a parody image of convention. Man chases woman; woman runs towards the church. The language is the traditional language of the chase ('hound', 'quarry', the 'vulgar women' enjoy the 'sport', and at the reception it is referred to as a 'race'). During the conversation at the reception, Birkin (who has not yet fully learnt to distinguish true spontaneity from false and praises the bride's flight for its spontaneity) rejects competitive patriot- ism as 'old hat'; but the pacificism which is set against it by Hermione is a mechanical reaction which betrays personal incoherence. Hermione, who in the first chapter is described as wanting to maintain her position 'among the first' in society and in culture, thinks that between nations the 'spirit of emulation' can be done away with; and when Birkin assists her in her argument with Gerald, by extending the image of the hat, Hermione exposes her actual resemblance to what she is ostens- ibly rejecting. If someone snatched her hat from her head, she says, she would kill him.

The most extended analysis of the old ideals centres round Thomas Crich, who is, in a form of symbolism characteristic of this book, which I shall discuss in a later chapter, literally dying. A rather degenerate kind of pity, which Lawrence always took to be centrally Christian, has dominated the life of Crich and at the time of his death becomes his ultimate means of self-protection. His own experience, on Lawrence's analysis, has shown that the pity 'was wearing thin', but he clings desperately to it as his only protection against the chaos of changing values. 'Before the armour of his pity really broke, he would die, as an insect when its shell is cracked.' The protracted process of his death becomes symbolic of a futile attempt to continue to assert the old values, which are in fact moribund. Crich's pity cannot be shown in action, since it belongs to the past, but in the analysis of it offered by Lawrence, it is seen as destructive both in the private and in the public worlds. In his wife's view, his life's purpose seems essentially parasitic: 'He would have no *raison d'être* if there were no lugubrious miseries in the world, as an undertaker would have no meaning if there were no funerals.' But the power of his pity is such that she cannot escape a kind of inhibited antagonism. Inwardly she rebels against his philanthropy, but against his love for her she cannot rebel; so she is held 'like a hawk in a cage', apparently submitting but inwardly fierce. His love projects an idealised image of her as a 'white snow-flower', but that only intensifies the actual 'destructive light' in her, so that not only is her real nature imprisoned, but she becomes deeply antagonistic towards him. The relationship Crich tried to base on love becomes one of 'utter interdestruction'.

In his public life, as an industrialist, Crich originally saw himself as a benevolent patriarch, the master who has power over ordinary men for their own long-term benefit, who is, both through organising what they could not organise and through charity to the needy, ultimately his servants' servant. As a creed, this already becomes incoherent during his own lifetime, as a result of the general secularisation of Christian ideas: human equality comes to mean equality of material possession. 'It was a religious creed pushed to its material conclusion. Thomas Crich at least had no answer.' Crich sees that it conflicts with his Christianity, that it is to make material possession an idol, and he knows it makes for organisational chaos. But his paternalistic Christianity provides him with no answer to the claims of men asking for equality of possession – and at the same time he has no desire to give up his own goods. So he is trapped into self-contradiction, bringing the troops in like the other mine-owners, and at the same time distributing cake and milk in undesired quantities to the locked-out miners and their families. As historical analysis, the treatment of Crich's experience is not very authoritative, but as an account of the incoherence between Christianity and the pursuit of industrial ends in a modern society, it is very cogent. In theory, the end of modern industry is very like that of Utopia – except that no serious attempt is made to eliminate the three evils of Pride, Greed and Sloth.

The function of Crich in the economy of the novel is to represent the Christian model of man as moribund both in the private and in the public worlds, though already, in the first two chapters, attitudes deriving from vulgarised forms of it are shown as remaining tenacious. The most complex reactions away from it are to be found in the major characters I shall discuss later, but I want to look first at the three locations which Lawrence uses to focus conceptions of 'progressive' alternatives. The first and the most obvious is the Bohemian London of the Halliday circle. In the two chapters (6 and 7) dealing primarily with it, Lawrence seems to be in some danger of trying to represent its puerile triviality too directly. Halliday and Libidnikov are both repeatedly referred to as young, Minette is frequently said to look like a child, and their behaviour is deliberately represented as adolescent – the self-conscious nudity and Halliday's inability to hold his drink. Since we are shown this behaviour at some length, these chapters have seemed to some critics tedious. But the Bohemians are in fact to be seen more precisely as making the most inept of a series of attempts in the book to establish an alternative value-structure from that of industrial society as organised by the older Crich. At the level of comedy, these would-be flouters of bourgeois morals are shown at Halliday's flat surrounded by a mixture of Futurist paintings and 'ordinary London lodging-house furniture' – drinking tea. At a level crucial to the structure of the book, Halliday's relationship with Minette is an ugly variant of that between Crich and his wife – based on a crude oscillation between pity and cruelty, servility and power – and although he wants to react against popular values, he has no idea of any positive alternative.

Halliday has power over Minette through exploitation of pity. When Gerald asks her what hold Halliday has over her, she replies, 'he *made* me go and live with him, when I didn't want to. . . . He came and cried to me'. But the demand for pity in fact puts Halliday in the power of Minette: 'Minette was becoming hard and cold, like a flint knife, and Halliday was laying himself out to her. And her intention, ultimately, was to capture Halliday, to have complete power over him.' Minette in turn gains power over Gerald, through her 'look of a violated slave', which rouses a pity contaminated with the will to dominate: 'The sensation of her inchoate suffering roused the old sharp flame in him, a mordant pity, a passion almost of cruelty.' But she is using the relationship with Gerald to strengthen her hold over Halliday: Gerald is too much of a man for her; Halliday she can master. Halliday is, as she tells Gerald, a baby, and the relationship is therefore dominated by the woman. Minette's is the crudest case in the book of the female-dominant form of relationship later diagnosed by Birkin in conversation with Ursula: 'Proud and subservient, then subservient to the proud. . . . It is a tick-tack, tick-tack, a dance of opposites' which leads nowhere. Halliday certainly has no idea where to go: as Minette tells Gerald, 'He waits for what somebody tells him to do. He never does anything he wants to do himself – because he doesn't know what he wants.'

Bohemia is essentially group life, a rather cosy group life, in which the conventions are very crudely related to those of the world it ostensibly rejects. Gerald's first impression is that its life is freer, but he, who belongs to the world of industry, has little difficulty in learning the changed rules. 'Here one did as one was possessed to do' – that is, one does not act with real individuality, but as the others do – so Gerald walks about Halliday's flat with self-conscious nudity copied from Halliday and Libidnikov. 'He was so conventional at home, that when he was really away, and on the loose, as now, he enjoyed nothing so much as full outrageousness. So he strode with his blue silk wrap over his arm and felt defiant.' Halliday himself is described by Birkin, in the Breadalby chapter, in terms of 'tick-tack': 'Either he is a pure servant, washing the feet of Christ, or else he is making obscene drawings of Jesus – action and reaction – and between the two, nothing. He is really insane.' Birkin is referring here to a time when Halliday had actual 'religious mania', but he remains 'pure servant' to Minette and a quotation in my last paragraph shows continued degenerate self-sacrifice ('Halliday was laying himself out to her'). His reaction phase remains dominated by Christian concepts. The significance of the frequent description of his physical appearance as 'broken' is made explicit at the beginning of chapter 7: 'He had a rather heavy, slack, broken beauty, dark and firm. He was like a Christ in a Pietà.' Towards his Arab servant, he had acted like a Good Samaritan ('We found him in the road, starving') – only he has to borrow other people's money to do so effectively. The whole Bohemian endeavour is an inept attempt to invert the values on which it is in fact parasitic.

The group of intellectuals gathered at Hermione's house, Breadalby, also conceive of themselves as progressives, in reaction against contemporary society. Their talk, we are told, is often 'anarchistic', and one of their longest reported conversations concerns 'a new state, a new world of man. Supposing this old social state *were* broken and destroyed, then, out of the chaos, what then?' With comic bathos, what is offered in the next sentence by Sir Joshua is the secularised version of a Christian idea already found by Crich to lead to chaos – 'the *social* equality of man'. Hermione's version, which follows a little later, is even a little less secularised – '*If*. . . . we could only realise, that in the *spirit* we are all one, all equal in the spirit, all brothers there – the rest wouldn't matter.' As in the Bohemian setting, there are recurrent images of water, a world alternative to the dry land of ordinary society. Libidnikov seems to Gerald like a 'water-plant' with limbs like 'smooth plant-stems'; yet he inhabits a world of common lodging-house furniture and tea. The Breadalby group indulge in temporary immersion in Hermione's pools, but through Gudrun's eyes we see them as amphibious lizards, sitting in a row on the bank. Specifically, she sees the would-be progressives as extinct forms of life – Sir Joshua 'belongs to the primeval world, when great lizards crawled about'.

Like Bohemia, it is a group form of life – they swim 'together like a shoal of seals'. Thinking themselves free and advanced, they are in fact more bound by the past than conventional society. Hermione says, '*to know* . . . is really to be happy, to be *free*'. Not only does this show personal incoherence again (in chapter 3 she was arguing that knowledge destroys life), but it is given the lie by the image of the house itself. The introductory description is of a Georgian house in a quiet and ordered estate, 'unchanged and unchanging', away from London and from the mining areas. To Gudrun it appears 'complete', 'as final as an old aquatint'. Birkin too can appreciate its beauty – 'how lovely, how sure, how formed, how final all the things of the past were – the lovely accomplished past – this house, so still and golden, the park slumbering its centuries of peace!' But as his thoughts unfold, the finality and peace of it become oppressive – 'what a snare and a delusion, this beauty of static things – what a horrible, dead prison Breadalby really was, what an intolerable confinement, the peace!' As Ursula has already perceived, the conversation there is only free in the sense that a canal runs freely: she becomes wearied by what she sees as 'a canal of conversation rather than a stream'. In the same way, Birkin saw that Bohemia was essentially restricted despite its illusion of freedom from convention. When Gerald asked pruriently if the Bohemians were 'loose', Birkin replied, 'In one way. Most bound, in another. For all their shockingness, all on one note.' The image which most fully renders the Breadalby alternative to the world of Crich's mines is of a game of chess. Birkin reflects, 'how known it all was, like a game with the figures set out, the same figures, the Queen of chess, the knights, the pawns, the same now as they were hundreds of years ago, the

same figures moving round in one of the innumerable permutations that make up the game. But the game is known, its going on
is like a madness, it is so exhausted'. The game is inherited from
the past: for all their intellectual pretensions to progressiveness,
the behaviour of the group is as fixed by inherited convention as
the house is static in its unchanged beauty. It is a very decorous
game: the players are less inept than Halliday, but the rules are
not even as different from those of ordinary high society as
Bohemia's crude inversion. Gerald fits in even better than he did
in Bohemia. It is a game so divorced from real contact with life,
that they can discuss what the French word would have been that
was rendered as 'hurriedly' in an English translation from the
French version of a Russian novel – until 'the maid came hurrying
with a large tea-tray. The afternoon had passed so swiftly'. As
Halliday seemed to Birkin 'insane', so this is 'like a madness'.

   The most rigorous attempt at 'tick-tack' rebellion against
society comes at the end of the book, the attempt offered by
Loerke, who is significantly only temporarily at the location
which helps to define him, since he is a more real Bohemian than
Halliday's set, the son of a man who 'wouldn't work for anybody',
who has no private income to form the basis of his parasitic
existence, but had to make his way by 'begging, begging
everything'. It is partly this which makes him attractive to
Gudrun – 'He seemed to be the very stuff of the underworld of life.
There was no going beyond him.' To her, he seems to have
achieved real detachment from the kind of world inhabited by
Crich and his employees: 'Everybody else had their illusion. . . .
But he . . . dispensed with all illusion. He did not deceive himself
in the last issue. In the last issue he cared about nothing, he was
troubled about nothing, he made not the slightest attempt to be at
one with anything.' There is a grain of truth in this, but it is to a
large extent merely an illusion about himself, which Loerke
projects and Gudrun is deceived by. To Ursula he explains with
condescension that his statue of the girl on a horse is pure
art-form, quite detached from the world in which horses and girls
are capable of feeling – 'it is part of a work of art, it has no relation
to anything outside that work of art . . . it has no relation with the
everyday world of this and other . . . they are two different and
distinct planes of existence'. But Ursula has in fact seen past this
illusion that through art one inhabits an alternative world. The
indifference to life is exposed, by the art of the statue, not as a

stance of superiority but as necessarily incurring brutality to the living. Caring about nothing includes caring nothing about people, and in practice that means the kind of brutality rendered in the horse. As Ursula says, 'The horse is a picture of your own stock, stupid brutality, and the girl was a girl you loved and tortured and then ignored . . . You can't bear to realise what a stock, stiff, hide-bound brutality you *are* really, so you say "it's the world of art".'

On Birkin's analysis, Loerke emerges as a less inept Halliday. His power over women, Birkin tells Gerald, derives from the 'fascination of pity and repulsion' exerted by the figure which, like Halliday's, is frequently referred to as 'boyish': 'He is the perfectly subjected being, existing almost like a criminal. And the women rush towards that.' He is further gone in corruption, but the tick-tack pattern remains clear: 'He *hates* the ideal utterly, yet it still dominates him.' The girl in his statue, and the only women he says he can use in his art, are 'small and fresh and tender and slight', and although the hatred is clear in the brutality of the horse, the girl is sitting on it. The man can brutally destroy the girl, but the brutality requires the vulnerable idealised beauty to destroy. Loerke does not actually exist in indifference but in reaction. As his relationship with Gudrun develops, he is more clearly related to the Breadalby alternative, merely carrying that, like Halliday's tick-tack, a stage further. He and Gudrun 'took a sentimental, childish delight in the achieved perfections of the past . . . they played with the past, and with the great figures of the past, a sort of little game of chess, or marionettes, all to please themselves.' These two, who are, in Birkin's language, further down the river of corruption than any others in the book, live in aesthetic reconstructions of the past. Their relationship is essentially a game – 'they wanted to keep it on the level of a game, their relationship: *such* a fine game'. What they seek in each other is merely a version of Hermione's knowing. Loerke says he would give everything 'for a little companionship in intelligence' Gudrun a little later replies, 'It is the understanding that matters. What they mean by understanding is collaboration in the illusion that playing aesthetic games with the past and brutalising the present represent a truly avant garde mode of life, some sort of way forward.

Despite his really rootless Bohemianism, the complete absence of the cosiness of the Halliday and Breadalby circles, and the sense in which he is still moving further down the river of corruption, Loerke represents an essentially dead end. As Gudrun sees, 'There was no going beyond him.' It is no accident that his art is sculpture – a passive girl on a 'stock still' horse and the frieze, which represents a 'frenzy of chaotic motion', in the most rigid of materials, granite. But his case is not only the extension of Halliday and Breadably further into their particular cul-de-sacs. In him the tick-tack is most completely fulfilled. The art, which he partly takes as his route of escape from the social structure he hates, is also its servant. Like both Halliday and Breadalby, he is parasitic, in that industry is paying for the frieze; but the circle he has prescribed is more complete, for the frieze is actively contributing to the mechanising effect of industry on human life. 'Art should *interpret* industry, as art once interpreted religion,' he says, and the interpretation his own frieze offers is to show even leisure, which Gerald thought an area for individual choice, to be an extension of mechanical action: when a man is at a fair such as his frieze represents, 'the machine works him, instead of he the machine'. 'Serving a machine, or enjoying the motion of a machine' – that, according to Loerke, is 'what god governs us'. For himself his art is an escape; for others it is a means of enslaving them more fully to industry: the treachery is complete. In the language of the review I quoted at the beginning of this chapter, the alternative 'picture' offered by the most advanced progressive is more certainly the death and neurosis of all than Crich's degenerate Christianity: mechanised man in granite.

The more complicated behaviour of the major characters, Gerald and Gudrun, can be seen more clearly in relation to the simple tick-tack of Bohemia, Breadalby and Loerke. The centre of Gerald's case is that he wills to go on, but since he does not know where to go to, the will becomes an end in itself. Initially he tries to carry one stage further the process of his father; when that fails, he turns to Bohemia or Gudrun. Birkin rather harshly analyses Gerald's tick-tack as mines and Minette; Gerald replies, in a 'queer, quiet, real voice', 'part of me wants something else'; but he never finds what it is.

The initial image of Gerald's will is given in the chapter called 'Diver', which starts with a description of Ursula and Gudrun walking through a 'soft drizzling rain' and natural surroundings in which the dominant impression remains one of softness. Gerald's figure cuts sharply through it in a 'white arc' of human assertion. 'The whole otherworld, wet and remote, he had to himself. He could move into the pure translucency of the grey, uncreated water.' He enjoys the nothingness of the water in which his willed movements can be free and clear. But ultimately the nothingness overwhelms him. The radical aimlessness of his will is already diagnosed by the sisters a few pages later. To Ursula's, 'He's got *go*, anyhow,' Gudrun replies, 'where does his *go* go to?' and the only answer to that is, 'It goes in applying the latest appliances!' The line of thought is pursued in the next chapter, the conversation between Birkin and Gerald on the train to London. Birkin challenges Gerald directly: 'What do you live for?' Gerald's reply is: 'I suppose I live to work, produce something, in so far as I am a purposive being. Apart from that, I live because I am living.' Production of material goods is the only end he can conceive, in so far as he is a purposive being, and when Birkin asks the next, obvious, question, 'when we've got all . . . we want . . . what then?' all he can reply is that we have not got there yet. A means can become an end, but only temporarily. A few pages later, the same essential question comes in different words: 'wherein does life centre, for you?' This time Gerald's reply is: 'I don't know – that's what I want somebody to tell me.' That is why he fails: Birkin thinks he will eventually be able to tell Gerald; Lawrence thought each individual had to find out for himself.

In the extended analysis of Gerald in the chapter 'The Industrial Magnate', in which his father's fatal illness begins, we are shown the development of his 'ethics of productivity' (Birkin's phrase) by tick-tack reaction against the older Crich's industrial paternalism. In his youth 'he rebelled against all authority'; in young manhood he toyed with progressive sociological ideas whose 'interest lay chiefly in the reaction against the positive order, the destructive reaction'. But when he is asked into his father's firm, he reacts against the earlier reaction: authority and order, as imposed by himself, become the principles of his life. To some extent this remains reaction against the values of his father. To the older Crich, the miners are 'his sons, his people'; to Gerald they become merely instrumental, merely functioning parts of the machine which he controls. 'As a man as of a knife: does it cut well?' He consciously rejects the Christian values of love and equality as 'old hat'. Yet in a broader perspective, it is a purely mechanical extension of the process which had begun in his father's time. The 'mechanical equality' developed by the miners

out of a secularised Christianity led to chaos: Thomas Crich
paralysed between recognition of the need for authority in
organisation and his dying Christian ideals. Gerald salvages the
organisation by removing the vestigial Christianity; equality is
old hat and the machine functions better without it, to the benefit
of all. In that way, he can give the miners more of what they want
than they could get by their own means of equality of possession.
If all serve the machine in the most efficient way, all get more
material goods. Gerald's personal satisfaction in it lies in the
victory of will over matter: 'What he wanted was the pure
fulfillment of his own will in the struggle with the natural
conditions.' But it becomes a surrogate religion for the miners as
well, since it is the fulfilment of the process they also helped to
develop out of dying Christianity. Gerald 'represented the
religion they really felt. . . . there was a new world, a new order,
strict, terrible, inhuman, but satisfying in its very destructive-
ness. . . . It was what they wanted. It was the highest that man had
produced, the most wonderful and superhuman . . . something
really godlike'. This is not unlike the interpretation of industry
offered by Loerke's frieze, except that to Gerald every man should
be free to 'look after his own amusements and appetites' after his
contribution to the working of the machine is made. But that
difference, together with the fact that Loerke, as an artist of sorts,
can go on making new things, is crucial. Once Gerald has
succeeded in perfecting his production machine, he has, in the
world of work, nothing left to struggle with: he has no end left. So
he becomes more dependent on the private world of appetite – his
relationship with Gudrun – focusing on that the will to dominate,
which has lost its former outlet.

The crisis comes at the time of his father's death. It has been
reached by the simple fruition of his own purpose. 'Once or twice
lately, when he was alone in the evening and had nothing to do, he
had suddenly stood up in terror, not knowing what he was.' There
follows the terrible experience of looking in the mirror and seeing,
behind his healthy blue eyes, the reflection of his own emptiness
and purposelessness. But the crisis is intensified by his father's
dying, since Gerald remains essentially a reactor, not an agent.
The 'unifying idea of mankind', against which he reacted to form
his own mechanical order, is dying with his father. In a sense he
wants this, as he has always wanted to destroy it – 'He somehow
wanted this death, even forced it.' Yet at the same time, he is

fighting death himself, since the annihilation of the old order removes all vestige of human purpose from his own tick-tack achievement: all that will remain is the 'superhuman' machine, which no longer needs its captain. So he has to 'see through' his father's death, in part metaphorically inflicting it, in part sharing it. 'As the fight went on, and all that he had been and was continued to be destroyed, so that life was a hollow shell all round him, roaring and clattering like the sound of the sea, a noise in which he participated externally, and inside this hollow shell was . . . the great dark void which circled at the centre of his soul.' The difference between father and son is that the older Crich has his ideals to cling to in his final assertion against death; Gerald has only his will itself. He has nothing to fight death *for*. There is only his will against the void which is within him. It is in desperation that he turns to Gudrun.

The radical split in him which makes this possible has been present from the start. As he reads a newspaper, waiting for the train in chapter 5, we are told of a 'dual consciousness running in him' which irritates Birkin. Specifically, there is a duality between the daylight Gerald, who organises the public world with propriety, and in reaction against that an attraction towards corruption, which he keeps separate or refuses to admit. He is fascinated by the 'grossness of spirit' he finds in Bohemia and the 'disintegration', the 'prophane' knowledge of evil which he sees in Minette in particular. The duality is registered in his response to the African carving at Halliday's flat: it seems to him 'rather wonderful', but he has also to reject it as 'rather obscene'. He is shocked when, with Birkin's help, he sees its meaning ('he saw Minette in it. As in a dream, he knew her') and refuses to admit that it is 'high art' – 'he wanted to keep certain illusions, certain ideas like clothing'. Only his physical clothing can be voluntarily discarded.

What attracts him to Minette is the combination of vulnerability, recklessness and a mockery directed at Halliday, all of which flatter his male pride and excite his prurience. But Minette is too small for him; his dominance throughout the relationship with her is registered, according to Lawrentian mythology, in references to a resistant strength at the base of his spine. In Gudrun he sees essentially a more potent version of Minette: at the extempore ballet performed at Breadalby, 'The essence of that female, subterranean recklessness and mockery penetrated his blood. He could not forget Gudrun's lifted, offered, cleaving, reckless, yet withal mocking weight.' The consequent reaction away from Minette is carefully placed after Birkin's analysis of Halliday's 'action and reaction' (quoted p. 234 above). It is followed a few pages later by the analysis of Gerald's tick-tack as mines and Minette; but Gudrun cannot offer him the 'something else', which in reply he says he wants. When Birkin tells Gerald that Gudrun would know the Halliday-Minette set, he adds, 'She was never quite that set – more conventional in a way.' Gudrun herself has already betrayed the nature of her conventionality while trying to disown it in conversation with Ursula: 'the really chic thing is to be so absolutely ordinary, so perfectly commonplace and like the person in the street that you really are a masterpiece of humanity, not the person in the street actually, but the artistic creation of her'. Her tick-tack is as dependent on convention as Gerald's: it merely carries her a stage further away. As he lives near the mines and slums it in Bohemia, so she lives in Bohemia and slums it in Beldover. She can offer no way forward, only distorted copies of old pictures.

In the famous episode at the level-crossing, it seems possible that the two halves of Gerald's life are becoming integrated. The exertion of his will over the terrified mare, as the trucks from his mine clank past, is clearly an extension of his victory of mind and machine over matter and nature; but the presence of Gudrun with her 'black-dilated, spellbound eyes' and language such as 'keen as a sword pressing in to her' equally clearly give the struggle a sexual significance. The same will seems to dominate in both spheres. But the effect on Gudrun even here is temporary: before the struggle is fully over, she has already become 'quite hard and cold and indifferent'. She enjoys the extreme experience of 'blood-subordination', but manages nonetheless to maintain her aesthetic detachment from it: 'through the man in the closed wagon Gudrun could see the whole scene spectacularly, isolated and momentary, like a vision isolated in eternity'. In a similar way, in the following pages, the two halves of Gudrun's life are brought together – the loathing for the vulgar life of Beldover and the attachment to Bohemia – into a new vision of the miners ('In their voices she could hear the voluptuous resonance of darkness, the strong, dangerous underworld, mindless, inhuman. . . . The voluptuousness was like that of machinery, cold and iron'). But her passive, aesthetic means of control is no more effective than

Gerald's active, physical means: the chapter ends with her oscillating between attraction to the colliers' world and reaction away from it.

The first really decisive encounter between them follows in the next chapter, 'Sketch-Book'. It opens with a descriptive passage, associating Gudrun with the mud and the succulent water-plants, which were used metaphorically of Halliday and Libidnikov. Gerald in effect enters Gudrun's world, and in it she is not just cold but dominant. The action dramatises this with a delicacy which is more common in the book than critical concentration on the more laboriously symbolic passages permits one to remember. Hermione asks patronisingly to see Gudrun's sketch-book, and as Gerald tries to take it from Hermione, it falls into the water. Gerald, trying to recover it, loses all his male dignity ('He could feel his position was ridiculous, his loins exposed behind him') and Hermione's temporary victory is very completely eclipsed by Gudrun's cutting expression of indifference about the book. Gerald is profoundly impressed by Gudrun's power over Hermione – but Gudrun is equally aware of an ascendency over him: 'they were of the same kind, he and she, a sort of diabolic freemasonry subsisted between them. Henceforward, she knew, she had her power over him'.

This power is more obviously manifested in the chapter 'Water-party', where she actually strikes him, as Minette struck the young man at the Pompadour, to demonstrate her lack of fear. But the analysis of Gerald's dependence on Gudrun, as a result of the failure of his male purpose with the mines, is now carried much further. It has frequently been pointed out that Lawrence indicates the unnaturalness of female dominance through the preceding incident of Gudrun's erotic dance in front of the (castrated) bullocks. But this is part of a whole structure of contrasts with the relationship between Birkin and Ursula. Gudrun speaks as she strikes Gerald: ' "That's why," she said, mocking.' On the previous page Birkin has been mocking Ursula with a grotesque dance, and Gudrun's striking Gerald has clear reference back to the preceding chapter, in which the male Mino, with Birkin's approval, cuffs the female stray cat. In the sexual relationship, Gudrun has complete dominance over Gerald. The words 'unconscious' and 'mindless' are repeatedly used of Gerald, and he speaks submissively the words Birkin would not speak to Ursula, 'I'm in love with you.' Gudrun can still keep half her mind disengaged from the struggle: 'On the edge of her consciousness the question was asking itself, automatically: "Why *are* you behaving in this *impossible* and ridiculous fashion?" ' The whole water-party, in which this episode is taking place, is being run by Gerald, and even in that male world of social organisation and management of affairs, Gudrun has to take over: Gerald's hand has been crushed by a machine, so Gudrun has to row their boat. After the accident, when Gerald has exhausted himself in a futile attempt to find the drowned couple, Gudrun watches him climb out of the water 'slowly, heavily, with the blind, clambering motions of an amphibious beast, clumsy'. He is defeated in both worlds, water and land, Gudrun's and his. His orders are over-ruled by Birkin, and Thomas Crich, calling Gerald 'my boy', assumes control of the rescue.

By the time of the next decisive stage in the relationship between Gerald and Gudrun, Gerald has no alternative but to enter Gudrun's world. In the chapter 'Death and Love', his belief in the mines and the daylight purpose they represent has become impossible: the relationship with Gudrun has become, in his repeated word, 'everything' to him. They walk in the dark and stand, at Gudrun's desire, beneath the bridge where the common colliers kiss their sweethearts. According to one of the basic patterns of her tick-tack, they act almost exactly in the conventional way, the only difference being that she is conscious of doing it better. It is also in the dark that Gerald makes his way 'blindly', having 'lost the path', through the allegorically named village of Whatmore, to the grave of his father ('one centre' where there is 'nothing for him') and from there to the bed of Gudrun. The potentially rather too obvious symbolism here is very finely subdued by the comedy of Gerald's escapade in the Brangwen house. The Napoleon of industry, the diver who could prescribe that sharp white arc into the uncreated water, sneaks like a sordid fornicator past the sleeping father with 'supernaturally keen' senses and 'infinitely careful feet' – into the bedroom of his mistress's brother by mistake. On the way out next morning, Gudrun has to manage things for him, to warn him to leave his boots off till he is downstairs. He has fully entered her world of imitation commonplace, but he remains comparatively inept in it. The consummation itself marks a further stage in the progression of Gudrun's dominance. To Gerald she becomes a mother-figure: 'The lovely creative warmth flooded through him like a sleep of fecundity within the womb. . . . Like a child at the breast, he cleaved intensely to her.' As at the episode with the mare at the crossing, Gudrun becomes in reaction cold and separate: 'She lay in intense and vivid consciousness, an exhausting superconsciousness. The church clock struck the hours, it seemed to her, in quick succession. She heard them distinctly in the tension of her vivid consciousness.' As he dresses, he seems to her ridiculous, but she is 'saved' by the reflection that it 'is like a workman getting up to go to work. . . . And I am like a workman's wife'. Gerald at least gains a form of 'self-sufficiency' from his surrender to Gudrun; she remains unchanged, since she views the whole experience, in her usual manner, from an aesthetic distance.

The protracted culmination of the relationship in the setting of the Alps is dominated by the reductive vision of Gudrun. In a sense Gerald's death in the white waste of snow is the final projection of his own daylight will: the white arc is swallowed up by the white wilderness of resistant matter, which there remains no point in resisting. But Gerald goes there with some glimmer of hope that Birkin's concept of final marriage might save him. From the start, Gudrun debases the idea of the joint excursion to 'an outing with some little *type*', and that is virtually what she succeeds in reducing it down to. At the stop in Paris on the way, she enjoys the artificial life of a super-Bohemia: 'Of course, everybody got fearfully drunk – but in an interesting way, not like that filthy London crowd' – the interest lying chiefly in a speech by a drunken Roumanian on how glad he was to have been born. Gerald she enjoys as a Don Juan, 'a whole saturnalia in himself'. What she wants from him is essentially an image, an image she can know and so retain her power over; as an individual, she fears he might have power over her. So the relationship is either dominated by her images, or characterised by a struggle for power.

In the Alpine hotel she enjoys the image of his reflection in a mirror, 'tall and over-arching – blond and terribly frightening', but cannot turn and actually face him – 'she would fall down at his feet, grovelling at his feet, and letting him destroy her'. Finally, of course, Gudrun destroys Gerald, but there is a protracted period during which the urge to destroy is mutual. At the time of Gudrun's vision in the mirror, Gerald is obtusely unaware of it, but progressively he becomes more conscious of a desire to kill Gudrun, and they become fixed in a tick-tack of destructive will, an 'eternal see-saw, one destroyed that the other might exist, one ratified because the other was nulled'. For Gerald, there is no possible living escape from this tick-tack. 'He could see that, to exist at all, he must be perfectly free of Gudrun, leave her if she wanted to be left, demand nothing of her, have no claim upon her. But then, to have no claim upon her, he must stand by himself, in sheer nothingness.' And that he knows he cannot do. The only possible end is a literal enactment of the emotional effect of the relationship ('what a perfect voluptuous consummation it would be, to strangle her, to strangle every spark of life out of her, till she lay completely inert, soft, relaxed for ever, a soft heap lying dead between his hands'), or, more completely, his own death in both worlds simultaneously ('I didn't want it, really', he says of his attempt to kill her). What he wants ultimately is 'to go to sleep' finally, 'to go on, go on whilst he could' into the snow, until his go has finally gone.

Gudrun survives not only because she is ultimately stronger, but because she can go on making pictures. In the earlier stages, Gerald can serve as the subject of the pictures: 'He would be a Napoleon of peace, or a Bismarck – and she the woman behind him' – though even as she projects this image, looking at him as he lies asleep, she reacts against it: 'at the same instant, came the ironical question: "What for?" ' But as her will to know him becomes fulfilled, she has to move beyond him. 'In him she knew the world, and had done with it. Knowing him finally she was the Alexander seeking new worlds. But there *were* no new worlds.' The image of Gerald as Don Juan becomes equally exhausted: 'his Don Juan does *not* interest me. I could play Dona Juanita a million times better than he plays Juan. . . . Gerald is so limited, there is a dead end to him'. Only Loerke can offer what seems to remain, since he is not the subject of pictures but a collaborator in making them. But Gudrun is painfully conscious of the ultimate sterility which her life is reduced to. 'The terrible bondage of this tick-tack of time, this twitching of the hands of the clock, this eternal repetition of hours and days – oh God, it was too awful to contemplate. And there was no escape from it, no escape. . . . All life, all life resolved into this: tick-tack, tick-tack, tick-tack; then the striking of the hour; then the tick-tack, tick-tack, and the twitching of the clock-fingers.' It is not merely Gerald who is as mechanical as his own machines – 'What were his kisses, his embraces. She could hear their tick-tack, tick-tack.' Her own reaction from him is the same: 'She never really lived, she only watched. Indeed, she was like a little, twelve-hour clock vis-à-vis with the enormous clock of eternity – there she was, like Dignity and Impudence, or Impudence and Dignity.' Loerke and Gudrun making sardonic pictures of Gerald's dignity are themselves merely tick-tack, and she knows it, though even this 'picture pleased her'. At the end, she is not literally dead, like Gerald, but trapped in a continuous process of reductive mockery within the shell of apparent conformity – 'the last subtle activities of analysis and breaking down, carried out in the darkness of her, whilst the outside form, the individual, was utterly unchanged, even sentimental in its poses'. When Ursula meets her after Gerald's death, 'Gudrun hid her face on Ursula's shoulder, but still she could not escape the cold devil of irony that froze her soul. "Ha, ha!" she thought, "this is the right behaviour." ' There was at least some dignity in Gerald's end; in her reaction Gudrun has acquired the obscenity of Loerke. Her picture-making is certainly the death of all humanity.

14 *Women in Love*: Life as End

In *Women in Love* Lawrence shows reaction against the old ideals to be as mechanical and sterile as the perpetuation of them. The older Crich dies, but so does Gerald, and the alternative of Loerke, towards which Gudrun's path leads, is represented by an image of mechanised life carved in granite. Action and reaction lead only to perpetual tick-tack, mechanical motion destructive of life. What Lawrence offers instead is in terms of imagery a waiting for the old to die and the new to emerge in its own time, in the way that a deciduous tree sheds its leaves and puts forth new ones in the spring. The image recurs frequently, not only in *Women in Love*, but throughout Lawrence's writing, particularly at this period. For example, in a letter to Lady Ottoline Morrell of 9 September 1915: 'let the old die altogether, completely. It is only the new spring I care about, opening the hard little buds that seem like stone, in the souls of people. They must open and a new world begin. But first there is the shedding of the old, which is so slow and so difficult, like a sickness'.[1] In the novel, this process is, of course, represented in the relationship between Birkin and Ursula.

Critical discussion of that relationship has, I think, been seriously disabled by a strategic mistake by Lawrence, the omission of anything corresponding to the Prologue which he discarded.[2] No one who has compared the slack expository prose of the Prologue with the economy of the first chapter could doubt his judgement in rejecting that particular draft, but the consequence of providing no substitute is that the reader is inadequately alerted to the shortcomings of Birkin, and so also to the nature of the growth he has to undergo. It is not that Lawrence only partly distances himself from Birkin, as has often been said, by making him too much of a preacher – 'addressing a meeting' as he is shown in the 'Class-room' chapter – he is, before his relationship with Ursula flowers, deeply sick. But because Lawrence has very largely to use him as a spokesman, it is, without the Prologue, very difficult to understand the sickness. The underlying problem of form is perhaps insuperable. The new ideal does not, by definition, evolve out of the old, so there can be no form analogous to George Eliot's. Yet it does grow – like new leaves – it is not preconceived, so there can be no narrator who has, as it were, got there before the characters (the Prologue, among its other faults, was too much in such a style). But mere reaction against what already is, leads, as in the cases of the other characters, to mere tick-tack. So Birkin has in effect to know what he wants but not yet have it; and there is some difficulty in knowing what one does not already have and can see embodied nowhere else, either directly or indirectly.

This is Birkin's state in the Prologue. 'His fundamental desire was, to be able to love completely, in one and the same act: both body and soul at once, struck into a complete oneness in contact with a complete woman.' But 'this is what no man can do at once, deliberately. It must happen to him'. Meanwhile he is trapped into incoherent tick-tack. His essays on education are brilliant, and he becomes an inspector of schools. But education, as he sees it, is growth towards some social, religious or philosophical ideal, and he has come to regard mankind as passing through a stage not of growth but of decay and decomposition. 'It is impossible to educate for this end, impossible to teach the world how to die away from its achieved, nullified form. The autumn must take place in every individual soul.' Yet he does not want himself to die, and he even feels bound by the constraints of the dying order of values. He feels physically attracted to men, spiritually to women, but will not acknowledge fully to himself the homosexuality forbidden by the old order ('I *should not* feel like this'). To some extent this split is caused by Hermione's over-spiritual love, but it is not, as one might gather from all we later see of Hermione, entirely her fault: '*Whenever* (my italics are justified by the context) it was a case of a woman, there entered in too much spiritual, sisterly love; or else, in reaction, there was only a brutal, callous sort of lust.' The relationship with Hermione is a tick-tack of tenderness and destruction, the pity and cruelty of Halliday and Minette: 'After he loved her with a tenderness that was anguish, a love that was all pain . . . he turned upon her savagely, like a maddened dog.' From the intellectual, spiritual love Hermione can offer him, he reacts violently towards the physical corruption which half-attracts Gerald to Bohemia: 'He went to other women of purely sensual, sensational attraction, he prostituted his spirit with them.' Like Gerald, he comes to regard his work as ultimately futile – 'the whole process . . . was pure futility, a process of mechanical activity entirely purposeless, sham growth which was entirely rootless' – and so, like Gerald, he becomes neurotically dependent on the relationships of private life. Like Gudrun, he channels his unconventionality into a mixture of mocking and imitating the ordinary: Hermione is conscious of 'something jeering and spiteful and low' in him, 'a deep desire to be common, vulgar, a little gross'. In an early draft of chapter 1, the Gudrun-like mock-conventionality is more explicitly a radical betrayal of individuality: 'He was always being somebody else, not himself . . . therefore he was never real.'[3] In short, this early Birkin is an incoherent tick-tack between Breadalby and Bohemia, intellectual wind and reactive corruption, potentially a Gerald, potentially a Gudrun, only a little more determined in his pursuit of what Gerald calls 'something else'.

That is, as it were, the raw Birkin, but in the novel as it stands we never see him in this state; what we see is a man already in the process of developing away from it, still partly governed by tick-tack, but gradually escaping. For the reader's benefit more than his, he knows what he must reject and roughly what he wants; as a character, his most important action is waiting for the unknown to unfold. Lawrence's main means of representing the unfolding are the erratic growth of the relationship with Ursula – erratic partly to conceal the need for knowledge by Birkin of the end before he reaches it – and setting up a wide-ranging series of resemblances and differences between Birkin and other characters, in such a way that Birkin's nature and his achievement with Ursula can be defined for the reader without incurring tick-tack behaviour by the truly liberated characters. I shall look at these two means in turn, but I need first to show that Lawrence did intend Birkin to seem sicker, before the relationship with Ursula flowers, than the novel without the Prologue leads the reader to suppose.

The dominant impression is of a man who exposes Hermione as a fraudulent intellectual, who admires spontaneity, who is more intelligent than Gerald, who does not fit in Bohemia (when Gerald and Libidnikov look equally '*comme il faut*', Birkin looks a 'failure in his attempt to be a properly dressed man'), who will not go 'trooping off in a gang' at Breadalby, and who at the end of the

Breadalby chapter seems finally to have washed himself clean of Hermione's taint by rolling naked among the hyacinths. But this is not basically a naturalistic novel (as the hyacinth episode surely shows), and when at the very end of that chapter we are told that he is ill, we are no more to take it on a purely literal level than we are to take the death of Crich.

He obviously gets the better of the argument with Hermione in the class-room, but equally clearly he is not free of her: they go off together after it, leaving Ursula behind. What Hermione wants essentially is to exert a power over Birkin which will conceal from herself her own vacuity. As she walks up to the church in the first chapter, we are told, 'when he was there, she felt complete, she was sufficient, whole. For the rest of the time she was established on the sand, built over a chasm.' In the Breadalby chapter, this is clearly related to Crich's clinging to his ideals: like him she is fighting to the death to protect an image in her head: 'because of [Birkin's] power to escape. . . . She hated him in a despair that shattered her and broke her down, so that she suffered sheer dissolution like a corpse, and was unconscious of everything save the horrible sickness of dissolution that was taking place within her, body and soul'. But in the early chapters, Birkin has not escaped, and indeed Hermione's power over him remains potentially considerable as late as chapter 22, when she controls the cat Mino. In those early chapters, Birkin is in tick-tack relationship with her. In the first, he feels 'ultimate dislike and . . . acute pity' for her. At the reception, he replies 'dutifully' when Hermione directs the conversation towards him, and he rescues her from Gerald as it proceeds. Even in the class-room, where he is fighting her, he is meeting her fundamentally on her terms, arguing in words that verbalised animalism is self-contradictory. As he does so, he is entangled in a tick-tack of cruelty and pity – 'He looked at her in mingled hate and contempt, also in pain because she suffered, and in shame because he knew he tortured her. He had an impulse to kneel and plead for forgiveness' – a tick-tack which bears a close resemblance to that between Halliday and Minette.

The conversation with Gerald in the train gives a dominant impression of a man who has much to teach Gerald; but in an important respect, he is in much the same predicament. When he has asked Gerald where his life centres, he goes on, after Gerald's reply, 'I know . . . it just doesn't centre. The old ideals are dead as nails – nothing there. It seems to me there remains only this perfect union with a woman – sort of ultimate marriage – and there isn't anything else.' Hermione cannot achieve that 'ultimate marriage', and Birkin is, like Gerald, on the way to Bohemia. The misanthropy he expresses at this stage is not altogether discarded, and I shall return to discussion of it later, but the mood of 'let mankind pass away – time it did' is explicitly said to be sick: 'His dislike of mankind, of the mass of mankind, amounted almost to an illness.' In Bohemia, we see him again in the process of attempted withdrawal, but he is there, he is well-known to all the circle, and in the letter read aloud by Halliday in the much later chapter, 'Gudrun in the Pompadour', a letter which dates either from this period or a little earlier, the language very clearly relates his reaction against Hermione's mental relationship to the degraded sensuality of the African carving in Halliday's flat: 'in the great retrogression, the reducing back of the created body of life, we get knowledge and beyond knowledge, the phosphorescent ecstasy of acute sensation'. Gudrun is affronted by that reading of the letter largely because it represents the position she herself is then in: as she leaves the café, the colour of her hat is described as 'like the sheen on an insect'. When Birkin recalls the carving in 'Moony', as 'one of his soul's intimates', he remembers its 'beetle face' as a particular image of the dissolution and corruption it represents. As for Breadalby, I have already quoted Birkin's reaction away from the house as a prison (p. 236 above), but the reaction is preceded by a sense of the beauty of the place ('how final all the things of the past were – the lovely accomplished past'); and to the outsider Ursula, Birkin seems one of those who dominate the way of life centred there: she is exhausted by the 'powerful, consuming, destructive mentality that emanated from Joshua and Hermione and Birkin and dominated the rest'.

The blow on his head from Hermione, which has the effect of largely freeing him from her, is clearly the culmination of a destructive will on her part. But it cannot be blamed wholly on her: Birkin has contributed a full share to the tick-tack of which it is the climax. He goes to her room feeling he had been 'violent, cruel with poor Hermione. He had hurt her, he had been vindictive'. As in the relationship between Gerald and Gudrun, the destructive urge is mutual, and the fact that the woman strikes hardest is no sign of superiority in the man. In the note he writes to her afterwards, he says she was right to hit him – 'because I know you wanted to'. He is still thinking in terms of crude spontaneity

here: more objectively she was right because it was merely a direct
expression of a relationship in which both parties equally swing
between pity and cruelty. The rolling in the hyacinths is in a sense
a washing himself clean from that relationship, but it is not
altogether a return to the health of nature from the claustrophobia
of Breadalby. There is an element of neurotic withdrawal, a
tick-tack reaction away from the intellectual social intercourse he
enjoyed there to a 'dread' of other people. 'He did not want a
woman – not in the least. . . . Here was his world . . . nothing but
the lovely, subtle, responsive vegetation and himself. . . . he
rejoiced in his own madness, he was free.' He is not certainly free –
Hermione still has him under her thumb four chapters later, in
'Carpetting' – but he is certainly somewhat mad, sick, ill (all three
words recur).

I have, of course, been emphasising the vestigial sickness of
Birkin more than Lawrence does: my argument is that Lawrence
does not express it sufficiently strongly for his own purposes to
readers unacquainted with the starker picture of the discarded
Prologue. But by the time the two major relationships between
Birkin, Gerald and the two sisters have begun to develop,
Lawrence has more adequate means of registering, through his
form, that Birkin is rightly orientated, but only fitfully in actual
grasp of what he seeks. In particular, Ursula can challenge him,
and the Gerald–Gudrun relationship can run in parallel, providing implicit commentary. Both means are working in the chapter,
'An Island', which constitutes the first really crucial stage of
Birkin's relationship with Ursula. The preceding chapter is
'Sketch-book', which begins with Gudrun 'knowing' the water-
plants and Ursula watching the butterflies, 'unconscious like the
butterflies' themselves, and which ends with the dominance of
Gudrun over Gerald first established. The symbol which is
opposed to the submerged sketch-book with its pictures of
water-plants is the flotilla of daisies floating on the surface of the
water like stars, and Birkin can be given explicit knowledge of
what it signifies – 'freedom together' – more safely than in the
earlier chapters, because Ursula can be used to confirm that his
knowledge is incomplete. As before, he knows himself he is sick –
'One is ill because one doesn't live properly – can't. It's the failure
to live that makes one ill' – but the symptoms can be more clearly
indicated through Ursula. When he says, 'Mankind is a dead tree,
covered with fine brilliant galls of people', 'Ursula could not help

stiffening herself against this, it was too picturesque and final' – that is, it is too like the vision of Gudrun. Birkin's concept of 'freedom together' will lead them beyond what Ursula calls 'love' and beyond the battle for dominance of the Gerald–Gudrun relationship; but he is as yet too deeply wounded by the total misanthropy of tick-tack reaction against Breadalby socialism to be able to envisage very clearly the means of achieving it. His theories are eventually vindicated, in modified form, but his theories do not get him off the island which is one logical conclusion of them: Ursula persuades him to leave it, with her. What he wants cannot be willed into existence: even *his* theories lead to a very dead end – the death of all mankind, 'a clean, lovely, humanless world.' In the last resort he has to wait for what he wants to happen.

Yet he does have to want it with a sense of purpose, as the end of the same chapter and the one which follows ('Carpetting') show: to the extent that he is over-passive, Hermione, and following Hermione's example, Ursula, become destructively dominant. In 'Carpetting', Birkin says theoretically that a woman, like a horse, should resign her will to the 'higher being' of a man; but in practice Hermione very completely organises his furnishings for him. The chapter ends with Ursula torn between a 'sort of league' with Hermione and a bond with Birkin which 'at once irritated and saved her'. From then on it is 'a fight to the death' between her and Birkin – 'or to a new life'. That metaphor is the one which perhaps most crucially distinguishes between the two relationships, Gerald–Gudrun and Birkin–Ursula. It is a fight, not to destroy but to renew life, and the means of achieving the different end is Birkin's fitful awareness of ideas of the end – in particular 'star-equilibrium' in relationship, male dominance within that equilibrium, and the individual integration of each of the characters involved. Discussion of whether such ideas are adequately different from the pictures which are 'death' I shall defer till a later chapter.

It is well known that Lawrence regarded these ideas as essentially inter-related: extensive quotations from essays and letters written at about the same time as *Women in Love* have been put forward as proof by other critics, and I shall not repeat them. In the novel, I do not think the inter-relation is quite satisfactorily established, because the nature of the raw Birkin is not entirely clear in what was published. If one does envisage the raw Birkin,

the connections are clear: he was involved in an inter-destructive
tick-tack with Hermione, in which she was actually dominant,
causing him to react away from her spirituality towards Bohemian
corruption: no balance, female dominance, individual incoherence. From that confusion he derives his theories, and the
theories, which *as* theory are only reactive tick-tack, are gradually
discovered in practice as the relationship unfolds. But as the novel
stands, I do not think that, for example, a crucial passage in
'Moony' is comprehensible. The stoning of the moon and the
related conversation concern 'star-equilibrium' and female
dominance, but half-way through the chapter, Birkin suddenly
finds himself face to face with a choice between the 'long African
process of purely sensual understanding, knowledge in the mystery of dissolution' and 'another way, the way of freedom. There
was the paradisal entry into pure, single being'. That choice,
between sensuality and integration, has no established connection with 'star-equilibrium', though it is not difficult to make it by
supplying Lawrence's deficiency with some critical generosity.
The much more difficult matter raised by the last quotation I have
made – whether what matters is the 'way', the 'entry' (that is, the
becoming) or the 'being', the process or the state, is a question I
shall also postpone till a later chapter.

The development of the relationship is obviously a process, and
I shall now trace its outline. The terms are set up broadly in
'Mino'. As so often in this book, the significance of the chapter is
confirmed by contrast with the one which precedes it. 'Carpetting' opens at the mill where Birkin's new rooms are to be, where
there are the canaries silenced by cloths over their cages, which
make them think it is night. This gives the cages a 'strange
funereal look' and Hermione laughs at the ease with which the
birds are deceived – 'Like a stupid husband.' Ursula laughs with
her. Hermione then dominates Birkin, despite his theory. 'Mino'
opens with an image not of death but of new birth, used of Ursula:
'She had fallen strange and dim, out of the sheath of the material
life, as a berry falls from the only world it has ever known, down
out of the sheath on to the real unknown.' Birkin makes explicit
the commitment to the unknown: 'there can be no calling to book,
in any form whatsoever – because one is outside the pale of all that
is accepted, and nothing known applies. One can only follow the
impulse, taking that which lies in front.' But he then explains
what he knows he wants: a 'freedom together' ('like a star

balanced with another star') and the male dominance, registered here more substantially than in the preceding chapter, by the behaviour of the cat Mino to the female stray. Ursula, of course, challenges the balanced stars with her understanding of love (which to Lawrence means merging into one-ness) and rejects the cat's behaviour as bullying egoism. The chapter ends with Birkin temporarily and partially submitting – agreeing to say he loves Ursula. But the submission is qualified in a way which makes it crucially different from the submission to Hermione in 'Carpeting': his voice includes both 'irony and submission' – a provisional approximation to balance.

'Water-party' primarily concerns Gerald and Gudrun, and I have already referred to the defining contrast made between Birkin's mockery of Ursula and Gudrun's dominance over Gerald. In addition, it helps to clarify Birkin's dilemma. He is himself aware of a problem created by his own foreknowledge of what he wants. 'There was always confusion in speech. Yet it must be spoken. Whichever way one moved, if one was to move forwards, one must break a way through.' Without speech, there can be no move forwards to fuller human relationship; with it, there is perpetual danger of misunderstanding – in particular a tick-tack reaction by Ursula, against the true meaning of his ideas, towards female dominance and a conception of love as merging. At the same time, there remain in himself vestiges of tick-tack reaction against his own idealised vision of balance: as they kiss in the road, he feels overwhelmed by an extreme desire which tends towards death – 'fulfilled and destroyed [like Gerald later in 'Death and Love'], he went home away from her, drifting vaguely through the darkness, lapsed into the old fire of burning passion'.

At the beginning of 'Sunday Evening', Ursula is in a state comparable with Birkin's island misanthropy: the desire for the death of the old order (the other adults have gone to church on Sunday evening) becomes distorted into a desire for personal death, without any underlying image of the death of a seed which is the birth of a new life. Like Birkin's, her vision resembles Gudrun's: 'all life was rotary motion, mechanised, cut off from reality. There was nothing to look for from life . . . One could look out onto the great dark sky of death with elation, as one had looked out of the class-room window as a child'. The second half of the chapter shows that she has not only caught this part of Birkin's

disease, but is also reacting dangerously against a more healthy
aspect of his vision. This is registered through the behaviour of her
brother and sister: the boy is willing to be kissed by Birkin; the girl
feels 'mistrust and antagonism' and will not be touched by him.
The chapter ends with Ursula withdrawn into a passion of hatred
towards Birkin.

The next is called very directly 'Man to Man'. Birkin, again
quite seriously ill, is reacting against Ursula's withdrawal into
female hostility. He understands her rejection of male dominance
and of the 'balance in separation' as a version of Hermione's will
for power, a will which held him imprisoned in tick-tack and a
form of possessive love which merges individuals instead of
liberating them: 'Hermione, the humble, the subservient, what
was she all the while but the Mater Dolorosa, in her subservience,
claiming with horrible, insidious arrogance and female tyranny,
her own again, claiming back the man she had borne in
suffering. . . . And Ursula . . . was the same. . . . It was intolerable,
this possession at the hands of woman . . . the horrible merging,
mingling self-abnegation of love.' His image of 'two beings
constellated together' remains in his head; but theory cannot
create the reality. In reaction against this failure, he sees his
relationship with Gerald for the first time as a 'necessity inside
himself . . . to love a man purely and fully'. But the degree to
which he can rely on the relationship with Gerald is thrown into
very serious doubt by the analysis of Gerald in the following
chapter, 'Industrial Magnate'.

'Rabbit' stands as a foil to 'Moony'. Gerald's will moves further
in the direction of self-destruction, as he dominates not the female
mare of the earlier chapter but the male rabbit, for Gudrun; and
the physical violence, culminating in the deep scratches on the
arms of both, registers the destructive sensuality in which they are
both, in Gudrun's word, 'initiate'. In contrast, 'Moony' is
inconclusive. At the end Birkin and Ursula are no closer than at
the beginning: they have merely caught a further glimpse of what
they seek. At the beginning, Urusula is in a state of confusion,
divided between enjoyment of isolation and fear of it. The moon,
which becomes the focus for several lines of thought in the book, is
at first a symbol of the isolation she enjoys: 'the strange brightness
of her presence, a marvellous radiance of intrinsic vitality, was a
luminousness of supreme repudiation, nothing but repudiation'.

Yet, as she goes for a walk to Willey Water, she becomes afraid of it, with the 'white and deathly smile' on its sinister, triumphant face. As she looks at its reflection on the still water, she dislikes it: 'It did not give her anything.' So there is not a complete contrast with the previous chapter when Birkin throws the stones, trying to shatter the reflection: he is not entirely opposing Ursula, as Gerald is entirely serving Gudrun; the destruction of what the moon represents is half-desired by Ursula too, though her mind is not yet clear enough for her to know that. What it does represent, in addition to Ursula's isolation, is both aspects of the kind of love which made Birkin ill in 'Man to Man': his references to Cybele, the Syria Dea, make it clearly a symbol of female dominance, and the action of the fragments of light in the detailed physical description make it equally clearly a symbol of merging, of individuals becoming absorbed into a single static whole. What Birkin wants is for Ursula to give herself to him – 'that golden light which is you – which you don't know'. But words divide them again – she takes him to mean he wants her to serve him and to assert himself over her – and they are only provisionally brought together, more on her terms than his. He submits to saying he loves her; they sit 'together in happy stillness'; and that, by tick-tack, kindles 'the old destructive fires' in her.

When, later in the chapter, he goes to the Brangwen house to propose marriage, she has reverted entirely to the 'complete bright world of her self alone'. She passes through a phase of destructive intimacy with Gudrun: 'they continued radiant in their easy female transcendency, beautiful to look at', like the moon, but destructive of all around them – 'the father seemed to breathe an air of death, as if he were destroyed in his very being'. Female assertion against the male culminates in Gudrun's reductive summing up of Birkin as a man with whom it would be impossible to live. But Ursula reacts back again, against the reductiveness of Gudrun – 'This finality of Gudrun's, this dispatching of people and things in a sentence, it was all such a lie.' 'So she withdrew away from Gudrun and from that which she stood for, she turned in spirit towards Birkin again.' But although she has now fully understood what he wants, she is not sure that the 'mutual unison in separateness' is what she wants, and the chapter ends inconclusively with Ursula drawn towards a vision of love as mutual abandon, mutual servility. She has understood the theory, but in practice she is still dancing in the tick-tack of dominance and service, 'proud and subservient, proud and subservient', which he had rejected in 'Mino'.

In 'Gladiatorial', Lawrence seems rather seriously confused about his own intentions. A famous letter to Katherine Mansfield[4] makes it quite clear that Lawrence himself believed in male friendship but had not found it: 'I believe tremendously in friendship between man and man, a pledging of men to each other inviolably. But I have not ever met or formed such friendship.' Birkin clearly shares this belief and this failure: he says frequently throughout that he needs Gerald, and Gerald always fails him. But in the chapter 'Gladiatorial', Lawrence seems to be gravely confused about whether the friendship would really be good for Birkin or not. It is not that he leaves a question mark over it, as he does at the end of the book. We are told explicitly, 'The wrestling had some deep meaning to them – an unfinished meaning' (that is, a developing, not a static meaning – therefore a deeply important one in Lawrence's structure of values). Yet the language of the chapter seems to give the lie to this. The language of will is insistent – 'one ought to wrestle . . . one should enjoy what is given . . . we should enjoy everything'. Birkin, like Gudrun, admires Gerald visually – 'He was looking at the handsome figure of the other man.' The effect of the wrestling is both to dis-integrate the individual (Birkin 'was divided entirely between his spirit, which stood outside, and his body, that was a plunging, unconscious stroke of blood') and to merge the two men (the language is of 'oneness', 'penetrate', 'interfuse', 'necromantic foreknowledge', and the imagery of 'net' and 'prison'). Moreover, the placing of the chapter between 'Moony', where Ursula's female hostility is encouraged by Gudrun, and 'Woman to Woman', where she is half-corrupted by Hermione, seems to indicate that the value of the relationship in all three cases is negative: that it propels Birkin and Ursula together by reaction against those of their own sex who can only offer what they want to reject. The sentence following the one I quoted about Birkin looking at Gerald seems to confirm this – 'But really it was Ursula, it was the woman who was gaining ascendence over Birkin's being, at this moment' – and the rest of the chapter is conversation about man-woman relationships. Lawrence seems to want the relationship to hold more than negative value; but the novel does

not let him. I am not convinced that it is the novelist who is the
'dribbling liar'.[5]

'Excurse' is, in most critical accounts of the book, taken to be
the climax of the Birkin–Ursula relationship. But 'Woman to
Woman' and 'Excurse' need, I think, to be taken together as the
positive alternative to 'Death and Love', which immediately
follows; and 'Excurse', though obviously climactic in a sense,
remains part of a process which continues beyond it. In 'Death
and Love', Gerald turns in desperation, from the failure signified
in the death of his father, to Gudrun. 'Woman to Woman' stands
as a summary of the death which Birkin has passed through, to the
new life with Ursula begun in 'Excurse'. Hermione is very clearly
related to the dying Crich, in an image which, as I suggested
before, underlies much of the thought of this book. 'She was a leaf
upon a dying tree. What help was there then, but to fight still for
the old, withered truths, to die for the old, outworn belief. . . . The
old great truths *had* been true. And she was a leaf of the old great
tree of knowledge that was withering now. To the old and last
truth then she must be faithful even though cynicism and mockery
took place at the bottom of her soul.' For her own purposes (to
alienate Ursula from him) and for the benefit of both Ursula and
the reader, Hermione summarises what Birkin *was*: she uses the
present tense for her own purposes, but what she is summing up is
the tick-tack raw Birkin. 'He lives an *intensely* spiritual life, at times
– too, too wonderful. And then come the reactions. . . . That which
he affirms and loves one day – a little later he turns on it in a fury of
destruction. He is never constant, always this awful, dreadful
reaction.' The real Birkin to her is the Breadalby Birkin – 'Rupert
is race-old, he comes of an old race'. But as she continues in
thought, sitting in 'antagonistic silence' with Ursula, she is fully
aware of the reactive other side of him: 'This violent and
directionless reaction between animalism and spiritual truth
would go on in him till he tore himself in two between the opposite
directions, and disappeared meaninglessly out of life.' Ursula can
see perfectly well through Hermione's advice to her, to the
Breadalby half-life: 'Hermione was like a man, she believed only
in men's things. She betrayed the woman in herself.' And she
knows the consequences for Birkin: 'You don't give him a
woman's love, you give him an ideal love, and that is why he
reacts away from you.' But the analysis confirms a real doubt in

her mind – 'And Birkin, would he acknowledge, or would he deny her?' What she sees, when he arrives, seems to be a Birkin still wholly under the power of Hermione – the cat Mino obeys 'la lingua della Mamma' and the tea-cups and old silver seem 'to belong to an old, past world which they had inhabited together' and still seem to inhabit, to the exclusion of Ursula, who feels an intruder. So she leaves in reactive anger. In this she is mistaken, though we have no means of knowing she is till the next chapter. Birkin does not react against Hermione in a tick-tack analogous to Gerald's turning from his father's grave, but can still enter her world though he is no longer of it. He explains himself in the argument in 'Excurse': 'you can only revolt in pure reaction from her – and to be her opposite is to be her counterpart'. True freedom must include freedom from mechanical reaction.

'Excurse' opens in a mood of casual despair, contrasting with the 'fixed idea' which drives Gerald to Gudrun in the next chapter. 'Why bother! Why strive for a coherent, satisfied life? . . . Why bother about human relationships?' As Ursula repeats the analysis of Birkin's tick-tack she learnt from Hermione, it shakes Birkin's own sense of having developed beyond it: 'It was true, really, what she said. He knew that his spirituality was concomit-ant of a process of depravity, a sort of pleasure in self-destruction.' And he is thrown back on a view of Ursula as she was (that is, what Gudrun actually is to Gerald in the next chapter), 'the perfect Womb, the bath of birth'. But there is an element of absurdity – registered in the car stopped in mid-road while they argue ('they did not see the ridiculousness of their situation') and the cyclist who interrupts a particularly intense moment with a cheerful 'Afternoon' – in a squabble based on pictures of what they *were*. The resolution simply happens. 'He wanted her to come back'; she wants to come back, and comes. The imagery of birth is obviously clear in itself, but defined further by contrast with Gerald's return to the womb with Gudrun ('as if he were bathed in the womb again'): Birkin is 'as if born out of the cramp of a womb'.

I regret I am not one of those critics who can muster admiration for the passage in which Ursula discovers Birkin to be 'one of the sons of God' by stroking his arse. The best I can find to say in defence of it is that its meaning is clarified a little by reference to the corresponding passage under the bridge, where Gudrun's fingers move across Gerald's face, extracting knowledge of him

('Her soul thrilled with complete knowledge. This was the glistening, forbidden apple, this face of a man'). In contrast Ursula's fingers move 'unconsciously', discovering what remains a mystery – 'not a man, something other, something more'. It remains a mystery. Secondly, I think it needs to be noted that Birkin 'did not like this crouching, this radiance – not altogether. It was all achieved, for her'. Contrary to Ursula's misunderstanding of his ideas, Birkin has never wanted *crouching* before the male; and the word 'achieved' is a danger signal in this book: completion means death; only continued process is life. This is, I think, why the notorious description of Birkin driving his car like an Egyptian Pharaoh with Greek head and arms is so badly written. In trying to describe a state, Lawrence is being false to his own vision and merely doing symbolic arithmetic (Egyptian sensuality plus Greek intelligence equals whole man). The end of the chapter is obviously climactic in a sense, but there remains a degree of incompletion. The promise we expect to be fulfilled as they drive into the forest ('They would give each other this star-equilibrium which alone is freedom') *is* fulfilled in the night; but next morning, at the end of the chapter, 'They hid away the remembrance and the knowledge' of the night. The new birth has taken place – happened – in this chapter, after the last reverberations of Birkin's verbalising have died away. But the life which has been born is an unfinished process (as the chapter title, contrasted with the tick-tack finality of 'Death and Love', clearly indicates). I shall return in the following chapters to the implications of this, and discuss there how far the process is developed in what remains of the book. The relationship as it exists in 'Excurse' is the end in only one sense: the end is a beginning of a new form of life.

I want to conclude this chapter with a few pointers to the other means Lawrence has of distinguishing the development of living purpose from tick-tack. I hope that the structural analysis I have sketched already constitutes partial explanation for the resemblances between the characters who are re-born and those who are not: the raw Birkin was very deeply afflicted by tick-tack, and his sickness continues quite far into the book; Ursula only comes to understand him gradually – largely by reaction; and the birth has to happen after the understanding, not merely as a result of it – after the fight, not during it. But there is a further reason for potentially misleading resemblances. A fundamental argument of the book is that tick-tack leads nowhere, however long it is pursued, even when every possible reaction seems to have been tried. That part of the book is almost like *Rasselas*: every route, every attempt to dodge past by antithesis, is blocked off. Yet Birkin and Ursula have come through. Inevitably, what they reach, and the routes they take, will bear resemblances at some points to aspects of a comprehensive survey of the permutations of reaction. But the differences are crucial, and they can be used by Lawrence as an important secondary means of defining his elusive meaning.

One of the effects of the 'star-equilibrium' on Birkin and Ursula is to integrate them as individuals. The raw Birkin is an incoherent mixture of Breadalby and Bohemia; through the union with Ursula, they each become whole and integrated. A corrupt approximation to integration is most consistently to be found in Gudrun. She is always seeking completion, a finality of vision which will contain the essence of things, statically. This is why it is she, of the four main characters, who finds the Alps most congenial: 'she wanted to climb the wall of white finality. . . . She felt that there . . . among the final cluster of peaks . . . was her consummation. If she could but come there, alone . . . she would be a oneness with all, she would be herself the eternal, infinite silence, the sleeping, timeless, frozen centre of the All'. But it is a reductive form of completion – I have quoted before her view of Birkin, from which Ursula recoils ('This finality of Gudrun . . . was all such a lie').

The integration of the living characters includes an acceptance of the corruption within life: Ursula is troubled a little by what seems 'degrading' in the 'licentiousness' of their sexual relations in the Alpine hotel, but accepts it on reflection as a necessary part of inclusive experience – 'she was unabashed, she was herself. . . . She was free, when she knew everything, and no dark shameful things were denied her'. This is related to, but also opposed to, the deliberate pursuit of corruption, sensuality as a complete end in itself, as represented most extremely in the African carving. Birkin explicitly rejects the 'long African process of purely sensual understanding, knowledge in the mystery of dissolution'. The thinking of the raw Birkin included the Bohemian cult of deliberate primitivism of this kind, but he rejects it, and even in the letter Halliday reads out, he wrote of a 'living desire' to leave the flowers of mud behind.

'Star-equilibrium' includes a full acceptance of the other, as well as integration of the individual self. Thus Birkin 'had taken [Ursula] at the roots of her darkness and shame – like a demon, laughing over the fountain of mystic corruption which was one of the sources of her being, laughing, shrugging, accepting, accepting finally'. The sick version of this is Gudrun's desire to 'know' Gerald – 'if she could have the precious *knowledge* of him, she would be filled', she thinks in 'Death and Love'; by 'Snowed Up' she knows him so finally that she has exhausted all he has to offer, and so turns to Loerke. Full acceptance requires full giving – that is what Ursula finds most difficult. Gerald gives himself so limply to Gudrun that he is like a baby turning to its mother, not an equal giving to an equal. New birth requires a prior death. Birkin's death-phase is his protracted withdrawal from Hermione. Ursula's reaches a more obvious climax in 'Sunday Evening': 'She knew all she had to know, she had experienced all she had to experience, she was fulfilled in a kind of ripeness, there remained only to fall from the tree into death.' But for both of them death has to be gone through: there is no other escape from tick-tack. The Gerald–Gudrun version of this is 'seeing it through'. Gerald says of his involvement in the death of his father, 'Somebody's got to see it through, you know'; Gudrun says to Ursula in the Alps, 'the only thing to do with the world, is to see it through.' They observe the death-process and try to stand back from it to do so; Birkin and Ursula pass through death to life. Finally, the refusal to accept the death-process within the self leads to the will to inflict death on the other – the inter-destructive struggle which ends in Gerald's literal death.

An exhaustive list of this sort of definition by near, but crucially incomplete, resemblance would become tedious. I will mention only a few more to emphasise the extent to which the method is used. Gudrun mimics conventionality, as I showed in the last chapter, partly to mock it, partly because she is not deeply creative enough to do anything really different; Birkin follows conventions in sensitive deference to others – he asks Brangwen if he may marry his daughter, and to Ursula's annoyance he continues to show what he calls 'decency' to Hermione. Gerald is incoherent, remains divided in effect between what Birkin calls 'mines and Minette'; Birkin is flexible, able to respond to differing situations in suitably different ways. We are told this on first introduction: 'He affected to be quite ordinary . . . taking the tone of his surroundings, adjusting himself quickly to his interlocutor and his circumstance.' Birkin is 'indifferent' in the sense that he is not dependent on others in a predatory way; Gudrun is 'indifferent' in the sense of being cold – for example at the level-crossing scene with Gerald on the mare – and her form of indifference is taken to uglier extremes by Crich's youngest daughter Winifred and by Loerke. Birkin and Ursula are 'isolated'; and again Winifred and Loerke are more isolated. Winifred is 'quite single and by herself, deriving from nobody.' In chapter 1, Gudrun's misanthropy is expressed in hatred of the people watching the wedding – 'She would have liked them all annihilated, cleared away, so that the world was left clear for her' – and this continues through to the vision she shares with Loerke of the earth split in two by a 'perfect explosive'. In chapter 2, Birkin says, 'People don't really matter'; but he is expressing only the negative side of a commitment to life beyond loyalty to his own species. The implication of that is another matter I shall discuss in Chapter 17. But before that I wish to raise certain other questions about the form of the book.

15 *Women in Love* : Fiction as Fantasy

I have done with exposition. In chapters 13 and 14, I have tried to clarify Lawrence's view of the meaning of human life as embodied in the book most widely agreed to be his best novel; what I wish to do in this chapter and the next is to examine, in reverse order, the adequacy of that view and the competence of his form to express it cogently. One of the recurrent arguments of the present book concerns the capacity of the fictional form to discipline fantasy – the fantasy of everyone (including the author) as projected in the characters or personas, and the fantasy of the author, which fiction-making of its very nature permanently tempts away from the recalcitrant world men inhabit. Lawrence's form in this novel seems to me to suffer from a disabling lack of such discipline. I will consider the book first as a version of utopia.

Lawrence's letters of the period of conception and writing of *Women in Love* abound in references to the establishment of an actual utopia, in response to what he saw as the conclusive collapse of the old world in the catastrophe of world war. His hopes of founding an actual new community divide roughly into three phases. In February 1915, he wrote to Lady Ottoline Morrell: 'I want you to form the nucleus of a new community which shall start a new life among us.'[1] This was to be an elite group ('We will be aristocrats, and as wise as the serpent in dealing with the mob'), led mainly by himself and Bertrand Russell, to whom he wrote in July of the same year: 'A new constructive idea of a new state is needed *immediately*. . . . You must work out the idea of a new state, not go on criticising this old one.'[2] By August, it was clear that Russell would not be adequately ductile: 'Russell says I cherish illusions, that there *is* no such spirit as I like to imagine, the spirit of unanimity in truth, among mankind. He says that is fiction. . . . Russell and Lady Ottoline . . . are traitors.' So the idea of a 'little nucleus of living people'

was abandoned: not even the elite could agree among themselves.
Around the turn of the year he was thinking in more desperate
terms of either a reduced group of four, including Middleton
Murry and Katherine Mansfield, or of himself and Frieda alone.
Thus in December 1915, he wrote to Katherine Mansfield: 'I
want you and Murry to live with us, or near us, in unanimity. . . .
Let us all live together and create a new world.'[3] In January the
'new world' is only *'moi-même* et Frieda'.[4] His 'Rananim',[5] as he
called his utopia, was to be neighbouring cottages in Cornwall,
with Murry and Katherine Mansfield, though it was not easy to
sustain accord even with them. The final phase was a return to a
more ambitious idea, a group emigration to Florida. Again it was
the other people who spoilt Lawrence's otherwise perfect vision. 'I
tell you my Rananim, my Florida idea, was the true one. Only the
people were wrong.'[6] Two months later the solution seemed clear:
'What I want is for us to . . . live apart, away from the world. It is
really my old Florida idea – but one must go further west. I hope
in the end other people will come.'[7] Different people would surely
not be so obstinately wrong – 'We want [Esther Andrews] to go
with us to America, and to the ultimate place we call Typee or
Rananim. There is indeed such an ultimate place.'[8] By the time he
wrote the letters I have last quoted from, *Women in Love* was
finished, but the book itself was, at different times, effectually a
prophecy of the utopia ('Shall keep the title *Women in Love* [*Dies
Irae* was for some time a provisional title, with deliberate
eschatological overtones]. The book frightens me: it is so end-of-
the-world. But it is, it must be, the beginning of a new world too'[9])
and a utopia in its own right ('I know it is true, the book. And it is
another world, in which I can live apart from this foul world
which I will not accept or acknowledge or even enter'[10]). The man
Lawrence of this period quite clearly wished to leave a world he
considered dead and deadening, and to found or find a utopia
somewhere – in England, in Cornwall, in Florida, in California, in
his fiction.

   In the book, there is often direct talk of a utopia. At Breadalby
there is discussion 'about a new state, a new world of man', a new
world which, like most latter-day utopias, is chronologically
rather than geographically distant from present-day Europe and
therefore envisaged as a possible future ('Supposing this old social
state *were* broken and destroyed, then, out of the chaos, what
then?') Sir Joshua puts Russell's case – the *'social* equality of man'

– and is opposed by Gerald with his vision of a mechanical social structure based on production plus personal freedom out of working hours. Birkin does not on this occasion speculate very far, but is clearly thinking along the Lawrentian lines which so exasperated Russell: 'In the spirit I am as separate as one star is from another, as different in quality and quantity. Establish a state on *that*.' A *state* based on star-equilibrium is a utopia indeed. But we hear no more of that. More characteristically, in 'Man to Man', Birkin is thinking of a small-scale utopia for the elect alone. As he muses to himself on his sick-bed, he thinks, 'There is now to come the new day, when we are beings each of us, fulfilled in difference.' And to Gerald, a little later in the same chapter, he expands a little on the essentially a-social conception of his utopia: 'Instead of chopping yourself down to fit the world, chop the world down to fit yourself. As a matter of fact, two exceptional people make another world. You and I, we make another, separate world.' But it is of course with Ursula that the real utopia is envisaged. In 'Excurse', Birkin's use of the word 'nowhere' four times in as many sentences seems to indicate that Lawrence was consciously recalling the meaning of the word 'utopia'. 'I should like to go with you – nowhere. It would be rather wandering just to nowhere. That's the place to get to – nowhere. One wants to wander away from the world's somewheres, into our own nowhere.' From his responses to Ursula's doubts, it does not seem likely that Birkin has a very distinct idea of the nature of his nowhere. 'There's somewhere were we can be free – somewhere where one needn't wear much clothes – none even. . . . there is somewhere – there are one or two people –'. When Ursula persists with the question of where this will be, he falls back firstly on travelling as an end in itself, since its destination is nowhere – 'Let's wander off. That's the thing to do – let's wander off' – and secondly on a wholly metaphorical utopia – ' "It isn't really a locality, though," he said. "It's a perfected relation between you and me, and others – the perfect relation – so that we are free together." ' But since they then proceed to write their resignations from their jobs, it is already clear that it is not in fact to be wholly metaphorical: they do literally desert the commonwealth ('we'd better get out of our responsibilities as quick as we can').

   This is clarified further in the chapter called 'A Chair'. After they have bought the chair, both Ursula and Birkin regret it: Ursula because it belongs to the past ('And I hate your past'),

Birkin because he does not want to live in a 'definite place. As soon as you get a room, and it is *complete*, you want to run from it'. They are agreed a little later that they do not want to 'inherit the earth'; what they want is 'a whole other world'. The home, which the couple they give the chair to want to build, constitutes the somewhere neither can tolerate. It is quite clear that in an at least partly literal sense, they wish to live in a nowhere. The rest of the chapter then takes up a question also touched on in Birkin's remarks in 'Excurse', the question of whether the utopia can include a few others. It is raised again at the end of the book, of course, but there is not, on this matter, any development beyond the inconclusive conclusion of this chapter. Ursula thinks no others are needed; both agree that it is hopeless to try to force others to join them; but Birkin is unsure whether or not he wants others (in particular Gerald), tending on balance to believe he does.

In the final chapters such disagreement between Birkin and Ursula as there is on the nature of utopia centres mainly on whether it is a state or a perpetual journey. Numerous critics have made us acquainted with the terms of Lawrence's philosophy, according to which passivity is characteristically female, activity male. That there should be this difference is to some extent a condition of their sexual relationship; but the novel would seem to indicate that Birkin is really right, that utopia is perpetual journey. On the way to the Alps, the difference is already clear: Ursula looks forward to 'the unknown paradise . . . a sweetness of habitation'; Birkin 'was overcome by the trajectory'. 'What was beyond was not yet for him.' We are prepared for an anticlimax to Ursula's hopes by what she sees as the day dawns, while they are on the train – 'This was an old world she was still journeying through. . . . No new earth had come to pass'. Only when they reach the snow-covered mountains does she feel, 'this was the other world now'. But this other world is essentially the static, dead world of Gerald and Gudrun. Birkin is uneasy almost throughout about what he calls 'the stillness, the cold, the frozen eternality' of the Alps; Ursula can only temporarily enjoy their static beauty; only Gudrun wholly desires the 'white finality' which becomes a very literal finality for Gerald. By the time Birkin and Ursula leave, she is thinking in his terms, and the only resistance comes from Gudrun. 'I think,' says Ursula to Gudrun, 'that Rupert is right – one wants a new space to be in.' Gudrun replies that Birkin's way is no route to a new world – 'to isolate oneself with another person isn't to find a new world at all, but only to secure oneself in one's illusions'.

Gudrun has already been used much earlier, in 'Threshold', as a means of forestalling criticism of the enterprise, with the intention of disarming it. She and Gerald are mocking Birkin from the back of his car: 'he believes that a man and wife can go further than any other two beings – but *where* is not explained . . . they go beyond heaven and hell – into – there it all breaks down – into nowhere'. The tone of cheap mockery continues into the later chapter: as the conversation with Ursula continues, Gudrun tries, characteristically, to close it – 'Go and find your new world, dear. . . . After all, the happiest voyage is the quest of Rupert's Blessed Isles.' Her vision, as always, is intended to be reductive (she sees in static pictures, unable to envisage life as process), and we are clearly meant to recoil from it, as Ursula does. But in a sense she remains right – the couple continue on their journey to what Birkin himself called 'nowhere' – and we see no more of the process. The novel does in effect ask us to accept the voyage to nowhere as an end, believing on trust that the process, which is traced no further, makes the voyage worthwhile.

In his *Study of Thomas Hardy*, Lawrence wrote, 'The degree to which the system of morality, or the metaphysic, of any work of art is submitted to criticism within the work of art makes the lasting value and satisfaction of that work.'[11] This is not really how Gudrun's criticism, or any other criticism, is meant to function within *Women in Love*: we are intended to recoil from it and consequently believe more fully in the basic 'metaphysic'.

It is not difficult to understand why utopia has to take on a new status in Lawrence's book. In all three of the other fictions I have considered, the utopian dreams are ostensibly desirable, but are finally rejected in favour of a return to the old world – the world which man has a responsibility to inhabit, and which, on the deepest reflection, turns out to be also more desirable, despite all the shortcomings which have been highlighted. Lawrence rejected the old world quite consciously, in this book and in general: the old world was dead leaves on a winter tree; their only natural role was to fall off and make way for new growth. At the same time there was for him no transcendent end, no 'choice of eternity' which could put a sublunary utopian enterprise into perspective. The only alternative to the dead old world was a living new one on earth. He had to go to utopia: there was nowhere else to go.

Yet he knew also that utopia is no place on earth. In later books, he made attempts to pretend that it could be located, which are admired by no readers capable of recognising the achievement of *Women in Love*. In this book, voyaging is both an indispensible metaphor and a literal necessity. A place is necessarily static: to stay in a new one, such as the Alps, is only the tick-tack counterpart of staying in the old one. Birkin and Ursula do not want to go home; for a fundamentally related reason they cannot make a new home elsewhere. If life is to be permanently a process, the fictional image of it cannot be one of inhabiting utopia; it must be of a voyage to no place.

Travel functions metaphorically in all four of the fictions I am discussing in the present book. In those of More, Johnson and George Eliot it has an ultimately pejorative force – one travels into fantasy; one returns to reality and responsibility. In Lawrence's novel, travel has become necessarily the desirable end. When the ultimately important end (the 'choice of eternity') is fixed from the start, the journey is in a sense fruitless: human nature being as it is, the individual has to make the journey, but he does not discover anything radically new. In searching for utopia he gets nowhere, but he perceives, with greater clarity, another goal, which he knew of before he started. In George Eliot's book, the ultimately important end is not objectively fixed, but it is quite definitely fixed in the author's mind. The important journey of Maggie is therefore to that end: the journies into fantasy help to clarify by negatives the really desirable route – the way home. But in Lawrence the end is fixed neither absolutely nor relatively: the important thing is to be living, not dead. Life is process; therefore what matters is not the destination as such, but the process of the journey. Travel is not necessarily a good, since it can be an image of tick-tack (the 'flit' to the Alps is Gerald's trip to Bohemia writ large; Gudrun finds there an extreme of the finality she has always sought); but travel as understood by Birkin and Ursula becomes an indispensible image of the commitment to the unknown, which in its earliest stages can be represented as the willingness of the seed to drop off the tree, through death, into new life.

I shall return in the next chapter to other implications, but in terms of form the consequence of these shifts in the status of utopia, and of the journey to it, is that they can no longer operate as means of containing fantasy. When utopia is plainly a never-never land, the raw human desire to go there can be disciplined within the form by means of irony. A bit of Hythloday or of Rasselas exists in every man; the ironies directed at Hythloday's tale and at Rasselas's search are means of preventing that bit from leading the whole man by the nose. In *The Mill on the Floss*, an analogous educative discipline takes place inside the novel: the kind of ironies Maggie experiences in the escape to the gypsies, for example, enables her eventually to resist the seductive fantasy of the drift with Stephen. I argued earlier that the ending is a lapse into authorial fantasy: the utopian discipline operates on Maggie, but not entirely on George Eliot, whereas in More's book it operates very plainly on the author through his role as character. But in *The Mill on the Floss* that breakdown only occurs at the end. In *Women in Love*, the utopia cannot operate as a means of discipline at all. The ordinary world is wholly moribund and to be cast off, so that the living characters can go to utopia. So the utopia cannot be contained within an ironic structure which can control fantasy by return to the ordinary world. In the other three books, one can make a distinction, clearly demonstrable from the text, between fantasy and the fiction which contains and more or less adequately disciplines it. In *Women in Love* the distinction between fiction and fantasy breaks down, since there is no formal means of registering it. Lawrence in effect goes with Birkin and Ursula to nowhere.

But utopian irony is only one means at the disposal of a writer of fiction, by which he can impose discipline upon himself. The difficulty Lawrence is in is more radical: the dogma, upon which the form embodying it must depend, virtually requires an absence of self-discipline. Lawrence himself, of course, did not see his situation in such negative terms. In his vocabulary, the difference is between vital, fluid art and dead, contained art. He is perhaps clearest in a letter of 1925, but two well-known essays of the same year, 'Art and Morality' and 'Morality and the Novel' express the same ideas. 'I don't care a button for neat works of art. . . . I can't bear art that you can walk round and admire. A book should be either a bandit or a rebel or a man in a crowd. . . . An author should be in among the crowd, kicking their shins or cheering on to some mischief or merriment . . . whoever reads me will be in the thick of the scrimmage, and if he doesn't like it – if he wants a safe seat in the audience – let him read somebody else.'[12] In *Women in*

Love, the contained form of art – art which is, as it were, framed, so that the reader can see its content in perspective – is quite deliberately attributed to Gudrun as a means of indicating her limitations as an individual. Near the beginning of the first chapter, she 'wanted to be quite definite', a desire which is radically characteristic of her, and the first stage of the conversation between the two sisters is, like many later ones, closed by Gudrun. ' "Exactly," she said, to close the conversation.' Still in the same chapter, we have her characteristic vision of people: 'She saw each one as a complete figure, like a character in a book, or a subject in a picture, or a marionette in a theatre, a finished creation.' Her own art treats of small figures which can be completed; when Hermione asks to see her sketch-book, she is reluctant, 'for she always hated to have her unfinished work exposed'. Outside her art, her vision is analogous. I have already quoted her sight of Gerald at the level-crossing through the 'closed wagon' of the guard's-van. As she leaves for the Alps she sees London in a similar way, 'having glimpses of the river between the great iron girders' of a bridge. The static, framed vision represents metaphorically the finality she constantly desiderates in life. The relation is made particularly clear for us in 'Flitting': 'She suddenly conjured up a cosy room, with herself in a beautiful gown, and a handsome man in evening dress who held her in his arms in the firelight, and kissed her. This picture she entitled "Home". It would have done for the Royal Academy.' As always, her pictures are reductive: this is hardly an adequate picture of home – it is ironically more like a man and his mistress, the role she is at that time reacting against with all the passion concentrated into the word *'type'*. Against *her* there certainly is a recurrent irony operative: the picture imagined by this avant-garde girl, for whom the London Bohemia is too small, would have done for the Royal Academy. But she is used as a means of directing irony, and the kinds of perspective it can provide, away from the vision embodied in the *open* characters.

There are other kinds of art referred to in the book, which help to define the nature of Gudrun's even more clearly. The most obvious is Birkin's highly unfinished drawing of the catkins: all he wants to do is to emphasise the essential – other details do not matter, and he is unconcerned when Ursula says the crayons will make the books 'untidy'. What he wants to learn from the Chinese geese he copies at Breadalby is 'what centres they live from – what they perceive and feel' – he wants, in the words of the letter I quoted above, to be 'in the thick of the scrimmage'. Even the corrupt art of the African figure at Halliday's flat represents a 'process' to him, a process towards dissolution. The defining opposite, the culmination of Gudrun's static art, is Loerke's frieze in granite. The relation of art to the life of Birkin and Ursula, the counterpart of Gudrun's picture of 'Home', comes in the chapter called 'A Chair': 'You have to be like Rodin, Michael Angelo, and leave a piece of raw rock unfinished to your figure. You must leave your surroundings sketchy, unfinished, so that you are never contained, never confined, never dominated from the outside.' It is, of course, no part of my argument that Lawrence lacks art. I have indicated, not only in this paragraph, but repeatedly in the preceding chapters, that the book is a very closely-woven texture of significant cross-references. What Birkin and Ursula are not is defined with great art by flexible combinations of resemblance to and difference from other characters. We see Gudrun with a completeness her own art has. My point is that the 'piece of raw rock unfinished' in this book is the relationship between Birkin and Ursula – that is, the centre of the book. It is an essential part of its very conception that this *cannot* be finished. It is in that respect that it most radically differs from Gerald's and Gudrun's. So we cannot, within the structure of the book, stand back from it. The vision which it embodies *cannot* be subjected to discipline by the author himself.

Utopian ironies are only one means of self-discipline; I will illustrate Lawrence's predicament further by considering others which I have discussed in relation to More, Johnson and George Eliot. In *Rasselas*, I argued, chance provides an important discipline on the form of fantasy projected through the characters, and in *The Mill on the Floss* external event constitutes a challenge to the author which I termed *resistance*. In *Women in Love*, there is a distinction between chance and fate which is very interesting, but which has no effect of discipline or resistance. Fate and related words are used repeatedly of Gerald, Gudrun and their relationship. The colliers exert a strange power over Gudrun, half-attracting her, half-repelling her – 'awaking a fatal desire, and a fatal callousness'. Gerald is established very early as a virtually fated character. The word fate is not used on either occasion, but at the end of chapter 2 Birkin tells Gerald he is essentially a 'murderee' – 'You seem to have a lurking desire to have your gizzard slit' – and in chapter 4 Ursula cannot accept Gudrun's opinion that it was by pure accident that Gerald shot his brother when a child. The desires to kill and to be killed are his by fate. The drowning of his sister in 'Water-party' seems to Gudrun to be '*bound* to happen'. When Gerald creeps into the Brangwen house in 'Death and Love', 'she knew there was something fatal in the situation, and she must accept it', and the words 'fate' and 'fatal' recur in that chapter with the degree of frequency which is a notorious characteristic of Lawrence's prose. The word 'fate' is of course not used in the normal, external sense: it is used chiefly to indicate a psychological or moral attitude of the characters. For example, in the following chapter ('Marriage or Not'), Gerald 'was ready to be doomed. Marriage was like a doom to him . . . He was willing to accept this'. This is carried through to the end: Gerald 'wanted so to come to the end' that he virtually wills his death. 'Lord Jesus, was it then bound to be . . . !' But it has also some external force, clarified by Birkin as he reflects on Gerald's death: 'The eternal creative mystery could dispose of man, and replace him with a finer created being.' Gerald and Gudrun are doomed in the sense that the mastodon was doomed.

The Birkin of the early part of the book is almost in Gerald's condition in this as in other respects: he sits in Hermione's room with his back to her – virtually submitting to the doom of the blow on his head. But his later behaviour, and the development of the relationship with Ursula are characterised not by fate but more by accident. Most of their meetings occur by chance – Ursula finds him in 'An Island' after wandering at random; similarly in 'Moony'. Later in 'Moony' he goes to ask her to marry him and finds himself speaking first to her father about it, by 'accident', as he says to Gerald. The climax in 'Excurse' occurs largely by accident – Birkin has almost given up caring ('Why not drift on in a series of accidents – like a picaresque novel?') – and the resolution to the argument that follows simply happens. Ursula makes the implication explicit in talking to Birkin about his hopes for a few other people joining their 'freedom together' – 'it must *happen*. You can't do anything for it with your will. You always seem to think you can *force* the flowers to come out. People must love us because they love us – you can't *make* them'. In other words, acceptance of accident is an aspect of committing oneself to the true current of life; if one starts willing, one becomes, like Hermione, a dead leaf clinging unnaturally to a winter tree. The image underlying Lawrence's dogma is not one of a struggle to evolve, but one of waiting for the new to happen, for the buds to burst of their own accord.

So chance does have a very important role in the structure of the fiction: the distinction between fate and chance helps to define the difference between Gerald and Birkin; Birkin's acceptance of chance is an aspect of his commitment to the unknown – of his voyage to utopia. But of course *that* role precludes the use of chance as a discipline on the fantasy of utopia. Accident has become part of the basic design, as is clear from Birkin's reflections in chapter 2, when he is thinking about Gerald having killed his brother: 'Why seek to draw a brand and a curse across the life that had caused the accident? . . . or is this not true, is there no such thing as pure accident? Has *everything* that happens a universal significance?' Of course, in all good fiction, virtually everything that happens has significance. But in George Eliot's form a (generally) credible course of events acts as a partial restraint on the desire to re-shape the brute world according to her own model. In Lawrence's form, even what merely 'happens' is an integral part of the basic model. What merely happens is in fact the desiderated part of his model; so it *cannot* function as resistance to it.

The same point has to be made about Lawrence's use of narrative expectation. In *Rasselas*, as I showed at length, broken expectation acts as a check on the confidence of the characters and the reader in their ability to find a way through. In *Women in Love*, it cannot, since Lawrence uses it for a different purpose. The relationship between Gerald and Gudrun follows a highly predictable course, from love at first sight (' "Good God!" she exclaimed to herself, "what is this? . . . am I *really* singled out for him in some way?" '), through suburban fornication, to fatal 'flit' to the Continent, which completes the story. In contrast, we expect the relationship between Birkin and Ursula to be unconventional, and find our expectations are broken, when he gives her rings, speaks 'first to her father, as it should be, in the world', and they formally marry – then broken again when their story is not completed, and the book ends with an inconclusive conversation between them. But this, of course, is part of the basic demonstration of how Birkin and Ursula come through. Gerald and Gudrun believe themselves to be reacting away from the past (Gerald goes to Gudrun's bedroom from his father's grave; Gudrun cannot

stand her father and her old home), but in fact are trapped in a
tick-tack pendulum swing away from and back to the conventional. Their relationship is really only the kind of exaggerated
version of the commonplace, characteristic of bad art, which
Gudrun always wanted ('how much more powerful and terrible
was his embrace than [the colliers'], how much more concentrated and supreme his love was, than theirs in the same sort!')
Narrative expectation is fulfilled because the relationship is
trivial, and the story closes because the way of life is as dead as the
convention. In the case of Birkin and Urusla, we do not get
obvious unconventionality because the way through tick-tack is
not by reaction; so the pattern of their story unexpectedly includes
an observance of the old forms, partly accidental and partly
charged with new meaning. But the old aesthetic form of narrative
completion is broken, because the way through is to new life, not
to finality. Broken expectation functions as a means of showing
the way through; it therefore cannot function as a means of
breaking confidence in one's ability to see the way through. The
ending of the book has frequently been taken, very naively in my
view, as pattern-breaking – a form of modern art truer to the
indeterminacy of things than the closures of more traditional
fiction. Actually it is a very fundamental part of Lawrence's
pattern; and as such it cannot operate as a discipline on the
fantasy which I take that pattern to embody.

In discussing *The Mill on the Floss* I wrote of the way character
can work as *resistance* to authorial fantasy in the naturalistic form
of the novel: George Eliot cannot cheat by making Tom a too
grossly maimed human being – if she did, the discord with the
conventions of her form would cause the reader aesthetic
dissatisfaction. It is very well known that Lawrence consciously
discarded those conventions in *Women in Love*, looking, as he
thought, for means of expressing something deeper. The classic
exposition of his intention is the letter to Edward Garnett of 5 June
1914. 'You mustn't look in my novel for the old stable *ego* – of the
character . . . don't look for the development of the novel to follow
the lines of certain characters: the characters fall into the form of
some other rhythmic form, as when one draws a fiddle-bow across
a fine tray delicately sanded, the sand takes lines unknown.'[13] The
famous image of carbon, which I have omitted from my quotation, emphasises Lawrence's intention of going into a deeper
reality; the part of his statement which I have quoted shows the

concomitant reductive consequence. The 'other rhythmic form' is Lawrence's dogma: character development of the kind found in the traditional naturalistic novel no longer constitutes any resistance to dogma. An extreme instance is the death of Thomas Crich. His death is not like Tulliver's, which George Eliot obviously included as part of her artistic intention, but to which her form required her to make the other characters respond credibly. Crich dies because Lawrence wishes to register the death of the old order of values, and the form exerts no restraint on Lawrence's wishes. On the contrary, it even permits him to make Mrs Crich say absurdly to her children, over the death-bed, 'None of you look like this, when you are dead! Don't let it happen again.' Lawrence wishes to say that Crich looks unnaturally young when he dies, because his values never allowed him to live properly. In a naturalistic novel, such a response would be incredible: the writer would be forced to refine his meaning. But Lawrence's form offers no resistance to his dogma. In the famous essay on 'Morality and the Novel', Lawrence wrote, 'If you try to nail anything, down in the novel, either it kills the novel, or the novel gets up and walks away with the nail.'[14] In this novel the 'dead' characters are absolutely nailed. Hermione never moves other than 'slowly'; Halliday is 'broken'; Gudrun always wants to close things. The dogma of the book is that they are incapable of walking away; the form nails them. They are not characters of the kind one finds in naturalistic novels; they are more like walking collocations of symbols which Lawrence can arrange into any pattern of his choice.

In some kinds of fiction, it does not matter that the characters or personas lack independence. The figures in *Rasselas* need not function as independent characters since they have equal fictional status and Johnson has other means of discipline which I have discussed. But what we have in *Women in Love* is a kind of two-tier system, in which most characters are nailed down by a structure of symbols, from which they have no means of escape, whereas Birkin and Ursula alone are granted independence. The 'carbon' of Hermione determines that she will always be imprisoned by her will; the 'carbon' of Birkin determines that he will escape. This simply reflects an absolute difference which Lawrence postulated between them (Birkin has 'life'; Hermione has not). The postulate has no external validation (in the way that the Christian thought underlying *Utopia* and *Rasselas* had, for their authors, external validation): Lawrence needs to make it good through the 'art-speech' of his novel. But the form of 'art-speech' he chose offered no challenge which could make him question or discipline the raw postulate. His position as narrator is analogous to that of Hythloday, not More: the rules of the form change according to the needs of the case he is making. Europe cannot be changed by wise counsel; Hermione can never really understand Birkin. Utopia has achieved the perfect state of the commonwealth; Birkin and Ursula have come through. When More doubts the difference can be so cut-and-dried, the answer is, 'You should have been there'; in Lawrence there can be nothing analogous to the irony of that answer. Hythloday and More have unequal fictional status, which More uses to challenge the raw postulate; Birkin and Hermione have unequal fictional status, which Lawrence has expended in expressing the raw postulate. More has external validation for the grounds of his challenge; Lawrence has only his 'art-speech' itself to validate his postulate; and he wilfully discarded the means of *resistance* incorporated in the form of George Eliot, who had similarly to rely on 'art-speech'.

This seems to me a very serious defect of form; but the situation is in fact worse than I have so far described it. There is *basically* a two-tier division between the characters, but Gerald does not actually belong as absolutely to the tier of the damned, as Hermione. From beginning to end of the novel, Birkin believes that there is some possibility of saving Gerald, and Gerald himself has both a desire for 'something else' and the sense that Birkin is the man who can help him find it. Yet the whole symbolic structure built up round Gerald – the associations with whiteness, snow, machinery, violence, destruction, and so on – so effectually imprisons him that it is impossible to believe, from the 'art-speech', that he could have escaped. According to the form, he was really doomed before the beginning of the book, even before he killed his brother – his nurse says he was already at six months old 'a proper demon'. It would seem that Lawrence did not entirely want to show an absolute division between damned and elect, and that his form, so far from refining his vision, actually simplified and obstructed it. I showed this happening in particular in 'Gladiatorial' (pp. 260–1 above). Lawrence seems to want to say there that the relationship between Birkin and Gerald is healthy and good for both, but his form will not let him introduce that complication. On the larger scale, it will not let him show a

Gerald who we can believe could go either way. Lawrence did not want to nail him; the form inexorably nailed him. The form of 'carbon' characterisation does not stretch the author beyond the limiting confines of raw human fantasy; it actually makes the fantasy-world more cramped.

A parallel point can be made about the structure of the book around a series of symbolic or semi-symbolic episodes. An intelligent narrative form can constitute resistance to the simplifications of fantasy-models – for example, a narrative structure which could include a more naturalistic kind of social intercourse would obviously have facilitated the development of a more substantial relationship between Gerald and Birkin. Instead, we have a series of isolated episodes, most of which, in addition to characterising either the Gerald–Gudrun or the Birkin–Ursula relationship, form part of a continuous definition by contrast, as the relationships unfold. I have given examples in the preceding chapters. This gives the novel a great intensity (many readers would say an exhausting intensity, since the book is of such length); but it means again that the pattern is all, and that it is reductive – Gerald is trapped by the sequence of contrasts as much as by the symbols which dog him.

I wish to conclude this chapter with a consideration of Lawrence's aesthetic purposes in this novel. To some extent his situation is similar to George Eliot's: like her he has recourse to no external conception of Purpose, so any sense of purpose has to be generated inside the novel. In the case of George Eliot, I expressed that as helping the reader to develop, like Maggie, towards a fuller humanity. It might seem, from some of his explicit statements, that Lawrence's intentions are similar – though of course his conception of what constitutes a fuller humanity is rather different from hers. Thus against her famous, 'If Art does not enlarge men's sympathies, it does nothing morally', it might seem obvious to set his equally famous remarks in chapter 9 of *Lady Chatterly's Lover* – '[The novel] can inform and lead into new places the flow of our sympathetic consciousness, and it can lead our sympathy away in recoil from things gone dead'. The derivation of this view of the moral effect of literature from Wordsworth is clearer in *Studies in Classical American Literature*: 'The essential function of art is moral. But a passionate, implicit morality, not didactic. A morality which changes the blood, rather than the mind. Changes the blood first. The mind follows later, in the wake.'[15] The language here is obviously not Wordsworthian, but the thought is clearly a variation on Wordsworth's concept of the education of the feelings. Yet is this really what happens in *Women in Love?*

Clearly George Eliot's belief, that the extension of sympathy is in itself a good, has gone: our sympathies are more led away in recoil from things gone dead, than extended. This is the case even with Gerald. Birkin weeps over his body and thinks in terms which seem oddly sentimental in a novel which rejects old beliefs – 'Those who die, and dying still can love, still believe, do not die. They live still in the beloved. Gerald might still have been living in the spirit with Birkin, even after death.' But the point is, he is not still so living – he let go Birkin's hand. 'If he had kept true to that clasp, death would not have mattered'; but he did not, so he is reduced utterly to 'cold, mute Matter'. His death causes pain, since (Birkin believes) he could have chosen differently; but fundamentally 'he left the heart cold'. There is obviously no need to argue that sympathy is not asked for any of the metaphorically dead characters. It would be equally superfluous to argue that the book does not work like *Utopia* or *Rasselas* – the way through is not by clearer thought: even Birkin's thought corrupts. But is the ostensible conclusion – that the purpose of the novel is to make the reader's sympathetic consciousness move towards Birkin and Ursula – correct?

We come back here to the shortcomings of 'carbon'. Birkin and Ursula do not, by deliberate choice on Lawrence's part, exist for us in the way that George Eliot's characters exist. When Maggie suffers, we are made to share her pain – those 'keen moments' of her childhood and adolescence are re-created by George Eliot's art in such a way that we live through them vicariously, taking in both their immediate effect and their cumulative influence on her development. When Birkin is on his sick-bed, we are not in any emotional way anxious for his recovery: the sickness only exists really on the metaphorical level. We do not so much feel what it is like to be Birkin sick, as think through his problems with him. At the most basic level of response to fiction, we are on the side of Birkin and Ursula, and against Hermione, Gudrun and all other threats to the resolution of the hero-heroine relationship. But the absence of a narrative level discourages the reader from feeling the kind of suspense which draws a sense of concern for the safe resolution. In fact, as the pattern of structural contrasts begins to build up, it rapidly becomes clear that that relationship is as certain to succeed as the Gerald–Gudrun relationship is to fail. Our interest becomes more an intellectual one – how can tick-tack be circumvented? – than an emotional one based on sympathy for the individuals and concern for their future. Because such sympathy and concern are absent, we do not, in the George Eliot manner, feel with Birkin and Ursula. It is clear enough that Lawrence wishes us to regard them as healthy and the rest as diseased, but in so far as the novel draws us towards their attitudes and away from the others', it does so by a rhetoric of symbolism, not really by a compulsion of sympathy, a feeling with them. We cannot really live vicariously in their relationship since we have not experienced what it is like to live their individual lives.

This need not necessarily matter very much. Fiction does not have to work by extending the reader's sympathies: neither *Utopia* nor *Rasselas* works in such a way. But Lawrence wants, rather desperately, to change the orientation of people: the old values are dead and the only hope lies in a renewal of the kind represented through Birkin and Ursula. There is, consequently, a messianic dimension to his book, which he tries to objectify and contain by means of Ursula's gibes at the 'Salvator Mundi' trait in Birkin. Opinions differ on the degree of his success in this, and since they have been extensively published, I will not expound the one I share – that the diction of superlatives and repetition is oppressively didactic, and the attempt to shift responsibility onto Birkin is unsuccessful; though since we do not feel with the characters, I doubt whether Lawrence had much alternative, as he wanted to change human values so substantially. But it is here that his difficulties become most acute. The image underlying his thought about the human predicament is, as I have said before, of waiting for a tree to put out new leaves, or for a flower to grow. Yet he sees his fiction, not only in the critical comments in which his own awareness of what he is doing is unsteady, but as the fiction itself makes obvious, as a means of persuasion – of persuading the reader to abandon the old and commit himself to the new and unknown. But as Ursula observes in 'A Chair', one cannot '*force* the flowers to come out'. A reader who *tries* to blossom, on the basis of what he reads, will turn out like Hermione, not like Ursula. Birkin only breaks through when he stops trying to think his way through and waits for it to 'happen'. 'Star-equilibrium' comes through perfecting relationship, not through the images of perfecting relationship which are all that can be derived from a book. The images are not static – they have not the kind of reductive effect of Gudrun's images – they are of process (of stoning a moon which perpetually re-forms, of travelling, and so on). But even inside the book they have the status of commentary on relationship, not of actual relationship; outside the book they have obviously only that status.

So the purposes embodied in the art of this book seem to me to oscillate between preaching and the expression of defiant resignation. Part of Lawrence wants to convert people to life; part of him knows that that is self-contradictory. A major intention of More and Johnson is to teach the reader how to think; George Eliot wants to teach him how to feel; despite the hyperboles in Lawrence's essays about the status of fiction ('The novel is the one bright book of life'), he has left it with little to do. His mood was very black when he wrote *Women in Love*. 'It has been the round of publishers by now, and rejected by all. I don't care. One might as well make roses bloom in January, as bring out living work into this present world of man.'[16] But he would not give up – 'We must live through, for the hope of the new summer of the world.' The genuineness and the tenacity of his belief in the future of life saves his enterprise, despite its self-contradiction, from any degree of absurdity; in chapter 16 I shall discuss its adequacy.

16 *Women in Love*: 'I want to be disinherited'

There is no doubt that Lawrence regarded not only the state of human civilisation in his time, but also his own response to it, as very nearly desperate. The voyage of Birkin and Ursula to utopia is put forward not with any sense of confidence but because 'there isn't anything else'. The phrase I have just quoted comes from the conversation between Birkin and Gerald in the train. Birkin has said that the old ideals are dead and there remains only 'ultimate marriage'. ' "And you mean if there isn't the woman, there's nothing?" said Gerald. "Pretty well that – seeing there's no God." "Then we're hard put to it," said Gerald.' On the showing of *Women in Love* we are indeed. Gerald's sphere of activity, mechanical production of material goods, is an empty sphere. Birkin's – education – seems equally pointless, since 'You can only have knowledge . . . of things concluded, in the past', and the past is dead. Between them, their activities touch on the whole range of human purpose, material and (in the broad sense of the word) spiritual. Both turn from their public activity to very limited personal relationship, as the sole remaining location of meaning in life, the difference lying only in the degree of desperation indicated by the timing. Gerald runs to the dead end of his industrial purpose and *has* to turn to Gudrun; Birkin finds Ursula and decides then to resign from his job. In Gerald's case, Lawrence shows that this makes him disastrously dependent on Gudrun; I do not think Lawrence faced with full honesty the fact that Birkin's case, with its equal lack of independent activity, makes him equally dependent on Ursula. But he knew clearly enough it was a *pis aller*: he had wanted Russell to collaborate in reforming society, and he wanted the utopia to include others; even Birkin, at the stage of desperation reached at the end of the novel, still believes he wants 'eternal union with a man too'. But he does not find it; and Lawrence, as he wrote to Katherine Mansfield, did not either.

Ostensibly, the concept of 'ultimate marriage' in isolation is an odd one. By the time he wrote *Women in Love*, Lawrence had almost comprehensively rejected the Christianity in which marriage has a traditional place. To Lawrence, Christian love implied a 'merging', which impinged on the vital autonomy of the individual; self-sacrifice was a form of tyranny or blackmail; even the War was only made possible through the fault of Christian concepts ('This is what the love of our neighbour has brought us to, that because one man dies, we all die . . . Christianity is based on the love of self, the love of property, one degree removed. Why should I care for my neighbour's property, or my neighbour's life, if I do not care for my own?'[1] But when Birkin speaks of the 'finality of love' in the chapter on the train, he is not to be taken to be expressing an idea belonging to his tick-tack phase – two chapters after 'Excurse' he agrees when Gerald says the 'married state' is 'final'. Lawrence of course rejected any notion that marriage was to be a 'bond' – 'It is an absurdity, to say that men and women *must love*.' But in the essay I have just quoted from ('Morality and the Novel', 1925), a permanent union of man and woman is described as the 'central clue to human life'.[2] The phrase recurs in 'A Propos of *Lady Chatterley's Lover*' – 'marriage is the clue to human life' – the essay which perhaps most clearly expresses the two basic reasons why, of all the old ideals, Lawrence wished to salvage this one. Firstly it is a means to freedom; secondly it is a means of contact with the universal rhythm of life. 'It is marriage, perhaps, which had given man the best of his freedom . . . It is a true freedom because it is a true fulfillment.' 'Marriage is the clue to human life, but there is no marriage apart from the wheeling sun and the nodding earth . . . And does not the changing harmony and discord of their variation make the secret music of life?' 'Sex is the balance of male and female in the universe, the attraction, the repulsion, the transit of neutrality.'[3] Marriage is the means to full freedom, the balanced individuality (the 'freedom together' of balanced stars) which is the only location of human life (since only individuals live), and the means of sharing in the universal interaction of male and female, which Lawrence believed to be the basis of all life. Only as an end is it dead. When Birkin talks of it being 'irrevocable', Ursula calls this 'the old dead morality', but he replies, 'No . . . it is the law of creation.' The end, towards which it is the means, is life itself.

In some of his essays, Lawrence is more explicit than is appropriate in the novel. 'Why the Novel Matters' is the location of the famous phrase, 'Nothing is important but life.'[4] In 'Aristocracy' the point is made in language which relates more obviously to the terms I have used in the present book: 'All creation contributes, and must contribute, to this: towards the achieving of a vaster, vivider cycle of life. That is the goal of living.'[5] The word 'goal' recurs in 'Education of the People': 'life is unfathomable and unsearchable in its motives, not to be described, having no ascribable goal save the bringing-forth of an ever-changing, ever-unfolding creation'.[6] Life itself is, for Lawrence, the ultimate end; and he saw very clearly that as such it should become the basis of his moral thought. He says so explicitly in 'Him with his Tail in his Mouth': 'This we know, now, for good and all: that which is good, and moral, is that which brings into us a stronger, deeper flow of life and life-energy: evil is that which impairs the life-flow.'[7] Good is that which makes for life; evil is that which obstructs life. This is, of course, a very natural conclusion. In the Christian view of the world, some things are more important than life: there is a transcendent End which gives life its meaning, but which under certain conditions 'impairs the life-flow'; and then life ceases to be the ultimately important consideration. George Eliot tried to retain the Christian order of values without the transcendent End from which they derive: specifically she set self-denial against the 'life-flow' between Maggie and Stephen. I have a deep respect for that attempt, but I fear it necessitates the kind of cheating I analysed earlier. It is possible to construct logical arguments, but I doubt very much whether it is possble to persuade many people, that it is more reasonable to sacrifice oneself than to seek what Maggie calls 'fulness of existence', when there is no transcendent end which makes 'fulness of existence' relatively insignificant. I fear it is unlikely to affect any but those who already wish to find 'the way home'. Lawrence's position is more obviously coherent: since the Christian end has gone, self-sacrifice has gone with it. 'Fulness of existence' becomes the end. As far as I know he did not comment in print on the Maggie–Stephen relationship, but from his view of *Anna Karenina* it is possible to be confident of what he would have said: 'the greater unwritten morality [as opposed to the social

code] . . . would have bidden Vronsky detach himself from the
system, become an individual, creating a new colony of morality
with Anna'.[8] If life is the ultimate end, it becomes a moral
obligation, overriding any particular social code, to do what most
fosters life – to sacrifice not oneself but what impedes life. That
makes sense; but there are consequences.

Many of these consequences are actually clear in *Women in Love*;
but the novel does not adequately register the significance of
them. For example, Birkin and Ursula have no children. Obviously, the form of the book as we have it could not include the birth of
children; but this is not a how-many-children-had-Lady-Macbeth
question. If the 'greater . . . morality' underlying a novel is 'for
life' (I will use that vague phrase for the sake of brevity – the
quotations above define it), the absence of literal birth cannot
pass unnoticed. The question is in fact raised in Bohemia –
Minette does not want the baby she is carrying – but the absence
of true creative spirit in Bohemia, which it signifies there, is not
subsequently contrasted with Birkin and Ursula in this respect.
The question is also raised in the first chapter, between Ursula
and Gudrun, and closed with a provisional negative. The
difficulty cannot be removed by arguing that Lawrence deliberately left the question open, as he tries to do with the relationship
of Gerald to Birkin. This is not left explicitly open at the end; it is
simply ignored. Nor can one possibly say that the answer is too
obvious to need inclusion – as at the concluding marriage in a
Jane Austen novel, for example. From what we do gather of the
way of life which awaits Birkin and Ursula, the conditions for
successful upbringing of children are very conspicuously absent.

If we turn to other writings by Lawrence, there is evidence that
the omission was by no means a matter of temporary absent-
mindedness. He can, of course, write with great penetration about
parent–child relationships, but in his visionary mood, his attention is concentrated on the man–woman relationship. In terms of
imagery, the flower matters more than the fruit. Thus in the
'Study of Thomas Hardy': 'The final aim is the flower . . . Not the
fruit . . . but the flower is the culmination and climax, the degree
to be striven for. Not the work I shall produce, but the real Me I
shall achieve, that is the consideration; of the complete Me will
come the complete fruit of me, the work, the children.[9] More
baldly, in 'Morality and the Novel', children 'result from the
relationship [of man and woman], as a contingency.'[10] In a way

this makes very good sense. If life is the ultimate end, then the climax to be striven for may well be the moment of flowering relationship, when life is most intense – and the fruit will follow by course of nature. But images only work within limits: human children do not grow quite like fruit. Or to use Birkin's image, how do children fit into 'star-equilibrium'? Lawrence did, of course, find a magnificent image elsewhere – the arch formed by Tom and Lydia for Anna in *The Rainbow*. But Birkin and Ursula could not be the pillars of an arch: they have nowhere to stand. They have nowhere by choice ('I want to be disinherited') because they want to be free – 'freedom together' is a fundamental desideratum throughout their relationship. That freedom includes freedom within the relationship – freedom from the clinging kind of love which Ursula thought she wanted in the phase when Birkin sees her as another Magna Mater, a tyrant threatening to imprison him as much as Hermione had done. But motherhood requires mother-love, and although that does not mean it will necessarily taint the man–woman relationship, it can hardly not affect it at all. To come outside Lawrence's vocabulary: having children incurs responsibilities which seriously restrict freedom. There is a very real dilemma here, which is simply not confronted. Why should a couple spoil the flower stage of their relationship, the moment, for them, of the most intense 'fulness of existence', for the sake of children who will restrict them? On the other hand, an ethic in which 'life' is the term of greatest value is rather disastrously crippled if the most 'living' do not in the most literal sense create life. To go back to Lawrence's symbolism, the rejection of home can represent cutting oneself free from the restrictions of the dead past, but if one follows its implications through, it is also in effect cutting oneself free from the restrictions of the living future. We are really back with the problem which most troubled the Utopians: if pleasure for oneself, or life for oneself ('the real Me') is one's individual end, how can the commonwealth, or the wider 'cycle of life', be sustained?

In different forms, this problem overshadows the whole book and dominates the ending. Birkin and Ursula resign from their jobs. This is not a sudden whim: Birkin had provisionally decided on it as early as chapter 11 ('An Island'). The work of both is in education, an area where, if at all, the young could be saved from the death of industrial mechanism and tick-tack rebellion. Very deliberately, they reject this possibility, in favour of securing their

own freedom from the whole structure of established society. As
Birkin says in 'An Island', 'I don't care a straw for the social ideals
I live by, I hate the dying organic form of social mankind – so it
can't be anything but trumpery, to work at education. I shall drop
it as soon as I am clear enough – tomorrow perhaps – and be by
myself.' The only qualification the rest of the book offers to the
misanthropy registered in the title of that chapter is to change
'myself' to 'ourselves'. Ursula's reply at the time makes an
important point. ' "Have you enough to live on?" asked Ursula.
"Yes – I've about four hundred a year." ' Freedom together
depends on a private income: Lawrence was completely honest
about that. But I do not think it is really the *most* important point.
To be free together, Birkin and Ursula abandon not just adults,
who have some responsibility for the society they constitute, but
children, who could be educated to create what Lawrence
believed to be a better one. This is indeed to desert the
commonwealth ('we'd better get out of our responsibilities as
quick as we can'). Again, it is entirely coherent: 'responsibility',
like 'duty', is a word belonging to a dead vocabulary. Paternalistic
'duty' dies with Crich; 'responsibility' to maintain mechanical
order dies with Gerald. Self-sacrifice is a corrupt means of
achieving power, like Minette over Halliday, Hermione over
Birkin. Submission to such imperatives of the dead moral order
would constitute that evil 'which impairs the life-flow'. Yet the
problem remains: commitment to 'life' seems to entail a
selfishness which 'impairs the life-flow' at the most literal level,
through the young.

Birkin and Ursula do not only resign from their jobs: they reject
the whole society they were born into ('I want to be disinherited').
Birkin wants to save Gerald, but he has no lasting concern for
anyone else. This is not merely metaphorical. They are, at one
level, rejecting the values that society stands by; but the rejection
is also based on the theories of 'disquality' shared by Birkin and
Lawrence. There is, of course, obvious truth in those theories: in
terms of gifts (in Lawrence's language, in terms of capacity for
life) men are very unequal. There is much to be said for the
honesty with which Lawrence confronts the problem of a
de-Christianised democracy. In the sight of an omnipotent God,
the inequalities between men are insignificant; remove His
perspective and the inequalities become great. But the way
Lawrence follows the argument through is not very palatable to a

liberal conscience. In 'Aristocracy': 'Life rises in circles, in degrees. The most living is the highest. And the lower shall serve the higher, if there is to be any life among men.'[11] In *Women in Love* we are not, fortunately, taken into the politics which derive from that line of thought; we stop short at the point made explicit in the 'Study of Thomas Hardy' – 'let those that have life, live'[12] (and the devil take those who have not life). But in political terms even this is desperate. Essentially it is the attitude of Hythloday. Most people are going to get wet in the rain anyway: the only effect of going out to persuade them to stay in the dry is to get wet oneself. The truly wise man (or the most living) will just leave them to it and go his own way. There is no return to public duties, to Abyssinia, to home: 'I want to be disinherited.' The soul 'is to go down the open road, as the road opens, into the unknown, keeping company with those whose soul draws them near to her, accomplishing nothing save the journey, and the works incident to the journey, in the long life-travel into the unknown'.[13]

The metaphor of travelling goes so deep that it becomes virtually literal: Hythloday will always be a traveller; Birkin and Ursula are committed to wandering. For Lawrence himself it became completely literal. 'Why come to anchor? There is nothing to anchor for. Land has no answer to the soul any more. It has gone inert. Give me a little ship, kind gods, and three world-lost comrades. Hear me! And let me wander aimless across this vivid outer world, the world empty of man, where space flies happily.'[14] The comprehensive misanthropy expressed by Birkin in 'An Island' is, according to my analysis of the structure of the novel, to be taken as diseased, one of the last throes of his tick-tack phase ('If only man was swept off the face of the earth, creation would go on so marvellously, with a new start, non-human. Man is one of the mistakes of the creation – like the ichthyosauri'). When he thinks in the last chapter in similar terms ('God can do without man. God could do without the ichthyosauri and the mastodon'), it is plain that the reference is only to Gerald and his like ('the mystery could dispense with man, should he too fail creatively to change and develop'), for Birkin and Ursula have changed and developed. But there is never any doubt about leaving all but the three (which becomes two when Gerald fails) to the process of destruction, which according to the novel is well-advanced. In practice, the 'life', to which Lawrence and his characters are committed, comes down to an unemployed,

childless and friendless couple wandering in freedom together to
no place. The facts are there, with deeply admirable honesty, in
the novel; the significance of them is not, in my view, made
adequately plain by the form – and Lawrence's own subsequent
way of life makes me doubt whether he fully grasped it at all. The
predicament was diagnosed by Imlac: 'He who has nothing
external that can divert him, must find pleasure in his own
thoughts. . . . He then expatiates in boundless futurity. . . . Then
fictions begin to operate as realities . . .'.

The consequences of taking life as the ultimate end include
some very grave ones; what might make it worth accepting them?
For Lawrence himself, I think it is clear that the main reason was
that it seemed to salvage some vestige of faith. 'Primarily I am a
passionately religious man, and my novels must be written from
the depth of my religious experience.'[15] That is a remark from a
letter of 1914, but he said the same thing many times elsewhere.
The details and the formulations of his belief underwent many
changes, but essentially it was in a God unfolding through Life.
Thus in 1911: 'There still remains a God, but not a personal God:
a vast, shimmering impulse which waves onwards towards some
end, I don't know what. . . . When we die . . . we fall back into the
big shimmering sea of unorganised life which we call God.'[16] And
in 1927: 'Creation is a great flood, for ever flowing, in lovely and
terrible waves. In everything, the shimmer of creation, and never
the finality of the created. Never the distinction between God and
God's creation, or between Spirit and Matter.'[17] I do not wish to
add to the very large number of expositions of Lawrence's articles
of faith. The essential point is that it elevates Life to the status of
the Unknown to which the individual will must submit. This is
fundamentally a religious attitude: Life becomes a god whom the
individual has an obligation to obey, an end greater than the
desire of any self-centred individual. This is what saved Lawrence
from the absolute despair which his analysis of contemporary
society and the failure of his utopian enterprises would otherwise
have entailed. 'None of us knows the way. The way is given on the
way. . . . I must submit my will and my understanding – all I must
submit, not to any other will, not to any other understanding, not
to anything that is, but to the exquisitest suggestion from the
unknown that comes upon me. This I must attend to and submit
to. It is not me, it is upon me.'[18] It is this submission to the
Unknown which distinguishes Birkin most radically, even in his

sickest periods, from the 'dead' characters who seek to know, to confine, to complete, to control ('Let mankind pass away – time it did. The creative utterances will not cease, they will only be there'). It is this that most fundamentally accounts for the changeableness which continues to disconcert even Ursula. This is why he cannot get what he knows he wants till he waits for it to happen. This is why his relationship with Ursula remains 'open', uncompleted, moving 'onwards towards some end, I don't know what'.

The actually religious content of Lawrence's beliefs has, I think, more expositors than converts. What really attracts those critics and readers who find him not only a greatly gifted novelist but also the great interpreter of life in our time (I am of course thinking of Leavis and his followers) are the vestigial religious attitudes and concepts which the vagueness of his beliefs – the way in which God can become Life and Life can easily lose its capital letter – makes it seem one can retain without any actual religion at all. Most fundamentally, there remains in Lawrence *hope*. Humanity has driven itself into a dead end, but life (Life) is larger than any man or indeed all men. Creativity is manifest in nature, even if God is not; creativity is manifest in the works of a man of Lawrence's obvious genius; creativity may therefore eventually triumph over man's present self-destructive lunacy – though one cannot see how, so it remains a matter of hope. But since that is the location of hope, the obligation of critic and teacher becomes one of fostering creativity. 'Life' cannot retain the fully Lawrentian implications of its capital letter – his *faith* in Life, entailing unquestioning submission to the Unknown, cannot be accepted – so waiting for rebirth to 'happen', after the universal destruction of the old forms, will not do. Consequently, there is that crucial difference between Lawrence and Leavis which Michael Black has recently commented on:[19] Leavis the dedicated educator, living and working in his native land; Lawrence, like Birkin, dedicated to Life but not to many people, wandering in search of the Unknown, to no place. In Leavis, creativity has in effect become the end (the 'case' of T. S. Eliot is that he 'denies human creativity'; the essence of Lawrence's superiority is that he offers 'an exaltation of creative Life'). Without Lawrence, it would be very difficult indeed to sustain the hope (since Eliot, the only other great English creator of our century, is involved in that crucial 'defeat of intelligence' in denying creativity); with Lawrence,

Leavis seems to me to be conditioned uncritically into accepting the modern idea that creativity entails the creation of new values. In the past, creativity lay in the rediscovery of the old values which lesser men continually obscure, the translation of them into the contemporary language lesser men have debased. That is what Eliot tried to do in his *Four Quartets*, and the defeat in them seems to me to lie not where Leavis locates it, but in the use of an inappropriately fashionable form – a form which involves pretence that the author himself does not know where he is going as he writes, and so incurs aesthetic irritation when the reader finds out in the end that he did know from the start. Leavis's situation is in fact radically paradoxical: the writer from whom he believes he most fully takes his bearings rejected the old moral order, in which words such as 'duty', 'responsibility', 'dedication to work' belonged, and went off to no place; yet Leavis does not desert the commonwealth – he returns to it, to expound, with great dedication and responsibility, the teaching of the man who did desert. That is paradoxical; but at this stage of my book, I need hardly say which of the two men I admire more.

Nor can Leavis's response be reduced to such myopia as I have so far implied. There are in Lawrence many other desirable attitudes, as well as hope, derived from beliefs which few can share, but seemingly accessible to those who cannot accept older beliefs. The most obvious, perhaps, is his emphasis on the unimportance of material goods. The mechanism of production and consumption, the radical materialism which makes it possible for the phrase 'standard of living' to retain no other connotations than economic ones, all the greed, philistinism and spiritual poverty which Leavis sums up in his notorious but very useful phrase 'technicological-Benthamite civilisation', are emphatically rejected by Lawrence as false gods distracting attention from what ultimately matters – the life which can be experienced only through relationship with other living beings. The attitude towards the other beings is to be one not of exploitation but of respect. Relationship is not a matter of one dominating the other, but of each respecting the other, in such a way that neither's freedom is reduced and both discover more than can lie within an enclosed self. Egoism is as much a sin in Lawrence as in Christianity. Self-fulfilment, achieved through Lawrentian relationship, is scarcely a Christian end, but it can conveniently focus an attempt to amalgamate Christian and

certain kinds of Romantic thought (found particularly in Blake).
Even the distinction between the saved and the damned has a
clear counterpart in Lawrence (the hope of being saved is much
curtailed; but the beliefs of some religious sects through the
centuries have shown that that can often increase its intensity).
Even though the damned are not individuals in any sense that
counts, the individual matters – a means seems to be retained of
resisting the de-humanising effect of rigid social and political
organisations and theories. Honesty remains a virtue and hypocrisy a vice, in the sense that living by the old forms seems to
involve a lie. If one omits the Christian doctrine of sin, one can say
that failure to live entirely by professed Christian standards is
hypocritical. Birkin says in 'An Island': 'By their works ye shall
know them, for dirty liars and cowards . . . if what they say *were*
true, then they couldn't help fulfilling it.' The alternative to
hypocritical Christianity is honesty to the complex reality of life,
which includes the 'roots of shame' as well as tenderness. As
criticism of Christian belief this is not intelligent, but it has the
apparent effect of snatching Christian values from under the
Christian's nose. And the advantage of the Lawrentian modification is that, in the words of Birkin I have just quoted, a true
individual *can't help* being virtuous: he has only, spontaneously, to
be his perfect self. 'Could I, then, being my perfect self, be selfish?
A selfish person is an impure person, one who wants that which is
not himself. Selfishness implies admixture, grossness, unclarity of
being. How can I, a pure person incapable of being anything but
myself, detract from my neighbour?'[20] Yet the true individual is as
free as modern man could wish from the incumbrance of a fixed
code: 'Everything is relative. Every Commandment that ever
issued out of the mouth of God or man, is strictly relative:
adhering to the particular time, place and circumstance.'[21]
Without irksome rules, one has only to submit to the unknown
(the Unknown easily loses its Lawrentian capital letter) to gain,
spontaneously, access to much which a liberal humanist would
want to salvage from the Christian structure of values. It is only
the damned (impure persons) who doubt that a perfect self, being
itself, could be in danger of becoming selfish; and since they do not
matter, their criticisms can safely be ignored. But there are
problems.

No one who has read any of Lawrence's expository prose can be
unaware of the insistent repetition of the words 'God' and 'Holy

Ghost'. They do not, of course retain their Christian meaning, and they hardly appear at all in *Women in Love* – for Birkin, 'there's no God'. But I do not think Lawrence's thought can really do without them. In the expository prose he sometimes uses them metaphorically, but often he does not: he believes quite literally in a creative force to which man ought to submit, and the state of perfected relationship between man and woman, man and nature, is quite literally, for him, the location of the Holy Ghost. I will not multiply quotations of the kind made above – evidence is to be found throughout both volumes of *Phoenix* and in the *Letters*. In *Women in Love* religious language is seldom used literally, but Birkin does use it in the last chapter ('the mystery which has brought forth man and the universe . . . is a non-human mystery, it has its own great ends, man is not the criterion. . . . God can do without man') and religious metaphors are very deep in its structure – the dying into life, the creative force that dispensed with the mastodon, the submission to the unknown. I do not think they could be removed; and unless they are believed to be more than metaphors, the reader has to make an equally difficult leap of faith. To take up the point at the end of my last paragraph, for example, for Lawrence a perfect self is preserved from becoming selfish because he is living in the Holy Ghost. But if one does not believe in Lawrence's conception of the Holy Ghost, one has to believe that a self can become perfect by purely human process, that it can remain a self without becoming selfish, by human – human what? I almost wrote 'human will', but human will leads in the direction of Hermione. One has to believe that the pure relationship will maintain the non-selfish individual, and the two individuals in the relationship will spontaneously maintain the purity of the relationship. 'Star-equilibrium' certainly does involve circularity. If one believes that the relationship is a form of God – the Holy Ghost – it is not hard to believe it can perfect man in such a way. But few of his readers share Lawrence's belief about the Holy Ghost; most of them, like Leavis, silently omit language of that kind in all but the most innocuously metaphorical form. The problem of belief in human self-transcendence which consequently confronts them is easy to conceal, but formidably difficult to overcome. Who can really believe, now, in any form of human self-perfectibility? Yet this is not the only problem. Birkin without Ursula is trapped in tick-tack; but not all Birkins find Ursulas in a world in which the unknown is not God and Birkins and Ursulas are very thin on the ground. In other words, the trust in the Unknown, which as I showed is very deep in the structure of the book, will not reliably lead to the relationship through which alone the self can be transcended, unless the Unknown is effectually providential. The Unknown cannot really lose its capital letter. Again the point is easy to miss when one is responding to a fictional structure with at least some of the inbuilt conventions of fiction. But there are problems in deriving beliefs from fictions without accepting the beliefs underlying the fictions.

I am assuming on the basis of published criticism (there being no other means of proof except a census), that virtually no-one can accept the details of Lawrence's theology as theology. The predicament of those who would like to meet him half-way is not much easier. Trust to the Unknown is, I think, the indispensible core – the article of Lawrence's faith which one could not discard without rejecting (as faith) the whole. In an obvious sense any religious faith is in the unknown, the humanly inconceivable because the beyond-human. But in Christianity, for example, the unknown God has revealed what of Himself it is helpful for man to know. To those who cannot accept Lawrence quite literally as a prophet, revealing that Law is from the Father and is Female, Love from God the Son and is Male, and so on, the Unknown has to be the absolutely unknown. On the showing of *Women in Love*, that incurs a willingness to desert man if the Unknown seems ready to discard him, like the mastodon. To trust an Unknown that far requires greater faith than any of the traditional monotheistic religions. How could one know that such an Unknown could be trusted in *any* way? What else would it discard, along with man?

I do not think, then, that Lawrence can actually offer what in Leavis's account of him he would seem to offer – that is, an interpretation of life fundamentally in accord with traditional Western European attitudes, without religious beliefs. If one has neither the traditional beliefs, nor Lawrence's own, his view of life demands more, not less faith. There are other difficulties. As I said at the beginning of this chapter, the relationship of Birkin and Ursula was put forward as a *pis aller*; as Leavis clearly sees, it is therefore unjust to criticise Lawrence for not having 'solved the problems of civilisation that he analyses'[22] by creating that relationship as a model. On the other hand, it is not unfair to point out self-imposed difficulties.

If life is taken to be the ultimate end, then clearly intensity of life is to be desired. 'Let those that have life, live.'[23] But does one live more intensely by being or by doing? If by doing, then there is a very grave deficiency in the situation of Birkin and Ursula at the end. If things are really so very bad, there is little that could be done; but that should not stop Lawrence from showing a serious effect on the relationship. He expresses no awareness of any serious effect. In some of the expository essays, in fact, he asserts the primacy of being over doing. My last quotation is from the 'Study of Thomas Hardy'; on the previous page, Lawrence writes of man's basic urge as the desire to *be* – kings 'had opportunity to *be* [and] were not under the compulsion to do'. In a letter to Russell, he wrote, 'Don't *do* anything any more – but for heavens sake begin to *be*.'[24] But elsewhere he clearly realised that this entailed problems. In another essay, he saw that 'what a man *is*, is measured by what he can do. . . . If you *are* something you'll *do* something, *ipso facto*'.[25] Yet Birkin resigns his job and goes wandering. At the theoretical level of the essay, the solution seems easy – 'If a man, whether by thought or action, makes *life* he is an aristocrat.' The examples are Caesar (action) and Cicero (thought). How a writer can 'make life' is clear; how a soldier can is less clear, but discernible; how an inspector of schools can is obscure. I am not being facetious: the problem is deep-rooted. If one's *end* is life, there are few pursuits *in* life which further that end. In this novel we do not have only problems in civilisation which Lawrence (of course) cannot solve; we have also problems Lawrence made for himself. To take life as one's end may seem to be liberating; in practice it is very restricting. It leaves one with little to do except be.

At the end of his second book on Lawrence, Leavis concedes that 'Lawrence's distinction between the necessity of work and the opportunity to *be* involves a simplification.' But he does not think this affects the presentation of Birkin: Birkin is not, 'like Lawrence, the growing tip itself', but his recognition that 'there *is*, or ought to be, one, and his uncompromising concern for it gives the significance to his life'. 'That is, he is in his individuality "created" and self-responsible, which is inseparable from recognising his basic responsibility in relation to life – to the life-issue.' If one is not a writer ('the growing tip') the possibilities of doing are restricted to being 'created'. I do not think this will serve. The whole question is begged in that shift from 'self-responsible' to 'basic responsibility' – the shift from Lawrence's ethic to Leavis's. Birkin is not responsible in the way Leavis is: there is no work he can do, which will further his end and Lawrence's. The main reservation Leavis wants to register about the 'simplification' is historical. In Lawrence's time, he thinks, 'more ordinary people' were able to *be* through work in a way now impossible. The example is from 'The Fox'. That will not do: the problem is built into Lawrence's own thought. If life is the end ('Nothing is important but life') any doing which does not serve that end ('making life', like an author writing books which redirect the flow of human sympathies) is an obstruction to the being which is what remains of the end. The root of the problem is not really that Western European civilisation is in such a bad way that Birkin can find no fruitful work within it; it is that the terms of Lawrence's thought prevent Birkin from undertaking any work which reduces his freedom to *be*. He wants to be disinherited so that he can more fully be. Yet being without doing is hardly possible to man, as Lawrence gives away when, with clearly unintentional absurdity, he lets Ursula say, 'I think it is much better to be really patrician, and to do nothing but just be oneself, like a walking flower.' The dilemma seems to me very closely related to the one encountered by Mill in his *Autobiography*. 'Ask yourself whether you are happy, and you cease to be so. The only chance is to treat, not happiness, but some end external to it, as the purpose of life.' Then 'you will inhale happiness with the air you breathe'.[26] The way to achieve intensity of life (if that is what one most wants) is not pursuit of being, but pursuit of some other end, which will constitute purposeful activity; then one will *be* not a walking flower but a man. But Lawrence, unlike Mill and like Hythloday,[27] lacked the ability to criticise his own terms of thought. He was clearly uneasy, but he could not, for long enough, stand back, and perceive that to take being as one's end is to travel to no place.

This problem becomes most plain at the end, but it is impending throughout the book. Lawrence's art, as many of his critics have shown, is essentially an art treating of process. The most powerful of his writing almost always concerns a process rather than a state – the stoning of the moon is an instance about which Mark Kinkead-Weekes has written with particular sensitivity:[28] the smashing and re-forming of the image of the moon enacts the process of conflicting forces which is central to the

Lawrentian philosophy set out in the expository essays of this period. It is an art which enables Lawrence to write with a power unequalled by any other English novelist of this century about the formative stages of a relationship. If he had envisaged any end beyond the formation of a sexual relationship, it might have enabled him to do even more. But since he does not, he is in a dilemma: does the process end in a perfect relationship (a state)? or does the relationship remain process (imperfect)? Outside Lawrence, of course, this is not a real problem: a relationship between living people is obviously a continuous process. But inside Lawrence's work it is a real problem, because the relationship is simultaneously a means and an end. The imagery which dominates the expository prose does not help. The lion and the unicorn are in process of fight; the crown is their state. The waves, the flow, the fire bring forth a flower. Such images let Lawrence get it both ways, and dazzle the reader. But the novel gives him away. The vivid part of the treatment of Birkin and Ursula concerns the formative stage of their relationship; in the last hundred pages they become shadowy. In 'Moony' Birkin reflects to himself, 'There was the paradisal entry into pure, single being'; the process of entry is paradisal only in the ironic sense that it comprises argument between man and woman; of the being we learn nothing.

In fact there is confusion about whether after 'Excurse' there is a continued process or a state. In 'Flitting', it seems there is a state ('a new, paradisal unit regained from the duality . . . both caught up and transcended into a oneness where everything is silent, because there is nothing to answer, all is perfect and at one'). On the first page of 'Continental', it is process again ('as yet she was only imminent'); on the third, it is state again ('the peace and the bliss in their hearts was enduring'); near the end, it is process again ('they were never *quite* together, at the same moment, one was always a little left out'). This confusion does not result merely from a local failure of imagination in these chapters: it is inevitable inside Lawrence's world. The process is towards a perfection of being; but there is no being in this life which is not a process. Human life is not like a flower which has one moment of perfection; it continues after the 'paradisal entry'. It will not do to posit a state of being as the flower of existence: when,becoming has become, it dies. Nor will the image of orbiting stars help to solve the problem. Orbit is maintained because there are contrary forces, centripetal and centrifugal. As an image of developing relationship that is of value. But Birkin and Lawrence want it to represent also a relationship that has 'come through'. Ostensibly it reconciles state and process – there is both balance and movement. But it depends on contrary forces. This is fine so long as there are contrary forces (such as in 'Moony'); but after the 'paradisal entry' there are no longer contrary views of what their relationship should be like. Outside Lawrence this does not matter: there is plenty else for contrary views to focus on, providing the energy for continued process. But Birkin and Ursula can hardly be supposed to go on quarrelling for the rest of their lives about whether Gerald could have been saved or not; and nothing else is of any consequence to them, except the next stop on their journey to no place. If the only issue worth bothering about is the nature of a sexual relationship, there either has to be continued opposition within it – as when the stray cat defies Mino and is hit – in which case there can be no 'we have come through', only perpetual coming and going; or, when the desiderated relationship is achieved, the opposition necessary to process collapses – and with it the relationship. Lawrence does not consciously confront this problem: for a hundred pages he prevaricates with imagery of seeds which never germinate and undeveloped hints of Birkin and Ursula being not yet 'quite together'. Critics who praise his art as an art of process have much to show us; but to accept it unreservedly as such leaves much concealed.

The final difficulty in Lawrence's vision I want to show returns us to the beginning of my discussion of his book. He wanted to reject preconceived models of man; he wanted man to unfold, like a flower, in response to the Unknown. But man cannot become in the way a flower becomes, because his nature includes the capacity and the need to intend. A person does not just unfold: even if he escapes the old models, and tick-tack reactions to old models, it remains in his nature to intend, and with respect to himself his intentions cannot be other than some form of model. Human nature inevitably includes the intention to be x; the only questions concern the character of x, and the strength of intention. It is easy enough to describe the model of man which Lawrence himself desiderated – spontaneous, integrated, responsive to surroundings, respectful towards other individuals, and so on. More importantly, model-making is built into the structure of the novel in the way Birkin projects ideas of relationship and the consequent 'singleness of being': if he did not project these models, intend to shape his own life by them, the 'star-equilibrium' with Ursula would not have spontaneously sprung into existence. Yet at a crucial point in his total model, Lawrence asks us to accept a totally unknown. To the relationship of Birkin and Ursula after 'Excurse', he gives no shape. I have just tried to demonstrate that the reason is that it is an impossibility, that Lawrence's thinking simply breaks down at this crucial point, the end to which the process is leading. But even if my argument is rejected, there is no doubt about the lacuna. What it profits a man to gain 'star-equilibrium' we do not know; all we do know is that it has cost him the rest of the world. Maybe the world is well lost; but since men live in time, I think I should need to know how Birkin and Ursula would grow old in 'freedom together' before accepting Birkin's model, even as a *pis aller*.

17 Conclusion

It is quite common for critics to conclude with avowals that they had no preconception of where their enquiry would lead them. I am not ashamed to confess that I had my end in view before I started. I wanted to show how one's conception of the end of man affects one's view of what he should be like, what he should do, and how it affects the possibilities of fictional form. To More and Johnson, the end of man was revealed, and self-proposed alternative ends are appraised by reference to that – the commonwealth or a choice of life leading to personal happiness. For George Eliot, the end was not divinely revealed, though it was inherited; and because it had not the status of revealed truth, it had to be made appealing through the rhetoric of form. The end had to be re-created within the form; and the form consequently could not function so completely as a means of appraisal; but her particular form, with the kinds of resistance which I have analysed, constitutes an at least partially successful discipline on the fantasies of self-proposed ends. In Lawrence, the end is self-proposed, not inherited; so it has to be not only made appealing but entirely generated within the form. So the form cannot function as resistance: in effect it advocates fantasy. In the three earlier writers, fiction works as a means of containing fantasy – recognising that it is a part of man's nature, but a part which needs to be held in check through self-consciousness. In Lawrence, the distinction between fiction and fantasy has disappeared – the fiction embodies the fantasy.

It will be clear that I regard the position of More and Johnson as the most secure, and also that I share it. But of course in our time many believe it untenable. George Eliot and Lawrence represent possible alternatives. It is no part of my argument that it is impossible to construct coherent ethical schemes without recourse to an idea of the end of man; but I do not think that man will ever be able to get permanently out of his head the question which echoes through Leavis's second book on Lawrence, 'What for – what ultimately for?' Of course, proximate ends will serve for long – for example, a rise in the 'standard of living' – and in my Introduction I pointed to the oscillation between a wholly negative answer to that question and money, which is now very common. But for those who need more, George Eliot and Lawrence represent two massive efforts of human intelligence to stop short of despair without opiates. To borrow again a phrase from Wordsworth's preface to the *Lyrical Ballads* which I have quoted elsewhere, they each attempt to stand as a 'rock of defence for human nature'. George Eliot tries to 'keep hold of'[1] a Christian model of the end of man without recourse to actual Christian belief; Lawrence sees that the model without the belief is moribund and tries to salvage from the last end short of despair – life – those vestiges of the model which can remain (fidelity to 'ultimate marriage', respect for the 'other', and so on). Beyond Lawrence, I can see only despair, or that most fantastic of all beliefs, the human self-perfectibility which must underlie any optimistic humanism.

I have already criticised the endeavours of George Eliot and Lawrence separately. I want to conclude by contrasting their advantages. The chief advantage of Lawrence's thought is that it is more self-sufficient and coherent. George Eliot offers a static model of man (which on her own showing in *The Mill on the Floss* requires external validation) within an evolutionary frame of thought. Lawrence offers a dynamic model (man must go where 'life' leads him) within a way of thought coherently based on the concept of process. An advantage which clearly derives from this is that Lawrence can reject dead values and (in his image) preserve the kernel, from which new life will grow. For example, he can reject degenerate charity (Crich's industrial paternalism and personal oppression) and preserve respect for the 'other' ('freedom together'). This fits both with his own philosophy of process and with the observable history of man, the way values have differed in different societies, through history.

The correlative disadvantage in Lawrence can be put in the form of a question. If the model is not static, what can authorise change? It will not do just to say 'life', because men think: change in man's self-image has willy-nilly to be intended. George Eliot glimpsed this problem in fact in her treatment of Protestantism in *Romola*: who has authority to say the old authority is no longer valid? Equally difficult: what happens when a new value conflicts directly with an old one? Lawrence is in no doubt: the old automatically goes. Ursula, near the end, even feels resentful towards her own memory: 'She wanted to have no past. . . . What had she to do with parents and antecedents?' But I doubt whether Leavis, for example, would really assent to this. To be specific, there is apparent in these four fictions a shift, corresponding to a general cultural shift, from self-discipline for the benefit of the community, to self-fulfilment despite the community. George Eliot very deliberately turns backwards, as Maggie rejects Stephen's arguments. In *Women in Love*, the commonwealth is deserted so that Birkin and Ursula may have life, may develop 'singleness of being' through 'freedom together'. If such a complete reversal as that may be admitted, what of the old values will be abandoned next? Already formidable problems come in its wake. What is the difference between authentic self-fulfilment by Birkin and selfishness in a mere egoist? How does an individual know what is properly self-fulfilling and what is selfish in himself? How can one individual recognise another (who merits respect) from one of the dead (who does not)? Birkin is mistaken, according to the symbolism running from start to finish of the book, about Gerald. Moreover, these matters are less difficult in fiction than in life. In fiction one can have the fastidiousness of Birkin in 'Flitting': 'How could he say "I" when he was something new and unknown, not himself at all? This I, this old formula of the age, was a dead letter.' In life it is more likely to come out like: 'I will live my life and, if possible, be happy, though the whole world slides in horror down into the bottomless pit. . . . I will save myself, for I believe the highest virtue is to be happy.'[2] – or 'Other people don't matter very much. The chief thing is to be one's own real self.'[3]

To suggest that 'life' be the authority in settling such matters brings more problems than it removes. At worst, it can lead to the moral vulgarity of *Lady Chatterley's Lover*: the moral thing is what most promotes life. Connie and Mellors have more life than Clifford; therefore the moral right lies with them. That way lies atrocity. At best, it leads to the rejection of will from the model of man: the living act spontaneously; will inhibits spontaneity. That way lies loss of humanity. George Eliot is a determinist in the strict sense of the word: all human actions have causes. But that leads her to charity: Tom is partly but not wholly responsible for his bad behaviour to Maggie near the end. Lawrence is a determinist in a grosser sense. Hermione is not spontaneous; she wills to be spontaneous and so is doomed to fail; therefore she is a dead leaf. Essentially there are two classes of people, the living and the dead. If you are dead, there is no chance of willing yourself alive. The dead are not to be pitied but deserted: pity for the dead is decadent charity. Ostensibly, submission to the unfolding of life offers a greater fullness of being. Actually, if the status of will is so drastically reduced, man becomes the prisoner of his immediate feelings. Lawrence puts his side of this argument most clearly in 'A Propos of *Lady Chatterley's Lover*'[4]: 'Our education from the start has *taught* us a certain range of emotions, what to feel and what not to feel . . . The higher emotions are strictly dead. They have to be faked.' All control of raw feeling is hypocrisy; the cultivation of virtue as represented in Maggie is a process of faking. The living are naturally good through a series of spontaneous 'delicate act[s] of adjustment on the soul's part'[5]; the rest are non-starters. How delicacy is achieved without will, I find in theory obscure; for the 'living' the problem of evil just evaporates. But as one of the dead, I could presumably not recognise one of these paragons – aristocrats as Lawrence calls them – if I met him. I should mistake him for an egoist.

In More and Johnson, the existence of a transcendent end makes simultaneously possible an acceptance of the conditions of a brute world, resistant to the desires of human fantasy, and a moral absolutism, a refusal to accommodate in questions of moral importance. In George Eliot, both possibilities are very largely retained: her fiction almost entirely disciplines fantasy, and in her fiction her moral thought is based on *virtue*, not, as she seems to have said in some misleading abstract comments, on impulsive response to particular cases. In Lawrence, both possibilities are lost. He effectively inhabits utopia, and the basis of his moral thought is as crucially dislocated as the Utopians': taking 'life' (for 'the real Me'), like taking pleasure ('first of all for yourself'), as one's ultimate end, can hardly be made the ground of a consistent, let alone an intransigent charity or fidelity. When one's ultimate end is so changed, all proximate ends are radically affected, and he has left himself, like the Utopians, no external restraint.

In short, Lawrence has already thrown away so much of what I should like to call human, and has so little means of holding on to what remains, that I should not want to follow him. If I did not believe in the same End as More and Johnson, I should go home with George Eliot, not to no place with Lawrence.

Notes

CHAPTER 1   INTRODUCTION

1. *Proust and Three Dialogues with Georges Duthuit* (1965) p. 103.
2. Frank Kermode, *The Sense of an Ending: Studies in the Theory of Fiction* (1966) p. 4.
3. Op. cit., p. 63.
4. Op. cit., p. 64.
5. Op. cit., p. 40.
6. Op. cit., p. 39.
7. Op. cit., p. 41.

CHAPTER 2   *UTOPIA*: FORM AS MODEL

1. J. H. Hexter, *The Vision of Politics on the Eve of the Reformation* (1973) p. 119.
2. David M. Bevington, 'The Dialogue in *Utopia*: Two sides to the Question', *Studies in Philology*, vol. 58 (1961), pp. 496–509.
3. That is, the letter printed in all of the first three important editions.
4. In his stimulating article, ' "Si Hythlodaeo Credimus": Vision and Revision in Thomas More's *Utopia*', *Soundings*, vol. 51 (1968), pp. 272–89, R. S. Sylvester points out that Hythloday 'wrested permission' from Vespucci to be left behind: his exile is completely self-willed. One might add that the contrast is carried through in great detail: the church More attends in Antwerp is Nôtre Dame, 'the most crowded with worshippers'.
5. *Proverbs* 29.11.
6. This has, of course, only superficial verbal resemblance to what in modern Protestant circles is called 'situation ethics'. In 'situation ethics', the ground of action is dependent on the situation; in More's view, the ground of action exists previously and independently, and one acts accordingly as far as the situation will permit. According to 'situation ethics' More should have forgiven Henry VIII and accepted his new queen and new title as Supreme Head of the Church in England. Hythloday would charge either to precipitate self-martyrdom, or back to Utopia. More used the law as long as the law could preserve his life; when the law was abused, More would not change the ground of his action.
7. *Matthew* 5.45–6.
8. 'More' is frequently taken to be foolish at the end of Book II when he says that the abolition of money 'utterly overthrows all the nobility, magnificence,

splendour, and majesty, which are, in the estimation of the common people, the true glories and ornaments of the commonwealth'. But this opinion is not his – he explicitly attributes it, without injustice, to the 'common people' (*publica est opinio*). Abolish such things and the common people, as opposed to austere intellectuals, will not like it: the point is not at all foolish.

CHAPTER 3 *UTOPIA*: THE PLEASURE ETHIC

1. Edward Surtz, *The Praise of Pleasure* (1957) p. 199.
2. *John* 18.36.
3. *The English Works of Sir Thomas More*, eds W. E. Cambell *et al.* (1931), p. 473.
4. Op. cit., p. 463.
5. Op. cit., p. 477.
6. *Responsio ad Lutherum*, ed. John M. Headley (1969) pp. 277–9.
7. *The English Works of Sir Thomas More*, p. 381.
8. Op. cit., p. 381.
9. Op. cit., pp. 381–2.
10. Op. cit., p. 393.
11. Op. cit., p. 394.
12. R. W. Chambers, *Thomas More* (1935), p. 128.
13. See p. 47 above.

CHAPTER 4 *UTOPIA*: PROXIMATE ENDS AND MEANS

1. *The English Works of Sir Thomas More*, p. 477.
2. J. H. Hexter, *More's Utopia: The Biography of an Idea* (1952), p. 70.
3. 'Treatise on the Passion' (Mary Basset's translation), *The Works of Sir Thomas More* (1557), p. 1358.

CHAPTER 5 *UTOPIA*: FORM AS DISCIPLINE

1. Harry Berger discusses *Utopia* in these terms in his article 'The Renaissance Imagination: Second World and Green World', *Centennial Review*, vol. 9 (1965), pp. 36–78. I do not share his wish to make a double distinction between 'green world' (Utopia), 'second world' (the actual world as represented within *Utopia*) and the actual world completely outside the book. The second and third are obviously not the same (More did not meet Hythloday in Antwerp); but More does not exploit the difference (as other writers have), whereas the interplay between the first and the second is central to the meaning of the book.

2. Berger (op. cit., p. 68) says wittily, 'The Utopians are handed the classical inheritance in the Aldine edition.'
3. R. J. Schoeck, 'More, Plutarch, and King Agis: Spartan History and the Meaning of *Utopia*', *Philological Quarterly*, vol. 35 (1956), pp. 366–75. 'I would suggest that the dating of Utopia's history at precisely 1760 years is an ironic signal that there was once a king who had made so radical a proposal as the redistribution of land and the cancellation of debts, and for this proposal . . . that Spartan king had been put to death.'
4. E. F. Rogers, *St Thomas More: Selected Letters* (1961), p. 85.
5. Op. cit., p. 64.
6. I quote from the translation by Leonard F. Dean (1946) as reprinted in *Essential Works of Erasmus*, ed. W. T. H. Jackson (1965), pp. 381–2.

CHAPTER 6   *RASSELAS*: FORM AS MODEL

1. *Little Gidding*.
2. This has been discussed interestingly by Earl Wasserman in 'Johnson's *Rasselas*: Implicit Contexts', *Journal of English and Germanic Philology*, vol. 74 (1975), pp. 1–25.
3. I am of course referring at the cost of simplification to general norms. The major writers commonly introduce complications to disturb the reader's basic expectations for particular purposes. In addition, it is in Swift notoriously difficult to perceive precisely where the excluded middle position lies and how to arrive at it.
4. Luis de Urreta, quoted by Donald M. Lockhart in ' "The Fourth Son of the Mighty Emperor": The Ethiopian Background of Johnson's *Rasselas*', *Publications of the Modern Languages Association*, vol. 78 (1963), p. 522, n. 21.
5. I am indebted here to an unpublished essay by John Hutchings, a dead friend for whom my 'real love' is 'yet not diminished'.
6. W. Jackson Bate, 'Johnson and Satire *Manqué*', *Eighteenth-Century Studies in Honor of Donald F. Hyde*, ed. W. H. Bond (1970), pp. 145–60.
7. Arieh Sachs, in *Passionate Intelligence* (1967) first pointed out the function of the analogy. The aviator says, 'How must it amuse the pendent spectator to see the moving scene of land and ocean . . .'. His fall prepares us for the failure of the philosopher.
8. Reinhold Niebuhr, *Discerning the Signs of the Times* (1946), p. 115. For reference to this passage of Niebuhr I am indebted to the essay by John Hutchings cited in note 4 above.

CHAPTER 7   *RASSELAS*: ENDS

1. This conflicts with the statements in chapter 2 that all the inhabitants of the Valley except Rasselas were 'pleased with each other and with themselves', and that 'few of the Princes had ever wished to enlarge their bounds'. Chapter 2 is supported by the view of the 'old instructor' of chapter 3: 'You, Sir, said

the sage, are the first who has complained of misery in the *happy valley*.' Imlac's remark is supported by Nekayah, who tells Rasselas in chapter 14 that she is 'equally weary of confinement' in the Valley. Either Johnson changed his mind as he was writing, or he wished to restrict the reader's knowledge in this respect to what Rasselas discovered. I am unable to find conclusive evidence.

2. Gabriel Marcel, *The Mystery of Being*, translated by G. S. Fraser (1950), pp. 211–12.
3. Review of *A Free Enquiry: the Works of Samuel Johnson* (1825), vol. 6, p. 65.
4. 'On the Death of Dr Robert Levet'.
5. Chester F. Chapin shows that Johnson was influenced in this aspect of his Christian thought by Pascal in particular. There is such remarkable similarity that Chapin's case is indisputable. But the line of thought is, of course, to be found very widely in the Christian thought of most ages. See Chester F. Chapin, 'Johnson and Pascal', in *English Writers of the Eighteenth Century*, ed. John H. Middendorf (1971), pp. 3–16.

CHAPTER 8 *RASSELAS*: FICTION AND ACCEPTANCE

1. Emrys Jones was the first to emphasise the importance of chance in this part especially and in the book as a whole. See his article, 'The Artistic Form of *Rasselas*', *Review of English Studies* (1967), vol. 18, pp. 387–401.
2. *Paradise Lost*, Book VIII, 66–178.
3. I think it probable that Johnson was either deliberately or unconsciously recalling Gulliver's dreams about what he would do if he were granted the immortal life enjoyed (as he thinks) by the Struldbruggs in Book III.

CHAPTER 9 *THE MILL ON THE FLOSS*: PURPOSE WITHOUT PURPOSE

1. *The George Eliot Letters*, ed. Gordon S. Haight (1954–6), Vol. 6 pp. 216–17.
2. *Essays of George Eliot*, ed. Thomas Pinney (1963), p. 379.
3. I quote from the Penguin translation, by R. J. Hollingdale (1968), pp. 69–70.
4. 'The *Antigone* and Its Moral', *Essays of George Eliot*, ed. Thomas Pinney (1963), pp. 261–5.

CHAPTER 10 *THE MILL ON THE FLOSS*: FICTION AND FANTASY

1. 'Amos Barton', ch. 7.

CHAPTER 11 *THE MILL ON THE FLOSS*: NATURALISM AND PURPOSE

1. The qualification is registered in an earlier *Middlemarch* epigraph (to ch. 4):
   1st Gent.: Our deeds are fetters that we forge ourselves.
   2nd Gent.: Ay, truly: but I think it is the world
           That brings the iron.
2. *The George Eliot Letters*, ed. Gordon S. Haight (1954–6), vol. 4, p. 300.
3. Op. cit., vol. 3, p. 111. The preceding quotation from Wordsworth is taken from *Letters of William Wordsworth*, selected by Philip Wayne (1954), pp. 47–50.
4. The nature of George Eliot's determinism is discussed definitively by George Levine in 'Determinism and Responsibility in the Works of George Eliot', *Publications of the Modern Languages Association*, vol. 77 (1962), pp. 268–79.
5. *The George Eliot Letters*, ed. Gordon S. Haight (1954–6), vol. 6, pp. 216–17.
6. Op. cit., vol. 4, p. 300.
7. Barbara Hardy, '*The Mill on the Floss*', in *Critical Essays on George Eliot*, ed. Barbara Hardy (1970) p. 46.

CHAPTER 12 *THE MILL ON THE FLOSS*: 'WHICH IS THE WAY HOME?'

1. J. S. Mill, *On Liberty* (1859), ch. 3. I quote from the Everyman edition (1910), p. 115. The following quotations are from pp. 118, 119, 117, 120, 127.
2. *The George Eliot Letters*, ed. Gordon S. Haight (1954–6), vol. 3, p. 366. 'The highest "calling and election" is to *do without opium* and live through all our pain with conscious, clear-eyed endurance.'
3. See my quotation from her letter of 1876, on p. 154 above.
4. Barbara Hardy, '*The Mill on the Floss*', in *Critical Essays on George Eliot*, ed. Barbara Hardy (1970), p. 48.
5. See Bernard Paris, 'George Eliot's Religion of Humanity', *ELH*, vol. 29 (1962), pp. 418–43 and *Experiments in Life: George Eliot's Quest for Values* (1965). My quotations from Lewes and from George Eliot's letter referring to his work are taken from the article in *ELH*, p. 422.
6. Quoted above, p. 155.
7. Friedrich Nietzsche, *Beyond Good and Evil* (1886), quoted from the Penguin translation by R. J. Hollingdale (1973), p. 185.
8. The phrases quoted here come from a letter of 1859 (*The Letters of George Eliot*, ed. Gordon S. Haight (1954–6), vol. 3, p. 231).
9. Bernard J. Paris, 'The Inner Conflicts of Maggie Tulliver: a Horneyan Analysis', *Centennial Review*, vol. 13 (1969), pp. 166–99.

CHAPTER 13 *WOMEN IN LOVE*: DEAD ENDS

1. Review of Trigant Burrow (1927), in *Phoenix* [vol. I] (1936), p. 380.

CHAPTER 14 *WOMEN IN LOVE*: LIFE AS END

1. *The Collected Letters of D. H. Lawrence*, ed. Harry T. Moore (1962), vol. 1, p. 365. In subsequent notes I shall refer to this edition simply as *Letters*, and give only page references since the numbering is continuous through the two volumes.
2. The Prologue was published by George H. Ford in *Texas Quarterly*, vol. 6 (1963) and is reprinted in *Phoenix II*.
3. Published by George H. Ford as ' "The Wedding Chapter" of D. H. Lawrence's *Women in Love*', *Texas Quarterly*, vol. 6 (1964), pp. 134–47.
4. *Letters*, p. 565.
5. *Phoenix II* (1968), p. 426.

CHAPTER 15 *WOMEN IN LOVE*: FICTION AS FANTASY

1. *Letters*, p. 311.
2. *Letters*, p. 354.
3. *Letters*, p. 402.
4. *Letters*, p. 411.
5. *Letters*, p. 440.
6. *Letters*, p. 483.
7. *Letters*, p. 497.
8. *Letters*, p. 499.
9. *Letters*, p. 482.
10. *Letters*, p. 477.
11. *Phoenix* [vol. I] (1936), p. 476.
12. *Letters*, pp. 826–7. The two essays referred to can be found in *Phoenix* [vol. I] (1936), pp. 521–32.
13. *Letters*, p. 282. The image I refer to in my following sentence is: 'There is another *ego*, according to whose action the individual is unrecognisable, and passes through, as it were, allotropic states which it needs a deeper sense than any we've been used to exercise, to discover are states of the same single radically unchanged element. (Like as diamond and coal are the same pure single element of carbon. The ordinary novel would trace the history of the diamond – but I say, 'Diamond, what! This is carbon.' And my diamond might be coal or soot, and my theme is carbon).'
14. *Phoenix* [vol. I] (1936), p. 528.
15. Reprinted in *D. H. Lawrence: Selected Literary Criticism*, ed. Anthony Beal (1956), pp. 400–1.
16. *Letters*, p. 505.

CHAPTER 16   *WOMEN IN LOVE*: 'I WANT TO BE DISINHERITED'

1. *Letters*, pp. 459–60.
2. *Phoenix* [vol. I] (1936), p. 531.
3. *Phoenix* II (1968), pp. 502, 504.
4. *Phoenix* [vol. I] (1936), p. 534.
5. *Phoenix* II (1968), p. 483.
6. *Phoenix* [vol. I] (1936), p. 608.
7. *Phoenix* II (1968), p. 428.
8. *Phoenix* [vol. I] (1936) p. 420.
9. *Phoenix* [vol. I] (1936), p. 403.
10. *Phoenix* [vol. I] (1936), p. 531.
11. *Phoenix* II (1968), p. 483.
12. *Phoenix* [vol. I] (1936), p. 426.
13. *Studies in Classical American Literature* (1923), ch. 12. Reprinted in *D. H. Lawrence: Selected Literary Criticism*, ed. Anthony Beal (1956), pp. 402–3.
14. *Sea and Sardinia* (1923), Penguin edn, p. 52.
15. *Letters*, p. 273.
16. *Letters*, p. 76.
17. *Mornings in Mexico* (1927), Penguin edn, p. 61.
18. 'The Reality of Peace', *Phoenix* [vol. I] (1936), p. 670.
19. *English*, vol. 26 (1977), pp. 23–40. Mr Black is reviewing F. R. Leavis's book, *Thought, Words and Creativity: Art and Thought in Lawrence* (1976), from which I quote later in my paragraph.
20. *Phoenix* [vol. I] (1936), pp. 432–3.
21. *Phoenix* II (1968), pp. 421–2.
22. F. R. Leavis, D. H. Lawrence: Novelist (1955), p. 29.
23. *Phoenix* [vol. I] (1936), p. 426.
24. *Letters*, p. 433.
25. *Phoenix* II (1968), p. 477.
26. World's Classics edition, Oxford (1924), pp. 120–1.
27. See pp. 78–9 above.
28. Mark Kinkead-Weekes, 'The Marble and the Statue: the Exploratory Imagination of D. H. Lawrence', in *Imagined Worlds*, ed. Maynard Mack and Ian Gregor (1968), pp. 371–418.

CHAPTER 17   CONCLUSION

1. The phrase is from the letter to Payne, quoted on p. 154 above.
2. *Letters*, p. 424.
3. *Letters*, p. 1211. In the novel this can be attributed to Birkin's sickness – he says in the second chapter, 'People don't really matter.' But if it is sickness, Lawrence had still not recovered in 1929.
4. *Phoenix* II (1968), p. 493.
5. *Fantasia of the Unconscious*, Penguin edn, p. 54.

Index